**AMERICAN
DREAMS,
AMERICAN
NIGHTMARES**

AMERICAN DREAMS, AMERICAN NIGHTMARES

CULTURE AND CRISIS IN RESIDENTIAL REAL ESTATE FROM THE GREAT RECESSION TO THE COVID-19 PANDEMIC

DANIEL HOROWITZ

THE UNIVERSITY OF NORTH CAROLINA PRESS Chapel Hill

© 2022 Daniel Horowitz

All rights reserved
Set in Utopia and Meta type by codeMantra
Manufactured in the United States of America

Library of Congress Cataloging-in-Publication Data
Names: Horowitz, Daniel, 1938- author.
Title: American dreams, American nightmares :
culture and crisis in residential real estate from the
Great Recession to the COVID-19 pandemic / Daniel Horowitz.
Description: Chapel Hill : The University of North Carolina Press,
[2022] | Includes bibliographical references and index.
Identifiers: LCCN 2022017104 | ISBN 9781469671499 (cloth) |
ISBN 9781469671505 (paperback) | ISBN 9781469671512 (ebook)
Subjects: LCSH: Housing—United States—History—21st century. |
Residential real estate—United States—History—21st century. |
Recessions—United States—History—21st century. | COVID-19
Pandemic, 2020—Economic aspects. | COVID-19 Pandemic,
2020—Social aspects. | Real estate business—United States—
History—21st century. | United States—Economic conditions—2001-2009. |
United States—Economic conditions—2009-
Classification: LCC HD7293 .H55 2022 | DDC 363.50973—dc23/eng/20220718
LC record available at https://lccn.loc.gov/2022017104

To Ben Horowitz and

Sarah Esther Horowitz,

with love and admiration

CONTENTS

List of Illustrations *ix*

Preface *xi*

Acknowledgments *xvii*

Introduction *1*

1. Housing Central: HGTV *22*

2. The Power of Positive Real Estate Workshops *53*

3. From *Realtor Magazine* to the *Financial Times*: How Print Media Covered the Global Financial Crisis *87*

4. Journalists, Filmmakers, and the Gendering of Looking Backward *126*

5. Looking Up and Down: Anthropology, Horror Films, and the Financial Crisis *163*

6. New Media and Residential Real Estate *184*

   Coda. From the Great Recession to the COVID-19 Pandemic *210*

   Notes *231*

   Index *279*

ILLUSTRATIONS

View from the author's desk xii

Jonathan Scott and Drew Scott, *Dream Home* (2016) 124

National Association of Realtors, *100 Years in Celebration of the American Dream* (2007) 124

Dean Starkman, *The Watchdog That Didn't Bark* (2014) 124

Bethany McLean and Joe Nocera, *All the Devils Are Here* (2010) 124

Gillian Tett, *Fool's Gold* (2009) 125

Karen Ho, *Liquidated* (2009) 125

Melissa S. Fisher, *Wall Street Women* (2012) 125

Noelle Stout, *Dispossessed* (2019) 125

Las Vegas stripper and real estate investor in *The Big Short* (2015) 131

Protestors against "Wall Street crooks" in *Panic* (2018) 144

Gillian Tett in *Inside Job* (2010) 151

Foreclosed homes in *Inside Job* (2010) 153

Michael Moore in *Capitalism: A Love Story* (2009) 159

View of the sky in *Room* (2015) 178

View from low-level home in *Parasite* (2019) 180

View from high-level home in *Parasite* (2019) 180

Daniel Kaluuya fights for freedom in *Get Out* (2017) 182

The uncertainty of housing's future 211

PREFACE

Homeland, housing, and homes.

These words were very much on my mind in 2019 as I began to research and write about residential real estate and the devastation the Great Recession caused. Then came the pandemic. Like many others, including those who should have known better, in early 2020 I initially failed to realize how dangerous the world was becoming. While in Los Angeles on March 5, my wife and I had lunch with friends in the crowded indoor confines of the Central Market in the city's downtown. We took no precautions. On March 11, I wrote a letter in which I naively asserted that "I am not esp. fearful" even though I was "aware system in this case (masks, ventilators, messaging, testing) is not yet up to snuff."[1] By March 16, we had cut short our annual stay in Southern California as snowbirds and returned home to Cambridge, Massachusetts. On the 21st, my wife, the historian Helen Lefkowitz Horowitz, and I participated in our first Zoom meeting—seven more followed in the next nine days. The new regime had begun.

When I returned to research and writing, I focused on how print media had covered (or, more frequently, failed to do so presciently) the global financial crisis of a dozen years before. I began to contemplate what changes were yet to come from the combination of the Great Recession and the pandemic, particularly what would happen in the homes where Americans lived. From then until now, I had to wonder what normality was like before the pandemic and what normal life would be at some point in the future.

If my research and writing was professional since that fateful spring, it was also very personal. I was among the most fortunate. We had returned to Cambridge because our doctors are there, though it turned out we did not have to consult them except on routine matters. My lockdown companion was the woman I first met on February 28, 1960, and still love deeply and dearly. Our financial situation soon strengthened as we spent less, saved more, and benefited from robust stock and real estate markets.

View from the author's desk. Photograph by the author.

We hunkered down in a safe and comfortable place. An infectious disease doctor who worked at Massachusetts General Hospital lived down the hall from our apartment. He easily convinced the condo board to keep me and my neighbors safe—initially by not allowing anyone but caregivers to enter the building.

During the pandemic, I was among the luckiest. The privileges of homeownership allowed me to escape the worst outcomes of the recession and the pandemic. Literally and figuratively, I had the space to explore, research, and write amid the inspiring treasures and trinkets in my home office. My desk faced what remained a familiar site. Bookcases contained volumes that fascinated and inspired me. Just above the computer screen, I could see on an eye-level shelf one of my favorite collections: miniature cars, including a model of a 1955 Chevrolet convertible that reminded me of an actual one I had driven across the country with two friends in the summer of 1960. We'd ended up at the Democratic National Convention in Los Angeles, witnessing the creation of the Kennedy-Johnson ticket. To the left of the bookcases hung two framed covers of the magazine *Judge*. One from 1905 conveyed worries about immigrants bringing "Filth," "Vice," and "Anarchy" into America. The other lamented the impending reelection of William McKinley in 1900.

At the top of the bookcase, on the right, stood another collection—this one of miniature buildings, including those at world's fairs and the Empire State Building with King Kong next to it, ready to climb to the top. And to the left, three pictures—of Helen and me at our wedding on August 18, 1963; of the two of us fifty years later; and of our children, Ben and Sarah, before they left our home in Northampton, Massachusetts. Love and work, as Sigmund Freud said.

Like many writers, I begin a book project with a clear idea of what interests me but a somewhat vague notion of what I will find and where I will find it. In some ways, this turned out to be true in this case, but with one big difference. Well into this project, the COVID-19 pandemic disrupted the lives of billions of people around the world; far less significantly, it also disrupted the course of my research and writing. After all, losing physical access to libraries paled in comparison with how hundreds of thousands of Americans lost their lives, scores of millions their livelihoods, and almost all of us our sense of well-being. Yet, as I hunkered down, relied on delivery of books from the public library, purchased others from online vendors, scoured the internet for research materials, and learned to use Zoom to keep in touch with friends and family, I also had abundant time to think about the larger implications of my research into residential real estate in the early twenty-first century.

Near the beginning of the pandemic, with friends in a book group, I read Laura Spinney's 2017 *Pale Rider: The Spanish Flu of 1918 and How It Changed the World*. Above the first line of the introduction, Spinney placed a quote from Terence Ranger's 2002 *The Spanish Influenza Pandemic of 1918–1919*: "The brevity of the influenza pandemic of 1918 posed great problems to doctors at the time. . . . It has posed great problems to historians ever since." Below she underscored how devastating that earlier pandemic was, infecting as it did "one in three people on earth" and killing up to 5 percent of people worldwide. As many as 100 million people, maybe as high a number as those who died in the twentieth century's two world wars. Perhaps, she wrote, it was "the greatest tidal wave of death . . . in the whole of human history." Spinney insisted that "the Spanish flu is remembered personally, not collectively. Not as a historical disaster, but as millions of discrete, private tragedies."[2]

Beginning in 1974, I had taught the second half of the American history survey. I am sure that I never mentioned the Spanish flu when I lectured on the years surrounding World War I. Rather, I focused on fights between interventionists and pacifists, the suppression of civil liberties, and the conflict's aftermaths. "War is the health of the state," Randolph Bourne wrote in 1918 during the presidency of Woodrow Wilson. "It automatically sets in motion throughout society those irresistible forces for uniformity, for passionate cooperation with the Government in coercing into obedience the minority groups and individuals which lack the larger herd sense."[3] I used those words in a public lecture at Smith College right after 9/11. I repeated them as I wondered out loud about their implications for the presidency of George W. Bush.

Reading a history of the Spanish flu pandemic of 1918–19 as the more recent pandemic wreaked havoc on lives around the world made me as a historian aware of the difficulty of integrating into a comprehensive historical narrative a dramatic tragedy that might seem like a one-off. So, in 2020, as I looked at what I was doing in my work on residential real estate in the early twenty-first century, I began to wonder about how to integrate seemingly singular events into a longer historical narrative—specifically, how to put into context 9/11, the Great Recession, and the COVID-19 pandemic, to say nothing of painfully polarized politics capped by the election of Donald J. Trump to the presidency in 2016.

Homeland, housing, and homes.

Three events have thus far helped define the twenty-first century: 9/11, the Great Recession, and the COVID-19 pandemic. The 9/11 terrorist attacks shocked the nation and began a seemingly unending war on terror. The Department of Homeland Security was established fourteen months later, but the attacks had already made Americans insecure about their homeland. That said, their anxieties seemed to focus more on the homeland in general than specifically on their individual homes. The situation changed sharply with the global financial crisis of 2007–8, tied directly to a housing bubble that had formed in the years after the immediate crisis of 9/11 had faded. A dozen years after the Great Recession that cost many Americans their homes after they found themselves unable to pay their mortgages, the meaning of home came once more to the fore as we faced the direct, palpable fear of the virus that lurked outside, and possibly even within. Homeland, housing, homes, inextricably linking public events here and abroad with the fundamental concerns of day-to-day living.

American Dreams, American Nightmares explores the multifaceted relationships between U.S. residential real estate, the Great Recession, and the COVID-19 pandemic. Drawing on a variety of sources—movies, TV shows, real estate workshops, journalism of the time and retrospective books, anthropological studies, and websites such as Airbnb and Zillow—I illuminate how a worldwide economic crisis and, later, a worldwide pandemic have reshaped how and where people live. These two events connected the global, national, and local. They intensified or initiated long-term and transformative trends, among them the tension between the reliance on the federal government and on free markets; America's place among nations; patterns of where Americans lived and how they worked; presidential leadership and partisan alignments; the relationships between diverse groups of Americans—men and women, parents and children, baby boomers and millennials, African Americans and whites, the rich and the poor, those who live in cities with robust economies and those who do not, and the power of new media and technologies in our lives. By better understanding how culture shapes the political, social, and economic aspects of homeownership, my hope is that we will be able to find new ways to ensure that safe, comfortable homes are more widely available than they are at present.

ACKNOWLEDGMENTS

Ever since I left the home where I grew up, I have lived in four dorm rooms, four college or university apartments, six rented apartments, three rented houses, three homes that Helen L. Horowitz and I owned, and five condo units that we purchased, including one we never lived in. Friends, housing offices, realtors, and mortgage companies have made it possible to do so—and I suppose this variety of residences has provided me with varied real estate experience that helped me write this book.

However, more important to whatever this book accomplishes is the help others have provided me as a scholar.

I carried out much of the research online, but librarians at Harvard University, Smith College, as well as the cities of Cambridge, Massachusetts, and Pasadena, California, did their best to get materials to me under difficult circumstances. Alas, the pandemic made impossible on-site research I had hoped to do in Waco, Texas; Orange Country, California; Las Vegas, Nevada; and at Than Merrill and Robert Kiyosaki workshops.

As usual, Judy Smith, Lynn Dumenil, and Helen L. Horowitz were my writing buddies who figuratively sat on my shoulder as my fingers hit keyboard keys and literally helped improve my prose and sharpen my arguments. In addition, there are many who nudged me along with encouragement and suggestions, among them Michelle Chihara, Ilana Gershon, Valeria Giacomin, Larry Glickman, Ben Horowitz, Sarah E. Horowitz, Jeffrey Jones, Julia Mickenberg, Helaine Olen, Maureen Ryan, Anya Schriffrin, Bruce Schulman, Steve Swidler, and Danny Walkowitz.

I had the extraordinary pleasure of teaching at Smith College for almost a quarter of a century, and that invigorating association continues to yield rewards. I am grateful to the college's Committee on Faculty Compensation and Development for continuing to support the scholarship of retired faculty members—modest financially but significant symbolically. It was at Smith that I met Ken Hafertepe, now a professor of museum studies at Baylor University and someone who has written prolifically on the history of architecture. Ken responded positively to my request that he read the chapter on HGTV's offerings. At critical moments, Rick Fantasia, a sociologist at Smith, helped me think through key issues. When I posted on Facebook a shout-out to those interested in what I was doing, the response was gratifying. Anna Campbell helped me understand how the sausage was made from the perspective of someone who had worked for HGTV for eight years. Christen Mucher joined the faculty shortly after I retired and then brought to her reading of the discussion of HGTV her abundant skills as a scholar, an editor, and an observer of the channel's offerings. After a decade of successfully working together on political campaigns and then reading a draft of the introduction, preface, and coda, Kim Probolus deployed her extraordinary skills as an editor to make useful editorial suggestions and, more importantly, pushed me to clarify my arguments and helped me find my voice. Anne McNeill, whom I taught when she returned to Smith College as a member of its transformative Ada Comstock Program, brought to the reading of a draft of the entire manuscript her passionate engagement, sharp intelligence, and more than ample ability to save me from major and minor mistakes. I am fortunate that Beth Prosnitz was willing to take time from her graduate program in sociology at University of Texas at Austin to reveal to me what it meant for someone whose own work is on real estate in Nepal (plus her command of housing on TV and on the ground in contemporary America) to apply her extraordinary editorial skills as she probed and urged me to deepen and clarify my argument. She revealed to me her stunning ability to move easily between lowly data and high theory.

Building on a friendship that has helped sustain me for decades since we were both in the Pioneer Valley, I called upon Peter Agree for help in thinking about writing a book and getting it published; hardly to my surprise, he did not disappoint. Peter introduced me to Peter Brown, who, having read several chapters, encouraged me to think about how to capture and sustain the interest of readers, something he did so successfully with *How Real Estate Developers Think* (2015).

When I was working on *Entertaining Entrepreneurs*, I had the good fortune to audit classes at the University of Southern California's Marshall School of Business, including ones by Christina Lubinski. The time I spent at USC's Lloyd Greif's Center for Entrepreneurial Studies, with Christina as my primary guide, helped me understand what the field of business history offered me. More recently, her reading of chapter 6 has reminded me of what I learned in her classroom and in ensuing conversations as she generously brought her astute intelligence and commanding knowledge to bear on the project.

With this project, I had to rely on people, most of whom I had not known before. Daniel Fridman engaged me in lively and suggestive exchanges about the role of financial self-help workshops. Abby Rapoport, who knows Waco well, applied her abundant editorial skills to chapter 1. With his usual keen eye and intelligence, Ken Lipartito urged me on at a moment when I thought my manuscript would never turn into a book. To a reading of chapters 3 and 4, Max Fraser brought his skills as a journalist who had reported on housing during the Great Recession as well as a historian who could return to the scene of the crimes as I reported on them. He thus offered exceptionally thoughtful and probing suggestions about how I might clarify and strengthen what I had written. As the dean of analysts among those who have written on how journalists covered the financial crisis, Dean Starkman also commented usefully on drafts of chapters 3 and 4, with interventions that were astute, probing, knowledgeable, and immensely helpful. Daniel Guttentag's terrific scholarship on Airbnb prompted me to open a conversation with him and eventually to ask him to read chapter 6. His full and careful response made clear to me that his acuity and expertise extended well beyond the study of tourism to include a wide range of factors driving transformations in housing. Focusing on chapters 4 and 5, James Stone both urged me on and helped me understand what might make them work more effectively. David Luberoff, deputy director of Harvard's Joint Center for Housing Studies, having read the introduction, chapter 6, and the coda, responded with a combination of extraordinary dedication, an impressive command of the relevant literature and issues, and editorial suggestions.

The kindness of strangers continued with economists. Three of them, all of whom study housing, read relevant chapters and commented usefully on them. The fact that we occupy different disciplinary worlds reminded me that as a historian I have a tendency to rely on storytelling and on the hope that the marshaling of evidence makes clear how I judge house flipping workshops. On the other hand, what struck me was how perceptive and helpful their responses were. Kyle Mangum guided me through the implications of recent research on speculation and house flipping. He also urged me to clarify and extend both my analyses and evaluations. As did Mangum, Craig Depken II wished (as do I) that we had data on the impact of the seminars on those who attended them. In addition, Depken read two relevant chapters with care and then responded astutely and urged me on. Chandler Lutz, whose work focuses on financial economics, read and commented on a draft of the entire manuscript—an act of extraordinary generosity. Moreover, I admired and benefited from his encouragement and astute suggestions. Our email exchanges across disciplinary boundaries reminded me how extraordinarily lucky I was to have the benefit of his attention, editorial skills, and commanding knowledge of relevant research, especially when he pointed to useful correctives to what I report. It was Lutz who suggested I look at the work of economists who emphasize the importance of expectations as a cause of higher home prices. That led me to Paul S. Willen and Christopher L. Foote, with whom I carried on informative and immensely clarifying email exchanges.

Anthropology of the financial world plays a significant role in this book. What set me off in that direction was that, at a key moment, David Gordon alerted me to the work of Gillian Tett at the *Financial Times*, a suggestion that over time opened up a whole world for me to examine. First, I turned to Don Brenneis, a dear friend and colleague since our days at the Claremont Colleges. He graciously agreed to read three relevant chapters, to which he responded with useful suggestions and abundant encouragement. I also discovered Melissa Fisher, whose work of two decades places her in a central position as a scholar who focuses on the intersection of gender, finance, and anthropology. In responding to chapters 3, 4, and 5, she marshaled her skills as an editor, anthropologist, and broadly informed observer of the worlds of finance.

Along with the kindness of friends and strangers, being financially secure and having good health was of immense importance as COVID-19 threatened the lives of so many others. In addition, regular Zoomathons played a critical and much-needed role in helping me thrive in the midst of the pandemic. Zoom conversations with Helen L. Horowitz, Monroe and Aimée Price, Betsy and Ted Rogers, Ted Stebbins, and Brenda Shapiro, though often focusing on shared interest in art history, could veer in unexpected and intriguing directions. Prepandemic (and I hope when we experience the new normal), our Boston-area Bookie group lifted my spirits and reminded me of the importance of new and old friendships with Florri Darwin, Fred and Joan Goldberg, Bob and Dale Mnookin, Joe and Meg Newhouse, and Al and Judy Warren. What replaced the winter gatherings of the Mardi Gris in Southern California's San Gabriel Valley were extraordinary conversations with David and the late Maggi Gordon, Sarah Hanley and Mac Rohrbough, Helen L. Horowitz, Perry Leavell and Barbara Oberg, François and Carol Rigolot, Bob Righter and Sherry Smith, Carl and Jane Smith, Pat Smith, and Sharon Strom and Fred Weaver. On a late June 2022 Zoom of the Huntington Library Scholars Seminar, Hal Barron, Nancy Buenger, Annick Foucrier, Dena Goodman, Kathy Kobayashi, Leslie Moch, Carol Rigolot, Lewis Siegelbaum, Carl Smith, Jane Smith, and David Zeidberg helped me think through key issues in the coda.

Helen L. Horowitz and I are fortunate to have two grandsons—Aaron Horowitz and Adam Liebman—who on weekly Zooms intrigued us with their virtual presence and engagement, as well as their ability to learn and remain resilient under the conditions COVID-19 imposed.

Once again I was fortunate to have a book published by the University of North Carolina Press. With tact and skill, Mary Carley Caviness, Cate Hodorowicz, and Iris Levesque guided the project from typescript manuscript to published book. I am especially grateful to Erin Granville for the wisdom, intelligence, and tact she deployed in the final stages of book making. Emily Shelton's extraordinary skills as a copyeditor were abundantly apparent in ways that prevented me from making mistakes, improved my prose, and clarified my arguments. María García handled key editorial issues with great care and intelligence. Once again, but this time under the difficult circumstances that the pandemic imposed, Mark Simpson-Vos revealed how skillful editorial work and appropriate encouragement made it possible for me to conclude and then publish a book.

AMERICAN DREAMS, AMERICAN NIGHTMARES

INTRODUCTION

In *Letters from an American Farmer* (1782), his classic statement of what the New World meant, the Frenchman J. Hector St. John Crèvecœur celebrated what homeownership represented. "I never return home without feeling some pleasing emotion, which I often suppress as useless and foolish. The instant I enter on my own land, the bright idea of property, of exclusive right, of independence exalt my mind. . . . no wonder that so many Europeans who have never been able to say that such portion of land was theirs, cross the Atlantic to realise that happiness."[1] From before he wrote and for centuries after, many Americans associated where they lived with what Crèvecœur evoked: independence, happiness, private property, and exclusivity. To such a list we'd have to add that homeownership also represented a form of domestic capitalism infused with both moral values and wealth building; a commitment to hard work and family; and aspirations for membership in the middle class that in various combinations linked citizenship, a sense of belonging, and the good life.

Over the course of American history, writers have envisioned the home as everything from a peaceful refuge to a painful trap. In the nineteenth century, the Beecher sisters offered influential visions of home life. In 1869 Catharine Beecher wrote *American Woman's Home, or Principles of Domestic Science: Being a Guide to the Formation and Maintenance of Economical, Healthful, Beautiful, and Christian Homes*, an updated version of her 1841 *Treatise on Domestic Economy, For the Use of Young Ladies at Home and at School*. These books influenced and reflected what white middle-class women experienced and aspired to by offering a vision of domesticity that combined patriotism, scientific management of the household, and Christian evangelical commitments with practical advice. Her books helped their readers navigate the relationship between the female head of the house and her female servants. Harriet Beecher Stowe's 1852 *Uncle Tom's Cabin; or, Life among the Lowly*, a book written by her sister, offered a series of set pieces through which the author explored the dynamics of relationships between the wives of white slaveowners and enslaved African Americans.

A more modern version of the home as highly problematic came in Betty Friedan's 1963 *The Feminine Mystique*. Friedan put forward a negative example of domestic life when she wrote of the suburban home as a comfortable concentration camp. Like the books by the Beecher sisters, Friedan's book relied on separate spheres, a world of busy wives and absent husbands. Yet her vision differed markedly from those of the Beecher sisters. Her commitments were secular; her understanding of the relationship between consumer culture and domesticity negative; and her hopes for liberation from the home's clutches replaced inspired management of domesticity.[2]

How Crèvecœur, the Beecher sisters, and Friedan envisioned the home found some echoes in the domestic dramas that played out in the Great Recession and the COVID-19 pandemic. How the "bright idea of property, of exclusive right, of independence" exalted the mind persisted under conditions vastly different from what Crèvecœur celebrated in the late eighteenth century. The Christian evangelicalism of the Beecher sisters found some echoes in the early twenty-first century. However, what replaced the sometimes benign racial dynamics offered in *Uncle Tom's Cabin* was a pervasive and pernicious racism that shaped the lives of tens of millions of African Americans. Gendered divisions, albeit often weakened, persisted from Friedan's world into the next century. Yet if she described what she called consumer culture's "sexual sell," early in the new century the vastly expanded but often celebrated power of commercialism drove crises that were more broadly global than narrowly domestic.

This book, *American Dreams, American Nightmares*, contributes to and reframes what others have written on the Great Recession and the COVID-19 pandemic. It does so by placing the stories of these two momentous events in broader historical contexts than have many observers and by deploying interdisciplinary perspectives, drawing on HGTV, house-flipping workshops, print journalism, horror films, documentaries, anthropology, and new media. What replaced the perspectives that Crèvecœur, the Beecher sisters, and Friedan offered was the home as a financialized commodity inextricably connected to institutions and people around the world. During the pandemic, the home may have become a sanctuary from a dangerous world, yet in the midst of the crises of the new century it was hard to avoid comparing the home to a metal ball bouncing around a roulette wheel as it tried to find a rewarding resting place.

To be sure, history reminds us that over time the actual nature of the home has varied considerably. In the nineteenth century, in both mythology and actuality, citizens lit out for the Western frontier, where, through hard work, they hoped to prosper on a homestead. Enslaved African Americans tended a small plot of land they did not own on which they could raise crops and animals; once freed in the post–Civil War South, the federal government failed to provide their forty acres and a mule. Though less mythologized than other choices, throughout America's history millions of people have aspired to live safely and comfortably in urban settings. More frequently in the twentieth century and early twenty-first, domestic longing has focused on a suburban home with well-tended front and back yards.[3]

Throughout American history, the connection between homeownership and the American dream frequently bumped up against reality. Sometimes homeownership could be what Crèvecœur called "useless and foolish." And of course many people did not own their homes outright, since financial institutions frequently held their mortgages. In addition, natural disasters struck and, along with health crises and job losses, imperiled the ability of mortgage holders to make monthly payments. The value of residential real estate could go down as well as up. Homeownership could tie a family to a geographical location when better opportunities beckoned. Moreover, even though federal programs have provided those with low incomes with homeownership far beyond what free markets have achieved, a variety of forces have made it impossible for a hefty proportion of the nation's population, the poor and minorities especially, to enjoy the benefits of owning a home. Those who rent could be at the mercy of greedy or needy landlords. It turns out that pursuit of an "exclusive right" has actually excluded others, especially people of color and those of modest means, or of no means at all.

Over the long course of American history, the actions of public and private institutions have influenced where and how people live, favoring homeowners over renters, whites over Black and brown people, the native-born over immigrants, those in the upper and middle classes over those below, people living on farms and in suburbs over urban dwellers, and lenders over borrowers. In contemporary America, the power of conservation commissions, historical commissions, and local zoning boards that control the who, what, when, and how of residential choices is among the most significant factors shaping access to homeownership. Also among the influential private sector actors are financial institutions on Main Street, Wall Street, and in suburban strip malls as well as local real estate agents and the National Association of Realtors (NAR), the organization that represents them and protects their interests.[4] The federal government exercises power over people's choices in important and myriad ways. Through its ability to set interest rates, to some extent the Federal Reserve Board influences where people live by influencing borrowing costs and the rates of inflation in ways that in turn affect the price of residential living and the prospect for increased home values. Through the tax code, legislative and administrative bodies pick winners and losers in ways that usually favor the powerful and the well-to-do. Similarly, laws and how they are administered place some in advantageous positions and others in jeopardy.

Until the New Deal, the federal government influenced residential choices on farms more than elsewhere. Aided by the completion of a national railroad network, the conquest, slaughter, and removal of indigenous peoples to reservations opened up vast stretches of land to settlers who emigrated from Europe or coastal areas. The Homestead Act of 1862 shaped the allocation and development of land west of the line of initial settlements by offering settlers 160 acres of federal land in exchange for a small fee, five years of continuous occupancy, and a commitment to improve their holdings. Freed enslaved folks were offered what turned out to be empty promises, both the 40 acres and a mule and access to what the Homestead Act provided others. Before the 1930s, the federal government had a relatively minor and indirect role in shaping residential living in and around cities. With about two-thirds of those who did not live on farms renting rather than owning, rates of homeownership remained modestly low, which was also shaped by the fact that most mortgages were five years or shorter in duration, with substantial down payments required. With the exception of the promotion of rural homesteading, until the 1930s what came from the nation's capital was more about public relations than public policy. In 1917, the Department of Labor launched an Own Your Own Home campaign, and in response to the Russian Revolution, President Woodrow Wilson and the NAR advocated individual homeownership as an alternative to Communism's vision of collectivism. Then, in the 1920s, Herbert Hoover promoted a Better Homes in America movement that was backed by ample words rather than robust policies or funding.[5]

Except for the persistence and even strengthening of racist policies and practices that disadvantaged African Americans and others, the 1930s brought fundamental changes to residential real estate, some of which helped pave the way for what happened in the early twenty-first century.[6] With foreclosures accelerating and new construction stalled, the federal government acted, at first gingerly and then forcefully. In 1932, a year before Franklin D. Roosevelt started his presidency, Congress created a system of Federal Home Loan Banks that supported home financing by providing member financial institutions with services and liquidity. When Roosevelt took office, almost one in four homeowners faced foreclosure; however, the Home Owners' Loan Corporation (HOLC, 1933–54) helped stabilize housing markets by refinancing mortgages or selling foreclosed homes. New Deal programs strengthened housing markets in other ways, including by fostering appraisal and construction standards. They also led to a restructuring of the banking system that over time would enhance the flow of private capital to underwrite homeownership, especially for white suburbanites living away from major financial centers. The Federal Housing Administration (FHA), founded in 1934, developed twenty-year (later extended to thirty-year), low-money-down, fixed-rate mortgages that made it more possible for Americans to think of their homes as a way of building wealth by accumulating equity through more modest monthly payments. If that helped middle-class families live in free-standing homes, the United States Housing Authority, created in 1937, sponsored public housing for the urban working class. Legislation underwrote policies that federal agencies administered and that in turn would shape modern homeownership for decades to come. Most significantly for what happened early in the twenty-first century was the 1938 creation of the Federal National Mortgage Association, or Fannie Mae. As a government-sponsored enterprise (GSE) that offered implicit guarantees and lower capital costs, it became a powerful public-private partnership that strengthened lending institutions by purchasing and guaranteeing FHA-insured mortgages, especially for low-to-middle-income families. Then, in 1944, came the Servicemen's Readjustment Act, commonly known as the GI Bill, which provided no-down-payment, low-interest mortgages to veterans.[7]

Together, these policies benefited low- and middle-income white families at the same time that they discriminated against African Americans and others. Along with lax enforcement of remedial laws, what Richard Rothstein in *The Color of Law* (2017) calls "systematic and forceful" policies, legislation, and practices at all levels of government shaped racialized patterns of segregation in housing.[8] As Kenneth T. Jackson notes in *Crabgrass Frontier* (1985), the result of federal policies was "to segregate the races, to concentrate the disadvantaged in inner cities, and to reinforce the image of suburbia as a place of refuge for the problems of race, crime, and poverty."[9] Redlining under the New Deal strengthened earlier patterns such as restrictive covenants in suburbs (ruled illegal in the postwar years) and racialized zoning laws in cities. The practices of real estate agents, appraisers, bankers, and city officials and the resistance of white homeowners doubled down on these patterns of residential segregation. The FHA used urban maps to rank neighborhoods according to their attractiveness to mortgage lenders: Best, Still Desirable, Declining, and Hazardous. That last category redlined residential areas, home to immigrants and African Americans, that banks should avoid financing, including through mortgages backed by the federal government, thus sharply limiting the access to financing for African Americans and others.[10]

In other cases, how policies were framed and administered followed the patterns of what the title of Ira Katznelson's 2005 book calls out as *When Affirmative Action Was White*: government actions that benefited some and disadvantaged others.[11] Since home equity is the principal way most Americans accumulate wealth, over the long run discriminatory federal housing policies helped some groups accumulate it while making it difficult for others, principally African Americans, to do so. Moreover, federal policies made it possible for millions of whites to live in detached, automobile-dependent, single-family homes located on leafy plots of land while confining a significant number of Blacks and others to public housing and cramped urban apartments.

In the post–World War II period, the impact of these policies fully took hold, intensified by other factors as well. Savings and loan associations, real estate agents supported by the NAR, government officials, suburban developers, and the mass media joined in a concerted effort to boost homeownership, especially for whites moving from both rural areas and cities into rapidly developing suburbs.[12] American suburban development had begun in the 1850s and, courtesy of streetcars, trolleys, and commuter railways, attracted more and more people. Yet it was in the years after the end of World War II that the car-dependent suburb, first noticeable in the 1920s, became prominent and iconic. Indeed, most of the scholarship focuses on how the postwar period witnessed the explosive growth of American suburbs, which was important because of their close connection to the American dream in those years and because the financing of homeownership through mortgages there was central to the global economic crisis in the early twenty-first century.[13] In response to the housing shortage created by returning veterans, family formation, and the beginning of the baby boom, Congress passed the Housing Act of 1949, which promised, in the buoyant words of the U.S. Code, "the realization as soon as feasible of the goal of a decent home and a suitable living environment for every American family, thus contributing to the development and redevelopment of communities and to the advancement of the growth, wealth, and security of the Nation."[14]

The legislation underwrote the building of some urban apartments, but, as Gwendolyn Wright has noted, since government officials "associated healthy family life with nonurban settings," the focus was primarily on suburban ones with ample backyards. A 1945 article in the *Saturday Evening Post* provided evidence of what American families wanted: a mere 14 percent indicated they were willing to occupy an apartment or a home someone else had already lived in.[15] "No man who owns his own home and a lot can be a Communist," remarked Levittown developer William Levitt in 1950s.[16]

Powerful forces continued and accelerated familiar patterns that helped some but hindered others—above all, people of color, especially African Americans, but others as well, whom government policies, developers, local officials, real estate agents, banks, and white homeowners prevented from buying a home in the suburbs. To be sure, beginning in the late 1940s and continuing into the 1970s, federal legislation promoted urban redevelopment not only by clearing out supposedly blighted neighborhoods but also by subsidizing the construction of urban housing, providing rent assistance for tenants, and helping fund housing for the elderly.

Yet, in the postwar period, powerful forces intensified long-standing racial patterns of homeownership. The 1949 Housing and Urban Redevelopment Act and the 1954 Urban Renewal Act, by aiming to improve the quality and quantity of residential options in cities, with more promise than success, sought to integrate African Americans into the housing fabric of cities and to stem white flight to suburbs.[17] However, other, more powerful forces were at work, transforming urban landscapes in ways that disadvantageously impacted the urban poor, including many African Americans. Between 1949 and 1967, urban renewal uprooted almost three-quarters of a million families, African Americans among them disproportionately. The Federal Aid Highway Act of 1956 wiped out African American and working-class sections of cities, created geographical divisions between Blacks and whites, and made it easier for whites to stay away from cities and employers to move factories, stores, and offices away from urban centers. More generally, the ways cities subsidized and assessed properties, along with provisions in the federal tax code, such as deductions for mortgage interest and real estate taxes and the preferential treatment of capital gains on home sales, exacerbated inequalities of wealth and income and favored the financial interests of homeowners, the well-to-do among them especially.

In the postwar period, with the support of federal legislation and financing, developers plowed ahead. As part of the exuberance of the

American Century, particularly in the twenty-five years following the end of World War II, suburban life became central to national identity, albeit at the cost of hollowing out cities and diminishing urban manufacturing. Suburbs came in a relatively wide range of types, marked by clear class differences—the inner ring of older ones contrasting with the newer ones edging toward exurban living. Yet, in numbers, popular imagination, and among widely read social commentators, corporations that operated on a large, industrial scale, such as Levitt & Sons, took the lead in developing suburbs that offered homes to whites, including the children of immigrants, who were escaping cities as they began to rise from the working and lower middle classes. Located in what Dolores Hayden calls "sitcom suburbs," where shopping centers were powerful draws, they were "deliberately planned to maximize consumption of mass-produced goods and minimize the responsibility of the developers to create public space and public services."[18] The typical occupants of these car-dependent residences were single-generation families—middle-class and above, often (and stereotypically) headed by white men who commuted to work in large corporations while their wives and children remained in the home and at neighborhood schools. Initially many of the homes were small, averaging less than 1000 square feet and built on small plots of land. Eventually the size of typical homes and of the land they stood on grew, as did their distance from city centers.

Between 1950 and 1960, the number of Americans living in suburbs grew dramatically. Cities, especially in the Northeast and Upper Midwest, lost considerable numbers to nearby suburbs. For example, from 1950 to 1980, Manhattan's numbers slipped from 1,960,101 to 1,428,285. Not coincidentally, the population in the two counties to the east on Long Island escalated, from 948,894 in 1950 to 2,712,311 thirty years later. St. Louis and Detroit experienced the most dramatic population decreases, between 1950 and 2010, both falling slightly more than 60 percent. Not everyone who left places like New York City and Cleveland headed for nearby suburbs. Warmer weather, air conditioning, and the possibility of better jobs lured many Americans to Sun Belt cities in the South and the West. Among the most striking results of the massive postwar population shifts was the dramatic growth of suburban population in the epicenters of the financial crisis later in the new century. The population of Orange County, California, stood at 130,760 around 1940 and at 3,175,692 circa 2020. Statistics are similar for other places where developers turned raw land into sprawling suburbs: Las Vegas had only 8,422 inhabitants in 1940, but eighty years later the number was more than 650,000. In the same years, Orlando went from a mere 36,737 to around 300,000 (and to 2 million for the metropolitan area), and Phoenix from 65,414 to about 1.7 million.

Along with the postwar economic boom, all these forces—the policies of the federal government, the powerful mobilization of real estate developers and mass media, the momentous shifts of population from farms and cities to suburbs and from Rust Belt to Sun Belt, and the robust aspirations of homeowners—underwrote a dramatic increase in homeownership, figures driven in turn by age, marital status, family composition, class, and race.[19] From 1890 to the end of World War II in 1945, the rate of homeownership in the United States remained between 40 and 50 percent, with most people renting or living in institutional settlings. It began to rise significantly in the postwar period, reaching a peak just below 70 percent right before the financial crash of the early twenty-first century. Then it declined toward the low 60s, bottomed out around 2016, and began to rise again, albeit not to its pre–Great Recession heights.[20]

Late twentieth-century federal legislation attempted to address some of the persistent problems that prevented millions from achieving the American dream of homeownership. On paper, the Fair Housing Act of 1968—passed shortly after the assassination of Dr. Martin Luther King Jr.—banned redlining and more generally sought to prevent residential discrimination in the selling, renting, and financing of housing, including on the basis of race. As administered, however, what hobbled its effectiveness were limited powers of enforcement and outright obstruction from people ranging from high-ranking federal officials to on-the-ground sellers, neighborhood associations, real estate agents, and money lenders. Indeed, the impact of historic patterns of discrimination continues today.[21] The Housing and Urban Development Act of the same year failed to fulfill its promise of building or rehabbing tens of millions of residences over ten years, with almost one-quarter of them designated for households with low-to-moderate levels of income. As the historian Keeanga-Yamahtta Taylor has convincingly shown, powerful forces undermined these and other federal efforts to end racial discrimination and support housing options for African Americans in cities and suburbs. What she calls "predatory inclusion" underscores that, absent a sustained commitment by the federal government, real estate agents and financial institutions were able to pursue profits rather than inclusive justice. Deep-seated racism persisted despite new legislation, with policies that were supposed to support homeownership by African Americans actually ending up developing new means of exploitation. Despite its promise, urban renewal resulted, Taylor writes, in creating "the conditions for continued extraction as opposed to development and renewal." Given that "racial inequality was structured and embedded within the architecture of the system of buying and selling real estate in the United States," the attempt to substantially open up housing opportunities for African Americans in predominantly white suburbs was hobbled if not doomed.[22]

In the last quarter of the twentieth century and the very early years of the twenty-first, the federal government developed additional policies to increase homeownership for people of color and those with modest economic resources. The 1977 Community Reinvestment Act incentivized financial institutions to support home purchases in low- and moderate-income neighborhoods. In 1995 the Clinton administration put forward a robust proposal, the National Homeownership Strategy: Partners in the American Dream, which loosened restrictions on home loans as a way to make housing more affordable. Then, in 2003, President George W. Bush proposed the Ownership Society, which, in order to increase rates of minority homeownership, involved tax credits, help with down payments, and the promise of a robust public-private partnership to expand the availability of mortgages. To some extent these government programs and, more importantly, low interest rates expanded the opportunity for homeownership.[23] However, among the factors that limited progress was that the increase in housing prices outpaced the growth in household incomes and that the growth of housing stock, influenced by zoning and NIMBYism ("Not in My Backyard"), was not adequate, given the increase in population and people's aspirations.

Despite efforts to redress historic discriminatory patterns, on the eve of the 2008 financial crash the differences in rates of homeownership among groups were significant and consequential. For Blacks the percentage was 46; Latinx, 49; Asian Americans, just under 60; Native Americans, 56; and for non-Hispanic whites about 75, or more than 50 percent higher than for Blacks or Latinx. Even if we control for income, the gap (now at historically high levels) remains substantial, across all income levels but decreasingly so as they rise.[24] These figures are significant because, especially for people of modest circumstances, homeownership represents the most significant element in household assets. For middle-class Americans, home equity accounts for 60 percent of household wealth. Wealth is important because it enables a family to cushion adversity and pass security, status, and opportunities from one generation to the next.

The income gap across racial lines is serious enough—Black families earn approximately 60 percent of what white ones do. However, the gap turns into a chasm when we focus instead on wealth: a typical Black family's wealth is 10 percent of a typical white family's, around $8,000 versus $80,000. In other words, if African Americans earn about two-thirds of the wages of whites, they accumulate 10 percent of the wealth. Strikingly, the rate of homeownership among college-educated African Americans is lower than for households headed by whites who do not even complete high school. Moreover, the long-term consequences of public policies and the racist practices in the private sector persist over time. Among them are discriminatory lending practices, intergenerational wealth transfers, the ways the continuation of housing segregation affects the value of homes and educational opportunities, and the consequences of favorable tax treatment connected to homeownership. As the sociologist Thomas Shapiro has put it, the distribution of "wealth represents the sedimentation of historical inequalities in the American experience" and provides "a window to explore how our past influences the realities of today."[25] The consequences of all of this for African Americans are enormous and long lasting, sharply limiting their ability to accumulate wealth through homeownership and confining many of them to cramped quarters and neighborhoods where violence cuts their lives short, the lack of good job opportunities limits their livelihoods, and environmental degradation compromises their health.[26]

The celebratory emphasis on escalating percentages of homeownership and on suburban homeownership, as well as the focus on the persistence of discrimination against minorities, should not hide others left on the sidelines of the comfortable mainstream of residential living, some by forces beyond their control. In Frank Capra's 1946 *It's a Wonderful Life*, we watch as George Bailey (Jimmy Stewart) tells members of the board of a savings and loan association how moral and important homeownership is when he asks rhetorically, "Doesn't it make them better citizens?" He poses this question to Mr. Potter (Lionel Barrymore), a wealthy board member who wants to take over the family-owned bank. Potter opposed a mortgage to a taxi driver who was part of the "discontented, lazy rabble." In response Bailey remarks, "This rabble you're talking about, they do most of the working and paying and living and dying in this community. Well, is it too much for them to work and live and die in a couple of decent rooms and a bath?" Annie (Lillian Randolph), the African American maid in the Bailey home, is stereotypically offered up as a woman without a family, let alone a home of her own. However, it is not only "discontented, lazy rabble" and African American maids who had limited access to the American dream of homeownership after 1945.

These days a significant number of Americans live in circumstances that are not included in the celebratory discussions of homeownership.

Culturally, homeownership may be the apex of storied achievement, but the evidence is that for varied reasons this is not often the case—people live under other conditions temporarily, involuntarily, and less comfortably housed than others. We might begin with the 400,000 immigrants in detention centers; the 2.2 million people incarcerated (including as many as 100,000 in solitary confinement); and the 170,000 in mental institutions. In addition there are the more than 150,000 Native Americans on reservations; 1.4 million people in nursing homes; 640,000 seniors inhabiting retirement communities; 2 million residing in public housing; 8 million representing the estimated 40 percent of college students who live on campus; 4.5 million who live on farms; more than 18 million who live in trailers or other manufactured homes; and the more than 500,000 homeless people. Together, all these figures account for more than 10 percent of Americans, and there are additionally millions who reside in small towns, in condos they own, or in apartments they rent.[27]

Then if we forget all these folks and jump over the ample middle to which so much attention is offered, we come to the apex of residential living, to which the mass media attends more than scholars. Donald Trump was the first president since antebellum slaveowners to have his fortune—such as it is and theirs were—in real property. He moved between the White House; the 62,500-square-foot, 126-room mansion at Mar-a-Lago; his residence at the Trump National Golf Course in Bedminster, New Jersey; and the three-story penthouse in Trump Tower on Manhattan's Fifth Avenue. Perhaps from there he can see the most expensive residence ever sold in the United States, a penthouse overlooking Central Park that the billionaire Ken Griffin purchased for $238 million in 2019. Redolent of extravagant living threatened by the global financial crisis is the 2012 documentary film *Queen of Versailles*, hailed by one observer as "perhaps the single best film on the Great Recession."[28] David and Jackie Siegel dreamed of living in the mansion they were building on the outskirts of Orlando that was modeled on the royal residence outside Paris. However, when the Great Recession threatened the Florida timeshare fortune David had built, the Siegels had to halt construction as David focused on saving his enterprises in Las Vegas—like Central Florida, another epicenter of the real estate crash. The film dramatizes the results: construction stopped, servants fired, pets abandoned, and the results of Jackie's compulsive shopping strewn all over the residence.[29]

Another, more widespread example of risky financing was what I remember seeing on billboards in Northern California in 2006, promising people that they could get a home mortgage with little or no money down. At the time I understood how risky that was for the home buyer. It turned out that homeownership—or at least a safe and comfortable place to live, so central to American aspirations—was soon in danger for millions and millions of Americans. Perhaps at the time I realized the problem this might pose to an individual bank or mortgage company, but, naive me, I didn't anticipate the damage done to the banking system, let alone to the American and global economies.

Here is a relatively simple explanation along those lines.[30] Beginning in the 1970s, a perfect storm of globalization, changes in technology and public policy, as well as the increasingly unjust distribution of wealth and income, imperiled the economic health of vast numbers of Americans. In response, they borrowed money, including what was necessary to finance homeownership, higher education, and consumer goods. As a result, homeowners and financial institutions, respectively, took on greater and greater risk in order to borrow and lend money. Eventually, what turned out to be a fragile financial system collapsed, causing huge losses in homeownership and damage to the financial well-being of households, financial institutions, and the world's economy.

Now a more extensive explanation that focuses less on individuals and more on structural forces: From the mid-1940s until the early 1970s, the relatively widespread distribution of the fruits of sustained economic growth in the United States helped improve the financial security of Americans and in turn enabled more and more families to purchase more commodious residences using mortgages they believed they were likely to be able to afford. Then, beginning in the 1970s, a number of things changed. A momentous shift occurred in what most people could earn from employment and the wealthiest from investing. At the same time, deregulation meant financial institutions could grow more powerful and take on more risk, while consumers had less protection. New technologies not only facilitated the development, lending, and borrowing of increasingly complicated financial instruments but also imperiled jobs, especially in the manufacturing and service sectors. New modes of transportation and communication, changes in public policy, and globalization shifted production abroad and made it possible for capital to flow freely and quickly across national borders. The busting of trade unions, the more general erosion of labor's power and wages, the weakening of social welfare programs, and the rising cost of higher education, which outpaced inflation, endangered the possibilities of social mobility and economic security. Securitization and speculation in housing and stock markets, abetted by government policies including low interest rates and favorable tax treatment of capital gains, intensified class and generational inequalities. Notably disadvantaged are the approximately

72 million millennials born between 1981 and 1996. Having sought homeownership later than the baby boomers, they control only 4 percent of equity in real estate even though they are the largest generation of Americans.

Together these forces have fostered socioeconomic inequalities, jeopardizing the economic well-being of vast numbers of people, including many in the middle class. Increasingly homeownership was out of reach of many Americans, including the working poor, African Americans, and Latinx, as well as many millennials and those born after them. Simultaneously these forces dramatically increased the economic resources of the wealthy, the top 20 percent, and, even more significantly, the top 1 or 2 percent of Americans. In these contexts, the pursuit of "lifestyles" could barely paper over the painful costs of economic and social stagnation vividly seen amid the dual crises of the Great Recession and the COVID-19 pandemic.[31]

Something had to happen in order to sustain an economy in which private consumption, including of residential real estate, played such a prominent role. What took the place of social mobility and relatively secure jobs with decent benefits was debt that financed higher education, residential real estate, automobiles, extended vacations, and household goods. To finance such burgeoning debt, financial institutions had to develop new ways to lend people money and new ways to underwrite these loans. Lower interest rates (which over the long term came down from their 1970s highs) and access to borrowing helped create what some called a bubble and others a boom in the housing markets. Banks, publicists, realtors, and journalists fostered optimistic expectations about the future of housing prices. The result of all these changes was a riskier and more fragile economic system, one in which speculation was central.

Thus, the Great Recession of the first decade of the twenty-first century had many causes, prominent among them the aspirations and naivete of prospective homeowners, the avarice of people who ran financial institutions, and the federal government's actions and inactions. The result, clear for all to see by the fall of 2008, helped wreck not only real homes but also the house of cards built on complex and often inscrutable financial instruments sold to investors around the world and backed, at some distance, by home mortgages in America. Designed to spread and minimize risk, in the end financialization—the increasing prominence of the financial sector in the economy and the insidious spread of market orientation and uncertainty from financial markets to everyday lives—turned out to intensify risk instead.[32]

The efforts to increase rates of homeownership by decreasing requirements for underwriting mortgages made them available to borrowers whose ability to meet monthly payments was uncertain for most Americans, given factors such as the risk of losing a job or having to pay for unexpected costs, especially for health care. In the supposedly good old days, before mortgages became so highly securitized and leveraged, your bank or savings and loan association funded your mortgage, a simple and rather boring loan that it then kept on its books. This meant local bankers had to be as sure as reasonably possible that even over a thirty-year period you would be able to make the monthly payments. In the 1970s, the dual processes of deregulation and the invention of new financial instruments began to transform the businesses of borrowing and lending, including mortgages. The processes of financialization and securitization—fancy names for what happened—began at Salomon Brothers in the late 1970s with the development of mortgage-backed securities. Once-staid and now-aggressive investment banks such as Goldman Sachs and Lehman Brothers bought mortgages from local banks and then bundled thousands of them into bonds that could be easily assembled, repackaged, and traded.

This meant that the financing of homeownership was changing dramatically. A number of factors, including the demise of savings and loan associations due to speculation and regulatory failures, meant that there were fewer thirty-year fixed-rate mortgages and more with little or no money down, interest-only or balloon payments, and low initial teaser rates. The government and financial institutions allowed people to submit a minimal amount of evidence, or, in some cases, inaccurate data or none at all, for nonconforming loans. Patterns of compensation incentivized people, from investment bankers in Manhattan to storefront loan officers in suburbs, to cut corners dangerously. Banks and investment companies, aided by sophisticated technologies, invented ways of financing debt that were more and more complicated and risky. Prominent among them were derivatives: in effect, contracts involving bets upon bets upon bets backed at several removes by an underlying asset, including home equity. These often arcane financial instruments, lightly regulated or regulated not at all, tore asunder the relationships between derivatives and their underlying value as assets. Subprime mortgages were the riskiest, and their value rose from $35 billion in 1994 to $625 billion in 2005. Increasingly, mortgages originated not with local bankers knowledgeable about borrowers and local conditions but by local brokers, many of them inexperienced, who earned outsized fees by generating loans that were packaged and repackaged in distant financial centers into mortgage-backed securities whose contents, backed by exotic derivatives, were opaque and whose regulations were beyond the purview of federal agencies. By 2008 there was $683 trillion in unregulated derivatives.

The private rating agencies, charged with evaluating these instruments, were more interested in increasing their profitability than in carefully and accurately assessing risk. The web of financial institutions became more and more complicated, dominated by a few huge investment banks in Manhattan that, freed from the restrictions of the Glass-Steagall Act of 1933 that kept investment and retail banks separate, took on greater and greater risk as they dramatically increased their debt-to-capital ratios. Combined, all these changes meant that a retirement fund for thousands of Brazilian teachers could hold a mortgage on a suburban home in Las Vegas.

This tied together the fates of the global and local, which the historian Adam Tooze effectively captures in *Crashed: How a Decade of Financial Crises Changed the World* (2018). "Ground zero was America's housing market," he convincingly shows. "Triggered by the humdrum market for American real estate," the global origins and implications of the crisis rested in securitization, the complicated processes by which debts (and, in this case, especially residential mortgages) were pooled and packaged before being sold in layers to institutional parties in ways that made it nearly impossible to figure out the nature and value of underlying holdings. Known mainly only to specialists, a dizzying array of terms and what they represented played central roles in the collapse of the global economy. This was a crisis whose central driving forces resided in the complicated nexus that connected powerful institutions like Wall Street and the City of London banks, sovereign wealth funds, the Federal Reserve, the Bank of China, and the European Central Bank with mortgage-holding families in America's suburbs and pensioners in much of the developed world.[33]

The federal government only intensified already-risky arrangements, resulting in problematic policies that played critical roles in causing the Great Recession. After the burst of the dot-com bubble in early 2000 and the terrorist attacks on 9/11 in 2001, chair of the Federal Reserve Board Alan Greenspan eased interest rates nine times, from a high above 6 percent just after the beginning of the century to a low below 1 percent in 2004. In 1981, rates on thirty-year fixed-rate mortgages hit a peak just over 16 percent and by 2009 had fallen to 5 percent. Federal regulators, housed in an alphabet soup of overlapping agencies that did not always coordinate their efforts and instead often worked at cross-purposes, got mired in situations they decided not to control.

As a result of these and other factors, the value of residential real estate increased at first slowly and then dramatically. According to one authoritative study, the index number for national home prices rose from 64 in January 1987 to 100 at century's end. The pace then accelerated, with the figure peaking at 184 in the summer of 2006 before declining rapidly to 134 in early 2012.[34] The rise and fall were especially dramatic in suburban areas of Florida, Arizona, and Nevada. Take the extreme example of Las Vegas: In early 2000, the index of home prices stood at 100 and by early 2003 at 122. In just three and a half years, by July 2006, that figure was at 234. By March 2012, it had plummeted to 98.

Nationally the situation was similar, though less dramatically so. As the new century dawned and increasingly soon after, housing prices escalated while the incomes of most Americans remained more or less stable, in the process upsetting the historic relationships between family incomes and the cost of residential real estate. In 1967 the median price of new housing was just below 3 times median household income; that ratio peaked at 4.7 in 2005 and fell to a low point of 3.27 in 2011 before steadily rising to 4.37 in 2020.[35] To finance housing purchases, people took on more and more debt while financial institutions tried to manage the resulting risk by devising increasingly complex and arcane financial instruments. The dramatic rise in housing prices in cities and their suburbs, especially ones like Las Vegas, tempted considerable numbers of people to see a home not simply as a place to live but as a tradeable commodity. They could leverage short-term gains as they treated houses as a combination of cash cows and roulette wheels when they bought, sold, and borrowed. In the process, they took money out to pay for fancy cars and expensive vacations or doubled, tripled, or even quadrupled their speculative bets. After the ink had dried on paperwork and the dust had settled on construction sites, nationally 8 million homes had been foreclosed on and $7 trillion in home equity had vanished. The International Monetary Fund stated that the world experienced the destruction of more than $50 trillion in assets, a figure equal to the annual value of goods and services.[36] Statistics can only begin to convey the pain Americans faced: their dreams destroyed or put on hold, their lives upended, and their health and security at risk.[37]

The most intense phase of the global financial crisis came in late 2008 and early 2009, at the end of the presidency of George W. Bush and the beginning of Barack Obama's. In response, and together with Congress and the Federal Reserve Board, these two presidents took unprecedented steps to prevent an economic depression and stabilize housing markets. The short-term responses on the federal level both prevented a deeper downward spiral and helped make the recovery weaker than it might otherwise have been. What government bailouts underscored was the privatizing of gains and the socializing of risky losses, with both processes benefiting the wealthy and powerful—and with a populist outrage a prominent result.

This book begins where many Americans explore how to buy, renovate, sell, or flip a house: the cable TV network HGTV, its offerings caught at a particular moment in time. Focusing on three popular shows—*Property Brothers*, featuring the twins Drew and Jonathan Scott; *Flip or Flop*, starring Christine and Tarek El Moussa; and *Fixer Upper*, hosted by Chip and Joanna Gaines—makes it possible to understand some of the connections between the Great Recession and media depictions of housing choices, and perhaps actual housing choices as well. Chapter 2 looks at two real estate workshops and seminars that tens of thousands of Americans have enrolled in and that I have attended: Robert Kiyosaki's Rich Dad/Poor Dad and Than Merrill's FortuneBuilders. Relying on materials available in many media and on my own observations, this chapter explores modern-day versions of the storied tradition of positive thinking that goes back to Benjamin Franklin, Napoleon Hill, and Norman Vincent Peale. Promising financial riches and financial freedom, these workshops emphasize self-governance in a dangerous world even as they market reliance on the expertise and assistance of others. Like HGTV's offerings, they have played key roles in fostering optimistic expectations about the future of housing prices. Chapter 3 explores how print media—from *Realtor Magazine* to the *Financial Times*—have covered the relationships between homeownership and the emerging changes in the world of finance that together led to the Great Recession as the global financial crisis developed. Drawing on the retrospective evaluations of journalists and scholars, the chapter offers a critical evaluation of what print journalists accomplished and missed, bringing together the role of financial corporations and the federal government, the threats to the business model of print journalism, and the story of what most business writers failed to understand.

In chapters 4 and 5, the focus shifts to journalists who wrote books, anthropologists who carried out ethnographic investigations, and directors who produced documentaries as well as horror films. While most journalists who were meeting daily or monthly deadlines could not figure out how to devise stories that presciently—or even somewhat accurately—captured the unfolding global crisis, those who created books, ethnographies, and films more successfully conveyed information about the causes and consequences of the Great Recession in which the financing of American homes played such a central role. Chapter 6 offers a different take on the relationships between media and residential real estate, chronicling how new media threatened or promised to transform the residential real estate sector by shaping the way buyers, sellers, and intermediaries interacted. The years around the Great Recession were when disruption seemed to be everywhere as a wide range of technologically powered corporations impacted how and where people lived. Attentive to the impact of new technologies, especially the internet, the chapter concentrates on five areas: the buying, selling, and financing of homes; short-term rentals in popular cities and resort areas; the home as sanctuary; the home as workplace; and the racial, class, geographical, and generational dimensions of the impact of disruptive innovations in residential real estate.

Finally comes a coda in which I consider the impact of yet another early twenty-first-century crisis that impacted where and how people live. Although the long-term consequences of the COVID-19 pandemic remain uncertain, early indications are that HGTV and companies running real estate workshops reconfigured what they did when. More generally, I consider how the pandemic has influenced where people live, travel to, and work. We see what happens to commercial and residential real estate when tens of millions of people can work from home, use telemedicine to communicate with health care professionals, shop online rather than in brick-and-mortar stores, are put in danger by living conditions in prisons and nursing homes, leave cities for suburbs, and stay home rather than travel. Even more crucially and speculatively, the coda explores whether the pandemic ended up transforming institutions and policies that shape the economy.

A number of important themes remain threaded throughout the book. Again and again, it is hard to avoid the presence of race, class, and gender. African Americans play inescapable and often tragic roles in the history of homeownership in the early twenty-first century. They appear more prominently in the audiences of workshops than they do as hosts or aspiring owners on HGTV's shows. In striking contrast, the power of national legislation, local zoning, real estate agents, and racially based targeting of subprime mortgages have made racialized discrimination a powerful force in housing markets and in the lives of African Americans and others. At workshops salesmen make pitches to audiences with substantial percentages of women, while HGTV programs highlight traditional gender roles in which men do physical labor and women focus on decorative elements. In contrast, a group of women, including the anthropologist-turned-reporter for the *Financial Times* Gillian Tett, were among journalists who perceptively understood the financial crisis as it unfolded. And although documentaries on the financial crisis have featured women in problematic ways, several female anthropologists cast light on dark corners of the financial system. At least one of these scholars, Noelle Stout, overcame a feature that has plagued studies of the crisis: the focus on elites rather than on those who struggled with adversity far from the nation's capital and Wall Street. Tellingly, many studies of where people live (including this one at times) focus on homeownership of middle-class families rather than on where the very wealthy and the least fortunate among us reside, such as in prisons, detention camps, and homeless encampments, in the latter case.

Throughout, I have on occasion used the aspects of neoliberalism as a widely accepted shorthand, albeit a problematic term to which I have given specific substance.[38] From 1933 until the early 1970s, a New Deal order relied on strong labor unions, the nation's robust power in the postwar world, government social programs, and support for reasonably priced public higher education to promote—however imperfectly—economic security, social mobility, and a narrowing of the wealth and income gaps. In contrast, what followed was a different political economy, one that promised opportunity achieved by flexible working conditions, privatized risk, deregulation, free markets, mobile capital, and globalization. Also in play are the celebration of self-regulating markets and human agency; the commodification of just about everything; the psychological processes by which the economic dominates lives; the importance of mass media and new technologies; the waning of the industrial sector and the rise of financial and informational ones; the denial of systematic injustice; the ascendancy of consumption and private property over work and the public good or collective action; and the celebration of meritocracy, individualism, and entrepreneurship. Above all, what strikes me as missing from many of the varied texts that this book covers is sustained consideration of the impact of housing choices on climate change and visa versa.[39]

As the implications of the global financial crisis came into focus, social scientists and others speculated whether it would prompt a questioning of or even a turning away from the political economy that dominated for decades since the 1970s. After all, in 2008 the federal government had forcefully and massively rescued a faltering economy, despite the opposition of some political and business leaders.[40] Writing in 2012—when, of course, the longer-term future was not clear—three observers pondered the future of neoliberalism, noting that it "may have lost another of its nine lives in the Great Recession of 2008–2009," and yet "the most perverse legacy of the global crisis has been a further entrenchment of neoliberal rationalities and disciplines." However, "almost as suddenly as it had arrived," they observed, "this sense of a progressive new dawn evaporated. Worse than this, it soon became clear that the global crisis had set the stage for another neoliberal counteroffensive."[41]

Meanwhile, back at the ranch house, as Crèvecœur insisted, being at home fostered "some pleasing emotion," a feeling that at times can also seem "useless and foolish." He understood "the bright idea of property, of exclusive right, of independence." Because a home is both tangible and transcendent, simultaneously having a price and being priceless, the American dream pursued and even achieved through homeownership remains powerful, elusive, and worthy of understanding in all its twists, turns, and complications.[42]

CHAPTER 1
HOUSING CENTRAL
HGTV

"The Housing Bubble Burst All Over Reality TV" announced a *New York Times* headline in September 2018, a little over ten years after an especially dramatic moment in the Great Recession. "Back when banks were handing out mortgages as if they were lollipops," the reporter Steven Kurutz noted, referring to a period before the collapse of Lehman Brothers in August 2008, "the fun was in seeing what all that easy money could buy: 6,000-square-foot McMansions in freshly landscaped exurbs; high-rise condos with granite counters, marble tubs and top-of-the-world views." Even shows that had once focused on modest homes did so "to illustrate how easily those homes could be turned into cash machines." Then, with fear and foreclosures spreading, TV networks that broadcast and rebroadcast real estate reality episodes had to figure out how they could keep viewers tuning in. Soon after housing prices began to drop in very late 2006—at first slowly and then, by the fall of 2007, more dramatically—networks canceled some series still in production and no longer told audiences that remodeling their kitchens or bathrooms would automatically enhance their home's value. The last episode of *Flip This House* aired on A&E in mid-August 2009, and with the launch of *Rehab Addict* on DIY and HGTV in 2010, Kurutz reported, "viewers glimpsed a new spin on the old dream of happiness through home-ownership." The initial episode focused on an older house purchased in a foreclosure sale for $156,000—not in glitzy Manhattan or in sunny Las Vegas or Phoenix but in a modest Minneapolis neighborhood with snow still on the ground. A shift to more modest dreams and promises—from getting rich quickly to living more comfortably—had begun.[1]

Memories are imperfect, and by 2018 the signs in the world of HGTV and other networks were not entirely clear as to whether or not the depressing impact of the Great Recession was wearing off. "With the stock market roaring," Kurutz remarked, "the genre seems to be entering a gilded age." Both Netflix and Apple TV announced new programs that would leave "viewers gawking at out-of-reach luxury homes." The previous year, Chip and Joanna Gaines had stopped production of *Fixer Upper* after five extremely successful seasons in order to focus on their robust and sprawling Magnolia empire, which now included hospitality, design, shopping, publishing, and real estate enterprises, expanding nationally from their base in Waco, Texas. "Perhaps," Kurutz speculated, "like savvy investors, the couple sensed another bubble about to burst" in one corner of the real estate market, so they switched to another.[2]

This chapter focuses on three HGTV shows—*Fixer Upper*, hosted by Chip and Joanna Gaines; *Property Brothers*, featuring the twins Drew and Jonathan Scott; and *Flip or Flop*, with Christine and Tarek El Moussa as its celebrity stars, although it is often impossible to keep up to date with what is happening with all three couples in their enterprises and in their private lives. Combining education, entertainment, and entrepreneurship, they are among the most popular shows on this network, making it possible to explore the impact of the Great Recession on media depictions of homeownership.[3] A focus on this corner of reality television's real estate programming tracks a series of entangled issues: first, the shifts in HGTV's programming, in the ways these three shows emerged and then later how their stars turned their attention elsewhere; second, the impact of the Great Recession; and, finally, the consequences of a halting economic recovery. As cultural studies scholars Jean Bruce and Zoë Druick noted in 2017, "over the past decade" shows such as these were "arguably becoming one of the central and most ubiquitous ways in which the financial crisis and its aftermath have been imagined and represented in popular culture."[4] To a considerable extent, at a time of peril in the public realm, these three programs promise that housing entrepreneurship can provide Americans a private heaven on earth.

Property Brothers taught millions of Americans how they could benefit from what appeared to be all-too-easy renovations at a time when moving significantly up in the real estate market seemed difficult. *Flip or Flop* did likewise for prospective homeowners, even as it promised riches to house flippers. When the El Moussas divorced in 2017 and Christina flipped her marital status, she added luxury makeovers to her portfolio. This shift to higher-end properties revealed what happened when the waning of the collective memory of the housing market collapse made it possible for many TV shows and some homeowners to scale up dramatically. *Fixer Upper* brought success to Chip and Joanna Gaines, who created a twenty-first-century version of the Christian home. Part of the appeal of their episodes stemmed from their just-plain-folks style and from the fact that they lived in flyover territory, where houses, even when stylishly fixed up, would seem reasonably priced to many who lived on either coast.

Before the Great Recession began to roil the housing markets in 2007, to say nothing of the American and world economies, the A&E network had prominently featured *Flip This House* (2005–9). Going from city to city, the seventy-eight episodes exuberantly promised viewers they could make small fortunes by buying, renovating, and then selling residential properties. Prominent among the teams featured on the show was a group from New Haven, Connecticut, starring Than Merrill, who, after playing football for Yale and then the NFL, turned to buying, renovating, and selling houses. Successfully surviving the Great Recession, he continued to play a prominent role in the world of real estate workshops, which featured his book *The Real Estate Wholesaling Bible: The Fastest, Easiest Way to Get Started in Real Estate* (2014) and helped develop his company FortuneBuilders. Others were not so lucky, especially the millions whose financial and emotional well-being was undermined by the collapse of the housing market. On a more parochial scale, the Great Recession weakened the hold of the A&E network on real estate shows at the same time that it vaulted HGTV to a more prominent position. More globally, some claimed that house flipping—generally and as represented by *Flip This House* specifically—played prominent roles in the collapse of the residential real estate market and the broader markets in its wake. "House Flippers Triggered the US Housing Market Crash, Not Poor Subprime Borrowers," announced a 2017 headline. Although they did not directly connect the behavior of flippers with the encouragement of or examples provided by television shows such as *Flip This House*, detailed and rigorous studies made clear that it was "wealthy or middle-class house-flipping speculators who blew up the bubble to cataclysmic proportions," flipping houses to make a "tidy profit" before wrecking "local housing markets when they defaulted en masse."[5] Accused of exemplifying the forces that irresponsibly fed the excesses that caused the Great Recession, A&E, having broadcast the show for four years, now dropped it.

"Instead of the lux aspirational shows of the early 2000s," note two scholars, "post-crisis series increasingly highlighted ways to find economic value in newly straitened times. Strategies for fixing up properties, such DIY repairs and crafting, and how to cash in on the foreclosures and find treasure amidst the trash, often profiting at the expense of others, began to come to the fore."[6] The time had come not for exaggerated hopes but for more cautious approaches, which another network, HGTV, would most successfully exploit. For example, that network's show *Love It or List It*, launched in 2008, offered improvements rather than the promise of speculative gains. Its format involved a family that finds its current home problematic. An interior designer executes a renovation that she hopes will keep them in place while a real estate agent finds them what he hopes is a house that will convince them to sell and move. At the end, with the once-bickering designer and agent standing by, the couple decides whether to remain where they are (love it) or sell their house and move into a new one (list it). The timing of the program's launch could hardly have been more auspicious: the first episode aired on September 8, 2008, one day after the federal government took over Freddie Mac and Fannie Mae, the two corporations that guaranteed a hefty percent of American mortgages, and a little over three weeks after the massive, storied investment firm Lehman Brothers filed for bankruptcy.

Launched in 1994 as the Home, Lawn, and Garden Channel, HGTV soon dropped the word "Lawn" from its title. Now broadcast in many countries around the world and the third most watched cable channel in the United States, HGTV offers viewers a wide variety of programs that focus on residential housing.[7] Today the network connects advertisers hoping to convince viewers to buy their products and services with viewers seeking satisfaction or titillation as it combines education, entertainment, domesticity, homeownership, and the promise of financial gains. As much as any other source, aside from friends and family, the channel is where millions of Americans learn about buying, renovating, decorating, and selling places where they can live—more likely by owning rather than renting, and primarily in mid-range and above housing markets. HGTV is not the only network that features real estate shows, but its popularity and variety are prodigious, though not assured of smooth sailing. It is, noted the *New Yorker* writer Ian Parker, "a splendid, crenellated house in a neighborhood built on quicksand and termite tunnels."[8] Among its more than one hundred and twenty series are shows that feature well over a dozen approaches to flipping, with various couple combinations (sisters, brothers, a brother and sister, married couples, a real estate agent competing with a renovation specialist), makeovers of only kitchens and entire homes, tiny houses and big mansions; residences on beaches, lakes, and islands in North America and around the world. "For many of us," remarked a reporter in April 2018, "HGTV is the antidote to Fox News and MSNBC. In an era of political uncertainty, turmoil and real-life cliffhangers, who doesn't want to escape to an alternate universe where, with the right blend of shiplap and granite, you could achieve perfection in your home, and by extension, your life?"[9]

Given the real estate crisis that helped cause the Great Recession, HGTV had to reconfigure its business model. Back at headquarters in Knoxville, Tennessee, executives and producers decided how to navigate the troubled waters that swirled at the intersection of media and housing. It did so in many ways, but most immediately with *Real Estate Intervention*. First airing in June 2009, this show featured homeowners who were struggling to cope with a highly problematic housing market. Had it been broadcast five years earlier, its host remarked shortly before its premiere, "the show would [have been] about 30 seconds long." Now, in contrast, a real estate agent had to convince homeowners to lower their expectations (and asking prices) in distressed markets. As a reporter observed in 2010, this show represented "a midcourse correction for HGTV, a cable network that fed—and feasted on—the fantasies and delusions of the housing bubble and then, when that collapsed, went into austerity and atonement mode with series" like this one and others. The network was "getting its building buzz back, but gingerly. Most of the new series . . . focus on modest middle-class home sales and improvement projects."[10]

From diverse quarters came the accusation that HGTV bore some responsibility for causing the Great Recession. In 2009, *New York Times* reporter Brian Stelter noted that the channel had not broadcast house-flipping shows. Rather, having "celebrated the conspicuous consumption of the housing boom," it was "more closely associated than any other with the country's housing crisis and the perils of easy credit and living beyond one's means." In April 2008 a Miami University communications professor confessed that he was "ashamed to admit that I am obsessed with HGTV, which, for me, is classic potato-chip television." What caused him to regret that he could not prevent himself from gorging hours on end was that "as much as any corner of the television universe, HGTV reflects and in its way, I'd suspect, has helped fuel the unfettered consumerism and neoliberal politics that have helped put millions of Americans into foreclosure and bankruptcy and that are threatening the economic stability and environmental viability of our society."[11] From the journalistic belly of the beast, the *Wall Street Journal*, came the accusation that HGTV could be held partially responsible for the collapse of the housing market. In an op-ed titled "Blame Television for the Bubble," a Cleveland advertising executive called HGTV "an evil empire that never rests." After all, "it had pumped up the housing bubble by parading the most mediocre, unworthy-looking homeowners into our living rooms to watch while they put their tacky, run-of-the-mill tract home on the market for twice what they had paid and then went out and bought houses with price tags too obscene to repeat. You couldn't watch these shows," he continued, "without concluding that you must be an idiot and loser if you lived in a house you could actually afford."[12] Then, in March 2009, *Time* magazine named the head of programming for Scripps Networks—at the time the parent company of HGTV—as among those most responsible for the economic crisis. The accuracy of such accusations pales in comparison with the expectations that housing prices would increase, the policies of the federal government and financial institutions, and, more generally, the financialization of the American economy.[13]

So it came as no surprise that senior executives at HGTV had to think about the consequences of their decisions. "We honestly asked ourselves, 'Have we been part of this?'" remarked the then president of HGTV Jim Samples in the spring of 2009. "I think we reflected the enthusiasm that people had around their homes." But he insisted that it was an unfair stretch "to say that HGTV fueled a housing bubble." Arriving at HGTV in the fall of 2007 from, of all places, the Cartoon Network, by early 2008 Samples had instructed those he supervised to consider how to reconfigure corporate strategy in light of the collapse of the real estate market. "I felt it was important to really scrub the air to make sure we maintained our credibility with the viewers," he later declared. He and his colleagues proceeded carefully: tweaking some shows, dropping others, and adding new ones. Among the additions were programs that helped homeowners pay down their mortgages or sell their houses in a depressed market. Among those eventually featured were *Property Brothers*, *Fixer Upper*, and *Flip or Flop*.[14]

The stories of three of the most popular residential real estate shows—*Property Brothers*, with peripatetic twin brothers Drew and Jonathan Scott; *Fixer Upper*, with Chip and Joanna Gaines of Waco, Texas; and *Flip or Flop*, with then-married Tarek and Christina El Moussa of Orange County, California—provide windows into how, after the Great Recession, Americans explored homeownership and investing opportunities.[15] Before late 2007, when all seemed exuberantly well in the residential housing market, the future stars of HGTV's reimagining of reality television's representations of homeownership lived lives of relative modesty and obscurity, even as they harbored more ambitious plans. We can usefully explore how the collapse of the housing market drove the narratives of their lives as troubles in real estate prompted them to shift gears—choices made more possible and more lucrative by their emergence as featured figures on reality television.

Drew and Jonathan Scott of *Property Brothers*, which first aired in early January 2011, are identical twins, born in 1978 in Vancouver, British Columbia.[16] More than their paralegal mother, their father influenced their future careers. Long dreaming of starring as a cowboy on television until the twins arrived, he acted in and directed films before switching careers to become a youth counselor. He moved the family to a horse ranch thirty miles east of Vancouver, where he fixed up the property and early on encouraged his sons to help out by repairing fences and decks. Although at times on different career tracks—Jonathan as a contractor/designer and Drew as an entertainer—from their late teens well into their twenties they both aspired to be in show business even as they realized they needed day jobs to keep themselves afloat.

In their very first semester as undergraduates at the University of Calgary, they discovered the infomercials of Carleton Sheets, the immensely successful guru whose enterprises supposedly spent in excess of $250 million between 1993 and 2007 on TV ads in what a *New York Times* reporter in 2009 called "the alternate universe of late-night TV infomercials," where he "reigned supreme." With his best-selling book *The World's Greatest Wealth Builder* (1998) in hand, he made on-screen appearances and, to coaches, offered courses promising "how to make millions" with "NO DOWN PAYMENT," "No Credit," and "No Previous Experience."[17] The Scott twins spent $500 for the No Down Payment program Sheets had developed and, so inspired, at age eighteen quickly began to make money in real estate near where they went to college.[18] Taking some of what they earned from fixing up a rented apartment where they and other students lived, they began to flip houses early in the new century. Once out of college, they developed their residential real estate enterprises, with Jonathan focusing on running the business and Drew on becoming an actor. In 2004, with Jonathan's training as a contractor (and as an illusionist, initially on-stage and then on television) and eventually Drew's as a realtor, they launched Scott Real Estate, a firm that offered integrated one-stop services in buying, renovating, designing, staging, and selling homes. All the while, they dreamed of making it big in the entertainment world, with Drew working hard at pitching real estate–themed TV shows in 2008, if not even earlier. By 2010, they hit pay dirt, and on January 4, 2011, the Canadian network Cineflix premiered *Property Brothers*, which HGTV soon began distributing in the United States.[19]

By the time *Property Brothers* first aired, the implosion of the residential real estate market made it clear that on television the Scotts had to feature stories on how homeowners could achieve satisfaction with modest but fashionable domestic changes. Sheets had stoked their ambitions, and, as a *New York Times* reporter noted in 2009, he "embodied the bubble as much as Citigroup or Merrill Lynch did" for "millions of real estate wannabes sitting in their living rooms." Now that it had burst, he presided "over some holdings of his own that appear to be troubled," and with "his late-night profile . . . greatly dimmed, . . . the world that he so avidly promoted—easy real estate riches—is in shambles."[20]

Drew and Jonathan Scott well understood the challenges before them, especially because the city they knew as well as any other in North America was Las Vegas, where, in 2004, 40 percent of houses were being flipped. At one point, house flipping yielded robust returns on investments, but the tragically dire consequences of the practice were eventually apparent.[21] Just in 2005, there and elsewhere American homeowners took $750 million from residential real estate holdings and then spent most of it on personal consumption.[22] Nowhere was this more vividly portrayed than in *The Big Short*, the book Michael Lewis published on March 15, 2010, that served as the basis for a 2015 movie where a key scene took place. Both book and movie told the story of a group of savvy investors who successfully bet against the bubble in the housing market.

The Scotts had often visited the gaming capital in Nevada, where Jonathan settled in December 2008, apparently still more focused on a career performing on-stage as an illusionist than as a contractor magically transforming residential real estate. Although they filmed the show in many different cities, Las Vegas was central in their lives: they opened a branch of Scott Real Estate there, bought a home in a nearby suburb, and eventually developed at least two design firms located in the Southern Nevada metropolitan area: Scott Living and Dream Homes.

Perhaps with some dose of retrospective wisdom, they later told of how, as early as 2007, realizing that the housing market in the United States was overheated, they protected themselves by completing real estate projects and avoiding being overleveraged, even though their descriptions of the situation failed to convey how dire and frightening the real estate world around them was. They wrote in 2017, using surprisingly low figures, "When the bubble burst, lots of new construction projects were left half-finished, and scores of existing homes went into foreclosure when owners couldn't make balloon payments on their mortgages."[23] After all, the words "lots" and "scores" hardly encompassed the tens of thousands of homeowners and speculators who experienced the housing crash in Las Vegas. Prices there had begun their dramatic rise around 2003, peaked in 2006, and then dropped precipitously before hitting bottom in 2012 at a level about 40 percent below where they had once been.[24]

In 2017, a reporter told a different story—to my mind, one that was both more believable and more consistent with the narratives that the El Moussas and Gaineses offered. When in 2008 the real estate market crashed, and "with the housing market burning down," as Mark Wilson reported in the publication *Fast Company*, "just as Jonathan and Drew's commercial development firm seemed in jeopardy," the brothers received a call from a representative from a Canadian production company that soon led to the launching of *Property Brothers*.[25] Earlier in their lives, the Scott brothers had turned to real estate as insurance against being starving artists. Now they turned to real estate–oriented entertainment to protect themselves from the perils of real estate investing, albeit by combining their skills as entertainers and entrepreneurs.

Property Brothers, which now airs in the United States on HGTV and around the world in 150 countries, features Jonathan and Drew Scott, one a contractor who renovates houses and the other a real estate broker who negotiates their sales. Episodes show the Scotts working with a family to find their dream house. In some, Drew develops a plan to ready their existing house for sale, which Jonathan then carries out. They play similar roles with the house the family purchases—usually a fixer upper chosen from among the several options Drew identifies. As an illusionist, Jonathan works his magic, using high-end computer-generated images to show what the new domicile will look like when finished. In a dramatic ending, a rabbit is figuratively pulled out of the hat when the brothers reveal the results of their work, including decorating details about which family members appear to have had little say. It is, as Wilson colorfully remarked, "a relatively straight-laced home improvement show, which goes down easy en masse, like an addictive bag of saltine crackers interspersed with the occasional zany bro-hugging, sibling rivalry fest."[26]

A typical episode reveals the skills of the brothers and the show's drama. In the first season, aired in Canada in January 2011 and then six months later on HGTV in the United States, the episode "Contemporary Fixer Upper" featured a mixed-race couple who were expecting twins and living in Westchester County just north of New York City. Peppering their presentation with clever asides and carefully crafted remarks, the Scott brothers laid out the options. African American Sam and a white and very pregnant Monica had a budget of $880,000, which would enable them to move out of the house where they were currently living, though we are not sure whether they rented it, had to sell it right away, or perhaps had already sold it. They wanted a larger home that would accommodate their growing family. True to formulaic form, the couple presented the brothers with their wish list: a contemporary-style, move-in-ready suburban house distant from the city and near (never-seen) family members with at least four bedrooms, three or more bathrooms, abundant light, high ceilings to accommodate

Sam's stature, "a great kitchen," a large master bedroom with an ample en suite bathroom, a finished basement, and a large yard—all ready before the babies' due date two months away. As they often do, Drew and Jonathan opened the show by walking the apparently unsuspecting couple through a perfect home in order to make it clear that a house like it is way over their budget, so they should purchase and renovate a fixer upper. Oohs, aahs, and hosannas precede the property brothers' first reveal: the house costs almost twice what the couple planned on spending. "Rupees or dollars?" Sam asks, and Monica adds that the shock might cause her to go into labor.

Recovering but unsure that Drew can find and Jonathan can renovate a house that fulfills their dreams, they nonetheless go on a hunting expedition. What follows is a look at two possibilities: the "pink house" located near Monica's family and the "retro home" twenty minutes away but much larger. Both need what seem like major renovations, whose results are difficult for skeptical and unimpressed Sam and Monica to imagine. The couple finds the first just plain terrible—dated, pink, and boring. Jonathan has not yet persuaded the couple (who understandably cannot see beyond the clutter, dirt, cramped rooms, and poor taste) that he can work his magic, as he looks into the camera and tells the viewing audience that he "wants them to see the vision." The list price of $689,000, plus the estimated renovation costs, would keep this option within budget, but Sam and Monica insist on exploring other options.

Attention then turns to the farther away but bigger retro home, similarly hard to imagine as reconfigured, especially given a purple master bathroom and the disarray of a house that was abandoned long ago. It is also within budget, especially because there was a recent and substantial drop in its asking price. What "wows the parents-to-be," remarks a female narrator with a soothing voice, becomes clear when the brothers present a dazzling computer-generated version of the renovation: ample walk-in closets, a master bedroom with a stunning master bath, and an up-to-expectations remodeled kitchen, the result of torn-down walls—all with luxurious and elegant furnishings topping off what the brothers call their "dream family home." From "dated" to "stylish," either house could be "move-in ready" in five weeks, they reassure Sam and Monica, with little time to spare before the twins arrive.

The scene shifts as Drew and Jonathan sit down with the couple to discuss the two options, which are difficult to choose between because of the trade-off between the desirable location of one and greater size and more distant location of the other. Drew and Jonathan tell the expectant couple that they have "a few minutes to decide." Sam and Monica choose the retro home, which they get after what the narrator calls a "bumpy sale" that involves Drew skillfully negotiating and buyer and seller compromising, after Drew leaves and returns in about a minute of screen time. With babies due in six weeks and the renovation estimated to take five, magically the story moves forward—no problems with appraisal, inspection, or financing, and apparently a closing faster than the speed of sound. On day one, both Monica and Sam take sledgehammers to walls, with Drew calling her work "the wrong type of labor" for a pregnant woman to undertake. Pointing to "these babies to worry about," she makes it clear that "this reno is Sam's baby." Sam does indeed take over, with his physical labor, Jonathan's much more visible work, and that of the unnamed workers whom Jonathan calls his "crew." Yet, as they proceed, Sam insists on costly changes, and Jonathan makes it clear that they will have to be offset by additional funds or compromises elsewhere.

Then out of the blue comes a different kind of change order when Monica goes into labor two weeks earlier than expected. "Babies don't follow schedules," Sam reminds the audience. Pressure is on Jonathan, who, wonder of wonders, finishes the renovation not only on time but a week earlier than originally expected, and for just $2,000—less than one-fourth of 1 percent—over budget. Unlike in the real world, or even what commonly happens on other reality television real estate shows (and sometimes in other episodes of this show), there are no major surprises: no termites, faulty wiring, or damaged roof discovered. Nor, apparently, is there any cost for a week of workers laboring overtime. The episode ends with the four adults hugging. The reveals follow. The newborns make their appearance. The narrator goes over what major changes cost, especially the luxurious master bathroom, with its custom vanity ($3,800), dual sinks ($2,700), and glassed-in shower ($11,200). And then Sam and Monica get a look at what choices Drew and Jonathan have made—remarkably, from what I gather, without having consulted the homeowner parents. After all, we see the brothers selecting the twins' cribs and picking out colors, furniture, and accessories for the off-screen married couple. Add to that the lack of any attention to financing or any appearances of the couple's friends and families. All this is certainly not like what many of the more fortunate among those reading this book or my wife and I have experienced. After all, the processes of dramatically revealing the results of positive decisions were so important that the Scott twins named their magazine, launched in early 2020, *Reveal*.

As identical twin brothers located in Las Vegas, the Scotts represent a couple combination whose supposed foresight in apparent anticipation of the Great Recession seemed to protect them from the adverse impact of the crash in residential real estate just before reality television enabled them to transition to fame and fortune. In contrast, the appearances of the married couple Chip Gaines (b. 1974) and Joanna Gaines, also known as Jojo (b. 1978), on *Fixer Upper* enabled them to recover from the fate of being overleveraged as the housing crisis spread from Las Vegas to Waco. Both graduates of Baylor University—Chip majored in business and Joanna in communications—they met when he encountered her as the customer service representative at her father's Firestone dealership in Waco.[27] Her American-born, Roman Catholic father had met her Korean-born Buddhist mother in South Korea, where he was stationed during the war in Vietnam. Chip's father had climbed the corporate ladder at American Airlines to become a vice president before leaving for a more lucrative position as the CEO of an office supply company. While in Manhattan on an internship during her college years (and, later, during their honeymoon after their wedding in Waco), Joanna had fallen in love with the boutiques that excited her about the possibilities of home decor. A little over two years after she married Chip in the spring of 2003, she fulfilled her dream of opening her own design store in Waco. Inspired when still in college by the dream of becoming a serial entrepreneur, Chip quickly developed several businesses, including those renovating rental houses and flipping others for sale.

A turning point came in the late 1990s when his father, needing tax deductions to offset his dramatically increased income, bought the house in Waco where Chip lived and had him rent rooms to his college buddies and renovate the property. When his dad profitably sold the house and his parents gave him a few thousand dollars, Chip realized that he could fix up houses and then flip them. "Flipping houses," he wrote later, "wasn't exactly a 'thing' yet, so people thought I was crazy when I told them that was what I wanted to do for a living."[28] With his father helping to finance his real estate investments early on, Chip assembled a considerable portfolio of residential and commercial properties in Waco that he either renovated, rented, or flipped, or where he and Joanna actually resided. The Gaineses nurtured what Joanna called their "babies": both their businesses and their children, whose number eventually reached five.[29]

Able to shift from financing by family members to loans from banks and private investors, over time the reputation the Gaineses developed for successfully investing and then renovating properties grew significantly. Locals knew Chip as a shrewd, ambitious businessman, and Joanna as someone who offered customers—in retail and renovation—distinctive stylistic flourishes. "There's something about things from the past that just calls to us, that triggers a kind of longing," she wrote, with carefully selected items reminding "you of something—something from history, something from childhood, maybe something you lost." Her "calling," she had come to learn, was "creating beautiful spaces where families are thriving."[30]

In search of economies of scale and more than ample wealth, over time they had gone from flipping one house at a time to doing so with as many as ten simultaneously. Eventually they began to develop Magnolia Villas, thirty-six small homes for sale, financed by what Chip called "a huge line of credit" from a bank, with interiors Joanna would design, and whose construction Chip would organize as he relied on a crew that—using a racialized and gendered term—he called "The Boys." Then, in 2008, disaster struck, threatening their livelihood and the idyllic albeit hectic lives they had created. Chip remembered later that "the tidal wave of economic despair that had swept through the rest of the country" and affected already-weakened "housing developers in far-off places like Miami and Las Vegas, had finally reached Waco."[31] Federal government directives forced the bank to cut their line of credit in half, putting the couple in a seemingly impossible position. "We looked up and saw God right there with us," Joanna wrote, telling the story of how they began to dig themselves out from under excessive debt by drawing on their faith, their savings, and a loan from a local investor.[32] Not fully out of the bankruptcy woods, they benefited from a front-page article in the local newspaper that featured their development of Magnolia Villas. Cash flow became more promising when a local lawyer read the story and purchased the first villa they sold for his mother. Yet they still struggled with debt as they tried to become solvent. Overextended in their real estate holdings and with flippable homes remaining on the market for far longer than they had earlier experienced, they were coming to realize "that if we didn't reinvent ourselves, we weren't going to make it."[33] With people turning away from trading up to a better house and instead fixing up the one where they lived, Joanna and Chip realized they had to shift the focus of their endeavors from flipping to renovating.[34]

Then what must have seemed like a life-changing miracle happened, at a time when they were barely solvent. Despite their retrospective claim of more focused reinvention, the Gaineses were struggling to achieve a work-life balance while the work part continued to involve complicated webs of commercial and residential real estate operations that included buying, renting, renovating, and selling. Then, in early 2012, a woman from a TV production company saw blogs that highlighted Joanna's skills as a designer and the "organic" ways she and Chip worked together as a married couple renovating and flipping homes. She phoned Joanna to ask whether she and Chip had ever thought about doing a TV show.[35] The call seemed like a suspicious prank, and, notably, they did not then or in the future own a TV set.

Struggling financially but not knowing quite what to expect, they agreed. A crew came to Waco soon after to film a sizzle reel, a brief video that a production company uses to pitch a show to network executives. After a stilted start to unscripted filming, Chip and Joanna's playfulness and telegenic qualities came through, and the production company persuaded HGTV to support the shooting of *Fixer Upper*. The folks at the network saw the "authenticity" Chip and Joanna conveyed, though perhaps the show's location in a modest small city far from either coast also mattered.[36] After all, presenting houses whose prices seemed astronomical—as the Scott brothers had early on, when their show featured Toronto real estate—could well seem irrelevant to most Americans. In contrast, even when the Waco residential market recovered, it was possible to purchase a three-bedroom, two-bathroom house with 2000 square feet for $165,000. A full crew came to Waco, and the pilot aired in May 2013, with the first episode following in April 2014. As it had for the Scotts, albeit in a more dramatic fashion, real estate reality television had rescued the Gaineses from the plight the Great Recession imposed on millions of less fortunate Americans.

Fixer Upper, perhaps the most successful of these three of HGTV's shows, resembles *Property Brothers* in major ways but differs in others. It is not hard to figure out why a show featuring a married couple transforming houses in a modest-sized Texas city is so popular. After all, it features the familiar gender division of female designer and male contractor, but with the added advantage of what many consider charming married-couple banter. As one shrewd observer remarked, they were "in the tradition of Lucy and Ricky Ricardo and Homer and Marge Simpson": a "sensible, occasionally exasperated realist" and an "impulsive, enthusiastic risk-taker."[37]

Before the dramatic rise in the show's popularity, what might have attracted visitors to Waco, aside from the presence of Baylor University, was the Dr. Pepper Museum and Free Enterprise Institute.[38] Rare was the tourist—and even rarer the civic booster—who might pay attention to another historically important site: the nearby location of the tragic standoff between federal agents and David Koresh's Branch Davidian cult. Otherwise, the city had a down-home hometown at its center and unspectacular but appealing countryside not far away. And, above all, at a time when *Property Brothers* featured a couple with $880,000 to spend and $500,000 could not get you much if anything in major cities on either coast, in and around Waco a budget of $200,000 was enough to pay for a fixer upper fixed up.³⁹ "In Waco," remarked a reporter for BuzzFeed, "a regular person working a regular job can afford to own a regular home. Not a 500-square-foot apartment, not a Volkswagen van, but a *house*—with a *yard*."⁴⁰ As Drew Scott remarked, "I kind of don't like filming as much up in Toronto because the market is so crazy expensive that 90% of the U.S. and Canada can't relate."⁴¹

"If not for the financial crisis," suggested Steven Kurutz in the *New York Times*, "it's entirely possible that American TV viewers would never had heard of shiplap or considered Waco, Tex. a cool place to visit" or even live. The show's hosts, he continued, "popularized farmhouse chic—and with it, shiplap, a cladding material that was once used for barns—as they went about their inexpensive but stylish home renovations." Rather than featuring crown moldings, sleek furniture, and acres of granite, the homes they designed contained recycled materials, comfortable furniture, decorative items bought at a local antique emporium, and even some custom-built features that seemed refreshingly simple. *Fixer Upper*, the reporter for the cosmopolitan coastal newspaper claimed, "was markedly different in tone and purpose from the flashy home TV shows popular in the go-go years before the crash. With their focus on family (the couple has five children), the Gaineses became unlikely stars by celebrating the virtues of responsible home stewardship, rather than trying to turn run-down properties into profit centers"—although, in fact, they did that also.⁴²

A look at a typical episode underscores the craft and color that help Chip and Joanna Gaines attract such a vast and loyal following. In season 3, on March 29, 2016, HGTV broadcast the episode "Family Leaves the Bustling City for Quiet Simplicity," a title that captures the changes Cody and Katie Messerall hope to achieve by moving from Houston to what Chip calls "little bitty" Waco, where they went to college. Coincidentally, the couple's last name stands in contrast with the show's neater-all designs. As he does on many episodes, Chip announces that "we take the worst house in the best neighborhood and we turn it into our clients' dream home." Then Joanna draws the audience in by asking, "Do you have the guts to take on a fixer upper?"

At the beginning, we listen as Cody and Katie describe what they are looking for: a three- or, preferably, four-bedroom home on a large lot with a nice backyard, for a budget of $185,000—one-fifth of what Sam and Monica planned to spend in a suburb of New York City. Chip and Joanna show the couple three houses, one of which they will move into with their two young children, whom we see briefly and only at the show's start and finish. The show features instead minidramas of the Gaineses children, at the time four in number, in ways that enable their parents to celebrate traditional values. At the outset, the Gaineses try to instill teamwork, a work ethic, and a sense of responsibility in their young children by turning work into play as the kids rake leaves and then jump on a pile of what they have gathered. Later on, we see a familiar gendered division of labor when Joanna takes over childcare from an unseen babysitter while Chip works late to meet a deadline.

With each house, Joanna uses sophisticated computer-generated graphics to dramatize what a renovation will involve and how much each change will cost—usually enhanced curb appeal, walls torn down to improve flow and a sense of openness, fresh coats of paint, an updated kitchen, a commodious master bedroom with a stylish en suite bathroom, and, above all, Joanna's distinctive design elements, which usually include shiplap, carefully selected antiques, new lighting fixtures, redone floors, and attractive landscaping. We might call this "cottagecore," "Waco chic," or, as one observer labeled it, "Boho-Glam-Industrial Farmhouse," characterized by modern comforts, historic touches, and natural textures.[43]

Joanna and Chip call the first property they view, listed at $97,000, "the Chicken House" because current owners have a small chicken coop in the backyard. While this one is in relatively good condition, such is not the case with the second one, a fixer upper that is more stripped down than fixed up, so much so that a listing price of $45,000 mainly reflects the land's value. A discarded toilet sitting on the front porch earns it the name "the Outhouse." Finally, they all come to "The Wizard of Waco," a "funky" residence priced at $60,000 and so named because it has, instead of a yellow brick road approaching it, a multicolored walkway. After deliberations we have no access to, the Messeralls select the Chicken House—to my mind the least risky and most unimaginative choice.

Now the fixing up begins. While Joanna focuses on design, Chip serves as contractor and, apparently, chief laborer. We see him knocking down walls, fixing the roof, attaching bricks; nearby are his fellow workers, almost always faceless and with whom we almost never see him communicating. In contrast, we watch Joanna working carefully with two local artisans to design an herb garden. With the work still incomplete, Joanna meets with the Messeralls and uses a laptop and an elaborate computer program to reveal what the renovations will yield. As she often does, she then presents the new owners with a choice between optional add-ons, each costing just under $10,000: a shaded pergola overlooking the backyard or a chimney for a fireplace whose structure, seen from the outside, enhances the house's curb appeal and resale value. She also shows them the boutique-inspired design flourishes, involving elaborately specific choices of furniture, colors, and accessories that she has chosen without asking, from what we can see, for their advice or consent. Unlike what usually happens on *Property Brothers*, on *Fixer Upper* renovating often uncovers unanticipated problems—in this case, a leaky roof that is very expensive to replace.

With construction on the Messeralls' home just about complete, Chip adds finishing touches on the front porch while Joanna tells the faceless movers where to place the furniture. She then pays attention to interior decorative touches: placemats put on a table with place settings on top, flowers arranged, crockery and books carefully laid out on shelves and in nooks, and the herb garden installed. Then comes the most dramatic of reveals, what Chip at one point calls a "Revelation," featuring the original property pictured on life-size panels that are pulled aside to show the transformation as the new homeowners ooh and aah when they see what Chip and Joanna have wrought outside and inside. Hugs all around, and then the two couples enter the house, apparently with the Messeralls seeing for the first time the decor choices Joanna has made—including fabrics on couches and beds, light fixtures, wallpaper, pictures on the walls, tableware, antique accessories, and even a specially designed work area for Katie. "We want to be the first to welcome y'all home," Chip says near the end, "and we really hope you guys live happily ever after." The last words come from Katie as the credits roll: "It's a dream. It's literally a dream come true."

This episode, like others on *Property Brothers* and *Fixer Upper*, artfully mixes reality and artifice in familiarly patterned ways. Labor is gendered, and many laborers—female babysitters and male manual workers—are usually hidden from view. For anyone who has bought or sold a home, several things are striking. In order to sustain illusions, the turmoil and anxiety of home buying remain smoothly off-screen. Absent are the tensions that animate home buying and renovating for families (more so in expensive coastal cities than in Waco), negotiating sales and purchases, securing financing, trading off as costs escalate and surprises intrude. And, unlike what usually happens in reality but not on reality television, the home's transformation takes place in record time, six or seven weeks, and on schedule.

Several qualities give this episode and the series more generally their distinctive flavor. The Gaineses continually engage in friendly, often goofy banter. For example, at one point the couple bet five dollars on whether Chip will find shiplap hidden under wallpaper. After we see Chip nailing a five-dollar bill to the wall, we find out that Joanna had correctly guessed yes and would use her winnings to buy a burger, "double meat, double cheese, easy on the mayo." Moreover, in crucial ways, *Fixer Upper* is an extended advertisement for Magnolia-related enterprises: Chip wears a Magnolia T-shirt; Joanna commissions custom-made pots, making sure the word "Magnolia" appears prominently on each one; she meets new homeowners at the Magnolia offices; we see and hear of the fixing up of two Magnolia silos, 120-foot-high structures that once stored cottonseed and are now the iconic symbols that guide people to Magnolia Market next door; we watch a large "MAGNOLIA" sign being installed on another building, with Chip attaching the final A while Joanna stands below and remarks how "awesome" it looks. He reminds viewers that the "Silobration," as he calls it, is "just around the corner." Throughout, the producers lure us in with scenes of Waco, familiar to inveterate viewers like me: on the Waco Suspension Bridge, the *Branding the Brazos* sculpture that celebrates the cattle drive on the Chisholm Trail; the "ALICO" sign on top of Waco's tallest building, which, at twenty-two stories, was once the tallest west of the Mississippi; tranquil waters flowing, especially in the Brazos River; the Lone Star State's flag and, more frequently, U.S. flags prominently displayed; dramatic sunrises and sunsets. Again and again, we see scenes reminiscent of simpler times: cozy interiors; artfully displayed farm tools; quiet, low-key neighborhoods; the pleasures of farm life; walks or runs along wooded paths; and birds as well as flowers showcasing nature's bounteous beauty.

Above all, *Fixer Upper*—family-oriented, "natural" in its presentation, and aspirational in its promise—quickly served as the model for other shows to follow, which was not always easy to do. If, before the global financial crisis hit home, glitziness for the wealthy was prominent, for the time being comfort and hominess were in order for everyday Americans—or, at least, HGTV's version of homeowning citizens. The goal, despite the popularity of other shows and the reality of the Gaineses' life, was less about turning an ample profit and more about affordable, family-oriented life.

Compared with the Scott brothers and the Gaineses, Christina and Tarek El Moussa, the stars of *Flip or Flop* (2013), came to residential real estate reality television by a less drawn-out but nonetheless dramatic route. Born in California's Orange County in 1983, Christina Meursinge Haack started out working in real estate, where she met the two-years-younger Tarek El Moussa, who had grown up in the same county and, like Christina, had graduated from San Diego State University. They encountered each other at a Prudential Real Estate office in 2005, married in 2009, and then formed their own real estate agency. Along with a business partner, they soon purchased and then sold their first investment property for a 30 percent profit. Yet, with Orange County having one of the highest rates of home foreclosures in the nation, the El Moussas soon felt the pain of the collapse of the residential real estate market. When Christina was pregnant with their first child (Taylor Reese, born in 2010), they moved from a house that had a $6,000-a-month mortgage into an apartment that they, along with a roommate, rented for $700. On a whim and with the help of a friend, in 2011 they produced a sample tape on house flipping and sent it off to HGTV, which signed them up in 2012 for *Flip or Flop*.[44] Successfully flipping relatively modest houses on television took the place of unsuccessfully doing so in the local market. The decision to name the El Moussas' show *Flip or Flop*, with its suggestion that success and failure were both possible—maybe equally so—marked a significant change from *Flip This House*, to cite an example of an earlier show with a declamatory title celebrating house flipping.

Flip or Flop features Tarek and Christina buying houses in Orange County, many of them distressed, fixing them up, and then selling them. The show's promotional material, Steven Kurutz remarked in the *New York Times*, "made some viewers pause at the hubris" of airing a program about house flipping, a phenomenon that was a symptom and a cause of the housing crisis. "There was a lot of hand-wringing over that show," said Kathleen Finch, head of lifestyle brands for Discovery channel, then the owner of the HGTV network. "We didn't know how our audience would react to it." Among what made *Flip or Flop* compelling was that when the collapse of the housing market killed the El Moussas' careers as real estate agents, they recovered by flipping, which, despite the show's title, apparently rarely involved flopping. In Kurutz's words, "They began feeding off fellow casualties of the mortgage crisis, flipping foreclosures, short sales and bank-owned properties."[45] In short, what the episodes do is turn the tragedies of the collapse of the housing market into entertainment. And they did so at a time when federal policy and homeowner hopes underwrote national and personal benefits of improving the housing stock.

In a typical episode, Tarek bids for a distressed house at an auction, although the source of financing usually remains hidden. "The bigger the disaster, the better the makeover," he announces. Sometimes the El Moussas are not able to enter the house until they take possession, and when they do, they often find vermin, mold, and code-violating additions. Nonetheless, they plunge ahead, with Christina focusing on design, especially of bathrooms and kitchens, and Tarek on structures. Ultimately, they turn a hellhole into an attractive but usually modest-size home, complete with the standard glitzy bathrooms, landscape makeovers, and open-concept kitchens filled with granite countertops and stainless steel appliances.

Each episode ends with an open house and then a sale with the figures for costs, sales price, and profits flashing on the screen.

The episode "Toxic Flip," which aired on April 7, 2015, exemplifies the show's approach. Filmed in Garden Grove, Orange County, it features the El Moussas undertaking a risky renovation. "Ever since the market crashed," Tarek announces as the camera pans over distressed houses and Christina holds a child, "with a family to support" they had launched a new business, flipping houses. At the beginning, this and other episodes contrast a disaster of a fixer upper with iconic Southern California scenes such as people frolicking on an ocean beach (even though Garden Grove is at least a dozen miles away from the coast) or a street lined with tall palm trees.

After brief and seemingly uncomplicated negotiations on a smartphone, they purchase a house from a listing agent—one with three bedrooms and one bath, just under 1000 square feet in size, for the asking price of $255,000. They had seen it only from the outside, with its boarded-up windows and a yard filled with trash. Yet a careful examination of neighborhood comps convinces them that, with a maximum rehab budget of $30,000 and an anticipated sale price north of $400,000, this is a terrific deal. Once they have taken possession and enter it, they find—to their apparent surprise but not to mine—true horrors: not only a huge amount of trash that has to be hauled away but also "horrific" smells, asbestos, "toxic" mold everywhere, water-damaged walls and ceilings, dry rot, holes in the roof, termite infestations, serious faults with plumbing, and electrical problems that require rewiring the entire house. Costs go up on-screen, and days go by on a flipping calendar as we are introduced to the fully involved contractor Steve Cedarquist, CEO of Cornerstone Property Services. We see Tarek and Christina doing a higher proportion of the physical labor than they probably do when the camera is not rolling, contrasted with workers, who, as with the *Fixer Upper* episodes featuring the Gaineses, appear to be Latinx and whom we never meet. As usual the work is gendered: Tarek worries about expanding costs as he supervises construction, and Christina, generally in charge of design, pushes for costly, thoughtfully designed choices that will attract buyers.[46]

Apparently recovered from the shock of extra days and costs, the El Moussas work their magic, with Christina announcing the strategy of making the house look more ample than it actually is, principally by relying on indoor-outdoor features, especially a charming outdoor patio complete with a barbeque that Christina insists will make the house appear larger. To enhance curb appeal for buyers and to charm the audience with a cute family scene, Christina plants flowers with the help of their young daughter.

Then the couple sits down and goes over their prospects: with $60,000 in repairs, double their initial estimate, plus $15,000 in closing costs, they wonder if they will turn a profit. Yet, with a break-even point of $330,000, they somehow regain their confidence when they return to the issue of comparable houses in the neighborhood. With local housing prices supposedly rising (which they were then doing at a rate of about 3.5 percent annually in the county), they settle on an asking price of $429,900. Despite its small size, lack of a garage, and only one bathroom, the stylish and "literally brand new house" may well, Christina announces, have gone from being "*awful*, a total money pit, to potentially being one of our biggest net profits ever." Now Kayla De St. Jean and Natalie Moreno of Premier Home Staging do their magic as viewers see contrasting pictures of before and after. Next come prospective buyers, whom we hear commenting on the house's minuses and, more prominently, its pluses, precisely the ones the El Moussas had hoped would turn lookie-loos into buyers. Worried that they may have overpriced it, after three weeks the El Moussas nonetheless get an offer for the full asking price, though we are not privy to the buyer's identity, the financing, or the negotiations. The result is a profit of $97,000, which means a 38 percent gain on their original investment of $255,000, although we do not know how much it cost them to borrow the necessary funds or how they value their own time and labor.

Despite the show's title of *Flip or Flop*, my back-of-the envelope calculations, based on somewhat imperfect data provided by Wikipedia, suggest the episodes show many more flips than flops. Of the slightly over one hundred episodes, only two involved losses (one of $9,700 because of an undisclosed lien on the house and the other of $3,300); about half a dozen seem to be unsold, representing investments of somewhere between $2 million and $3 million. On the other hand, not including the cost of borrowed money or how much the El Moussas might take as salaries, profits seem to stand at about $70 million, some of which they shared with investors.[47] As is true with the other shows, here there is little or no attention to the struggles over negotiations, financing, and decorating, all more common in reality than on reality television.

By late in the second decade of the twenty-first century, the three pairs in the three shows had reached turning points, to varying degrees influenced more by their TV success than by the nation's recovery from the Great Recession. Ironically, it turns out that in the wake of such a transformative event, more than by simply investing in real estate, it was lucrative for these six people to build empires originating in and based on *Property Brothers*, *Fixer Upper*, and *Flip or Flop* in ways that underscore the inextricable connections between the economic reality of real estate and the entertainment that reality television offers.

The expanding fortunes that TV stardom brought the Scott brothers is the least dramatic of the three sagas. Key elements of the empire they have helped to expand were already in place before the first episode aired. Yet, before long, the original TV show was a relatively small portion of their enterprises. "We haven't stopped with *Property Brothers*!" their website boasts, since they developed "something for every family and just for you." *Brother vs. Brother* (2013) features the twins competing with each other as they mentor rival teams of home improvement specialists. At the end of each episode, the stars coming over from *Love It or List It* and *Flip or Flop* help winnow the field of its competitors. *Buying and Selling* (2012) presents a different model, the brothers operating as a tag team that enables a family to renovate their house for sale so they can buy a new one. In *Property Brothers at Home* (2014), anticipating a family reunion where the family members are "[their] own toughest clients," they renovate their 5,000-square-foot Las Vegas house, complete with a home theater, a putting green, a waterslide, and a pool with a swim-up bar. A more recent addition is *Forever Home* (2019). "On a mission to help couples transform their houses . . . where they can put down roots and happily spend their lives," the show's website announces, Drew and Jonathan take couples on tours of recently renovated domiciles so they can make decisions about their own plans.[48]

Additional enterprises underscore what the original *Property Brothers* show made possible and how over time that series occupied a relatively small corner of their endeavors. The list is growing and seems endless: a thirteen-city tour; books for adults and children; a sitcom based on their lives at one time under consideration on Fox; a design-oriented cruise, Sailing with the Scotts; Scott Living, a line of home furnishings that recently had sales in excess of $500 million; home furnishings sold on websites such as Wayfair and in brick-and-mortar stores such as Kohl's; Dream Homes by Scott Living, a firm that designs unique luxury residences for celebrity or CEO clients; and Casaza, an online home decorating site with rooms curated by a team of designers. All this hardly contains their ambitions, for in addition to other TV shows, there is an app, a radio program, several web series, short films, a board game, and the magazine *Reveal*. My earlier scholarship, especially *Entertaining Entrepreneurs: Reality TV's Shark Tank and the American Dream in Uncertain Times* (2020), helped me understand what the Scott brothers represent about American entrepreneurship, including branding, the process of using an iconic reference to build a series of related enterprises. Celebrity gossip attempts to keep up with their lives. Jonathan married in 2007, divorced six years later, and recently became romantically involved with Zooey Deschanel, whom he met on the set of *Carpool Karaoke*. Fans of celebrity gossip have wondered whether Drew and his wife, Linda Phan, would have children after their prominently featured destination wedding in Italy in May 2018.[49] The Scotts are peripatetic but based in Las Vegas.

Reality television also transformed the lives of Chip and Joanna Gaines. The success that they achieved fixing up other people's homes on television enabled them to end their show with the fifth season in 2018 and focus on their Magnolia empire. Central to their brand are family values and the town of Waco, with its Baptist commitments prominent at Baylor University and among its churchgoing citizens. Speaking with questionable accuracy in early 2019 about Drew and Jonathan Scott, a reporter announced that "the duo's net worth is estimated at a whopping $20 million," which "puts them at anywhere from two to four times as wealthy as fellow HGTV stars ... Chip and Jojo [who] have basically turned Waco, Texas, into a Disneyland for shiplap obsessives!"[50]

Success on HGTV's *Fixer Upper* made it possible for the Gaineses to achieve worldly success when they developed an extensive home-oriented empire as the nation recovered from the Great Recession, one that eventually included *Magnolia Journal: Inspiration for Life and Home*. Building on the popularity of their TV show, they developed a multifaceted, sprawling empire that transformed their lives and turned the city of Waco into a major tourist destination that by 2019 reportedly brought 50,000 visitors a week. "You Won't Believe the Crazy Number of Businesses and Projects Chip and Joanna Gaines Actually Have," announced a reporter in a May 2018 article in the online magazine ShowbizCheatSheet. Although, except on reruns, you can no longer to watch them "waging war against walls on demo day or installing shiplap on every available surface," the reporter noted, it hardly meant that "the duo [was] planning to disappear like tumbleweeds across the Texas countryside." What followed was a list of fifteen enterprises, beginning with the restaurant Magnolia Table and ending with a wallpaper line, in between them books, stores (online, locally, and at Target) offering furniture and accessories, and, in Waco, the Magnolia Market at the Silos, complete "with a flea market, retail store, food trucks, bakery, lawn for games, and frequent events like concerts and artist showcases. . . . It's a place you could spend an entire weekend hanging out and having fun."[51] In early 2019, the online magazine Simplemost, without acknowledging the irony involved in the contrast between the publication's title and the headline, announced "A Look inside Chip and Joanna Gaines' Empire," which reportedly had more than 750 employees.[52]

The Gaineses insist that their Christian faith inspired everything they did. As Charles Morris of Haven Ministries remarked in 2017, "Joanna was lonely and fearful about the future but learned how to find satisfaction and security in God's love," and her "relationship with Christ led her to glorify God in all things, including her parenting, the Magnolia Market, and what would later become *Fixer Upper*."[53] As a reporter remarked in 2019, the "Magnolia effect" has been transformative: "A small town made charming instead of claustrophobic, a haven for small businesses in place of never-ending big-box retail plazas. And for many who do come to Waco in a kind of pilgrimage to Magnolia, once they've spent time downtown, the experience morphs into something almost holy—an American civic ideal, remodeled for the 21st century."[54] Don't worry; all was not lost when *Fixer Upper* ended. As a *New York Times* reporter noted in the spring of 2018, the success of the show's stars provided the TV network "with a formula for filling the ratings sinkhole they'll leave behind: Make shows about charismatic twosomes from underexplored parts of the country."[55]

If every house renovation on *Property Brothers* and *Fixer Upper* has a happy ending, the story of the El Moussas as a married couple had an unhappy one, even as the waning of the Great Recession underwrote their success in reality television's real estate ventures. In May 2016, shortly before season 5 aired, the El Moussas separated soon after Tarek left their house in Yorba Linda following a tempestuous argument that led Christina to think he might take his own life. She alerted the police, who located Tarek. He claimed he had no intention of killing himself but was out on a hiking trail, carrying the gun to keep himself safe in case wild animals attacked him. Divorce ensued, an event that only served to intensify their celebrity status.[56]

But every post–Great Recession residential real estate story must have a more or less happy ending. In the spring of 2020, Tarek launched *Flipping 101 with Tarek El Moussa*, and in the fall he announced that he was planning to marry Heather Rae Young. Described on a media site as "buxom, leggy, and shapely blonde bombshell," the one-time Playboy Playmate of the Month had a starring role in the reality TV show *Selling Sunset* (2019).[57] While her divorce from Tarek was pending, Christina became romantically involved with Ant Anstead, host of the British TV show *Wheeler Dealers* (2003), which features the flipping of distressed cars rather than distressed houses. They married in late December 2018 at the Newport Beach home they purchased for $4.1 million. In May 2019 Christina appeared in the premiere of *Christina on the Coast*, a docuseries that featured her providing clients with what HGTV's press release called "luxe spaces filled with distinctive design elements and cool SoCal style." If Newport Beach was only twenty miles from Yorba Linda, with its median home price of $2.5 million it was many steps above the real estate cost and prestige ladder in Orange County, where the median price was just below $1 million. Equally great was the distance between houses renovated and sold on *Flip or Flop* and those designed on *Christina on the Coast*. "You may know me from flipping houses," remarked Christina Anstead. "But there's a lot more sides to me than that. . . . I'm helping people create beautiful new spaces to spend time with their families. There is something wonderful about reinventing someone's world."[58] By 2019, memories of the Great Recession had faded in some quarters. First airing on May 23, 2019, the new show was perfectly suited for a new era—in some places, a new Gilded Age. In the land of fairy tales, stories can end with unexpected twists. By September 2020 Christina and Ant, who had a child together, had split, less than two years after they married. Meanwhile, Christina continued to cohost *Flip or Flop* with her ex, and, if social media sites are accurate, she remains on good terms with him, even as her own personal saga continues.

Realty reality television is hardly real; after all, just as sellers stage a house to improve the chances of selling it at a favorable price, producers stage episodes of *Property Brothers*, *Fixer Upper*, and *Flip or Flop* to improve their chances of garnering good ratings and increasing advertising revenue. To be sure, Joanna Gaines defended the genuineness of *Fixer Upper*, saying that she was glad that the production company wanted "authenticity . . . because that was all they were going to get" from Chip and her. Yet she unconvincingly insisted that Chip could never be scripted and that she would never have agreed to do the show if she couldn't be herself. She went on to remark that "when there's heart and substance on a TV show, the drama just isn't needed."[59] Of the reality TV shows featuring homes, these may be among the more "authentic," but they are nonetheless highly orchestrated dramas. Not surprisingly, artifice, illusion, and invisibility play a central role in emphasizing authenticity as producers and editors choreograph episodes. Viewers are hardly privy to all that goes on off-screen, including the arrangements between star couples and home buyers, as well as the surely complicated financial arrangements that undergird episodes such as revenue from product placement, relationships between HGTV as a corporation and the players on the ground, and the staging of shopping for a home.⁶⁰ Specific dollar figures might flash across the TV screen in people's homes, but on-site financial reality was . . . well, more unreal, and easily fudged or hidden. Carefully editing hours of filming into minutes, the show uses scripts, music, repetition, screen shots, and pauses to provide drama in what are, after all, highly formulaic stories.⁶¹

Moreover, as already noted, on reality TV shows much is left out, hidden, or skewed—which may reflect how well producers of these shows understand what audiences want. The three shows fail to focus on people who cannot afford comfort, safety, and reinvention; they commonly picture educated, middle-to-upper-middle-class buyers, especially married couples with children whose purchasing power is out of reach for many Americans, more markedly so with *Property Brothers*. *My Lottery Dream Home* (2015) is hosted by the flamboyantly gay David Bromstad, and the hosts of *Nate & Jeremiah by Design* (2017) are a gay married couple. And if *Love It or List It* frequently features same-sex couples, the three shows under consideration in this chapter rarely do. *Fixer Upper* features buyers of many ethnicities, but it hardly gives an accurate picture of Waco's population, which is at least 32 percent Latino and 21 percent African American, while almost 27 percent live in poverty. The presence of a mixed-race couple in our sample episode of *Property Brothers* is not typical for these three shows.⁶²

If African Americans play such minimal roles on these shows as workers or buyers, elsewhere on HGTV the record is quite mixed.⁶³ Research done by HGTV reveals that 13 percent of the audience for its shows is African American and 5 percent is Latinx, but on these particular shows representation is far below those figures.⁶⁴ It is similarly notable that *Home Town* (2016), though it has featured African Americans as clients, more prominently involves white people (as hosts, store owners, or workers), even though they represent only 26 percent of the population of Laurel, Mississippi, the small town where it is filmed. Indeed, if the stars of the shows central to this chapter spoke up in response to 2020 struggles for racial justice, hosts Ben and Erin Napier of *Home Town* remained silent.⁶⁵ "*Home Town* seems like White Town," one observer remarked online.⁶⁶

Executives in charge of HGTV did make some attempt to feature African Americans, the most notable example being *Double Down*, which first appeared on HGTV in 2019 and stars the twin Downing brothers. "Born and raised on the South Side of Chicago by a Bahamian mother and an African-American father," their website informs us, they grew up "with family members who were homeowners in the Bahamas and Chicago" and who, when they were young, instilled in them "the value of property ownership." After they graduated from the University of Illinois at Urbana-Champaign, they returned to their hometown and became professional firefighters.[67]

"In their work as firefighters," their website reads, "the twins witnessed a need for community development and began to take action through real estate investment," beginning with one home before going on to renovating apartment buildings and then flipping their first property in 2013. They were committed to fighting "gentrification by purchasing, renovating and selling attainable, middle-class Chicago housing with a keen eye for architecture and design," their website states, apparently unaware of the ironic aspect of the statement. Though they have yet to build an empire on the scale achieved by their white twin counterparts, the Scott brothers, they have developed a portfolio of real estate investments in both Chicago and the Bahamas; worked "to educate the community on financial literacy and real estate investment through their 'Homecoming with the Downing Brothers' podcast, national college tour, community partnerships, and brand collaborations"; published a book, *The Downing Brothers: A Visual Strategy Guide for Real Estate*; and offered referrals to contractors and realtors, access to financing, and an online real estate course whose cost begins at twenty-five dollars. Thus, they represent an African American version of what the historian Ken Lipartito calls the evangelism of real estate wealth.[68] "It is their mission," their website emphasizes, "to shine a light on real estate investment as a feasible opportunity and provide resources to develop generational wealth. They are determined to leave the South Side of Chicago better than they found it. Anthony and Anton are endlessly motivated by their mantra: Dream. Plan. Execute."[69]

If we shift our attention back to *Property Brothers*, *Flip or Flop*, and *Fixer Upper*, we understand that these shows, along with the work of Marie Kondo and the magazines *Martha Stewart Living* and *Real Simple*, provide us with useful entries into the aspirations for stylistic simplicity that, though opposed to real messiness, are hardly so simple. The shows themselves, as well as the books that the Scott brothers and the Gaineses have authored, picture supposedly simple living and offer practical advice, but what they convey, especially in their illustrations, is actually more lavish than down-home ordinary.[70] It is hard not to be struck by what are by now clichéd choices that stand in opposition to how the shows—*Property Brothers* in particular and *Fixer Upper* less so—celebrate tailored uniqueness: open-concept kitchens with islands topped by granite; crown moldings above formal living and dining rooms; palatial bathrooms with the obligatory free-standing tubs, walk-in showers, and dual sinks. Reflecting the celebration of the private sphere as a safe harbor from a turbulent economy, the evocation of a couple imagining how they will use spaces where they can relax as they enjoy a cup of coffee or a rustic scene seems more aspirational than commonly experienced.[71]

All three shows showcase domesticity, but on *Fixer Upper* Chip and Joanna offer a more specific version, a contemporary vision of the Christian home and family, largely implicit on screen and more explicit in their books. One observer characterized this as an example of "Mompreneurs," reflecting not feminism but "Conservative Christian Femininity."[72] To begin with, the publisher of their two most personal books, *The Magnolia Story* and the cleverly and appropriately titled *Capital Gaines*, was Thomas Nelson, a Scottish company founded in 1798 and since 2012 part of HarperCollins Christian Publishing. Its website announces that it "is committed to one central mission: inspiring the world by meeting the needs of people with content that promotes biblical principles and honors Jesus Christ." Chip and Joanna attend Antioch Community Church, an evangelical congregation in Waco whose minister opposes same-sex marriage and supports the conversion of gays and lesbians into straight people. Their episodes have never, as far as I can recall, featured a same-sex couple.[73] In their books and on television the Gaineses do not invoke Christ's name, but they have threaded their writing with Christian themes, mentioning revelation, callings, and, more specifically, their gratitude to God. Yet at most other times, what they evoked was more subtle: the importance of lives centered around home cooking, "traditional" family life, and furnishings that tell the comfortably reassuring stories of those who live there. The private domestic space of a heterosexual married couple and their children becomes a haven in a dangerous and challenging world.[74]

One of her books, Joanna insisted, should "empower and motivate you to create a home that communicates the soul and substance of the people who live within its walls," because this is "the place where I am most known and most loved." When she was overwhelmed by conflicting obligations to business and family, she realized it was "time to go back to the fundamental things that ground me." So she stayed home more often, delegated more of what she had to do (to whom was left unspoken), and created in her garden one of her many "retreats."[75] Their own home really did become a "sanctuary," Chip wrote, a "place of peace and quiet . . . to go back to at the end of every day."[76] Joanna, who more frequently than Chip uses religious language to describe what they do, wrote that if she "ever needed proof that I should trust God with my dreams," that "certainly" came when "He turned my little dream, my mustard seed of faith" into all she and

Chip had created, before going on to mention not only a family-centered home but also the thousands of people who came to Magnolia Market and the local businesses the show's popularity supported. She and Chip were "able to channel" what she called "this growth" directly into "the town we love" when the folks in Waco "dedicated their time and energy to making beautiful items we showcase, from jewelry to furniture, to handmade signs and pottery." The most explicit invocation came at the conclusion of their book *The Magnolia Story* (2016). "In times of doubt or times of joy," Joanna remarked, "listen for that still, small voice. Know that God has been there from the beginning—and He will still be there until," followed by their ellipses and, then on a different line, the book's final words, "The End."[77]

If religion plays a mostly implicit but sometimes prominent role in the vision of domesticity the Gaineses offer, on all three shows race, class, and gender shape how work is portrayed. The shows usually reinforce traditional gender roles—not only by emphasizing the resourcefulness of Joanna's and Christina's consumer-oriented design skills as opposed to the talents more closely aligned with physical labor displayed by Chip, Tarek, and the Scott brothers, but also by focusing on the frequently conventional roles demonstrated by women and men among buyers.[78] We see labor and domesticity both as gendered and largely influenced by the hidden dynamics of class, race, and ethnicity. The principals of all three shows hire others to do most of the work, especially the hard physical labor. On-screen the manual laborers usually remain literally or figuratively faceless, and we rarely see the supervising member of each show's couple communicating with them. Although the three couples are celebrities who seem to perform ordinary tasks, their larger-than-life stature keeps attention away from the bigger problems that Americans face, such as precarious employment, which are more difficult to solve than are buying, flipping, or transforming a domicile on television.

In contrast is what Chip says in his 2017 book *Capital Gaines* of the Mexicans he worked with beginning in his mid-twenties. "We were a close-knit group. These were my boys," he remarks, using a vaguely racialized, diminutive word to describe grown men. He writes that "something about their culture and work ethic really resonated with me," as he countered common, racialized images of lazy immigrants from Mexico. He says that "when you roll up your sleeves and labor side by side with someone, your stereotypes and assumptions"—which he leaves to the reader's imagination—"fall away." He preferred spending time with "these guys" over his "college buddies, and at first, that struck me as strange." But eventually he "just owned the fact that" they were "some of my very favorite people" despite "their obvious differences," which also remain unacknowledged. He "respected deeply" his "great crew of Mexican guys," even though in TV episodes there is little evidence of his engagement with them.[79] The one exception is Chip's working with his sidekick Saul ("Shorty") Sanchez in later episodes before Sanchez left to launch his own remodeling business.[80]

Moreover, financialization and entrepreneurship suffuse and enable what these HGTV shows offer. New financial instruments such as mortgage-backed securities and collateral debt obligations occupied central positions in the tragic turmoil that caused millions of Americans to face bankruptcy, foreclosure, and eviction as the housing crisis intensified, beginning in 2007. Memories of what had happened earlier persisted even when these shows launched and then gained in popularity. Those in charge of mass media responded in predictably problematic ways. These three shows and others represent what media scholar Laurie Ouellette has called "recessionary entrepreneurialism," the ways real estate reality television focuses on the "opportunity to create and sell entertainment based on 'real life'" episodes.[81] As another media scholar, James Hay, notes more generally about the genre, "As ongoing training, advice, and rules," realty reality TV programs "operated as technology for the government of the self, *empowering* citizen-consumers to help themselves and in that way affirming the virtues of entrepreneurial entrepreneurship."[82] And two other media scholars observe that "film, television, and digital culture increasingly compensate for broad vulnerabilities of economic citizenship with gendered rhetoric of power, success, and family or community membership."[83] If we broaden our focus chronologically, what is striking is that after the global financial crisis that culminated in 2008, the financialization of real estate property rebounded, and it did so more unequally than before. Yet the fact that these three shows sustained their appeal reminds us that the more things can change, the more they can remain the same.

However, all that is off-screen, when buyers look at their options and make their decisions. After all, any significant emphasis on the precariousness of contemporary life would threaten the importance of these shows as entertainment. Watching budget figures flash and days flip on calendars, you would not know that for most people home buying and renovation involve making hard choices involving agony, already-stretched budgets, surprises, uncertainty, tension, and conflict. And the home's transformation is usually completed on time—something rarely experienced in real life away from reality television. Rarely, if ever, is there an unhappy ending: a final sale falling through, financing collapsing, a major problem discovered after occupancy, or buyers objecting to what one of the hosting couples has wrought. In a world filled with financial risk and unanticipated turns of events, the carefully calculated suspense of these shows rarely fools an inveterate and knowledgeable viewer who is skeptical about supposedly cosmetic changes that cost more than many American families earn in a year. It's not the inexperienced buyers but the seasoned stars who bear whatever risk there is, but then, judging by the lack of flops on the El Moussas' show, rarely is there any risk.[84] Also absent from the makeovers on these shows is any attention to environmentalism—almost no evidence of a commitment to recycling materials ripped out and thrown away as renovation proceeds, and, similarly, no attention to designing for energy efficiency.

On-screen, domesticity dominates as viewers voyeuristically enjoy the pleasures of searching for, buying, and enjoying all the comforts of a stylish home they might be able to afford, even if in the world off-screen uncertainty and unaffordability reign. As a media critic wrote in *USA Today* in the summer of 2011, "There is something very satisfying in watching people come to the realization that today's economy, and common sense, require adjusting expectations to reality while finding a pleasant place to live in the bargain. As a bonus, you get to recoil in horror at the worst houses, root for the best and guess which they'll pick."[85] Combining education, inspiration, and entertainment, shows such as these teach viewers how to be good self-governing consumer-citizens, even though (or precisely because) they are relying on the exemplary advice of professionals. Episodes celebrate domesticity of private spaces and the pleasures of home improvement as they connect citizenship, homeownership, and entrepreneurship.[86] In a televisual world where governments are absent, self-governance dominates with the marketing of the self and the home. You, too, can enjoy these pleasures, the episodes reassure viewers, making it possible to overcome adversity and achieve one version of the American dream of reinvention and upward mobility. The enjoyment of the sanctified private home involves comfort and self-expression in ways connected with the wisdom of financial success. For viewers this involves the guilty pleasures of voyeurism and dreaming. They can invade the privacy of others in order to enhance their own sense of satisfaction, even though such pleasures are complicated by jealousy and ambivalent judgments. As the literary critic Terry Castle has trenchantly remarked, watching "house porn" shows like these "could best be understood as a postmodern equivalent of traditional consolation literature," providing "a middle-class coping mechanism . . . a way of calming the spirit in bizarre and parlous times."[87] And she said this in March 2006, more than a year before the beginning of the Great Recession.

CHAPTER 2
THE POWER OF POSITIVE REAL ESTATE WORKSHOPS

In 2007, as the housing and mortgage markets teetered and then, before long, collapsed, stories circulated prominently of how avaricious and reckless mortgage companies underwrote home purchases by people who could not possibly make payments. "As a supervisor at a Washington Mutual mortgage processing center," a court case later revealed, "John D. Parsons was accustomed to seeing babysitters claiming salaries worthy of college presidents, and schoolteachers with incomes rivaling stockbrokers". He rarely questioned them. A real estate frenzy was under way and WaMu, as his bank was known, was all about saying yes."[1] In actuality, the causes of the collapse of the housing market and its ensuing reverberations were more complicated than a focus on irresponsible lending and borrowing would indicate, involving as they did factors such as the failures of federal regulators and private rating agencies, the undermining of the Glass-Steagall legislation that had kept investment and retail banking separate, the invention and widespread use of complicated financial instruments, the globalization of the market for mortgages, the prevalence of speculative investors, and the greed of lenders who garnered short-term income from exorbitant fees in ways that involved long-term risks.

Workshops and popular books that promoted a number of problematic strategies for making it rich in residential real estate were both a cause of and a response to the Great Recession. They bore some responsibility for stoking a heated and dangerous housing market that helped lead to turmoil in the residential real estate markets and, in turn, to the Great Recession. Then, in the wake of the crisis in the global economy, with the foreclosures fresh in their minds, these same books and workshops taught people how to capture opportunity amid adversity. They drew simultaneously on people's familiarity with reality TV real estate shows, on long-standing links between the American dream and homeownership, and on the hope that, in the years before and after the Great Recession, people could achieve financial freedom by successfully investing in housing. Among the many strategies that books and workshops taught was house flipping: buying a house in order to sell it quickly for a higher price, with or without renovating it. Before 2008, this churning took place when interest rates were low and housing prices were rising rapidly and, many thought, endlessly. People with favorable credit scores—and many without them—used home equity loans to make down payments (often a small percentage of the price of a home) and then took out a mortgage on a second, third, or fourth home. These conditions and practices made the housing market fragile, subject to downdrafts at least as dramatic as the boom in prices. Then, in the wake of the recession, books and workshops promised people that they, too, could recover and achieve economic security and well-being. Magically and ironically, if at one point real estate workshops intensified turmoil in the housing market, then later they promised to rescue people from its consequences.

A look at residential real estate statistics for one of the locations most adversely affected, the metropolitan area of Phoenix, Arizona, captures the dimensions of the roller coaster ride. From early 1981 until early 2004, prices had risen gradually, from an index number of 79 to one of 170. Soon the pace accelerated, peaking at slightly more than 294 by the end of 2006. From then until the middle of 2011, when they hit a low of 144, prices fell dramatically—a drop of about 50 percent in four and a half years.[2] Losing money is more painful than gaining it is pleasurable, a phenomenon that psychologists call loss aversion. So, even for those who stayed in place with the same roof over their heads, the quick and dramatic fall in housing prices could feel terrible. The greater tragedy befell those for whom bankruptcy and foreclosure ended their dream of comfortable domesticity, in some cases temporarily and in others forever.

Among the most sophisticated and authoritative analyses of the role of speculative real estate investing as a factor causing the Great Recession was one that came in 2017 from the behavioral economist Robert J. Shiller, who in 2013 won the Nobel Memorial Prize in Economics. In 2000 he had published *Irrational Exuberance*, a term coined by Federal Reserve Board chair Alan Greenspan in 1996. Shiller's timing was impeccable. As Greenspan had done four years earlier, Shiller warned about dangerously high stock market prices. The dot-com boom went bust one month after his book appeared. There and in other writings he explored how markets, subject to psychological forces, did not always act efficiently and rationally. His book's second edition appeared in 2005, this time warning about a bubble in residential housing prices. Then, in August 2006, just as home prices in areas like Phoenix were about to peak, he and a colleague cautioned that in the real estate market there was "significant risk of a very bad period, with slow sales, slim commissions, falling prices, rising defaults and foreclosures, serious trouble in financial markets, and a possible recession sooner than most of us expected."[3]

Although this was neither the first nor the last time Shiller warned about the consequences for the broader economy of the bursting of a bubble in real estate or the stock market, later on—with considerable justification—he could point out that he was right. He did so in May 2017 in a *New York Times* article titled "How Tales of 'Flippers' Led to a Housing Bubble" that underscored the emphasis on the importance of increased expectations as reflected on HGTV shows. He argued that the factors that economists usually relied on to explain housing prices, such as interest rates and building costs, did not adequately account for the fact that, adjusted for inflation, housing prices had risen 75 percent between early 1997 and late 2005. To understand the role that residential real estate played in the Great Recession, he pointed instead to "sociologically important narratives—like tales of getting rich through 'flipping' houses . . . that constitute the shifting mentality of the era." In the late twentieth century and early twenty-first, he wrote, Americans rarely used the term "housing bubble," preferring instead to embrace narratives that promised riches by leveraging what is known in the trade as "other people's money" (OPM) to make fortunes by flipping houses.[4]

Here's more evidence of the widespread prevalence of irrational exuberance. On January 9, 2007, a time when few people foresaw the arrival of what would later come to be known as the Great Recession, Rick Villani and Clay Davis published *Flip: How to Find, Fix, and Sell Houses for Profit*. With over 500,000 copies sold, their book captured a committed following. Part of the Millionaire Real Estate Series, *Flip* promised its readers not only riches but also personal satisfaction. As the dust jacket of a parallel book, Gary Keller's *The Millionaire Real Estate Agent* (2004), claimed in a way typical of self-help or how-to literature, "IT'S NOT ABOUT THE MONEY. . . . It's about being the best you can be!"[5] Like others who promoted house flipping, Villani and Davis, executives at HomeFixers ("North America's leading real estate rehab franchise"), claimed that it was easier to become wealthy in residential real estate than in the stock market. Although they acknowledged that "flipping a house seemed so much easier on those television shows," they nonetheless offered "a proven formula, a step-by-step process" that was "designed to take the risk out of the game."⁶ Well, such books (along with podcasts, websites, workshops, and television shows) may have created some millionaires and helped even more in their quest for self-fulfillment, but they also played a role in the housing crisis and its aftermath.

One of the first signs of what was ahead came in early 2007. On April 2, 2007, fewer than three months after *Flip* was published, the real estate investment trust New Century Financial declared bankruptcy, with over 3,000 employees losing their jobs as a consequence. In 2006 the company had written nearly $60 billion worth of mortgages, many of them subprime, to an escalating number of borrowers with poor credit histories, many of whom could no longer make their payments. A little over six months later the stock market reached all-time highs. The National Bureau of Economic Research (NBER) determined that economic activity peaked in late 2007 but waited until after the election in November 2008 to officially declare that a recession had begun. That it would turn into what was then the most serious economic crisis since the Great Depression was not yet clear.

Popular books and their related workshops provide the most visible and dramatic evidence of the allure of achieving the American dream by investing in residential real estate. Relying on materials available in many media and on my role as a participant observer, this chapter concentrates on two real estate workshops that tens of thousands of Americans have enrolled in and that I have attended: Robert Kiyosaki's Rich Dad, Poor Dad and Than Merrill's FortuneBuilders. Starting with a free two-hour meeting and then escalating to working with a personal coach for $30,000 or more, the sprawling enterprises built by Kiyosaki and Merrill promise riches and financial freedom to investors adversely affected by the Great Recession. In many instances, like reality TV programs such as *Storage Wars* (2010) that feature auctions of abandoned property, popular residential real estate how-to books, TV programs, and other workshops together represent efforts to deal with the detritus left in the recession's wake.⁷ Yet, as modern-day versions of the storied tradition of positive thinking that goes back to Benjamin Franklin, Napoleon Hill, and Norman Vincent Peale, they all emphasize individualistic self-governance even as they market the important of the expertise and assistance of others. Thus, like Americans who have celebrated individualistic ambition and achievement, they balance self-reliance with reliance on others.⁸

The most influential book on residential real estate investing—and foundational in the world of real estate workshops—is Robert T. Kiyosaki's 1997 *Rich Dad, Poor Dad: What the Rich Teach Their Kids about Money—That the Poor and Middle Class Do Not!*, written with the help of Sharon L. Lechter. The enterprises of Kiyosaki and Lechter paid some attention to house flipping and more generally promoted residential real estate as central to household wealth. Initially self-published, *Rich Dad, Poor Dad* remained on the *New York Times* list of best sellers for over six years. Translated into more than fifty languages, it has sold more than thirty million copies in more than one hundred countries. With some justification, Kiyosaki could claim it was the "number one personal finance book in history."[9]

Before the book's publication and for ten years after, Lechter partnered with Kiyosaki. In the late 1990s they formed the Rich Dad Company, for which Lechter served as CEO until 2007. Then, after suing Kiyosaki for not properly sharing the profits, she went out on her own and formed Pay Your Family First. "Whether it's receiving your first allowance, purchasing a home or strengthening a retirement nest egg," the company's website insists, "the basis for financial literacy and money management begins at home. Empowering families and households with . . . confidence," it continues, people had to realize that "the complexities of fiscal responsibility creates stronger communities and a wealthier future." And, I hasten to add, launching Pay Your Family First was the initial step in the development of Lechter's own sprawling, multifaceted empire, which involved making motivational speeches, developing board games for children, serving on presidential advisory panels, selling products issued under the YOUTH-preneur brand, and offering a wide range of ways of promoting financial literacy.[10]

A key moment in the development of her enterprises came in 2008 when she teamed up with the Napoleon Hill Foundation to publish *Three Feet from Gold: Turn Your Obstacles into Opportunities!* (2009) and to bring into print an updated version of Hill's legendary and immensely influential 1937 *Think and Grow Rich*. Hill claimed—probably inaccurately—that he had met Andrew Carnegie in 1908 and that Carnegie had helped him gain access to many of America's richest men. Then Hill, having supposedly interviewed them, based his book on the stories and wisdom that he claimed they had provided in a book that has sold more than 100 million copies. Inspiring Norman Vincent Peale, Hill's immensely popular book offered a version of mind control.

In 1938 Hill had also written, but not published, *Outwitting the Devil: The Secret to Freedom and Success*, which Lechter helped get into print in 2011. Because this book relied on Hill's claims that his conversations with the devil had enabled him to access the Devil's Code, neither he nor those who controlled the manuscript's copyright after he died in 1970 wanted to see *Outwitting the Devil* published. When the Napoleon Hill Foundation gained control over the right to publish it, its CEO approached Lechter about annotating it and making it available. The foundation seems to exist not as its title might imply, as a philanthropy, but as a business that offers Hill's books for sale and the opportunity to "Become a Certified Instructor of Dr. Hill's Philosophy of Success." On the home page of the foundation's website, I learn what Napoleon Hill had taught: "All the breaks you need in life wait within your imagination. . . . Imagination is the workshop of your mind, capable of turning mind energy into accomplishment and wealth."[11]

In the annotations Lechter offered to *Outwitting the Devil*, she talked of people "facing severe economic adversity" for the first time in their lives and how they might overcome the resulting "fear and self-doubt." She advised people to learn from adversity, for, as was true in the Great Depression when Hill wrote, people with the memories of the Great Recession still fresh in their minds could understand that "it is during periods of great stress that we find our will and our inner strength" that empowers them to find new paths to abundant success. She emphasized that success came from faith in oneself and not from government programs. Hill saw God "as the ultimate source for his overall philosophy of success," as others should do. In contrast, Lechter realized that she alone was responsible for her future.[12]

Before her edited version of *Outwitting the Devil* appeared, Lechter had already worked with the Napoleon Hill Foundation, on October 6, 2009, publishing under its auspices *Three Feet from Gold*. Appearing after General Motors' declaration of bankruptcy in early June and before December, when the number of home foreclosures hit an annual rate of almost 3 million, *Three Feet from Gold*, whose title referred to people who gave up even as they neared success, occupied a universe that closely paralleled Hill's books, both the one published when he was still alive and the one that would appear in 2011. The foreword to *Three Feet from Gold* came from Mark Victor Hansen, himself no stranger to the world of inspirational books, as the cocreator of the astonishingly successful series of *Chicken Soup for the Soul* among other self-help books. The Napoleon Hill Foundation, Hansen wrote, desiring "to provide renewed hope and courage for everyone during the current global economic crisis," set out to replicate Hill's path forward. The resulting book was written under the auspices of the foundation by Lechter and Greg S. Reid, a motivational speaker and author of inspirational books, including *The Millionaire Mentor: A Simple Way to Get Ahead in Your Work and in Life* (2003). Lechter and Reid told the story of a callous man named Greg whose life is unraveling. By chance, he meets a wildly successful but fictitious man who, the story goes, provides him with access to three dozen people, real live ones listed in the book, whom Greg interviews to find out how they turned obstacles into opportunities. Meeting with these "Masterminds," Greg learns how to be generous, compassionate—and successful. The two authors peppered their text with aphorisms Hill and others had articulated: "Before great success comes, you will surely meet with temporary defeat," or (P + T) × A × A = Success [(or Passion + Talent) × Association × Action = Success]. Toward the end of the book, they doubled down as they reiterated their message. "Act as if!— Have faith that your personal Success Equation will drive you to incredible success," which the authors and the foundation assumed would meld the financial and spiritual. They then ended the book on a similar note: "You are now *three feet from gold!*"[13]

As influential as Lechter has been, Kiyosaki built an even more robust empire that focused on getting rich through real estate. Born in Hawaii in 1947 into a Japanese American family, after graduating from the Merchant Marine Academy in 1969 Kiyosaki became a decorated Marine Corps officer for serving as a helicopter pilot in Vietnam in 1972. A turning point in his life came soon after, when he attended Werner Erhard's est seminar. Erhard had been influenced by Hill's *Think and Grow Rich*, as well as by the humanistic psychology of Abraham Maslow and Carl Rogers and the Americanized Zen Buddhism of Alan Watts. From the early 1970s until the mid-1980s, Erhard offered controversial seminars (one of which I attended with a friend who was a true believer) that involved the intense process of convincing attendees to abandon the path they had set out on and instead learn the true way forward. When he enrolled, Kiyosaki learned that his "misery" was due to "my lack of integrity and my not keeping my word," as he felt he had done when he acted irresponsibly in the military. In addition to encountering an example of how an entrepreneur could use intense "seminars" to make money, Kiyosaki recognized that "my 'changed life' went well beyond the two weekends I spent in the est seminar. I realized I had the power to create the best destiny for my life, or the worst. It was my choice."[14] Walking away from a sales job at Xerox that Poor Dad might have urged him to keep, in 1977 he launched his first company, as Rich Dad had taught him to do.[15]

The contrast between his two "dads," one a failure and the other a success, not only stood at the center of the narrative of his life but also served as the principal metaphor for his brand. His oft-told but not fully convincing tale contrasted his supposedly poor biological father with the life of the successful man, the father of his best friend, who as his Rich Dad served as the model for his life. Around when his highly educated father was fifty years old and already superintendent of education for Hawaii, he ran for lieutenant governor in 1971 as a Republican in a heavily Democratic state. After he was defeated, those in power reportedly blocked him from ever having a government job again, and even his supporters, fearing they would lose their jobs, supposedly betrayed him by deserting him. Trying his hand at business by purchasing an ice cream franchise, his father failed again. These were defining moments for his son, Robert wrote later, although he did not mention that his mother died at age fifty in 1971. "Here he was in the prime of life, highly educated but with a broken spirit," he noted of his dad. "As time went on," his dad "got angrier at himself and at the one-time friends that he felt had betrayed him."[16]

At least retrospectively, if not at the time, Kiyosaki believed shifts in public policy made people's future more uncertain. Nixon's decision to take the nation off the gold standard in 1971, he claimed, meant that millions of people would later suffer from the ravages of inflation. Three year later, changes in legislation governing retirement upended financial planning. The 1974 ERISA law that created 401(k) and other investing instruments, as well as the long-term shift from defined benefit to defined contribution plans, Kiyosaki argued, meant that people had to prepare for retirement without adequate financial education, which put them at the mercy of greedy advisers who claimed they were experts. "After ERISA," he insisted, "Wall Street had control over the country's retirement money, and most people had to blindly trust Wall Street because they simply didn't have the education and knowledge to understand how to invest properly."[17]

His father urged Robert, then in his late twenties, to return to school for a PhD and then get a government job. Instead, about this time, Robert, having attended the est seminar, rejected his father's advice. Knowing that more formal education had not worked for his Poor Dad, he followed the path of his Rich Dad, who, as a real estate investor, supposedly would become one of the state's wealthiest men because he did not allow anything to limit "his entrepreneurial spirit or his desire to mentor his son and me."[18] Initially, the younger Kiyosaki founded companies that quickly failed. Then, in 1985, the way forward began to become clear when he launched the Excellerated Learning Institute, which offered courses on investing and entrepreneurship. Selling that company nine years later, in the early 1990s he struck out on the path as an author, offering a real estate advice book, *If You Want to Be Rich and Happy, Don't Go to School* (1992). At some time between the late 1980s and the early 1990s, he worked for Money and You, a training program that offered financial wisdom developed by Marshall Thurber that drew on est's methods.[19]

Rich Dad, Poor Dad is one of more than two dozen books Kiyosaki has authored, but surely the most important. Written with the help of Lechter and composed in a chatty style, this 1997 publication pictured the world as a dangerous place from which only proper financial education could prevent people from failing. Poor Dads, committed to the belief "in a company or the government taking care of you and your needs," taught their children to pursue large doses of formal but irrelevant education and to lead lives chasing after consumer pleasures that did not lead to genuine happiness but to burdensome debt to financial institutions. In contrast, successful fathers, committed to "total financial self-reliance," wanted their children to learn "Lesson No. 1": if "the poor and the middle class work for money," in contrast, "the rich have money work for them." Employees, driven by a combination of fear and greed and full of anger at their bosses, were slaves to money and victims of governments that captured so much of their income. "They work very hard, for little money, clinging to the illusion of job security," he noted gloomily, "looking forward to a three-week vacation each year and a skimpy pension after forty-five years of work."

On the other hand, the rich minded their own business instead of someone else's. They acquired assets instead of liabilities. They knew how to minimize or avoid taxes even as members of the middle class were taxed to help the poor; lacking the access to clever lawyers and accountants, "the poor and middle class ... sit there and let the government's needles to enter their arm and let the blood donation to begin." Above all, the wealthy lived lives filled with freedom and security. The result between these contrasting worlds was such "a horrifying gap between the rich and poor that chaos will break out and another great civilization will collapse."[20]

With this book and its vision as his launch pad, it was the Rich Dad enterprises and the board game Cash Flow that brought Kiyosaki fame and fortune. Partnering with Amway, he created a multilevel marketing system, which some liken to a pyramid scheme. Indeed, although Kiyosaki has substantial investments in information technology, real estate, and oil, most of Rich Dad's income supposedly came from his franchising of workshops. It should come as no surprise to learn that lawsuits and exposés claim that his writings and seminars promote illegal and false nostrums, such as insider trading and tax fraud.[21] Those who question the presenters about the benefits of seminars sometimes meet hostile skepticism and even forcible removal from the scene. When an investigative reporter for Canadian public television asked Kiyosaki about the problematic promises and tactics the franchises offered, he vacillated between expressions of surprise and promises to investigate. However, above all he shifted blame to Whitney Information Network (later Tigrent), the controversial company that Kiyosaki used to franchise his seminars.[22] In 2013, one of Kiyosaki's many corporations filed for bankruptcy protection, and court documents appeared to show that his company had not paid the agreed-on share of the profits to Learning Annex, the corporation that sponsored his speeches and seminars.[23]

Unsurprisingly, Kiyosaki partnered with Donald J. Trump in his prepresidential years, and they shared beliefs in the gospels offered by Norman Vincent Peale and Napoleon Hill.[24] Their 2006 book, *Why We Want You to Be Rich: Two Men, One Message,* pictured a dangerous world where challenges to the middle class were omnipresent and powerful. Globalization, the shift from an industrial economy to an information one, threats to Social Security and private pensions, a health care system in crisis, federal budget and trade deficits, tax breaks for the rich, government programs that helped the poor, and new technologies could not make America become great again. In contrast, financial education that focused on real estate could rescue you by turning you into an active investor. The sections ascribed to Kiyosaki emphasized that, rather than working hard as an employee and placing money patiently and carefully in the stock market, savvy investors would use leverage provided by OPR (other people's resources). After all, though bankers will not lend you money to buy mutual funds, they "will line up to lend you money for investing in property."[25] Going against the advice of those who offered get-rich-quick schemes by house flipping, he recommended a buy-and-hold strategy that took advantage of a wide range of tax benefits. Flipping was speculation with adverse tax consequences, but buying and holding meant that "if your rental income goes up, you as an investor can refinance and draw on your appreciation as tax-free cash and have your tenant pay for the amortization of the new loan amount." Even though he advised staying away from the stock market, he tried to amplify his reputation by comparing his approach to that of Warren Buffett, because they were both "into compounding" returns and not sharing them with the government.[26]

Now came the pitch. Being a successful real estate investor was much preferable to being an employee and holding down a job, since it gave people more control over their lives. Just as his Rich Dad had mentored him, so, too, could the Rich Dad enterprises lift others, because their coaches provided "a one-on-one program that has produced phenomenal results." Since he could not possibly be a personal coach for every customer, he had created "Rich Dad's INSIDERS." For a fee people gained access to general information, and then for additional charges they could hire a "personal advisor" from one of Kiyosaki's corporations. There was nonetheless danger in the approach, hidden in plain sight but covered over with confident huzzahs. "Investing for appreciation is especially tragic," he acknowledged, particularly so "when the real estate market crashes, which it does on a regular basis," even though he did not make clear that using OPR would magnify the significance of the downward spiral.[27] Kiyosaki issued this warning not long before the real estate market crashed, especially in Arizona, where he lived.[28] Although in a 2004 book Trump warned that "love of leverage when the market crashes is what ultimately eats you alive," the general impression of the book they coauthored two years later was that you could build a fortune by investing in real estate aggressively and relying on other people's money. As a chapter title in their book shouted, "Getting Very Rich Is Predictable . . . Not Risky."[29] At the very end of *Why We Want You to Be Rich* appeared an advertisement, at the top of which stood a checklist with nine "Personal Goals." After firing your boss and starting your own business, it counseled, "flip a house"—which, of course, Kiyosaki had just warned against doing.[30]

At the same time, the future president launched Trump University, an example of for-profit education on steroids. First offering classes in 2005, it closed down five years later, charged with misleading promises and high-pressure sales practices. After the 2016 election, Trump settled the lawsuits against his "university" for $25 million. Court cases revealed the nature of the familiar business model, which was not unlike what we see with more successful real estate workshops. Emboldened by the success of the TV show *The Apprentice*, which was launched in early 2004, Trump was trying to amplify the power of his brand by developing Trump University. It offered "courses" in a rented spaces, perhaps an urban or suburban hotel. The initial seminar was free, but the instructors pressured those attending to sign up and pay for additional classes. About 7,000 customers did so, for fees that began at $1,495 for a three-day workshop. The instructors then "set the hook" by telling those attending that the initial workshop did not really provide Trump-like help, which only a more expensive "mentorship" would do and whose cost ranges as high as $34,995. The playbook told the instructors to "give them credit for taking a great first step. But don't let them think that three days will be enough to make them successful. . . . People will always take the path of least resistance," so "do not give them the option."[31]

Even though Trump claimed he had handpicked the instructors who would offer his very own "insider success secrets" that would enable attendees to get rich by using other people's money, the facts hardly matched the hype. The supposedly expert teachers had experience in sales rather than in real estate. Trump claimed he created the university as a charitable venture, even though he personally garnered $5 million of the $40 million in revenue. The instructors, who falsely claimed a personal connection with Trump, took home 10 percent of the fees the students paid. The instructors had students reveal what their assets were so they could know into what level courses they should be lured. During a lunch break at a three-day seminar, the attendees were to call their credit card companies and have their credit limit raised. Getting financing from other people's money turned out to be much more difficult than promised. Trump's lawyers claimed a 98 percent satisfaction rate, higher, they asserted, than Harvard students reported about their courses, even though one of every three enrollees demanded refunds.[32] The instructors "were unqualified people posing as Donald Trump's 'right-hand men,'" remarked a former employee. "They were teaching methods that were unethical, and they had had little to no experience flipping properties or doing real estate deals. It was a facade, a total lie."[33]

Kiyosaki's Rich Dad enterprises, some of which resembled Trump's, were but one of the forces—albeit a very important one—that shaped the optimism about residential real estate in the early twenty-first century. At a conference in 2003 or early 2004, David Berson, the chief economist of Fannie Mae, offered "a favorable outlook for the housing industry as a whole over the next decade." Americans, he predicted, "should be able to enjoy many opportunities over the next decade to successfully participate in one of the most exciting industries, the real estate industry."[34] This summary of Berson's remarks comes from Steve Burges, *The Complete Guide to Flipping Properties* (2004). Burges, an experienced investor in real estate, insisted that "his is *not* a get-rich-quick book," cautioned against no-money-down offers, and warned that house flippers needed to be sure they could service their debt. Nonetheless, he emphasized the importance of the "OPM principle: *other people's money*," including unlocking money through a home equity loan and lines of credit of your credit cards. He thus underscored the goal of controlling "as much real estate as possible while using as little of your own capital as possible.... The name of the game in this business is leverage." Even more unrestrained were the book's promotional promises. The back cover of the paperback led with the invocation of "fix and flip single-family houses for quick profit—and long-term prosperity," since the book provided investors with "the tools they need to build wealth safely and reliably."[35] Like Kiyosaki and Merrill, Burges correctly emphasized that leveraging investments in real estate was for most individuals one of the few ways of getting rich quickly—however precarious this might be as a strategy and however exaggerated their claims could be.

Researching this book, I attended several real estate workshops that promised me financial success. Before the pandemic drove them online, every week in scores of American locations these events took place. Before jumping in I tried to find reliable data on how successful I might be. I am not sure that what I quickly discovered is accurate, but here it is for flippers (but, alas, not for those who attend these workshops). According to one financial writer, the average gross profit margin from buying and selling a home was just under $30,000. However, higher returns were available. Flipping homes in the $100,000 to $200,000 range was especially promising, yielding as it supposedly did a 54 percent return on investment. Investors in Massachusetts and California were especially successful, averaging as they did in 2013 gross profits of $103,384 and $99,999, respectively. What matters are a command of knowledge about specific markets, access to a good contractor if you do not do the rehab work yourself, and time and patience. Then, of course, there is the much-heralded reliance on OPM. In response to an online question, there was a link to companies that would make personal loans. I learned that, depending on your credit rating, the interest rate would range from 5 to 30 percent. To be sure, not everyone was so successful, since nationally there is a 40 percent failure rate among house flippers. Moreover, it is not clear whether factored into the calculations is the time a flipper spends on buying and selling real estate or might spend earning money in another activity.[36]

On June 7, 2019, I attended my first workshop. I left Cambridge, Massachusetts, where my wife and I live most of the year, and drove nine miles to a Sheraton Hotel in suburban Needham. There I attended a free workshop offered by Rich Dad Education. By attending the workshop, I was entering an ample corner of a vast and complicated business empire that began in 1997 with the publication of Kiyosaki and Lechter's *Rich Dad, Poor Dad*. The sponsors of the workshop promised that I would learn lessons Kiyosaki and Lechter had earlier offered in a book whose title refers to the financial security they promised that readers could achieve by investing in residential real estate. They contrasted this with the job security Kiyosaki's father supposedly chased after, illustrated by pictures of construction workers flashing across the screen. The advertisement did this even though Kiyosaki's father was head of Hawaii's Department of Education. Claiming his father struggled financially and wanted his son to get a more formal education, the younger Kiyosaki contrasted him with his father's best friend.

His putative Rich Dad, though he did not complete high school, became wealthy by investing, including in real estate.[37]

Folks who attended such seminars, journalist Helaine Olen wrote perceptively, "are, in many ways, the confused survivors of the economic earthquake" of the early twenty first-century. Investing in real estate, Olen continued, "made people falling behind feel like they were players" whom seminar leaders urged to take action. In truth, however, "the vast majority were never going to be big winners but were instead destined to be the minnows of an economy that was increasingly predicated on financial sleights of hand."[38]

Such tricks of the trade were just what I witnessed as an attendee. With a world "in great financial volatility," I was told beforehand in a promotional email I received, I could learn the "Secrets the Rich Use to Get Richer You Never Learned in Schools" including "Ways to Fund Your Investments Using OPM (Other People's Money)." I had to come "prepared to learn a step-by-step system" that would reveal "how to put the dynamic principles of the bestseller *Rich Dad, Poor Dad* into vibrant action" in my life. The initial "Life-Changing Event" was free, but the promotional material informed me not only that Robert Kiyosaki would not be present but also that I would have the opportunity to purchase "additional products and services." If the free seminar was not sufficient, I learned, then I could climb a series of ladders, near the top of which was "Elite Training," which was "for investors and entrepreneurs who are interested in making that journey to the very highest levels of financial success." For $1690 I could start with an online course, "Fund, Fix, & Flip." Wait: there was more to come, since there are reportedly truly advanced programs that can cost at least $45,000.[39]

Thus, successive and successively more expensive "seminars" offer some investment instructions but focus more extensively on urging audience members to enroll in a series of ever more costly and perhaps more informative programs.[40] The small print in an email I received after registering made clear how difficult it would be to sue if I followed the workshop's advice and thereby jeopardized my economic well-being. The "curriculum," it insisted, despite also promising riches, "is avocational in nature and is intended for the purpose of the personal enrichment, development and enjoyment of, our students." The testimonials I would hear were "not typical, as each individual's success depends upon the unique skills, time commitment, and effort of each student."

As the appointed day approached, I received a series of texts, reminding me of the place and time of the seminar, asking me to confirm, and informing me that more than 700,000 people had preceded me. When I arrived,

I signed in and was handed a name tag that announced "My Legacy Is in the Making." The person who registered me said that more than seventy people had signed up, although they expected fewer would actually attend. Seated in one of those large, institutionally undistinctive function rooms that midlevel hotels rent out, I instead found myself among perhaps a dozen people. In my early eighties, I was by far the oldest of those attending. A quick look around revealed more women than men and more people of color than white people, and almost everyone was between their late twenties and late thirties. Once seated, at the appointed hour we watched a short video featuring Kiyosaki himself—out of date, I assumed, as we learned not to rely on the government (think of the crisis in the Veterans Affairs Department and not the Troubled Asset Relief Program) and to avoid becoming victims of the massive financial crisis, whose origins the video traced back Nixon's decision to go off the gold standard and not to the more recent one in which the bursting of the housing bubble played such a prominent role.

Then up to the front of the room strode "James": a tall and thin man, snappily but informally dressed and a glib, irreverent, fast, and colorful talker. Later on and back home, Google helped me identify him as James M. Smith, whose website held out the hope that he could put me on "The Fast Track to Financial Freedom." On a Facebook site he posted encouraging aphorisms such as "Champions Train, Losers Complain." A Facebook post by another person noted that Smith "wasn't afraid to talk about God or warn people about not believing in God." On the other hand, I discovered a Yelp post from a disappointed 2016 attendee who reported that he felt like he was "sitting in a church, where the speaker says what he wants and you have to hear those lame stories and try not to fall asleep."[41] Although I almost never sit in a pew and listen to a minister but participate in minyans and listen as fellow congregants conduct the service, I sat here attentively, a scholar rather than a potential real estate investor. A gifted storyteller and skilled inspirational speaker, Smith talked for almost two hours. He had set his smartphone to go off several times, prompting him to shift from one topic to another. Claiming he knew the Boston area well, he spoke glowingly of the wonderful life his financial success made possible. He traveled extensively, he said, including to the Caribbean, where he spent enough time looking for possible real estate investments to justify his using the trips' expenses as tax deductions. We learned he doubled his net worth every four years. But wait: eventually it was clear that bragging about his success had a larger purpose, offering those attending inspiration and help so they, too, might get ahead.

Following Kiyosaki's writings, Smith framed the contrast between what he had achieved and how he could help us fulfill our own dreams by emphasizing the dangers in the world we inhabited. He urged us to see the movie *The Big Short*. At a time when participants in the bond market were expecting very low rates of inflation, we learned that in eight years there would be a terrible crisis caused by runaway inflation (just keep in mind, he reminded us, how in Venezuela the government prints an abundance of $1 million bills). Unemployment, store closings, bankruptcies, soaring health care costs, political unrest, collapsing corporations, and a risk-filled job market—all backed up by statistics he offered—added up to a frightening picture of what surrounded and faced us. No longer could we rely on powerful institutions such as banks, major corporations, universities, or even real estate agencies. Again and again, he went back and forth between references to horrors and evocations of successes. Oh, and by the way, he had known Robert Kiyosaki for twenty-five years and counted Warren Buffett and Steve Forbes among his acquaintances. The message, sometimes implicit, was clear: you need someone like me to mentor you in this uncertain and dangerous world. In saying this, Smith, like Merrill and others, skillfully played on the pervasive sense among Americans and others of the troubles they faced as investors, citizens, and employees.[42]

Forty minutes into his presentation, Smith shifted to more practical matters. He told us that there would be a three-day seminar later in the month. Of course, he predicted, we would tell ourselves we could not attend because it would cost so much money and we did not have the confidence to believe we could achieve financial freedom. So he quickly reminded us that in the short term we could not trust the stock market, and, more ominously, he once again warned of the financial crisis coming in eight years. And now he suggested more fully the importance of mentors. He had mentored many people, he said, helping them make fortunes. It was at this point that I began to suspect (something confirmed later) that this free two-hour meeting and then the three-day seminar I would have to pay for would put me on the road to riches only by paying tens of thousands of dollars to hire a Rich Dad, Poor Dad–sponsored mentor. After all, James repeatedly told us, he made more money in a day than his own dad had in his lifetime. Quickly doing the math on my iPhone, I calculated that if his father labored forty years earning $20,000 annually, he would have lifetime earnings of $800,000. So if James, the son of this Poor Dad, worked 250 days a year for the reputed $800,000 his father garnered in a lifetime, his annual income would be $200 million. Oh, well, I thought, if James worked only one day a week, his annual income would be in excess of $40 million—and he would then not have to waste his time and energy making these two-hour presentations. Then, when I later googled James M. Smith, I found figures for the net worth of a person with that name, including from a real estate investment trust traded on the New York Stock Exchange—precisely the stock market he told us to avoid relying on.[43]

An hour and a half into the presentation and I had not really learned much—except that I should avoid taxes and sign up for the three-day seminar. To be sure, there were hints of what I should do. Hard assets are more real than paper ones. Because you cannot count on major institutions, especially the federal government, you need to be both self-reliant and reliant on the knowledge and mentorship that the Rich Dad, Poor Dad programs offer. Of course, Smith's statement about federal inaction contradicted the robust response the government had already made during the Great Recession and would again later in the pandemic. Though he never mentioned God or religion (but he did refer to the Bible), he made it clear he has used his vast wealth to support missions in the developing world. Although he continually emphasized his opposition to political correctness, again and again he mentioned that he has partnered with African Americans and that he did not care if you were here in the United States on a green card. He singled out these groups, I assume, because African Americans and immigrants had in the past proven to be receptive targets of these pitches.[44]

At last, with fifteen minutes to go, his pitch became more targeted. James pointed to a table on his right, complete with pictures of books on real estate investing. By signing up for the three-day seminar, I, too, could have access to the Rich Dad Reference Library, as well as to the Home Study portal. To underscore my potential future, he offered two examples of investment possibilities (mobile home parks and lease options), which were more complicated and more lucrative than simply flipping houses. He also reported that he had purchased an empty Payless store and turned it into an adult day care center that brought in income of at least $75,000 a month. And he had purchased a six-bedroom house for $600,000 and turned it into a group home in which six people paid $5000 monthly. Do the math: $6 \times \$5,000 \times 12$ months = $360,000 annually. He did not mention costs such as taxes, utilities, upkeep, and food. Yet he did emphasize that he hired women from the Philippines to run the house in exchange for the low wages that would mean so much when they returned home.

OMG, it sounds as if I might earn $300,000 a year on my initial investment of $600,000. What an ROI (return on investment)! OK, now I get it, the generational family dynamics. Kiyosaki's Poor Dad failed him, but his Rich

Dad transformed his life. So James had a father who barely made a decent living, but Kiyosaki's wisdom made him rich. Now it is your turn. Though someone failed you, you have learned from the seminar that you have your own Rich Dad, a mentor like James. A family drama unlike the one Freud offered but a family drama nonetheless, one that if properly understood promised not a less neurotic life but a more prosperous one. Freud never predicted that hours in therapy would bring psychic freedom, but a three-day seminar will put you on the road to financial freedom. With only hints of "elite" products off in the future, the next step is clear. The upcoming three-day seminar, which normally costs $495, can be yours for less than $200.

As I got up from my seat and headed to the exit, I faced a line of assistants seated at long table across almost the entire room, ready to sign me up. With difficulty I could bypass this arrangement and get out. This meant I had to go against what the Rich Dad, Poor Dad workshop website says: "You Can Make Money or Make Excuses. **The choice is yours**. Everyone wants to be rich, but only a select few will ever TAKE ACTION and get the financial knowledge they need to make their dreams come true. You can be one of that select few!" Perhaps I could avoid being one of the tens of thousands who were among the "select few," not only because I was attending in order to do research for a book but because my own dad was so successful in so many ways, as a businessman and civic leader. And, to boot, he had encouraged me to become a professor.

Several times during the two hours, Smith offered disparaging remarks about the real estate seminars inspired by the work of Than Merrill who joins Robert Kiyosaki on any list of real estate gurus who have built an empire in part on workshops. Merrill's life story is hardly as dramatic as that of Kiyosaki, nor is his vision so elaborately and rhetorically evocative. Nonetheless, the narrative of his life and the inspirational power of his vision help underwrite the power of what his ventures have wrought. Repeated endlessly on websites and at workshops, Merrill's life story builds on references to two achievements that are supposed to inspire confidence: his graduation from Yale and his career in the National Football League. A 2003 knee injury ended his professional football career, one that involved only a single season in the NFL and two in the NFL Europe League. Like most inspirational advice givers, Merrill told a story, albeit less dramatic than others, of failure and recovery. While playing for the Chicago Bears, he opened a Mexican restaurant in what he soon learned was an "entrepreneurial burp." Not having enough business savvy and hating the distractions and exhaustion that came from working up to fourteen hours a day off season, he realized that with both his NFL career and restaurant business faltering, he had to make "a *massive* change." After all, he insisted, everyone has experienced "moments that define your future and the path you ultimately choose to take." Remembering that he had always been passionate about real estate, he read books and enrolled in many seminars in order to learn more about the field. Partnering with a childhood friend and a Yale football teammate, Merrill launched his career in real estate—at first buying some rental properties and soon turning to flipping multiple houses simultaneously.[45]

Right away, in 2004, he formed with his business partners CT Homes in New Haven, Connecticut, a real estate investment company that along with the real estate education company FortuneBuilders Inc. forms the basis for his sprawling empire. His work with CT Homes brought him to the attention of the producers of A&E's *Flip This House*, on which he and his buddies appeared for three seasons (2007-9) as they flipped properties in and around New Haven. His future, however, lay not on television, but in investing in and educating about real estate, the latter through a familiar escalating staircase of workshops.

We can get a first glimpse of the approach available in his workshops by looking at his book: *Real Estate Wholesaling Bible: The Fastest, Easiest Way to Get Started in Real Estate Investing* (2014). Although lacking the personal drama of Kiyosaki's *Rich Dad, Poor Dad* and mostly focusing on practical strategies, Merrill's "Bible" nonetheless began by offering readers hope. Investing in real estate promised escape from jobs they despised and instead made it possible for them to achieve financial freedom and the opportunity to "spend more time pursuing your higher calling," whose nature he left undefined. Moreover, he insisted, real estate investors "are sexier, better lovers, and generally nicer people than any other type of investor." By "controlling your financial destiny," he promised, you can "ensure you don't fall victim to the shrinking middle class in America." He recommended finding a mentor who would "dramatically" enhance your chances of achieving financial success and joining "a mastermind group" of peers "with whom you can brainstorm and share best industry practices." To underscore the urgency of his message, he emphasized the familiar litany of frightening woes millions of American faced. Median household incomes were stagnant or falling; debt levels were growing higher and higher; globalization eroded job prospects; children were less likely to be better off than their parents. In short, the United States was "rapidly being transformed from a country of middle-class citizens into a country of government dependents." Instead, he held out the hope that reading his book "can help you avoid becoming a statistic" because, as has been true in the past, real estate "has been America's number one wealth builder."[46]

On July 11, 2019, I attended my first Than Merrill real estate class. I left our apartment in Cambridge and drove a few miles to a Holiday Inn in nearby Somerville. The location was far from fancy. In the Bunker Hill neighborhood close to several of Boston's most important historic sites, more immediately what marked its setting were highway overpasses, warehouses, and small commercial establishments serving working-class customers. As had happened with the Rich Dad, Poor Dad presentations, beforehand I was bombarded by reminders, although this time even slicker and more insistent. "Hey Daniel, this is Than," he told me personally in a text message without acknowledging that we were both Yale graduates. "I'm so excited you'll be attending my free real estate investing class." What followed was information that would help me "get the absolute MOST" from this experience. With a "free guest ticket," I could bring along "a spouse, business partner, or friend." After all, with my "financial future at stake," two heads were definitely better than one. Reminding me that Woody Allen had said "80% of success is showing up," I was encouraged to arrive early, when one of their "awesome greeters" would welcome me. This would ensure me a seat and launch me on the path to financial freedom as these sessions had already done for thousands of others across the country. Making sure I knew how "excited" he was for me, he made it clear he desired "YOU to be our next great success story."

Then and soon after came words of encouragement and offers of advice. My "VIP Success Package Is Ready!" I learned. Another religious reference reminded me that I could discover "The Twelve Commandments of How Wealthy People Think." Using typical language that reminded me of Norman Vincent Peale's *The Power of Positive Thinking* (1952), he urged me to overcome fears that held me back so that I would realize that "success starts in the mind!" I could download a copy of a "Money Resource Guide" that would tell me how to draw on OPM.

When I arrived, I found myself seated in the midst of an audience of perhaps forty people, most of them between their late twenties and their midfifties. About one-third were African American, and the audience had a roughly even gender division. Before we met the presenter, the session began with a film approximately five minutes long in which we watched a quick and hugely successful rehab of a home in Connecticut overlooking Long Island Sound. Of course, there were lots of disclaimers: this was no get-rich-quick scheme, and one had to learn how to manage risk and work hard. Education mattered. Moreover, "any testimonials showing our success or our students' success" were "not to be interpreted as common, typical, or expected" and some of them were "from students who" work as FortuneBuilders "coaches or trainers."

The presenter then appeared: Woody Wolden, who said he was from Pensacola, Florida, and informed us that, because the material was copyrighted, we could not take pictures or use a tape recorder. Perhaps in his midforties, I speculated, he identified himself as a real estate investor and an inspirational speaker. The absent Kiyosaki seemed ever-present in the other event, but Than Merrill was only seen figuratively, even though he had personally invited me here—though, of course, we learned that he had gone to Yale and played in the NFL. More so than James M. Smith from the Rich Dad, Poor Dad offering, Wolden deployed a clever interactive approach, though, apparently knowing little of the Boston area, he could not tailor his presentation geographically. Again and again, he relied on call and response: "When am I going to begin?" he implored. "NOW," we quickly learned to shout. Setting up drama to be reenacted later, he cleverly established the conditions for role-playing by singling out audience members—one to act as someone who, having lost his job, was desperate to sell his home before losing it to foreclosure; another, an actual contractor, to play the role of contractor; and a third to play a prospective buyer looking for a home she could fix up and sell.

Now Wolden took over. If James M. Smith had belittled Than Merrill, Wolden dotted his presentations by casting aspersions on HGTV for what he said was the network's unrealistic shows, which made real estate investing seem much too easy. He said this even though we later learned of a woman who started out with Merrill's FortuneBuilders and then went on to have her own home renovation show on HGTV. As was true in the Rich Dad, Poor Dad event, here I learned how dangerous the world was out there. Indeed, threaded throughout the two hours were references to a treacherous existence from which only financial education (not governments, banks, the stock market, or corporations) could rescue us. Yet, on the whole, the first hour provided much more practical information than Rich Dad, Poor Dad had.

Mixing drama and specific tactics, Wolden walked us though steps we could take to buy, renovate, and then profitably sell a property: sign a contract for a house someone was desperate to sell, use FortuneBuilders' Deal Analyzer to estimate costs and predict profits, figure out the expenses for fixing up the property, estimate the costs of holding the property before you could sell it, and then determine the price you would have to sell it for in order to make the profit you had in mind. All along the way, he insisted, we should rely on the labor and expertise of others—a contractor who could estimate the costs of renovation and later on make it unnecessary for you to wield a hammer like the male stars of HGTV shows occasionally did; the homeowner who would provide the figures for the carrying costs; a realtor who, relying on MLS listings, could give you the sales prices of comparable residences; lenders who were easier to borrow from than bankers; and a property manager whose work would enable you to enjoy your spare time. In the end, you had several options: buy, renovate, and sell, or, better yet, engage in what he calls reverse wholesaling: buy and then earn a handsome fee by selling the contract to a local investor. It all sounded free of risk and emotional roller coasters.

If this was the practical advice, what surrounded it was a series of fears (albeit not as ominous as what I learned in Needham) and hopes. Schools do not teach you how to achieve financial freedom, but Than Merrill's wisdom will. You have to fund your retirement, and to do so it's better to rely on what FortuneBuilders have to offer than on the stock market. Since it's likely that you have a dead-end job working for a boss who is not as smart as you, the goal is to avoid being an employee and instead become an owner, your own boss. You are doing this not for the money but for what money will buy—the ability to enjoy retirement, create a legacy for your family, and pay back to society.

With an hour to go, the focus shifted from offering practical advice to suggesting a path forward by generating the passive income that will make financial freedom possible. "Oh, I know," we heard, "friends and family members will do their best to dissuade you." To underscore his point, Wolden told of how years ago he had faced a similar situation when a buddy with whom he was attending a Than Merrill workshop tried to persuade him to leave and go instead to a bar and enjoy camaraderie. Wolden resisted, and told us we should as well, since he, too, was struggling then, and look at how successful he was now. My decision made me who I am, he insisted, and this can happen to you, too. Your lives change today, we heard him say as there flashed on the screen in small print a disclaimer and then pictures of those who took the next step and changed their lives. Stop being a know-it-all, he demanded. One hour and six minutes in came the revelation that there was no way a two-hour workshop like this could turn us into successful investors, and we needed what we would learn in a three-day seminar held over a long weekend at a nearby location. Going briefly through what we would learn each day, Wolden mentioned that wealthy people lent money to FortuneBuilders, which in turn had in recent years lent $250 million to investors like us. So, stop watching those TV shows, because the workshop would give us the tools and inspiration we needed.

Offered a hint about the importance of having a mentor (an "advanced coaching system," he called it) and, more importantly, of associating yourself with successful people, we could now see the light. Watching a video that showed scores of enthusiastic attendees at the next level of workshops, we learned of a Stanford University study that supposedly proved people earn what those they most closely associated with earned. The implication was clear: if we hung around with others at the three-day seminar (rather than with the losers who tried to dissuade us from taking the next step), then we could draw on their inspiration, energy, and positive motivation.

With thirty minutes to go, we learned that people were sitting in back of the room ready to sign us up. But if we waited until later, the three-day seminar would cost $500. For no extra money, we could bring a spouse or friend; even a third person was negotiable. Sign up now and it was ours for $197. The calculus was in our favor: ourselves and a guest for three days—that's $33 per person a day, and we would take home a bagful of helpful books. Compared with a college textbook—and, even more significantly so, with tuition for a college course—this was an incredible bargain. Moreover, just as Wolden had made clear earlier that many in his target audience were people whose lack of access to money prevented them from moving forward, he pointed to someone at the back of the room who could help those who could not readily afford $197 find a financial way forward. About two-thirds of my fellow attendees went to the back of the room to sign up; none that I could see needed special help to finance the next step.

With only a handful of us remaining in ours seats, Wolden persisted, telling us of other money-making schemes. Eventually he seemed to run out of steam. Just as at the beginning he had relied on a video, now he turned another one on. Flashing before our eyes, as had been true before, were pictures of people whose lives previous workshops and mentorship programs had transformed.

Persistent as a researcher who relishes work on the ground as much as online or in a library, on January 23, 2020, I attended another introductory workshop, this time in Pasadena, California, where my wife and I are snowbirds in the orbit of the nearby and high-minded Huntington Library, Art Museum, and Botanical Gardens. This time, the setting was much more upscale than the Somerville location: a meeting room in a Hilton Hotel within walking distance from the condo where we lived. Again, beforehand I was bombarded by a stream of text messages and emails filled with encouragement and promises. I did not recall that before the one I attended in Somerville, FortuneBuilders had provided me with testimonials, as it did this time—for example, a thirty-second video featuring an African American woman who appeared to be in her midthirties testifying that "after having two master's degrees and a doctorate" she was laid off. "I made a decision at that point that I wasn't going to work for anybody else again." What Than Merrill's programs offered was "a way to grow [her] income, where the other activities produced ways for [her] to keep a job."

Compared with the audience at the Somerville event, this one was larger and more diverse: perhaps seventy people, ranging from their midtwenties to their early eighties, and with a full complement of whites, African Americans, Latinx, and Asian Americans. Yet, to my surprise, if the audience was different, the presenter, I soon realized, was the very same Woody Wolden. Early on, he had us stand up and introduce ourselves to five others nearby—"as in church," he remarked. Immediately, this got me thinking about the relationship between capitalism and religion: What did it mean that Than Merrill authored a real estate bible; that he was the absent but frequently invoked deity who watched over us; that we participated in call-and-response exercises and listened to stories of rebirths; and that, at the end, we could sign up for a baptism that would occur later on?

Not surprisingly, the pitch was familiar, though I suspect that the differences or additions I offer here are due more to the imperfections of my earlier note-taking than to any variance in Wolden's method. He explained that the FortuneBuilders systems involved an approach clearly preferable to trying to learn from HGTV. There seemed less emphasis this time on how precarious the world was, and the insistent refrain of being an owner and not an employee seemed even more prominent—strikingly so, because I now had to assume that Wolden, a skilled salesman who went around the country making his pitches, was employed by FortuneBuilders.

As far as I could reconstruct my previous experience, Wolden had put forth only hints of future offers to separate us from our money, though it was possible that I now knew more about the increasingly expensive ladder of opportunities. This time, halfway through, he began mentioning the importance of mentors, personal and experienced coaches from whom we could learn. Even more striking—and something I do not think I heard in Somerville—was his discussion of the advantage of purchasing a franchise. After all, he asked, would it not be better to own a Subway franchise and not have all the risk and bother involved in opening your own sandwich shop? This way you could indeed be an owner and not a worker—an opportunity I assumed I might learn was possible were I to partner with

FortuneBuilders. It turned out that this free workshop was indeed the first step in what Wolden described as part of a relationship business, with an opportunity to partner with Than Merrill, who now had over 500 employees. He showed us success stories on a large screen, scrolling down to show ones in California we could identify with.

Then, at almost exactly the sixty-minute mark, came the real transition. Putting personal testimonials on the screen, Wolden reminded us that a two-hour session was not adequate to the task of our building fortunes; we had to sign up for a three-day workshop. Next came his personal story, which I did not remember from the Somerville session. Twenty-three years ago, when he was twenty-six years old, he'd been exhausted by a daily thirty-five-mile commute in Southern California from Long Beach to Glendale. He was making it in life, but not much more than just making it. The friend he had mentioned in Somerville said Than Merrill's workshop was "hogwash," but the pleasures of sitting at a bar awaited them. Someone came up to Wolden and said that taking the three-day seminar would change his life—even though it cost $1,000 then (compared to $197 now). He turned down his friend's offer and opted for the FortuneBuilders workshop.

Now we were into the familiar next steps. I watched as about 70 percent of the attendees walked to the back of the room and signed up for the $197 weekend workshop. Initially I stayed in my seat and listened to Wolden's presentation, one that underscored to me the fact that he was hawking an elaborate system that seemed to make buying, renovating, and selling carefree. Somewhat bored, I thought to myself that I needed to sign up, but not to achieve financial freedom. After all, there I was, ten years into retirement and with a good measure of financial freedom, but working as a historian sixty hours a week on projects that were far more rewarding psychologically than they could possibly be financially. No, I could sign up in order to pursue this as a research project. I talked to a sales associate, but the weekends available did not work for me. Sensing my reluctance, he made me an offer: let him charge me the $197, and I could go to any three-day workshop in the next twelve months. I was reluctant to make such a commitment, and, as a perceptive salesman, he knew better than to spend more time on me.

I assume that programs such as Kiyosaki's and Merrill's have successfully taught some people how to enhance their financial situations. Those who operate them offer examples of the stunning successes some of their followers have achieved, and yet, if they have hard and reliable data, it is not publicly available.[47] On the other hand, central to any evaluation are warnings familiar to anyone who understands multilevel marketing. As with Trump University, we began with a free presentation that lasted a few hours. Then we moved to a bargain rate three-day workshop. And then came steps up a ladder of offerings, which could apparently easily cost $50,000 or more. Along the way, we encountered many key elements of high-pressure salesmanship that rely on well-honed and skillful tactics: the pressure to make quick decisions, the offer of irresistible bargains, inspirational examples with disclaimers that noted they may not be representative but which nonetheless were convincing, and tantalizing promises of financial freedom. Especially interesting with FortuneBuilders was what I take to be their franchise model. Hinted at in the presentations I attended, this seemed to involve paying a substantial fee in order to become a coach or mentor, which could provide an income stream different from actual real estate investing. From Merrill's company, especially lucrative were the full range of products offered: not just the tip of the iceberg I witnessed but a wide range of real estate, investing, financing, legal, accounting, and educational services.[48]

With Kiyosaki's narrative and the Rich Dad, Poor Dad seminars, the criticisms are especially cogent but hardly surprising. Skeptics have called into question the accuracy of Kiyosaki's story about contrasting fathers, as well as whether he amassed a fortune and how his corporation's declarations of bankruptcy cast doubt on his business acumen and reliability.[49] Nor are the workshops beyond reproach. For example, in 2011 a reporter told of one woman's experience. Finding herself unemployed after a career in sales, Shawn Moody signed up for a seminar that promised "to teach people how to make a killing in real estate or other investments." However, an observer noted, "the only thing that ended up getting killed in Moody's case was a hefty chunk of her bank balance." And she was lucky, for others reported being out much more than that. After attending the free event and then signing up for a three-day seminar that cost several hundred dollars, once there they found themselves subjected to unrelenting pressure to spend even more for a combination of education and mentoring.[50] In 2012, a writer for *Forbes* let loose with a more expansive critique. Helaine Olen called Kiyosaki "one of the small-time wealth guru mountebanks" who built his own success by "telling his forever falling behind audience" how to succeed. "The schtick behind the Rich Dad books," she continued, "was that Kiyosaki was sharing secret money-making strategies of the wealthy with his wage slave readers. The tips ran the gamut from ridiculous to illegal and downright hurtful." As Olen reported after having attended a Rich Dad, Poor Dad workshop, the presenter was "telling us there is a way for us to go from wage slave, living paycheck to paycheck, to mega mogul, flying off on our dream vacation on a private jet."[51] With this and other programs, in order to figure out how much a customer can afford to spend, salespeople press them for information on their finances and encourage them to secure higher limits on their credit cards.

It is not very difficult to find similar critiques of Merrill's workshops. For example, on October 26, 2015, the Frugal Vagabond posted on the web a report titled "Undercover: Than Merrill's Fortune Builders." He reported that he sat "through a two hour slow-burn sales pitch that used misdirection, omission, and psychological tricks to place the audience in a receptive frame of mind, and ultimately, to extract $197 from a group of people who can ill-afford to spend it."[52] Much of what he said jibed with my own experience: like other wealth-building seminars, the workshop he attended used a slick presentation that provided much more inspiration than useful information to gullible people who rushed to the back of the room to put down their $197 for a three-day course whose lessons might be readily available for free online or at your public library.

Yet the Frugal Vagabond did tell me some things I had not learned or had only half realized when I attended the free workshops. He underscored that the presenter's use of call and response was a "compliance technique called 'Foot In the Door'" that put audience members in a mood that made them receptive to increasingly more complex requests, ending, of course, in the call to plunk down $197, followed, they hoped, by a response. He underscored what I suspected, that FortuneBuilders was offering "systems" (e.g., spreadsheets, checklists), the technical expertise that they promised would make investing in real estate less risky. Clearly, investing in a Chipotle franchise was wiser than opening your own taqueria. Unlike what I experienced, at the two-hour seminar the Vagabond attended, a representative of a private money-lending company appeared who would finance attendees' real estate investments at what the Frugal Vagabond believed were "very high interest rates." The Frugal Vagabond also made clear that those who took the next step would have the opportunity to enroll in a series of more costly programs, culminating in Mastery courses for tens of thousands of dollars that might actually offer useful information, albeit at what he called "insultingly disproportionate" costs. When I walked home from Than Merrill's event, I thought about how I would write up what I witnessed. In contrast, when the Frugal Vagabond returned to his car, he pondered how often "countless real estate gurus" gave similar presentations; how those who signed up would soon learn that a free three-day seminar provided them with little they could not learn elsewhere; and how climbing the ladder of ever-more-costly programs would impact, presumably in adverse ways, "their lives, their marriages, and their children."[53]

Elizabeth Youngling, an economic anthropologist who has attended even more real estate workshops than I have, has written perceptively about their promises of financial freedom and achievement of the American dream in the years since the foreclosure crisis of 2008. She confirms what I read in books by Kiyosaki and saw in workshops he sponsored: that, together, self-help traditions, hints of the power of evangelical religion, a belief that homeownership is central to achieving the American dream, the celebration of entrepreneurship, and familiarity with real estate–focused reality television promised to "turn the grim inequities" in contemporary America "into a platform for selling insider knowledge to people with limited financial resources and experience." Like her, I was struck by how presenters at two-hour workshops used varied strategies to convince audience members that they would achieve financial success with the help of what they offered. People like James M. Smith and Woody Wolden pictured a dangerous world out there, one in which it was no longer possible to rely on government handouts, formal education, or the stock market. What Kiyosaki's Rich Dad offered was clearly preferable to the false security and precarious comfort that his Poor Dad chased after. So, too, could audience members transform themselves from bored and struggling employees into happy and liberated investors—or, as Youngling put it, "a passive consumer can transform herself into an empowered market maker."[54] The pain and disruption of the crisis in residential real estate was fresh in people's minds. Yet books by Kiyosaki and Merrill, along with the workshops they launched, promised to turn struggling citizens, who had hardly recovered from the impact of the Great Recession, into prosperous investors.

In the end, it is crucially important to render judgments about the impact and meaning of TV shows such as HGTV's *Property Brothers*, *Fixer Upper*, and *Flip or Flop*, as well as seminars like those offered by the Rich Dad, Poor Dad and FortuneBuilders franchises. Such enterprises have inspired tens or hundreds of thousands of Americans and then impelled them into the worlds of real estate investing—often doing so in ways resembling how cults operate. Although it makes no sense to minimize the impact of these ventures, lacking rigorous studies, it is difficult to measure what they have wrought. Neither HGTV nor the operators of workshops are likely to carry out serious studies of the consequences of their efforts, and even if they did, they would be less likely to make them either publicly available or subject to exacting verification. Their impact on the national and global economies is not clear and probably not very significant. However, they do promise more than they can usually deliver and cost most people more in time and money than they can likely gain emotionally or financially.

Scholars have paid some attention to economics of house flipping. Some observers claim that flipping houses helped ease the housing crisis. In already-inflated markets, they argue, flippers may well make residences less affordable, yet in cities and neighborhoods with an abundance of neglected or foreclosed homes, speculative renovators add decent and affordable residences to the market. This may be especially true in places such as Tampa, Florida, or California's San Joaquin Valley, where flipped houses account for as much as 10 percent of residential real estate sales.[55] Indeed, in early 2020 an economist who specializes in the impact of house flipping on residential real estate emailed me about the benefits of the practice. He acknowledged that flipping can artificially inflate prices, yet he seemed to insist that the benefits outweighed the risks. By bringing together buyers and sellers, flippers did "provide liquidity"; in "many cases," their renovations added "value to the surrounding neighborhood. Like speculators and arbitrageurs in the financial markets," he concluded, "flippers provide capital that allows a more orderly residential real estate market. Without them, some homes would lie vacant for months or even years. The result would be decaying neighborhoods, increasing crime and vagrants settling in the area."[56]

In contrast, in what strikes me as the most rigorous and sophisticated study, four economists examined 3.5 million transactions in the metropolitan Los Angeles area between 1988 and 2009. Among the conclusions they drew was that two groups, middlemen and novice speculators, did not correctly anticipate the impact of the financial crisis. Middlemen were "welfare-enhancing," well informed, and rational investors who profited by taking advantage of market inefficiencies; "provide[d] liquidity to the market . . . purchasing from motivated sellers with high holding costs and waiting more patiently for the right buyer"; improved the housing stock, especially in older neighborhoods, by making significant physical improvements; and, overall, used their expert knowledge to take advantage of market conditions. They operated during booms and busts and during the latter they helped "to stabilize the market, effectively putting a floor on price declines and providing liquidity for many homeowners who may be desperate to sell quickly following economic shocks."[57]

Then there were novice investors, like the flippers energized by reading popular books or attending workshops. To these four economists, these investors were unable to foresee changing conditions, earned unexceptional returns, lost substantial amounts of money when the bubble burst, and promoted neither economic efficiency nor social welfare. With "very little prior experience in real estate investing," they were neither particularly skilled at bargaining nor well informed about market conditions, especially at anticipating when markets would peak. The many "amateur speculators" who jumped into the market for residential real estate early in the twenty-first century helped in the development of rapidly rising home prices and then contributed to the "bursting of local price bubbles over the next several years." By intensifying price volatility and destabilizing markets, they did nothing to enhance market efficiency and had "a negative effect on social welfare in the market."[58]

Additional evidence for the deleterious impact of some house flipping came from journalists Ben Casselman and Conor Dougherty, who tracked its impact on a neighborhood in southwest Atlanta where individual and corporate investors stepped in. Casselman and Dougherty told of how, within one year, a house changed hands three times in a once-prosperous neighborhood that the foreclosure crisis had devastated. It was now recovering as the impact of the Great Recession receded and the BeltLine began to develop as a multipurpose rail trail. Using a limited liability corporation, an individual investor purchased the residence for $85,000. After owning it for less than sixty days, he sold it for $134,000 to yet other investors, a couple who spent eight months fixing it up, then sold the renovated 1,600-square-foot residence for $324,000 to a couple with a young child who actually planned to live in it. Varied forces came together to cause such a dramatic rise in prices: not only the return of some modicum of prosperity to the city and the way public improvements enhanced the values of private property, but also the increasing attractiveness of the neighborhood to what the writers called "a new generation of young, affluent (and largely white) residents."[59]

However, beyond the impact of house flipping, other, more powerful forces shaped the markets for residential real estate, often dramatically driving up prices. Competing with individuals seeking a place to live and others flipping houses on a small scale were what Casselman and Dougherty called "a fast-growing industry that promotes investment in single-family homes: lenders who provide the capital, brokers who handle transactions, wholesalers who buy homes by the dozens and sell them before they even take possession." Private equity companies, often based in Wall Street, had "'taken an asset class that used to be something hokey and made it the real deal,' said Martin Kay, the founder of Entera," a company that enables people to "choose among hundreds of thousands of single-family homes as if they're buying stocks and bonds. Investors can build an online profile of homes they want—for example, those in an up-and-coming neighborhood in a city with lots of tech jobs, or affordable homes in middle-class neighborhoods in Texas—then make an offer with a click. Entera finds homes that fit that profile and facilitates the transaction: Ground agents assess the condition and location of the homes, while a team in Houston works to close the deal."[60] If we step back from the studies and reports we have on house flipping, we might find that, from an economic perspective, several conclusions are possible. In some instances, a win-win results, where the seller, flipper, and buyer all benefit because the investor acts as an intermediary who improves properties and enhances how markets function. On the other hand, what the flipper does is neutral in its effect. Then there are cases where an overly zealous and poorly informed intermediary with a short-term perspective does damage by contributing to a housing bubble and distorts capital markets without making investments that improve the quality of a property.[61]

What about the impact of TV programs, popular books, and well-attended workshops? They have brought many people with modest incomes into the market and in some cases helped improve their lives, even as in other instances they led to personal misfortunes. However much they might help some investors achieve financial freedom, residential real estate workshops, as one critic has colorfully insisted, rely on "the 'medicine show' seminar structure designed to upsell the audience to much more expensive add-ons."[62] Although there are few if any rigorous assessments of the impact of these specific efforts, my informed judgment is that the real winners in the game of residential real estate investing, including flipping, are corporations like Entera and private equity firms, along with the organizations that launched and supported Kiyosaki, Merrill and his partners, the Gaineses, the Scott brothers, and the El Moussas. Early in the twenty-first century it was easy for people to learn about fortunes made in residential real estate. This, plus the promise of expertise that HGTV programs and house-flipping workshops, surely inspired significant numbers of Americans to seek their own fortunes by investing in real estate. There obviously are cases of the resulting road from rags to riches. Yet the evidence from historical and contemporary studies (including the one that tracked millions of sales in Los Angeles) is that people with economic, social, and cultural capital are more likely to win at this game than those without such resources.

However, we also know that what flowed from some real estate TV shows and seminars affected the nation as a whole. As early as 2000 the U.S.

Senate carried out an extensive investigation focusing on house flipping. The conclusion was clear and ominous: con artists used a variety of fraudulent methods to take advantage of unsuspecting buyers. However, the ramifications threatened to move from individuals to the entire economy. "Flipping is spreading like a virus," Senator Susan Collins asserted, "that, if left unchecked, could reach epidemic proportions."[63] Yet it took a long time for that virus to reach that epidemic level—if that is what happened—and serve as a cause of the Great Recession.

What we do know is that, because memories are problematic, the stakes are high, since old patterns soon returned and new ones developed. "Six Years after the Great Recession, House Flipping Is on the Rise," announced a reporter for *PBS NewsHour* in a mid-October 2016 broadcast. This time would be different, he claimed, because, "while such rapid turnover helped fuel the housing crisis a decade ago, advocates and analysts say the current wave is helping to ease a shortage of affordable housing in some parts of the country."[64] Once again, best-selling books, along with their accompanying workshops and websites, helped fuel the quest, as they had earlier.[65] The empires that originated with Kiyosaki, Merrill, the Scott brothers, the Gaineses, and the El Moussas grew apace. Seeing opportunity and relying on new technologies, powerful hedge funds, private investment firms, and even financial instruments modeled on mutual funds, they placed heavy bets on house flipping. They may have enhanced market liquidity but they were often less-than-ideal landlords who undermined the prospects of individual homeowners. In mid-2019, for example, KKR, a global investment firm with over $150 billion under management, announced that it was doubling its earlier investment of $250 million in a company that already had $1.5 billion in short-term loans to house flippers. While the subheadline read that KKR was "positive and constructive on U.S. housing-related risk," the caption under the accompanying picture emphasized the risks, such as downturns in the housing market, problematic remodeling estimates, or flippers guessing incorrectly what homeowners wanted.[66] This contradiction underscores the powerful influence of corporate power in shaping the world of residential real estate and the risks that individual investors face.

Yet, stepping back, we can also understand how the enterprises developed by Kiyosaki and Merrill reflect, amplify, and promote the power of broader forces in play. Relying on fieldwork in the Rich Dad, Poor Dad world in ways that are more broadly applicable, the sociologist Daniel Fridman persuasively explored the nature and appeal of financial self-help programs in *Freedom from Work: Embracing Financial Self-Help in the United States and Argentina* (2017). He writes that to consumers of the advice that Kiyosaki and others offer, financial freedom does not mean merely or principally accumulating money but something connected to "realization, transcendence, and fulfillment... the critical individual autonomy without which one simply cannot be the architect of one's life." Following Michel Foucault, Fridman speaks of the pursuit of financial independence, not having to work for someone else, as part of "technologies of the self," one of "the many ways in which individuals turn themselves into targets of their own self-transformation" by systems of self-government that foster entrepreneurship, autonomy, and individualism in which self-help books and related resources play such a critical role. Far from the world of academic economics, someone like Kiyosaki is nonetheless an on-the-ground adviser on economics who provides both the imperatives and technical information that motivate followers and the tools that might make their success possible. Fridman thus usefully suggests that the appeal of these enterprises is less tangibly economic than deeply shaped by the cultural and social dynamics of entrepreneurial self-help offerings.[67]

In the wake of the Great Recession, Kiyosaki, Merrill, and their book-writing and television-appearing peers offer all comers the promise of recovering from the recession's ravages and then achieving financial freedom. They picture a world full of dangers, and they promise that buying their products and following their examples will free people from dependence on the federal government and on major financial and educational institutions. They deploy a wide range of appeals with historical resonance. They offer a contemporary version of a familiar tradition in which pitches offer get-rich-quick schemes. Their appeals are both religious and secular, drawing as they do on references to the Bible or God's plan, as well as the powers of salesmanship, fakery, inspiration, and the promise of earthly rewards. In some cases, they involve smooth-talking salesmen separating gullible people from their money.

One can only speculate how attendees and readers actually respond. Some are surely lookie-loos, eager to find something entertaining on a slow day. Yet the significant percentage of attendees of the two-hour presentations who went to the back of the room to lay down money for the next stage suggests more serious interest in learning how to make money by investing in real estate. Some might have pursued a get-rich-quick scheme or wanted to make a fortune. For others, extra income or a modicum of financial freedom seemed possible. In determining whether or not they took additional steps and, if so, how successful the programs helped make them, surely the precariousness of life in the early twenty-first century is a factor. But also relevant are the suggestions that there are secrets to success that the operations of people like Merrill and Kiyosaki can unlock. Although these operations point to the success some of their followers have achieved, quite appropriately they issue ample disclaimers. On its website, FortuneBuilders emphasizes that prospective investors follow the company's advice at their own risk since "there is no assurance that your earnings will match the figures we present." They offer "no guarantees as to your income or earnings of any kind, at any time" since what the programs depict "are NOT to be interpreted as common, typical, expected, or normal for the average student."[68] Yet surely many who climbed the ladder from free two-hour presentation to heights beyond might well say they were better than average.

Above all, these workshops, TV programs, and books emphasize individual agency, disciplined selfhood, and entrepreneurship instead of the connections between social change and communal responsibility. They promote self-governance even as they pitch reliance on the expertise and assistance of others. In a world shaped by globalization, the diminished power of the federal government, transformative technologies, and difficult-to-understand changes in the financial markets, they offer reassurance and riches achieved through relatively simple solutions to the problems millions of Americans face.

CHAPTER 3
FROM *REALTOR MAGAZINE* TO THE *FINANCIAL TIMES*
HOW PRINT MEDIA COVERED THE GLOBAL FINANCIAL CRISIS

From the blind optimism of *Realtor Magazine* and the ideologically driven analyses of *Forbes*, *National Review*, and the *Nation* to the often-insightful observations found in *Fortune*, the *Economist*, and the *Financial Times*, in the early twenty-first century writers struggled to cover dramatic, fast-changing, and unprecedented events connected with the Great Recession. An examination of these publications—as well as of *Inc.*, the *New York Times*, the *Wall Street Journal*, and *Business Week*—reveals a number of issues, including the changing dynamics in the way print journalists cover the economy, debates about the relationships between African Americans and housing, and the ideological battles over the role of federal policies. Certainly it is easier for a historian looking backward to understand what was going on than it was for most observers writing at the time. Given the complexities of the national and global economies, to say nothing of new financial instruments, accurately understanding the present and predicting the future requires an uncommon combination of luck and skill. It is, of course, unreasonable to expect that anyone would get everything right with admirable consistency. Yet, for a variety of reasons, some observers did better than others.

One barrier was the trap of playing the blame game. As finance journalist Dean Starkman has perceptively noted, this involves the evocation of EITB (everyone is to blame). "Sorry, everyone was not to blame," he observed in 2017. "'We' didn't all do it. 'Main Street' didn't succumb to a new tulip mania, and cheap credit didn't expose anything but the corruption and immorality of a financial industry that systematically put huge numbers of even credit-worthy borrowers into defective products." Sure, there were some borrowers who lied and cheated their way to mortgages and then tried to build a leveraged housing kingdom, but they were relatively few in number. Some observers characterized what happened as a "housing crisis." It is more accurate to call it a crisis in finance capitalism. The enormous proliferation in subprime mortgages and widespread fraud trapped people in commitments they could not handle, especially those on the margins of American society. Writers located themselves along a spectrum from cultural to structural explanations, the former tending to focus, for example, on the lure of the American dream and the latter on the overarching power of historical and institutional forces.[1] To be sure, while it is individuals who make decisions and wield power in history and in institutions, the force exerted often extends beyond individual action.

If some writers got mired in the dead ends of the blame game, ambivalent choices, a mixture of realism and optimism, and partisan political debates, others wrote with remarkable insight. To varying degrees journalists provided readers with information they needed to understand what was going on. At rare moments, they could anticipate the future, especially the serious consequences of the collapse of global markets and the way those working in financial institutions had turned mortgages of American homes into toxic, securitized assets. Old-fashioned pitches and newfangled patterns of institutional investing and financialization that were so profoundly reshaping how homes were bought and sold: this is what those who wrote for newspapers and magazines were trying to explain, especially between early 2007, before the collapse of New Century Financial, and late 2008, after the demise of Lehman Brothers and the American International Group (AIG). And now this historian, with the help of others' evaluations, can judge how well they did.

If journalism was the first, rough draft of history, ideological, institutional, and perspectival commitments often limited how effectively most of those who wrote for a representative group of major newspapers and magazines conveyed to their readers the nature and meaning of what was happening at key moments as the Great Recession developed. Of course, it is unreasonable for someone with the benefit of retrospective wisdom to expect too much. Events were so unusual and rapidly unfolding, and the forces that drove them were understandably difficult to comprehend. Still, print media can and should play a role in helping citizens and investors understand the world around them. Moreover, there were some outliers in an otherwise unimpressive story. Writers for *Fortune* and for two British publications—the *Economist* and, even more so, the *Financial Times*—offered coverage that, at its best, was accurate and insightful.

Beyond the ken of most Americans in the early twenty-first century were difficult-to-understand terms and the financial instruments to which they referred. As the British author John Lancaster noted in 2010, "Finance, like other forms of human behavior, underwent a change in the twentieth century, a shift equivalent to the emergence of modernism in the arts—a break with common sense, a turn toward self-referentiality and abstraction, and notions that couldn't be explained in workaday English."[2] Invented earlier but now increasingly prominent among them were collateralized debt obligations, credit default swaps, collateral rehypothecation, mortgage-backed securities, asset-backed commercial paper, and collateralized mortgage obligations. Throughout this book I discuss these concepts, which are not always easy to understand; after all, they are abstract, arcane, and complex ways of investing, invented in the late twentieth and early twenty-first centuries, that played a central role in the global financial crisis. I have done my best to explain them as I go along, but all that most readers need to know is that they involved bets upon bets upon bets, packaged and repackaged, that were supposed to reduce risks to investors and the capitalist system but did the opposite. What millions of Americans understood at the time was that where home prices were dramatically rising, there was a wave of refinancing where owners and investors used gains for a variety of purposes, including paying down credit card debt, going on vacation, or plain and simple but risky speculating. Those who invented and held the repackaged bets were more distant and less personal than the real estate agent who sold them their new home or the local bank that seemed to finance it. Americans may have known of Bank of America, the Dow Jones Industrial Average, and even the Treasury Department, but little did they initially realize the importance of New Century Financial, Bear Stearns, IndyMac, Countrywide Financial, Freddie Mac, Fannie Mae, Moody's Investor Service, Lehman Brothers, and AIG.

As the crisis unfolded, *Realtor Magazine* was the most blindly optimistic source, from which it would have been difficult to discover what events and institutions had major roles and responsibilities in the crisis that originated with the financing of America's homes and eventually caused a global Great Recession. In June 2006, under the headline "Great Partnerships: Finding the American Dream," Barbara Ballinger, a journalist with an MBA, told stories of how realtors helped prospective homeowners from around the country and in the process provided hints about the magazine's ideology and blinders. She focused on families for whom "the dream of owning a home seems beyond reach" because of poor credit scores, little or no money for a down payment, unreasonable expectations, or inadequate knowledge of funding options. "Fortunately," she insisted, "there are real estate salespeople out there who don't understand the words 'can't do.'"

They helped "turn dreams into reality despite high odds," often by arranging financing for future homeowners. Purchasing homes that ranged in price from $112,000 to $250,000, the five families whose stories Ballinger told now obtained "that white picket fence—and more": a more-than-ample backyard, separate bedrooms for each child, large closets, and the opportunity to pay down a mortgage instead of writing endless checks for rent. Celebrating National Homeownership Month by saluting the real estate agents "and the buyers they've helped, partners who truly understand the meaning of home, sweet home," Ballinger made clear that a central task of the National Association of Realtors (NAR) was helping real estate agents close the deal by securing financing, however risky it might be.[3]

Realtor Magazine, published by NAR, was not up to the task of accurately tracking the larger picture of the implications of new ways of financing residential real estate. The publication—"the official magazine of the National Association of REALTORS and the business tool for real estate professionals"—was sent out once a month to its 1.4 million members, many but hardly all of them involved in residential real estate. The writers and editors understandably seemed more interested in emphasizing the benefits of homeownership to buyers and realtors than in assessing the dangers to the economy more generally. After all, Ballinger did not make fully clear that the locally arranged mortgages taken out with a small down payment (or none at all), an unpredictable adjustable rate, a risky balloon payment, or a high subprime interest rate usually ended up in the opaque portfolio of anonymous investors who owned a tiny fraction of a financial instrument containing thousands if not tens of thousands of mortgages.[4]

Inevitably, institutional commitments shaped *Realtor Magazine*'s coverage of the Great Recession. In carrying out its mission "to empower REALTORS as they preserve, protect and advance the right to real property for all," the NAR and its house organ provided real estate agents with help they could use to sell more homes. They did so by offering practical information on tools for selling and financing, profiling successful realtors, recommending how to educate home buyers, and tracking relevant federal regulation and legislation.

It should hardly be surprising that throughout the period when the troubles in the market for residential real estate in the United States threatened the global economy, chronic optimism suffused the writing of those involved with *Realtor Magazine*. In 2005, David Lereah, then the NAR's chief economist, published *Are You Missing the Real Estate Boom?* With housing prices having apparently zoomed up in a recent year by 54 percent, he admitted that bubbles were possible—even though he also remarked that this could be the beginning, middle, or end of such a dramatic change. Addressing the reader directly, he insisted that "you need to take advantage of this once-every-other-generation opportunity *now*." Compared to what he saw as historically unprecedented evaluations in the stock market, he remained assured that there was "no such irrational exuberance in real estate today," using a term Alan Greenspan had popularized in 1996. Because the "real estate boom has got wings," readers should not "be fooled by any temporary pullback from" recent "record-setting numbers. I predict no major contractions in the housing markets for the foreseeable future," he insisted confidently—but, as it turned out, incorrectly—before going on to say there was no "national real estate bubble."[5] At the beginning of 2007, under the headline "On the Road to Recovery," he was quoted as saying that "if the second half of 2006 proved to be a tough period for residential real estate practitioners, the good news is, the bad news is mostly behind us."[6] Similarly, in an article published on May 1, 2007, a month after the collapse of the subprime mortgage lender New Century Financial, although Lereah acknowledged that "the frenzied lending environment of the past few years has led us to today's subprime mess," he nonetheless remained confident. "From a broader perspective," he asserted, "today's subprime problems are occurring against a backdrop of cyclically low mortgage rates and a growing, healthy economy, with jobs and liquidity plentiful. That suggests today's problems could stay contained."[7]

Retrospectively, *Time* listed Lereah among those to blame for the economic crisis. "He regularly trumpeted the infallibility of housing as an investment in interviews, on TV and in his 2005 book," *Time*'s writer correctly insisted. Lereah claimed that "he grew concerned about the direction of the market in 2006, but consider his January 2007 statement: 'It appears we have established a bottom.'"[8] NAR announced Lereah's departure in the spring of 2007 but he was one of many of NAR's optimistic celebrants at a time when there were already signs of trouble present and ahead. Then, in mid-November 2007, the savvy online financial publication *The Motley Fool* introduced an article under the headline "Housing Worse, despite Yelping NAR." In it, Seth Jayson remarked that "sometimes you have to wonder what's coming out of the water cooler" at the association's headquarters. Relying on foreclosure data provided by RealtyTrac, statistics on write-downs of mortgage-backed securities at major financial institutions, and bad news for holders of adjustable-rate mortgages, Jayson criticized the NAR for issuing "a slew of misleading press releases, all intended to jump-start a withering housing market and earn those Realtors a 6% commission." He provided a link to his earlier article, which tracked what he called the trade association's "hilarious history of ineptitude in predicting future home sales." In that article, published on September 11, 2007, Jayson stated that comparing NAR predictions with hard data about home sales revealed that NAR's economists provided "nauseating," "rosy-lensed," and "ever-optimistic" spin that meant their predictions were "as useful as ice skates in Iraq."[9]

After Lereah's departure, Lawrence Yun moved up from his position as senior economist to become NAR's chief economist. Although his assessments were somewhat more cautious than Lereah's and many of the headlines above his own articles, Yun continued in an optimistic mode even as troubles intensified. Thus, in the November 1, 2007, issue, he acknowledged some weaknesses in residential real estate markets yet believed that the problems with subprime mortgages were "contained [and] the trend lines are already contradicting many of the predictions of woe." The woeful prediction most on the mind of Yun and his associates at NAR came from the economists Karl E. Case and Robert J. Shiller, who formulated the Case-Shiller Home Price Indices, initially developed in the early 1990s, which offered widely accepted measurements of changes in housing prices based on data continuously collected from cities around the nation. "Beneath Market Punditry: Underlying Strength" ran the headline for an interview with Yun. "Dire predictions" of a dramatic collapse of home prices like those of Shiller, remarked Yun's associate, "do more than grab the attention of the media; they can shake consumer confidence and help make such predictions self-fulfilling as home buyers stay on the sidelines, pressuring sellers to lower prices—in effect fueling a downward spiral."[10] Writing in *Realtor Magazine* in June 2008, Blanche Evans reiterated the NAR's concern about the adverse impact of the work of Case and Shiller. "If the unemployment rate is historically low yet your customers are waiting for home prices to drop 30 percent before they buy," she wrote, "you've just been Case-Shillered." Wondering why reporters and financial analysts relied so heavily on their predictions as she hinted at darker forces at work, she speculated that "one reason might be its Wall Street seal of approval: It was launched to provide information for hedge funds."[11]

Elsewhere, *Realtor Magazine* doubled down on optimism by using a psychological explanation that even more dramatically minimized the power of brute economic forces or public policies. A few months before the attack on "market punditry," the popular financial guru Suzie Orman, though doubtful that the residential real estate market would soon recover, nonetheless located the problem not in global financial markets but in people's minds. She insisted that the subprime mortgage problems were psychological: it was "as bad as people perceive it to be. Reality doesn't matter, believe it or not. All that matters is people's perception."[12]

Throughout 2008, *Realtor Magazine* continued in a cheerleading mode, even as it was becoming clear to some that troubles in the market for residential real estate might threaten the collapse of the global economy. In early February 2008, Yun remarked that with interest rates low and "the FHA poised to regain some of the market share it lost to aggressive subprime lenders during the boom, a pick-up of demand is waiting in the wings."[13] In early May 2008, not long after the collapse of the major investment bank Bear Stearns, the magazine's cover announced that it was "Celebrating 100 Years of the American Dream." The July 1, 2008, issue offered a headline that talked of an "Economy: A Year of Repair, Then a Year of Growth." In the accompanying article, Yun remarked that "even though we're not out of the woods yet, by many signs we've put the worst behind us."[14] This issue appeared just as IndyMac, the nation's seventh largest originator of mortgages, was in its death throes. Then, a few weeks after the collapse of Lehman Brothers in September 2008, the magazine's cover featured "Destination Success!" as the location for its conference in Orlando, not far from Walt Disney World, "the Most Magical Place on Earth," and near one of the epicenters of the collapsing market for residential real estate.

Soon after, at the height of the financial crisis that put homeownership in danger for tens of millions of Americans and imperiled the financial well-being for at least hundreds of millions of others around the world, the coverage turned somewhat more cautious and practical. At the end of 2008, the publication hawked "Still Many Happy Returns for Home Rehabs," because remodeling and upgrades provided "stable paybacks, even in a slower market."[15] By April 2009, as the worst of the recession's impact on homeownership started to wane and real estate agents began to see better times, the cover featured "Right Tools Now: 274 Useful Tips and Tactics to Help Your Business Soar." Yet even as writers for *Realtor Magazine* doubled down on its long-standing commitment to offer practical advice, the larger faith remained intact. "Still Believing in Real Estate" ran the headline of editor in chief Stacey Moncrieff's November 1, 2008, affirmation. Speaking for those at NAR, she asked rhetorically if the organization was wrong to promote homeownership during "this trying economic time. . . . Were we wrong to do that [in the wake of] the warning signs of overzealous lending and [instead] use the influence of the magazine to urge greater caution? I don't think so." She had never, she reminded readers, "stopped believing in real estate ownership as both a wealth builder and one of the great pleasures of life."[16]

Moncrieff's article appeared in the midst of a meltdown in residential real estate prices. On the first day of November 2008, the Case-Shiller Index, which had reached a high of 184.6 in July 2006, was at 156.1. It hit a bottom of 133 in February 2012, which represented a decline of almost 28 percent, close to what Evans had earlier seen as highly unlikely, the result of unwarranted scare tactics. The Dow Jones Industrial Average had hit a low of 6595 in early May of 2009.[17]

All of these approaches—the optimism, the minimizing of bad news, the emphasis on the psychological, and the shift to the practical—reflected how NAR and *Realtor Magazine* responded to the turmoil in the market for residential real estate. Central to their mission was the promotion of the well-being of realtors and the health of the American housing market. To do so, they provided members and readers with practical information even as they avoided confronting and reporting on troubles in a sustained and realistic way. However, it is important to acknowledge that the optimism of NAR and *Realtor Magazine* shaped and, even more importantly, reflected the mien of most real estate agents. Earning a living and respect on the ground involves sustaining confidence day by day. The most ethical agents know well that their clients have trusted them with a momentous responsibility. In a profession where personal relationships and local knowledge matter so significantly, information about distant events, even pivotal ones, can be all too distracting. To sustain optimism—to show up at the office or an open house and to thrive in the face of tense bidding wars—is not simply a skillful necessity; for many agents, it is a habitual and essential way of life.[18]

Such an optimistic mindset and the seeming irrelevance of news about faraway political and economic events also help explains *Realtor Magazine*'s approach to policy issues. Readers could glean from its pages how NAR lobbied for legislation that would help curtail abuses and promote homeownership.[19] When writers discussed predatory lending, for example, their assumption was that real estate agents themselves, far from bearing any responsibility for selling homes to people who could not afford them, played a central role in educating buyers so that they would not make mistakes. Aside from avaricious lenders, the Case-Shiller indices, and some federal policies that could easily be corrected, there seemed few larger and more pernicious people, institutions, or forces at work within the real estate industry. With their attention understandably on the local and the personal, securitization, globalization, investment banks, pension funds, rating agencies, and hedge funds all remained largely out of sight. It was as if among those in charge of the real estate publication there was ignorance—at times seemingly willful—about the present and future of homeownership.

Compared with *Realtor Magazine*, business publications whose subscribers were more varied and whose focus was more general provided readers with coverage that by and large was more tempered and informative.[20] To varying degrees during 2007 and 2008, *Inc.*, a widely read monthly magazine that focused on small businesses; *Business Week*, which usually appeared weekly, as its title announced; *Fortune*, which in these years usually appeared twice a month; the biweekly *Forbes*; and the six-times-a-week *Wall Street Journal* all provided insights into the rapidly emerging story of the relationship between the financing of residential real estate and threats to the global economy.

Yet there were often limits to the explanatory power of what they published, some of these limitations inherent in business media's mission and others in the difficulty of accurately predicting movements in the financial markets. For those on a daily, weekly, or monthly schedule, it could be difficult to track major, long-term changes in a timely manner. In addition, central to all these business publications was a commitment to emphasize practical advice by focusing on specific investment opportunities and on individual organizations and their leaders. This meant that there was always something to celebrate or purchase—some specific choices that were attractive, in some cases helpfully so and in others wrongheaded. Above all, though less so than was true of *Realtor Magazine*, intrinsic in the perspective of these four publications was a commitment to optimism that could result in more feel-good stories than articles adequately warning of present and future dangers.[21] In some instances, these publications could explain the power of and dangers involved in the nexus between securitization, subprime mortgages, lax oversight by rating agencies, and problematic federal government policies.[22] Yet, in some of these publications more than others, there were often limits to understanding how serious the dangers were or how global their reach. The coverage in *Business Week* was, well, weakest. Until it was too late, its writers often assumed that troubles were confined to the housing market. More so than other business publications, only late in the game did it devote more than minimal coverage to derivatives. Throughout, it provided too little sense of either the global origins of the emerging crisis or its impact on the lives of ordinary Americans. Though recognizing what was going on at the southern end of the New York–Washington corridor, writers paid attention principally to Wall Street and, in the process, neglected to focus on loan originators, rating agencies, and endangered households. After all, for those in charge of *Business Week*—and, presumably, for its readers—what mattered most was the implications for stock market investors: what happened in corporate boardrooms and executive suites.[23]

Even a publication such as *Fortune*, which offered prescient warnings, could often quickly backpedal or qualify them.[24] Similarly, early on readers of the *Wall Street Journal* would have understood the power of securitization and the weakness of government oversight, but not so readily how powerfully risky this combination was.[25] Thus, in its pages in mid-June 2007, Steve Rattner, who almost two years later would play a key role in the government's rescue of the automobile industry, stood on the sidelines wondering whether the collapse of credit markets that began with subprime loans might "trigger the economic equivalent of a multi-car crash, in which the initial losses incur large enough damages to sufficiently slow spending enough to bring on a recession." In the end, using a metaphor that would turn out to be highly ironic, he concluded that "we have little choice but to sit back and watch this car accident happen," for it would be wrong for the Federal Reserve "to rescue imprudent high-yield lenders," who had to "learn the hard way." If they learned hard lessons, he nonetheless hoped "not too many innocent bystanders will share their pain."[26]

Such mixed signals—often characterized by equivocations, contradictions, articles with conflicting headlines, and hard-to-reconcile perspectives might immobilize investors but are understandable given the complexities and uncertainties of financial markets and, more generally, the economy. We can see evidence of this in the frequent tension between dire news and optimistic expressions. For example, writing in the February 2008 issue of *Inc.*, Amy Feldman acknowledged the dark clouds on the economic horizon that meant that many economists and corporate executives were "less than thrilled with the economic outlook and exude levels of pessimism not seen in years." Yet she insisted that entrepreneurs, "many of them as optimistic as ever," saw "the world through a different lens." She then reported on five executives at highly successful companies who "shared a sense of confidence that, if it's played right, an economic downturn can work in their favor."[27] Along similar lines, a writer for the *Wall Street Journal* answered in the affirmative the question posed in an August 27, 2007, headline that read "Can the Financial Markets Make a Comeback?" Ethan Penner, who had pioneered new methods of financing real estate, remained convinced that "securitization will survive and continue to grow significantly" despite "the current turmoil." Investment firms and the market more generally "will emerge stronger as a result of this period of dislocation," which was true in the long term but not sooner.[28] Likewise, in early May 2007, writing in *Forbes*, Kenneth L. Fisher, who ran a highly successful advisory firm and for one-third of a century wrote a column for the publication, listed the "small, petty, garden-variety suicidal excuses to miss the reality that this is a uniquely spectacular time," despite commonly heard shouts like "Subprime! Iran! High oil! Ben Bernanke's inflation babble! Profligate consumers! Soft landing! The yen carry!"[29] Even more strikingly, a mid-August 2007 issue of *Forbes* offered up competing and irreconcilable assessments by two different observers, with one writer calling what turned out to be early problems at Bear Stearns as a "scary portent" that would be a "watershed event," while the other insisted the global economy "continues to exhibit amazing resilience to events that in the past would have hurt it severely."[30]

There were other aspects of a pattern of seemingly irreconcilable perspectives. Even in the darkest times, there were successful careers to be emulated. Similarly, terrifying news sat in an uneasy relationship with tempting investment opportunities. Tellingly, the mid-September 2007 issue of *Fortune* contained half a dozen articles on, as its cover story announced, "The Business of Luxury" that should have sat uneasily with a series of less prominently placed articles that told "Tales of the Crash of 2007." Among them was one in which the author remarked that "even if the credit crunch passes without a major catastrophe, the prices of stocks, bonds and real estate have a long way to fall."[31] In mid-June 2007, subscribers to *Forbes* could read Carrie Coolidge's recommendation of the purchase of IndyMac, which specialized in offering highly risky home loans, at thirty-five dollars a share as "a bargain cast up by the subprime story" while "Mortgage Madness" was so prevalent. The share price soon began to cascade downward and hit zero in mid-2008.[32] In late August 2007, an article in the *Wall Street Journal* ran a headline that celebrated an investment adviser who two years earlier had warned of a "Credit Crunch" that caused him to sound the "Subprime Alarm." Yet he now insisted that with every bubble there were buying opportunities.[33] Of course, even in the worst of times, there are always investment opportunities to be taken advantage of. Even at the stock market's worst moments during the COVID-19 pandemic, people benefited from shorting most stocks or holding positions in Netflix or Amazon. So, too, in the midst of an earlier crisis, shortly after the collapse of Bear Stearns during the spring of 2007, readers of one issue of *Fortune* could learn that with the economy "On the Brink of Disaster," collecting vintage watches provided a "Safe Haven."[34]

If business publications often presented a tension between danger and opportunity, they could also find some person, institution, or policy to blame for economic troubles. In the fall of 2007, Peter Eavis at *Fortune* wittily explored this "blame game." He started with borrowers for whom getting rich in real estate had become "a national pastime." If in these years business publications paid relatively little attention to TV shows that clever observers called "real estate porn," he could not avoid highlighting trouble. He spoke of "Flip This House, Flip That House" as "stoking everyone's inner Donald Trump." Escalating home prices brought seemingly everyone into the game, including amateurs who, with all too little sense of risk, recklessly borrowed easy money to purchase several condos in hot markets such as Las Vegas. However, the buck did not stop there, which Eavis made clear as he moved up "the credit chain" that included mortgage brokers, moneylenders, appraisers, rating agencies, investment banks, hedge funds, and the Federal Reserve.[35]

If Eavis stood on the sidelines and understood all this as a game, others—especially those who wrote for the *Wall Street Journal*, *Forbes* (and, as we shall soon see, for the *Nation* and the *National Review*)—played the blame game less self-consciously. Of course, it should hardly come as a surprise that business publications featured writers with strong political positions or that, most frequently, they wrote conservative, pro-business stories in which meddling politicians and wrong-headed decisions of the Federal Reserve played prominent roles in preventing markets from operating successfully. Yet if *Inc.* paid relatively little attention to public policy, and *Fortune* and the *Wall Street Journal* did so in ways that could be restrained and even fair and balanced, in playing the blame game *Forbes* was persistently and forcefully ideological. And it was Steve Forbes, who followed his grandfather and father in running the magazine, who shaped the magazine's politics. While, generally speaking, those on the left blamed the excesses of the economic system for the crisis, conservatives like Forbes blamed the failures on the political system.

Nowhere was his position clearer than in his October 2008 essay "How Capitalism Will Save Us," published when the federal government had already stepped in forcefully to rescue the economy, soon after the collapse of Lehman Brothers and AIG and immediately following the moment when the Dow Jones Industrial Average suffered what was then its most significant loss in a week. Forbes claimed that the market crash and financial turmoil, which only later came to be known as key elements in the Great Recession, stemmed not from the excesses of capitalism or "the failure of free markets" but from dangerous government actions. He acknowledged the role of "greed and recklessness," including that of "mortgage bankers and of Wall Street packagers of subprime mortgages, as well as the excesses and misuses of exotic instruments," but insisted "all this came about because of government errors—regulatory and monetary." The Federal Reserve's lowering of interest rates fostered speculative bubbles, including in residential real estate. At the same time, he said, ill-conceived and meddlesome government regulations stifled innovation while high taxes undermined innovation, initiative, and the productive use of capital. Also contributing to the housing bubble, he said, were Fannie Mae and Freddie Mac. Freddie Mac originated in 1970 while the New Deal launched Fannie Mae 1938 as a public-private, hybrid institution charged with turning mortgages that banks originated into packaged securities for sale. In 1968 Congress transformed Fannie Mae into a private albeit federally charted corporation that bought conventional mortgages and repackaged them and then sold them as mortgage-backed securities. Together these two companies were GSEs (government-sponsored enterprises) that were partly federal government enterprises and partly private corporations that played a major role in the housing market and indeed in the American economy. According to Forbes, "Reeling politically from egregious accounting scandals, [they] decided they could justify their existence by becoming champions of 'affordable housing.'"[36]

For Forbes, going forward the solution was not, as liberals advocated, legislation guaranteeing costly health care, restrictions on corporate pay, ill-advised regulation of the financial sector, or criminalization of business failures. Rather, central to Forbes's recommendations were a strong dollar backed by gold, lower taxes, and the support of private enterprise. Yet, ironically, having claimed that only capitalism "Could Save Us," Forbes nonetheless offered a detailed discussion of how action by the federal government had in fact prevented a worldwide depression—and could have done so even more fully. "Belatedly, but thankfully," he commented, "governments recognized that the only way to get credit flowing again was for them to make quick and direct massive infusions of new equity into beleaguered banks, as well as commit to other emergency measures hitherto unimaginable." And he hoped that "sensible rescue efforts" would continue. Moreover, he believed that Washington should have prevented Lehman Brothers from failing. He berated rating agencies—to me a perfect example of private corporations supposedly acting in the public interest— for drinking the Kool-Aid and giving triple-A ratings that supported "Wall Street's appetite" for "fee-generating packages of subprime mortgages" that had become "gluttonous" and that, "thanks to securitization, [were] spread all around the world. The Fed and other bank regulators stood by as the bubble ballooned." Thus, though the policies that Forbes advocated for the future were quite conservative, and although he blamed government action for causing the crisis in the first place, he not only attacked the greed and gluttony of institutions of private enterprise but also advocated vigorous government intervention.[37] Like many Republican officials and conservative ideologues, in a crisis he sanctioned socializing public risk when to save capitalism they deemed it necessary to bail out financial institutions.

The dominance of the blame game, which focused on responsibility for the mistakes of the past and present and reflected one strategy that underwrote neoliberalism, could all too easily prevent writers in the business press from understanding the implications of the collapse of the American residential real estate market and the global economy for the future of politics. This was especially true of those who signaled one factor or only a few factors instead of understanding either a wide range or, more accurately, larger historical and structural forces. Among American business publications, there was, however, at least one exception that proved the rule: articles in *Fortune* by Bethany McLean. She came well prepared to the task of covering the financial crisis that began in 2006: starting out as an analyst at Goldman Sachs, in March 2001 she authored an article in *Fortune* that asked "Is Enron Overpriced?" and then followed that with a book, coauthored with Peter Elkind, *The Smartest Guys in the Room: The Amazing Rise and Scandalous Fall of Enron*.[38]

A little over three years after the book's publication in mid-October 2003, McLean began to warn that the dangerous relationships between subprime mortgages, securitization, and neglectful government and rating agencies could lead to a crisis in homeownership and financial markets. "While Marx may well be right that history repeats itself," she noted in November 2007 as she pondered the relevance of Enron's fall to contemporary events, "it rarely does so exactly."[39] Then, in a remarkable article published in the October 13, 2008, issue soon after the government agreed to bail out the giant insurance company AIG, Nina Easton, another *Fortune* journalist, presciently gazed into the future. The headline stated: "Main Street Turns against Wall Street: A Populist Backlash Is Changing the Country's Political Climate." Even though not all of her predictions were on the mark, Easton nonetheless understood that the bailouts of major corporations had set off "a populist backlash" that in the future would stoke anti-elitist views of government power in ways that would affect regulatory, trade, and tax policies.[40]

In many ways, the conservative, general-interest *National Review* played the blame game like *Forbes*, its equally conservative but more business-focused counterpart. They shared the central proposition that the cause of economic turmoil was not the failure of free market capitalism or long-standing structural problems that adversely affected many American households, but of irresponsible borrowers or wrong-headed interventions by the federal government driven by politicians who focused not on national well-being but on their own reelections.[41] Yet, compared with what appeared in *Forbes*, the articles in the *National Review* offered often more extensive and biting arguments. Writers attacked Democrats but hardly spared Republicans who were not sufficiently conservative. Several policies and institutions played prominent roles in the publication's analysis. The Federal Reserve Board's lowering of interest rates to what the writers considered dangerous levels had helped create asset bubbles, including in the market for homes. The 1977 Community Reinvestment Act, along with "thuggery from ACORN," the community-based organization that fought for social justice for low and moderate-income families, put tremendous pressure on lenders to underwrite problematic mortgages.[42] Fannie Mae and Freddie Mac, as prominent political commentator Charles Krauthammer wrote, "pressured" financial institutions "to extend mortgages to people who were borrowing over their heads."[43]

Even when the focus turned to securitization, which rarely occurred in the pages of the *National Review*, the blame fell not on avaricious capitalists but, in the words of a writer in late October 2008, "squarely on the doorstep of the federal government and the political activists working with it."[44] All these policies came together to cause trouble in the housing market, resulting in what the economist Thomas Sowell called a "cycle of dependency" in which the federal government had helped make seemingly affordable houses available to homeowners who could ill afford them.[45] In February 2008 the classicist and military historian Victor David Hanson attacked the privileged populists, "gloom-and-doom" Democratic candidates Hillary Clinton and Barack Obama, for offering a wrongheaded assignment of blame. They and their allies had played central roles in the "liberal efforts to increase homeownership rates." Yet their "pessimistic indictment" singled out the wrong villains. Liberals incorrectly insisted that "the home mortgage meltdown has not occurred because too many speculative buyers were hoping to flip houses for quick profits" or because of "the misguided attempts of government and lending institutions" to provide mortgages aspiring homeowners were unlikely to be able to pay for.[46]

If these assertions echoed what conservative writers offered elsewhere, some of what appeared in the *National Review* was often distinctive—and in ways that meant that, unlike subscribers to business magazines, from its pages its readers would have difficulty gleaning accurate information about the course, dimensions, and seriousness of the evolving crisis. To begin with, later and with unwarranted expressions of certainty, writers for the *National Review* denied or minimized the significance of what was happening. As he would do during the COVID-19 pandemic, Fox News anchor Neil Cavuto insisted that the media were responsible, in the earlier case for fostering a sense of exaggerated danger about subprime mortgages. In mid-October 2007, between the collapse of Bear Stearns and IndyMac, a reporter for the *National Review* remarked that Cavuto believed that mainstream media had cast a skeptical eye on Fox News because it was willing to "break from the media consensus" by asserting that "most of the media's hysterical coverage isn't justified by the facts."[47] Soon after, Larry Kudlow, who would become President Donald Trump's chief economic adviser, accused the Democrats and the "mainstream media" of not recognizing the strength of the national economy under the leadership of President George W. Bush.[48] In late January 2008, under a headline that put the word "recession" in skeptical quotation marks, the prominent investment adviser Donald L. Luskin cautioned against panicking because market turmoil offered "unique opportunities for those who can keep their heads while those around them are losing theirs. The so-called crisis in subprime mortgages," he continued, was "actually a very small economic problem in the scheme of things—equivalent in its dollar impact to the cost of reconstructing after Hurricane Katrina." Though it was "a tragedy for those directly involved," it nonetheless represented "really nothing in the context of our massive economy"—simply a "scare on Wall Street about exotic debt instruments" and hardly anything that "ought to throw the U.S. into a recession."[49] Even as late November 4, 2008, well after the collapse of Lehman Brothers and AIG, Thomas Sowell remarked that "the truest thing" John McCain had said during the presidential campaign was "The economy is sound." He continued by remarking that, just as it had done in the 1960s, "the political left has always known how to exploit temporary economic problems to create lasting institutions reflecting their ideology."[50]

Finally, when reading through the *National Review* for 2007 and 2008, it is impossible to ignore the emphasis on race, a topic not frequently explored in the publications under consideration so far. During the crisis in residential real estate, those on the left, most notably the Center for Responsible Lending, had emphasized how predatory lenders preyed on African Americans who aspired to become homeowners in part because of a long history of redlining that had put them in disadvantageous positions.[51] No one among conservatives more fully addressed this issue than Thomas Sowell, an African American economist and fellow at the Hoover Institution. We have already encountered him as a conservative who used strong language to support his arguments: in his deployment of "thuggery from ACORN" and "cycle of dependency." In an April 17, 2009, contribution, he laid some blame for the crisis in residential real estate on the shoulders of "politicians, the media, and community activists like Jesse Jackson" who earlier on had claimed that "non-whites" suffered in the housing market because of mortgage lenders. This had put pressure on banks to lend to "more low-income and minority" buyers, which in turn "led to lower mortgage lending standards, more risky mortgages, higher default rates, and the collapse of financial institutions that brought these" riskier mortgages and the securities into which they were bundled.[52]

Historically, African American newspapers and magazines had presented statements that countered the way mainstream and conservative media outlets often blamed the victims and minimized the impact of discriminatory residential real estate policies and practices. In the wake of the Great Recession, the communications scholar Catherine R. Squires set out to explore how a range of African American publications responded to the impact of the financial crisis on housing for African Americans.[53] Claiming that "none of the dominant media outlets—whether broadcast, cable, print or online—raised sufficient red flags about the burgeoning bubble," she wondered whether the historical role that African American media had played would in this instance "provide more alternatives to the neoliberal depictions of the crisis found in most mainstream news and financial media." She wrote, "What we could reasonably expect, given the black press's legacy of critiques of capitalist excesses and racial discrimination in the marketplace is that some significant proportion of black-oriented media would be on the front lines offering alternative, progressive responses to the crisis and its related racial disparities once the bubble burst." Well, it turned out that the situation was more complicated and disappointing, reflecting as it did a spectrum of responses that in many ways mirrored those found elsewhere.[54] In addition, technological and economic forces had changed the African American media landscape in ways similar to what happened more generally, closing down as it did some traditional and local outlets while creating others, including online resources and those that appealed to multicultural audiences.

Squires examined the coverage in three publications oriented to experiences of African Americans. *Black Enterprise* appealed to well-to-do African Americans and to those who aspired to achieve wealth through entrepreneurial success. Owned by the *Washington Post*, the *Root* was available online only. Supported by a nonprofit organization committed to economic and social justice, *Colorlines* saw its target audience as members of communities of color. If mainstream media often "framed the subprime crisis as the result of bad decisions by ignorant borrowers," including African American ones, "shady lenders," and misbegotten policies such as those supported by the Community Reinvestment Act, Squires asked, would the situation here be any different?[55] Not surprisingly, in response to the financial crisis, *Black Enterprise* paid little attention to failed public policies and avaricious financial institutions. To be sure, on occasion it acknowledged racial disparities in the financing of housing and criticized those who blamed African Americans for what had befallen them. Yet, overall, there was some blaming of the victims for their reckless behavior and little attention paid, as Squires put it, to "structural factors that contributed to the crisis hitting African American communities." Without mentioning Sowell's work, Squires criticized how *Black Enterprise* "replicated and reinforced the worst of the neoconservative blame games that circulated in the mainstream press."[56]

The *Root* stood at a midpoint in the spectrum of responses. On the one hand, echoing what one might read in *Black Enterprise*, it offered up advice on ways Black folks might learn from mainstream media and self-help offerings how to behave more prudently. More so than its entrepreneurial counterpart, it acknowledged how racial stereotypes and prejudicial financial practices placed African Americans in seriously disadvantaged positions in the housing markets. Nonetheless, Squires insisted that it "did not question the premise that homeownership is (usually) a win-win for individuals and society," embraced the vision of a wonderful ownership society, and advocated standard policies rather than progressive ones. In contrast, Squires showed that *Colorlines* provided the most convincing analysis of the implications of the Great Recession for African Americans; its writers made clear their objection to blaming African Americans and Latinx for what had befallen them and understood the long tradition of failed policies and practices. More importantly, writers for *Colorlines* placed their analysis in more transformative and progressive contexts than did the two other publications. Its "writers articulated the need for a paradigm shift in housing policy, not just reforms of the mortgage system" and "asked the question, why should everyone strive to be homeowners, asked its readers to remember the days when the phrase 'affordable housing' was in wider circulation," as well as recognized that decent rentals were an appropriate goal for achieving decent housing. They wondered out loud whether homeownership was an appropriate cornerstone of the American dream and whether indeed that dream was achievable in a society so riven by inequalities in wealth and income that made daily living for so many so precarious. Finally, unlike contributors to *Black Enterprise* and the *Root*, those who wrote for *Colorlines*, Squires contended, correctly acknowledged the importance of "attaching its critiques and recommendations for policy reform to activism and organization on the ground."[57]

Largely echoing some of what appeared in *Colorlines*, the *Nation* offered a leftist counterpart to the Right's *National Review*. Readers of the *Nation* could learn about the powerful dangers of securitization—earlier and more clearly than they could from the *National Review* or, indeed, from many publications. In explaining the causes of the housing crisis, the *Nation*'s writers blamed avaricious capitalists instead of craven politicians and celebrated rather than denigrated activists who fought against the exploitation of minority and low-income home buyers. They did all this in a way that, they assumed, highlighted rather than obscured key factors driving the global economy toward collapse.

Writing for the *Nation*, the investigative journalist Danny Schechter criticized those who cheered rather than warned. When "a financial tsunami, tied to the implosion of the subprime mortgage market" struck in the summer of 2007, he wrote almost a year later, "most media were asleep at the switch." Even though many newspapers, magazines, and TV programs focused on business, he insisted, they tended to write for the Wall Street supporters, "the very mortgage companies and financial institutions that were raking in millions from the bubble," rather than for the much greater number of citizens and consumers. "Tethered to a mission to pump up confidence, no doubt to support their advertisers," he continued, citing Jim Cramer of CNBC and the cozy relationships between realtors and publishers as examples. They ignored "realists and critics and play up the prognostications of insiders, usually perennial optimists who have been consistently wrong in their predictions."[58]

If writers for the *National Review* played the blame game, so, too, did their counterparts at the *Nation*—but they did so more self-consciously and, of course, with their own villains. In late December 2008, an unidentified writer said "Let's Play the Blame Game!" and then went on to criticize prominent right-wingers like Sean Hannity and Rush Limbaugh who blamed ACORN, Fannie Mae, Freddie Mac, the federal government, and the Community Reinvestment Act for the economic calamity, which had begun, they insisted, with subprime mortgages that made housing affordable to constituents who would keep the Democrats in office.[59]

In contrast, writers for the *Nation* placed responsibility not on government action but on the evils of capitalism and capitalists, especially those who wrote and underwrote predatory loans. Nowhere was this more apparent than in an early and stunningly prescient mid-July 2002 article by Bobbi Murray titled "Wall Street's Soiled Hands." Murray wrote at a time when nonspecialist readers might have struggled to figure out what was meant by "securitization," a word she used but whose consequences and global reach she and most others could not yet fully understand. She carefully explained how financial institutions, including Lehman Brothers, aggregated loans, including predatory subprime ones, and then bundled them into mortgage-backed securities that were in turn divided into tranches ranked according to the level of risk they supposedly represented. The hocus pocus involved meant that it was impossible for investors in a mutual fund or most experts to fathom the nature of ownership and responsibility, as a result threatening to undermine one of the bulwarks of claims that empowered ownership was central to capitalism. "The capital unscrupulously pumped from poor neighborhoods," she insisted, "by way of predatory loans whizzes along a high-speed pipeline to Wall Street to be used for investment." This might protect investors from risk, she concluded, although she avoided wondering about how far risk might spread.[60]

In the pages of the *Nation*, Murray was hardly alone in excoriating predatory lenders and the financial institutions that profited along with them. Throughout 2007 and 2008, writers criticized lenders who, they asserted, preyed "on the poor, the uninformed and minorities" while legislators in both parties stood idly by because lobbyists poured money into their campaign chests.[61] Working people struggled to survive while executives at major financial institutions lavishly lined their own pockets.[62] In the spring of 2008, the radical commentator Alexander Cockburn wrote that Barack Obama, Hillary Clinton, and John McCain had "scarcely made a centerpiece of their campaigns the outrageous and racist thievery practiced by Wall Street in the subprime scandals."[63]

Writers for the *Nation* criticized Democratic and Republican politicians for the spread of subprime mortgages and the adverse impact they had on those aspiring to become homeowners, African Americans especially. Redolent of the ways the Left offered a reverse image of the Right's vision, those who wrote for the *Nation* celebrated activists, especially Jesse Jackson, who fought to provide fair and widely available housing.[64] Readers could learn of how, as head of Operation Push, he led the uphill battle. In early 2008, an article quoted Jackson saying that, with the crisis in subprime lending "sinking America's economic ship like the Titanic," African American homeownership, especially as a factor in wealth building, was "the single largest economic issue of our time" and "a crime committed on Wall Street, made possible by complicity of the US government."[65]

As multiple crises intensified, so too did the *Nation*'s commitment to address the impact of financial turmoil on homeownership by African Americans. Thus, under the title "Subprime Swindle: How the Mortgage Industry Stole Black America's Hard-Won Wealth," an extensive mid-July 2008 cover story told the story of African American families in Atlanta who now encountered trouble as foreclosures and subprime lending made it harder and harder for them "to claw up the socioeconomic ladder and plunge into America's consumer culture."[66] As Jesse Jackson had remarked several months earlier, while predatory lenders and government agencies were looking the other way, the nation urgently needed bold plans to "save America's homeowners and stabilize our economy."[67]

If to a considerable extent the *Nation* conveyed the consequences of securitization and more specifically focused on the impact of predatory lending on African Americans, even more striking in its pages and elsewhere is the role that women played in offering prescient warnings and analyses. We have already learned of the work of Bobbi Murray at the *Nation*, and both Nina Easton and Bethany McLean at *Fortune*. We now turn to the coverage by Gretchen Morgenson at the *New York Times*, Meredith Whitney at the investment firm Oppenheimer, and Gillian Tett at the *Financial Times*.

In emphasizing gender analysis, I am neither advocating biological determinism nor relying on a single-factor analysis. After all, there were many prominent women who fed or celebrated the securitization beast. In addition, having highlighted the prescience of some women, it is also important to note that some men, including Mike Hudson, Richard Lord, and Mark Pittman, could also convey a pretty impressive understanding of what was going on.[68] In addition, the educations of four women underscore the importance of the liberal arts: not only Tett's training as an anthropologist but Morgenson's undergraduate education in English and history at St. Olaf's College; McLean's in English and math at Williams College; and Whitney's in history at Brown University. Gender is one dimension of the influence of being an outsider, something that the journalism historian Dean Starkman has noted in his discussion of Hudson, Tett, and Lord. To that list we can add Pittman, who began his career as a reporter covering police activity for the *Coffeyville Journal* in Kansas and did not join the staff of *Bloomberg News* until he was forty years old. Finally, having an adversarial and skeptical temperament also matters, as do ideological commitments.

Writing for the *New York Times*, Morgenson stood out as a writer whose coverage of the looming financial crisis was often impressive, even as some others in the paper focused on the blame game and concluded on an upbeat note despite the presentation of frightening evidence.[69] Morgenson approached the emerging crisis with abundant preparation: a job as a stockbroker for two and a half years in the early 1980s; a marriage in 1991 to Paul Devlin, who was then a managing director at Bear Stearns; coverage of the worlds of finance at *Money*, *Worth*, and *Forbes*. Then in 1998 she joined the staff of the *New York Times*, where, in 2002, she won a Pulitzer Prize in Beat Reporting for what the jury called her "trenchant and incisive" coverage of Wall Street.[70] As early as April 2007, a headline for her article on home loans announced "A Nightmare Grows Darker." In the article she mentioned "snazzy and newfangled mortgage loans" that had helped drive the rate of American homeownership to a historic high of almost 70 percent. She went on to emphasize that such loans, offered as they were to "borrowers with tarnished credit or spotty employment histories," rather than fulfilling the promise of creating an ownership society, as George W. Bush had advocated as early as 2003, were "turning the American dream of homeownership into a nightmare for many borrowers."[71]

If that article focused mainly on the risks to lenders and borrowers, shortly before, Morgenson had warned of broader consequences. On March 7, 2007, reporting about an increasing rate of delinquencies at Countrywide Financial well over a year before that firm failed, she remarked that because Wall Street packaged home loans in less-than-transparent ways, what "investors don't know about why the home mortgage securities market is in distress could fill volumes." Consequently, "only after fiery markets burn out do we see the risks that buyers ignore and sellers play down." Neither borrowers nor lenders, or even Wall Street companies that bundled mortgages, liked "to face ugly realities like financially ailing borrowers who are so strapped that nothing can save them." However, shrewd investors knew "that a reliance on fantasy will only prolong the pain that is racking the huge and important mortgage market."[72] Then, a few days later, writing of an optimistic prediction by an analyst about New Century Financial and Bear Sterns, Morgenson warned that Wall Street firms, credit rating agencies, regulators, and those at hedge and pension funds who invested in "pools of home loans" might not adequately understand that financial markets could significantly cause trouble for the American economy. New Century Financial collapsed in a few weeks; Bear Stearns, in almost exactly a year.[73]

Among the analysts for financial firms, Meredith Whitney stood out for her Wall Street street smarts. She worked for the financial firm Oppenheimer from 1993 to 2009 (with a break at Wachovia from 1998 to 2004).

As early as October 2007, she informed investors about the dangerous consequences that stemmed from the current real estate bubble. She saw it as resulting from highly problematic bank loans to which rating agencies had turned a blind eye. At that time, she correctly predicted what few believed: that Citi Group would have to cut its dividend. Later on, she added Bank of America and Lehman Brothers to her list of financial institutions that would have to write down the value of loans on their books. Then, in early August 2008, weeks before the Treasury took over Freddie Mac and Fannie Mae and Lehman Brothers and AIG collapsed, she was cited in a cover story for *Fortune*. A writer remarked that if "her peers keep searching for some sort of light at the end of the tunnel," Whitney "thinks the tunnel is about to collapse." With financial institutions greatly underreporting what they were losing, she predicted the onset of a "recession that will devastate the 10% of the population that became overextended during the housing boom." Whitney felt like she was "at the epicenter of the biggest financial crisis in history."[74]

Then there is the compelling story of Gillian Tett, who brought to her work at the *Financial Times* (as a freelancer initially and then on staff starting in 1993) an unusual set of skills.[75] She went to Tajikistan in the early 1990s to work on her dissertation in anthropology at Cambridge University, focusing on how Tajiks maintained their historical and cultural identities despite the control and surveillance of the Soviets. Not long after she returned to Cambridge in the summer of 1991, when a failed coup in August marked what turned out to be the beginning of the disintegration of the USSR, the *Financial Times* hired her to cover events there, reporting that familiarized her with economic, social, and political problems that plagued a former Soviet republic and the former USSR more generally.[76] When much later she struggled to understand complex financial transactions, she later reported that she said to herself, "You know what, this is just like being in Tajikistan. All I have to do is learn a new language. This is a bunch of people who have dressed up this activity with a whole bunch of rituals and cultural patterns, and if I can learn Tajik, I can jolly well learn how" foreign exchange markets work.[77]

As a journalist in Tokyo beginning in April 1997, Tett garnered firsthand experience of the consequences of Japan's Lost Decade, a period of economic stagnation that had begun in the early 1990s. In Japan, she was learning how to use anthropological methods to understand the financial world. Before long she turned what she found into a book—*Saving the Sun: A Wall Street Gamble to Rescue Japan from Its Trillion-Dollar Meltdown* (2003). She explored the collapse of the Long-Term Credit Bank of Japan, in which both the bank's placing money in risky real estate loans and the clash of cultures played such commanding roles.[78] Cumulatively these experiences taught her how to understand critically transformative historical events. Later on she remarked of events in 2007–8 that "the behaviour and the psychological mood of the markets" were "almost identical to what happened in the autumn of 1997 in Japan."[79]

Before she moved to New York in 2010, in the summer of 2003 Tett returned to London, where she continued to write for the *Financial Times*. In March 2005 the editors moved her from writing the "Lex" column to a seemingly low-prestige position covering obscure and infrequently examined capital markets for collateral debt obligations (CDOs) and other newfangled financial instruments. While still working on the "Lex" columns and thinking what separated the well-known from the "other," she later recalled, she wrote what came to be called "the Iceberg Memos," in which she distinguished the visible aspects of the capital markets, such as mergers and acquisitions to which business reporters paid so much attention, from the infrequently discussed securitized bundles down below. She understood that most journalists who studied high-flown finance relied on the fluff that the public relations staff of investment banks offered. So when she saw an invitation in her mailbox to an early 2005 conference of investment bankers in Nice, she realized that by going there she might be able to fathom the iceberg's unseen and little-understood underside. Once there, she had an odd sense that all this was familiar. Tett knew she could deploy what she learned as an anthropologist exploring people in their native habitats. Though, while in Tajikistan, she had to get past the KGB to understand local wedding rituals, now she could bypass PR personnel in order to explore the habits of financiers.

What she gradually figured out was that investment bankers saw the world as a place where a highly abstracted sense of money, disconnected from the lives of ordinary people, derived its power from a worldview with an origin myth and ideology. Listening to papers and then to chitchat during and after dinner, she learned that investment bankers believed they were benevolent revolutionaries. Starting in the 1980s, they claimed, they had developed instruments of securitization that by spreading risk made the economic system safer and more efficient. Yet she also realized that this invented story and the phenomena it represented were central components of the iceberg below the surface that few business journalists reported on, let alone understood. Initially, she and members of her staff wrote up their findings in what were essentially travel guides to the world of CDOs, but by

2006 she was increasingly concerned that what she was witnessing might eventually cause a financial crisis.

In thinking about how to turn what she saw into articles, Tett realized that there were none of the key elements that usually made for a good story—no facts, narratives, or people; in other words, a world that was too opaque and slow moving—and that reporting on it might seem like information that only insiders would appreciate. Moreover, without the help of what anthropology had to offer, she understood that the existence of separate silos (within and between investment banks, as well as within and between regulatory agencies) also made it difficult to grasp what was going on. Just as the Tajiks had their tribal loyalties, Tett remarked, so did those in the world she had begun to pierce. Perhaps a few at the top of the banking hierarchy could understand the situation holistically, but the vast numbers of those with Bloomberg terminals on their desks were detached from the broader implications and results of their work. Subprime borrowers in Phoenix or Orlando were offscreen. Boring stories about geeks were not the stuff of front-page news in the *Financial Times*. Its readers and those who inhabited the icebergs above and below the surface may have thought they lived in a frictionless and interconnected world, but that was only because of the power of "cognitive and structured fragmentation." Tett thought she might change all this, she remarked in 2008, by decoding the "cognitive map" of the world of finance and understanding it "holistically." She may have felt that, as an anthropologist, she was an "imposter," but her education had given her an "anthropological filter" that enabled her to understand the power of rituals, social structures, and ideologies.[80] She knew it was important to "put finance in a cultural context" by understanding that "money and the profit motive" were cultural rather than natural, and "to not just look at the areas of what we call 'social noise'—i.e. what everyone likes to talk about," but "at the social silences as well," a concept that the French sociologist Pierre Bourdieu had highlighted.[81]

In late March 2006, Tett first wrote of her discovery in Nice of what she called "the Morgan Mafia," whose existence she became aware of through her earlier reporting on CDOs. Like the bankers at Salomon Brothers that Michael Lewis had focused on in *Liar's Poker: Rising Through the Wreckage of Wall Street* (1989), those at J. P. Morgan had played crucial roles in developing weapons of mass securitization. At the conference in Nice, Tett had been baffled when she listened as "men (and the occasional woman) earnestly muttered about 'delta hedging,' 'correlation risk' or 'CDO squared.'" Except for the fact that billions of dollars were involved, she reported, "they might have been discussing nuclear physics or ancient Chinese." Gradually she learned that, ten years earlier at a meeting in Boca Raton, Florida, a group of bankers from J. P. Morgan had developed complicated financial instruments that were, essentially, bets on bets on bets that would, more importantly and ominously, change the financial world—and, though she could not guess it then, the global economy.

Toward the end of the long article, Tett wondered out loud about the long-term consequences of innovations in financial instruments. She noted that, with risk harder to assess, it was increasingly difficult for central bankers "to predict what might happen if a cataclysm did hit.... Could the world's trading system cope?" With "the next round of innovation" involving "derivatives of credit derivatives, or even 'derivatives cubed,'" she knew "one thing is certain: inside every moment of stunning success of Wall Street and in the City are the seeds of future decline."[82]

Tett's ethnographic work on the world of bankers had enabled her to understand, earlier and more clearly than most financial writers, the importance of securitization to the global economy and the risks inherent in bundled and opaque financial instruments. At a time when journalistic kudos went to those (mostly high-octane men) who wrote about the elevated status of financial news about mergers and acquisitions, she had turned her attention to credit default swaps and collateralized debt obligations because she believed that, as she said in an October 2008 interview, that was where "there was a revolution happening that had been almost entirely ignored."[83]

As she began writing about the risks from collateralized debt obligations and credit default swaps, she remarked in mid-April 2005, "Though financial markets are often stable, when turbulence strikes, it can hit with unexpected vengeance" as "correlation risk" accentuated "the danger that if one asset turns bad it could affect other assets in a snowball effect." Given how swiftly innovation occurred, government officials and rating agencies found it difficult to keep abreast of changes. Moreover, investors were lulled into a false and problematic sense of security. Defaults, she emphasized, do not always happen randomly, and "if one asset goes wrong, it can start a chain reaction" that would ricochet "through the financial system in unexpected ways."[84] From then on, she wrote articles in which she increasingly warned about a financial world in which many major players seemed oblivious to the heightened risks that instruments such as CDOs created. In early 2007 she remarked that if there was any lesson to be learned from the emails she was receiving from insiders, most of whom insisted on anonymity, it was "how much unease—and leverage—is bubbling, largely unseen, in today's

Brave New financial world."[85] As 2007 proceeded, her reporting took on an increasingly urgent tone.[86]

Between her first article on CDOs in April 2004 and the collapse of Lehman Brothers and AIG in mid-September 2008, the *Financial Times* printed about eighty of her pieces. Six weeks before the cataclysmic events of mid-September 2008, she brought together what she had learned in Japan in the 1990s and, more recently, on both sides of the Atlantic to help readers understand the seriousness of the impending collapse of global financial markets. The August 4, 2008, issue contained one of her articles under the headline "A Year That Shook Faith in Finance." In describing "the worst financial crisis seen in the West in seventy years," Tett explored how years of innovation in financial instruments led to an undermining of faith in a wide range of financial and regulatory institutions. The "vicious deleveraging spiral" meant it would require years to restore trust in the worlds of finance, "particularly given that so many of the assumptions underlying 21st century finance have turned out to be so dangerously wrong."[87] After virtually all observers understood the seriousness of what had happened, Tett deployed the commonly used term "zombie" to drive home how horrible the situation was. "For a world littered with corporate zombies," she wrote, referring to corporate debt, "is a not a world where activity is likely to flourish again soon—particularly when those half-dead companies are linked to their new 21st century bastard brethren, the zombie half-dead CLO."[88] Such vivid writing, along with her prescience, earned Tett a series of awards for her reporting. Yet her early warnings also earned her sharp (albeit, as it turned out, wrongheaded) criticism from those involved in the world of finance who worried about threats—journalistic or otherwise—to what turned out to be their own blind confidence.

Of course, Tett was hardly the only one to issue early warnings. In the early 1990s, when the Morgan Mafia was beginning its work, the respected investment banker Felix Rohatyn famously said that derivatives were the equivalent of "financial hydrogen bombs built on personal computers by 26-year-olds with MBAs."[89] As early as 2001, Joshua Rosner skeptically warned that "A Home without Equity Is Just a Rental with Debt."[90] In a 2002 paper, "The Run-Up in Home Prices: Is It Real or Is It Another Bubble?," the economist Dean Baker pointed to the potentially disastrous consequences of the second option.[91] As early as 2002, Richard Lord contributed articles to the *Pittsburgh City Paper* on predatory subprime lending before going on to publish *American Nightmare: Predatory Lending and the Foreclosure of the American Dream* in 2004. In 2003, Michael Hudson wrote in "Banking on Misery: Citigroup, Wall Street, and the Fleecing of the South" about the extensiveness of banks' investments in subprime mortgages. He then followed that up with a documentary he was involved in, *Maxed Out: Hard Times, Easy Credit and the Era of Predatory Lenders* (2006), and in his book *The Monster: How a Gang of Predatory Lenders and Wall Street Bankers Fleeced America—and Spawned a Global Crisis* (2010).[92]

There were plenty of other warnings, some of them early on. In 2004, well before she became a major political figure, Elizabeth Warren published *The Two-Income Trap: Why Middle-Class Parents Are Going Broke*, one of a series of her warnings, issued before and after the crisis emerged fully, about the financial fragility of American lives and the larger economy. In 2004 the FBI highlighted extensive fraud in the mortgage markets. In that same year David Rosenberg, the chief North American economist at Merrill Lynch, told leaders of the financial institution of a growing housing bubble, and Gary H. Stern and Ron G. Feldman published *Too Big to Fail: The Hazards of Bank Bailouts*. At a meeting of central bankers in Jackson Hole, Wyoming, in August 2005, Ragharum G. Rajan, the head of the IMF's research department, cautioned that deregulation and financial innovation could lead to a "full blown financial crisis" or "create a greater (albeit still small) probability of a catastrophic meltdown"[93] In his 2006 *Traders, Guns and Money: Knowns and Unknowns in the Dazzling World of Derivatives*, the Australian banker Satyajit Das used wit to explain the risky and arcane world of recently developed derivatives. Over time, he predicted, they would "turn out to be WMDs (weapons of mass destruction), causing large losses that affect markets, investors, and banks." He went on to declare that "perfect storms were lurking over the horizon: they would blow in suddenly, leaving death and destruction in their wake."[94]

The warnings intensified beginning in 2007. In May of that year, hedge fund manager William Ackman described how the bubble would burst in a presentation titled "Who's Holding the Bag?"[95] In late June 2007, Mark Pittman warned of dangers in the banking system in a Bloomberg article titled "S&P, Moody's Hide Rising Risk on $200 Billion of Mortgage Bonds."[96] As early as September 2006, the economist Nouriel Roubini warned of a crisis brewing that began with trouble in the American housing market.[97] In late October 2007, Allan Sloan wrote in *Fortune* of subprime loans packaged as mortgage-backed securities as comprising a "house of junk."[98] Then, in February 2008, Charles Morris published a book titled *The Two Trillion Dollar Meltdown: Easy Money, High Rollers, and the Great Credit Crash*. Soon after, Robert J. Shiller cautioned that the global financial crisis that would result from a bursting of the bubble in housing prices "could cause damage not only to the economy but to the social fabric—the trust and optimism people feel for each other and for their shared institutions and ways of life—for decades to come."[99] Danny Schechter produced two documentary films: *In Debt We Trust: America before The Bubble Burst* (2006) and *Plunder: Investigating Our Economic Calamity and the Subprime Scandal* (2008). In early 2008, the *New York Times* correspondent Peter S. Goodman began to understand the vulnerability in the market for employment and housing and the American economy when he visited a job center in Oakland, California.[100]

Of course, not all of these writers perfectly understood the present or accurately predicted the future, but, despite their warnings, boastful confidence remained prominent. A June 2007 meeting in Barcelona was titled "Global Asset Based Securitization: Towards a New Dawn!" Consequently, Tett's dissent led many—especially in the worlds of finance on Manhattan's Wall Street and in London's City—to denounce her. At the Davos meeting of the Global Economic Forum in 2007, Tett recalled that "one of the most powerful people in the US government at the time stood up on the podium and waved my article, the article that predicted the problems at Northern Rock," a bank in Newcastle that relied on mortgage-backed securities, "as an example of scaremongering."[101]

This brings us to another case of the gendering of financial news: the term "Davos Man," supposedly created in 2004 by the conservative political scientist Samuel Huntington, who perhaps had no intention of making the term derisive and problematically gendered. However, over time, some did gender it. For example, in 2017, Tett talked of the Davos Man who had no clothes coming out to play at the World Economic Forum, where 80 percent of the participants were male. Earlier, in 2009, when innovative capitalism had not been so fully criticized, she set the scene of fully clothed testosterone-driven men when she described "smooth-taking, white-toothed salesmen from large American banks, eagerly selling repackaged mortgage debt; self-deprecating British traders; and earnest, chain-smoking representatives from German insurance companies and banks. Their prey included asset managers from Italy, Spain, Germany, and Greece, often decked in elegant pastel colors. . . . A few regulators could also be spotted, conspicuous in looking generally dowdier than the bankers. Some of the biggest delegations, though, came from the three credit rating agencies that were drawing fat profits from the CDO boom."[102]

Did journalists fail to cover, foresee, and warn of the impending crisis? Some observers think so. Writing soon after the collapse of Lehman Brothers and AIG under the headline "Press May Own a Share in Financial Mess," the *Washington Post*'s media critic Howard Kurtz cited several reasons, though he mentioned Morgenson as an exception. Even though "the shaky house of financial cards that has come tumbling down was erected largely in public view," he wrote, "penetrating the finances of corrupt companies" was daunting. Some of what reporters had to explain, such as CDOs (or even synthetic CDOs), was difficult for members of a general audience to understand. In the often "ghettoized" world of journalism, reporters focused on threats to homeowners who held mortgages, but paid much less attention to the financial institutions that funded them. They might well worry about the power of advertisers, for, as one reporter noted, a magazine editor warned "that he couldn't sell magazines 'with a bucket of crap on the cover.'" Representatives of credit and regulatory agencies criticized the relatively little that reporters did expose, blaming them for being blinded by their politics. Indeed, Kurtz reported, "if these journalists shout too loudly, they can be accused of scaremongering and blamed for torpedoing the stock of outwardly healthy companies" or causing a run on banks. Getting too close to their sources, many reporters were often dazzled by the stock market's robustness and the apparent wisdom of Wall Street's wizards.[103]

Later on, evaluations of what went wrong confirmed and extended the evaluation Kurtz had offered in 2008.[104] A widely shared consensus emerged in the writings of the many scholars whose work focused on how well journalists covered this and earlier financial crises. Although they acknowledged there were exceptions that proved the rule, they nonetheless emphasized the failure of the community of business journalists to predict, let alone understand, the momentous dangers that deregulation and financialization posed to individuals and to the global economy. After all, since the late 1970s the financial sector had become increasingly prominent on Wall Street and in the nation's capital, to say nothing of its impact on the daily lives of Americans. With incomes for a broad swath of the American population stagnant, households increasingly relied on debt. From 1979 to 2005, a time when real GDP slightly more than doubled, revolving credit held by consumers (mainly on credit cards) increased from $11.3 billion to $826.6 billion, while mortgage debt increased from $673.4 billion to $12.15 trillion.[105] Before 1985, the financial sector had never earned more than 16 percent of the nation's corporate profits, but during the new century's first decade the comparable figure hit 41 percent.[106]

No one offered a more careful and comprehensive assessment of how the business press covered the global financial crisis than Dean Starkman in *The Watchdog That Didn't Bark: The Financial Crisis and the Disappearance of Investigative Journalism* (2014).[107] With more than twenty years of experience as an investigative reporter under his belt, including work that earned him a 1994 Pulitzer Prize, he headed the *Columbia Journalism Review*'s "The Audit," which critically assessed how the media covered the news. In the spring of 2009, he and his Columbia colleagues examined how nine of the most important business publications (including five under consideration here) examined "stories that could plausibly be considered warnings about the heart of the problem: abusive mortgage lenders and their funders on Wall Street." In the book that appeared five years later, Starkman summarized the findings. Like others, he distinguished between two kinds of business journalism. Access reporting relied on inside information, what journalists learned from talking with major players in the financial world, which they passed on to readers eager for what they considered useful inside dope. Access journalists emphasized the importance of speed, reliance on elite players and orthodox understandings, and undigested information useful to investors rather than judgment. In contrast stood accountability or investigative reporting, which, seeking information about powerful players rather than from them, relied on uncovering facts in order to offer analyses. Investigative journalism took longer, focused on the impact elites had on the lives of ordinary Americans, relied on skeptical informants who took contrarian positions, understood readers as citizens rather than as investors, and offered critical evaluations grounded in moral commitments.[108]

Although Starkman reached back to the muckraking of Ida Tarbell in the early twentieth century and then continued the story with developments at the *Wall Street Journal*, his coverage of the global financial crisis began in earnest in the 1990s and ended in 2007. My analysis of how journalists covered, or failed to cover, the global crisis, which focuses on the years 2007 and 2008, picks up where Starkman left off.[109] In the late twentieth century, he showed, accountability reporting played a significant role, as it operated in a "symbiotic relationship" with regulatory battles that offered an integrated approach involving both exposure and enforcement. In the first four years of the twenty-first century, he concluded, "the *best* business investigations were done." Ironically, if this was "the period *before* the true madness that engulfed the lending industry," it was in the following three years, "the period of the *worst* excesses," a time when subprime mortgages reached enormous heights, that he found "mainstream accountability reporting virtually dormant. The watchdog, powerful as it was, didn't bark when it was most needed."[110]

Starkman offered several explanations for what had happened. As regulatory efforts waned, so, too, did investigative reporting. As increasing numbers of Americans invested in the stock and bond markets, especially as their retirement portfolios grew, what took hold is what he called "CNBCization": rapid-fire and superficial reports of investment choices that relied on access to corporate titans like the ones on cable television. Finally, the business press, buffeted by competition from new media that undercut its advertising revenue, faced strong headwinds that, along with the other forces, undermined accountability reporting and strengthened its access counterpart. Indeed, the most severe threat to the ability of mainstream publications came in the middle of 2007 at the same time that the financial crisis accelerated. The migration of advertising revenues to digital sites such as Craigslist, Google, and Facebook caused major dailies like the *Washington Post* and the *Los Angeles Times* to reduce their numbers of journalists by 50 percent.[111]

Critics echoed Starkman's analysis when they lamented how the financialization of news and the reliance on advertising dollars drove an emphasis on stories of interest to investors or consumers rather than a broader range of citizens, especially nonelites. Like me, they also explored how reporters easily fell into the trap of giving credence to both sides of an argument. Caught up in competition from the twenty-four-hour frenzy of cable news and under tremendous pressure for scoops, reporters focused on the short term and had little time to step back and report on major trends or offer extended analysis.[112] All too easily and frequently, they both absorbed and conveyed the optimism and excitement of markets and of their sources among highly placed celebrants who were caught up in irrational exuberance. Under pressure from competition with internet-based sites, some financially strapped publications lacked the ability to hire a sufficient number of specialized and investigative reporters with the training, temperament, and skill to resist intellectual capture and understand arcane financial instruments. Access journalists failed to see the risks or corruption that led to the financial crisis. "We asked far too few questions about derivatives and risky changes to the banking system," remarked Jon Talton, an economics columnist for the *Seattle Times*, in early March 2009, "instead following mergers and slick new securities like star-struck sportswriters. We helped pimp the stock market as working Americans were giving up their pensions and embarking on a risky—and now ruinous—experiment."[113]

In contrast was the work of investigative reporters. To cite a few examples: Meredith Whitney understood how banks and rating agencies were deceiving investors. With her emphasis on icebergs and silos, Gillian Tett pierced through what access reporters conveyed as she put sectors of the investment world aside and looked below the surface. By relying on outsider skeptics like Joshua Rosner, Gretchen Morgenson shifted attention from compliant and orthodox sources to skeptical and unorthodox ones. Bethany McLean warned of the dangers of securitization as she built on her earlier skepticism about the hard-to-verify claims of Enron, whose corrupt operations were shrouded in mystery. Bobbi Murray and Michael Hudson exposed the fraud at financial institutions. Their work, and that of other investigative reporters, should have been useful to investors, but it was also important for all citizens to understand. As outsiders they offered more accurate analyses, in some cases because they were women and more generally because of their backgrounds and politics, shut out from or disrespected by men in power, and more aware of risk and corruption than most journalists, especially those at the center of the crisis.

Journalists' lack of training and expertise, especially if they were generalists with little command of what they were covering, made them more reliant on their sources. Most of them, even those covering finance, simply did not understand the complexities of financialization and deregulation. As Gillian Tett remarked in the fall of 2009, "A widespread assumption in the financial sphere that the debt and derivatives markets were simply too 'technical,' 'boring' or 'complex' to be of any interest to non-bankers. And in some respects, the bankers were quite correct to assume that. After all, there were almost no articles in the mainstream press about the wave of innovation or growth underway in debt and derivatives, precisely because the journalists (and their editors) tended to label these areas as excessively dull."[114]

The relationship between journalists and their sources remained an important factor. Surely there are times when the firewall between the editorial and business operations of a newspaper or magazine is breached, given the way publications need to rely on advertisers, especially from financial and real estate institutions. However, pressure can also operate in more insidious ways. "Intellectual capture" is easier, wrote Anya Schiffrin and Ryan Fagan, because of the uneven power relationships between reporters who "lack the analytic training to critique prevalent business perspectives" and "a dominant orthodoxy within the business community" that is widely shared by readers more interested in the short-term prospects of their portfolios than the long-term fate of the global economy. Focusing more on colorful personalities and stories with immediacy meant that analytic and longer-term evaluations got short shrift.[115]

Also operating was the power of journalistic conventions to shape coverage. It was easier to write a story about a specific corporation or its charismatic leader. As Tett noted at the time, "Twenty-first century journalism tends to assume that newspaper stories can only 'work' for readers or viewers if they feature stories about recognized, named individuals who can supply 'on the record' quotes, supplemented with verifiable facts and tangible events. Such elements," she continued, "can usually be found with stories about the stock market, where there are named individuals (company CEOs), events and facts (such as quoted prices)." In contrast, reporting on the world where financialization dominated not only involved sources reluctant to talk but also private and difficult-to-understand data. With "discrete events" that "seemed few and far between," these markets "did not create 'stories.'" An overheated market "did not meet the usual definition of a journalistic 'story,' since the subject matter seemed too complex, technical and dull, dressed up in a jargon that only bankers appeared able to understand."[116]

In crucial respects, the way the economic system tightly wove together the interests of media and financial institutions led reporters to celebrate heroic capitalists and booming financial markets. With *Bloomberg News* employing 2,300 business journalists; the *Wall Street Journal* more than 700; and the *New York Times* more than 100, it was easy for news itself, and not only in its specialized versions, to become financialized.[117] In specific terms, as one scholar asserted, journalists who focused on the world of business were careful to protect their careers by not rocking the boat and thereby contributed to the "adulatory cult of the chief executive" and ended up as "cheerleaders for speculative frenzy."[118] Or, as another commented, needing "to keep supply lines of information open, as part of the newsgathering process" bred "a coziness that naturally inhibits hard-hitting, critical reporting."[119] Moreover, reporters sometimes feared that writing about an impending financial disaster could make them culpable of adversely affecting markets. More generally and powerfully, reporters are subject to what perceptive observers call "cognitive capture"[120]; being "ideologically captured"[121]; suffering "from a form of Stockholm Syndrome"[122]; or "high source dependency."[123]

Nor were these the only factors to blame. Citing the work of Pierre Bourdieu, Tett writes of a "pattern of 'social silence'" that "ensured that the operations of complex credit were deemed too dull, irrelevant or technical to attract interest from outsiders, such as journalists or politicians." In addition, she suggests, since journalists lived in different silos from financiers on Wall Street, it was difficult for them to write about what they could only struggle to understand. Tett noted that, except for the *Financial Times*, most business publications paid remarkably little attention to complicated financial instruments between early 2000 and mid-2007 because they were "utterly geeky and dull." Of the more than 100 million articles published in that period, she revealed, only 1710 mentioned CDOs, and most of those appeared in highly specialized publications, resulting in knowledge not always being readily available and fully apparent to politicians, ordinary citizens, and most investors.[124]

The results of these relationships between reporters and their sources included suppressing criticism due to the way sources exercised control, adopting the language and viewpoints of financiers, and paying minimal attention to the perspectives of nonelites among the citizenry—or, as Schiffrin has put it, ignoring "the common man in favour of stories that glorify the titans of business and finance." Starkman put all this most cogently when he noted in mid-2009 that it was "far easier for news bureaucracies to accept ever-narrowing frames of discourse, frames forcefully pushed by industry, even if those frames marginalize and eventually exclude the business press's own great investigative traditions." In the end, he insisted, "missing are investigative stories that confront directly powerful institutions about basic business practices while those institutions were still powerful. This is not a detail. This is the watchdog that didn't bark."[125]

Of course, the view from the rearview mirror is always clearer than that from the newsroom in the midst of a crisis characterized by conflicting data, mysterious financial instruments, complicated plotlines, and massive uncertainty, all of which made understanding and predictability difficult at any one point in time. So it is perhaps unreasonable to expect reporters to be soothsayers, although some exceptional ones were. But, as Starkman remarks, "the expectation is merely that financial outlets do their best to report on *what is happening now*, including, one would hope, confronting powerful institutions directly about basic business practices. This is not complicated."[126] After all, in 2009, the headline of his article in *Mother Jones* asked "How Could 9,000 Business Reporters Blow It?" The answer was that much of mainstream press treated readers as investors hungry for inside dope rather than as citizens to be informed. "All the cheerleading and *Flip That House* fluff," he insisted as he referenced the popular reality TV show, "diverted resources from the real task at hand which he identified as "the good, hard-hitting arms' length stories."[127] On the other hand, there are different kinds of access journalism—at one extreme, those like Jim Cramer of CNBC and many print journalists who gained access to the rich and powerful but seemed to have no commitment to accountability; and those like Tett, who used her anthropologically informed perspective, and Morgenson, with her access to Rosner at the Center for Responsible Lending, for whom accountability was crucial.

What is revealed by the coverage of the coming of the Great Recession—especially the failures to do so effectively—are the complicated relationships between journalists, shifts in the business models of financial journalism, and the neoliberal order. Unbridled financial markets helped create the global crisis that threatened the well-being of billions of people worldwide. Ironically and tragically for themselves and their readers, writers were reporting on a problematic economic order while it was also transforming their careers and the companies that employed them. They might well see the handwriting on the wall, given the way internet and cable TV competitors, shifts in government policy, the growth power of fragmented markers, and lowered costs for entry into the media world threatened their futures.[128] By accelerating the shift to new media, including free social media sources, the Great Recession provoked a crisis for print journalism, which now had at its disposal fewer resources and talent. CNBC and Yahoo Finance were relatively well established, but BuzzFeed and ProPublica were launched in 2006 and 2007, respectively; Business Insider, owned by the German behemoth Axel Springer, appeared in February 2009. "While the media was reporting on the financial crisis," notes Schiffrin, "it also fell victim to it. Falling advertising and circulation, as well as increased competition from the internet, meant massive lay-offs and less in-depth reporting," which in turn could "increase the power of the advertiser and diminish the chances that day-to-day business and economic reporting will be critical of the conventional wisdom and the tycoons of finance. At the same time, publications seeking to save money on salaries are increasingly publishing opinion pieces and columns that they don't have to pay for, which may come at the expense of investigative reporting."[129] Yet, by and large, rather than connecting the dots that characterized these parallel universes, print journalists doubled down on their commitment to represent in often uncritical ways the worldview that their sources offered. Reliance on elite sources intensified the power of a market-based perspective.

The resulting lack of more extensive criticism by journalists of what they witnessed during the most serious economic crisis since the Great Depression underscores the power of the viewpoint that celebrated the frictionless movement of markets. The Great Recession exposed the ideological and cultural contradictions of capitalism, especially the disjuncture between a celebration of free-market capitalism and an embrace of government bailouts. As we have seen, even the free-market libertarian Steve Forbes—to say nothing of leading Republican officials like George W. Bush and Ben Bernanke—welcomed massive and unprecedented intervention by the federal government. Momentarily, all this suggested to some that, in the words of the media scholar Justin Lewis, "in a metaphorical nanosecond, one that seemed to slip away almost as it appeared, the enormity of the 'credit crunch' had the potential to bring the whole edifice of neoliberal capitalism crashing down." Lewis emphasizes that, while the crisis had "an identifiable line up of guilty men (and they were mostly men)," most journalists were not significantly "prepared to go in challenging the system that created these inequities." It was a time when reporters, moving beyond dramatic stories and personalities, might have questioned ideologies and the economic system they made seem self-evident.[130] After all, up for grabs was the fragile edifice of twenty-first-century capitalism, which had benefited so few and left so many behind. However, though there were some exceptions, both at the time and retrospectively, business journalists were more stunned and humbled by what they saw than awakened to what they had failed to cover. Overall, shaken and stirred, the journalists who covered the worlds of finance had missed the big story. Whether or not they had contributed to the bubble caused by globalization, new technologies, deregulation, and financialization, once it burst it was clear how significant the limits were to how well most of them understood and then both reported on and criticized what was happening. In order to explore alternative and more successful possibilities, we turn elsewhere: to anthropologists who carried out ethnographic work, investigative reporters who wrote books, and producers of documentary films.

Jonathan Scott and Drew Scott, *Dream Home: The Property Brothers' Ultimate Guide to Finding & Fixing Your Perfect Home* (2016).

Dean Starkman, *The Watchdog That Didn't Bark: The Financial Crisis and the Disappearance of Investigative Journalism* (2014).

National Association of Realtors, *100 Years In Celebration of the American Dream* (2007).

Bethany McLean and Joe Nocera, *All the Devils Are Here: The Hidden History of the Financial Crisis* (2010).

Gillian Tett, *Fool's Gold: How the Bold Dream of a Small Tribe at J. P. Morgan Was Corrupted by Wall Street Greed and Unleashed a Catastrophe* (2009).

Melissa S. Fisher, *Wall Street Women* (2012).

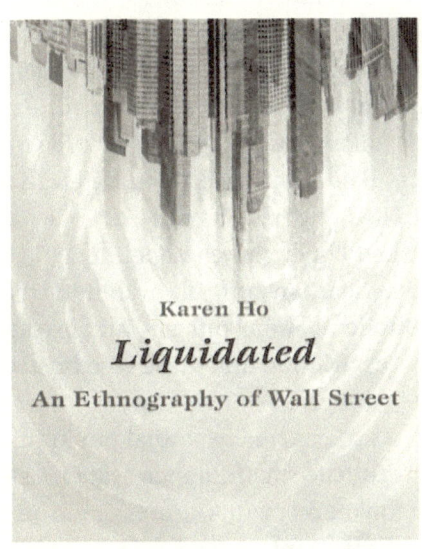

Karen Ho, *Liquidated: An Ethnography of Wall Street* (2009).

Noelle Stout, *Dispossessed: How Predatory Bureaucracy Foreclosed on the American Middle Class* (2019).

CHAPTER 4

JOURNALISTS, FILMMAKERS, AND THE GENDERING OF LOOKING BACKWARD

On March 12, 2009, Jim Cramer, host of CNBC's *Mad Money with Jim Cramer*, appeared on *The Daily Show with Jon Stewart* broadcast on Comedy Central.[1] The episode occurred less than a month after CNBC's editor Rick Santelli, standing on the floor of the Chicago Mercantile Exchange, called for the creation of a Tea Party because the federal government was "promoting bad behavior" by subsidizing "the losers' mortgages."[2] With his usual enthusiasms, gimmicks, and exaggerations, Cramer, like many on CNBC, had long hyped the stock market and individual stocks. The accuracy of what he and CNBC promoted proved problematic as the economy encountered significant headwinds and courted disaster. A telling moment occurred a year earlier, when the collapse of Bear Stearns approached, and Cramer kept touting its stock. "If I'd only followed CNBC's advice, I'd have a million dollars today," Stewart later remarked, "provided I'd started with a hundred million dollars." To Stewart, CNBC's operations smacked of what critics of business media elsewhere called "high source dependency" or "cognitive capture": slavishly parroting rather than critically evaluating the access offered by corporations, their public relations officers, and executives. Cramer took umbrage at Stewart's accusation that those who hosted shows such as his were in bed with their sources.

Yet *The Daily Show*'s host persisted. As the normally cordial but in this case angry Stewart observed, "I can't reconcile the brilliance and knowledge that you have of the intricacies of the market with the crazy bullshit I see you do every night.... I understand you want to make finance entertaining, but it's not a fucking game." Stewart called on CNBC to be "a powerful tool of illumination." Pointing out that Cramer and his colleagues knew how highly leveraged banks were, Stewart insisted that "you all know what's going on. You know, you can draw a straight line from those shenanigans to the stuff that was being pulled at Bear, and at AIG, and all this derivative market stuff that is this weird Wall Street side bet." And so "to pretend that this was some sort of crazy, once-in-a-lifetime tsunami that nobody could have seen coming is disingenuous at best, and criminal at worst." Driving home his points, Stewart told Cramer, "These guys were on a Sherman's March through their companies financed by our 401(k)s... and they burned the fucking house down and they walked away with our money rich as hell, and you guys knew that that was going on."[3]

Cramer responded by telling his host that financiers had lied to him, conceding that he had made mistakes, insisting that he wanted wrongdoers indicted, and admitting that he could have done a better job of foreseeing the collapse of the global financial markets.[4] Soon after, a group of progressives issued a statement that called on CNBC to provide "strong, watchdog journalism—asking tough questions to Wall Street, debunking lies, and reporting the truth" instead of doing "PR for Wall Street. You've been so obsessed with getting 'access' to failed CEOs that you willfully passed on misinformation to the public for years, helping to get us into the economic crisis we face today."[5] Ten months later, Stewart vividly hammered home his argument. "Let me see if I got this straight," he remarked in January 2010. "The only people who have fully recovered from the financial meltdown are the ones who caused the financial meltdown, and by recovered I mean apparently redipping their balls in gold."[6] In his discussion with Cramer and elsewhere, Stewart used colorful language, blunt statements, and satire to pierce through the veil of the media's claims of objectivity and promises by financiers in ways their defenders and well-established journalists could rarely do.

Stewart was right that Cramer missed the story of how securitization turned out to be a precarious house of cards that collapsed in 2008. Cramer had plenty of company, because few observers understood that a once sleepy bond market had become a vast and dangerous casino when it turned the stock market into a sideshow to which most journalists, investors, and regulators paid far too little attention. In the short term, assets were leveraged so much so that major financial institutions and shrewd investors stood to make outsized returns on their investments. Yet few people had accurate knowledge of the soundness of the individual mortgages contained within these holdings in which they had placed their money and their faith. Government officials either looked the other way because they felt they needed to remain optimistic, at least in public, or because they simply did not understand what was going on. The rating agencies Moody's, Standard & Poor's, and Fitch earned handsome fees by giving AAA ratings to packages that contained hefty percentages of high-risk mortgages.

Pension funds around the world unknowingly snapped up these seemingly safe investments, assured, as they had to be, of their safety. All hands were on board. Economists earned handsome consulting fees in exchange for intellectual justification of deregulation and securitization; politicians were glad to receive campaign contributions and listen to the reassurances of lobbyists; bankers earned huge bonuses. And, over time, so did those who originated and certified risky subprime mortgages that were unlikely to be paid off, especially when adjustable rates kicked in or incomes turned out to be precarious.

So, what the work of Jon Stewart reveals is that if we can't find that many sources in traditional print media or more rarely on major financially oriented TV programs that early on and soon after understood the global financial crisis, we must turn elsewhere—to filmmakers, book-writing journalists, and, eventually, to anthropologists. Much of their best work and wisdom depended on retrospective perspectives. In addition, the nature of the genres they relied on and their freedom to make clear their ideological commitments often allowed them to offer critical assessments. As a result, compared with what many journalists offered, there were important differences in how they described what had happened; whether and how they connected Wall Street, the nation's capital, and the lives of ordinary Americans; what moral and historical perspectives they offered; whether they understood their audiences as investors or citizens; if they worried more about systematic risk or corruption, or both; how they made complex and arcane financial instruments understandable; and what role gender played (and did not play) in their analyses in ways that revealed and hid what was going on. This is what a cultural historian does: juxtapose texts that illuminate and complicate each other to help us understand how culture operates during and soon after critical moments.

As a book, and especially as a film, *The Big Short* offered what were among the most clever and accessible explanations of what happened. As suggested by the title, it focused on shorting: the process of betting that an asset will fall in value and that those who shorted a holding would reap tremendous financial rewards. Michael Lewis's 2011 book *The Big Short: Inside the Doomsday Machine* served as the basis for the docudrama with the same title that appeared four years later.[7] Focusing on corruption at major Wall Street institutions, national rating agencies, and local loan originators, both book and film chronicled the story of a handful of hedge fund investors who by 2005 understood how dangerously leveraged the mortgage market was. "A few outsiders and weirdos saw what no one else could," we hear in the film; they looked at a "giant lie at the heart of the economy."

They realized how risky subprime loans were, risks intensified by their connections to new and arcane financial instruments, especially collateralized debt obligations (CDOs) and credit default swaps (CDSs). They gambled on their prediction that when interest rates rose in the near future, many who borrowed to buy residences with adjustable-rate mortgages would no longer be able to make payments. So they placed very considerable and highly leveraged bets that mortgage-backed securities and other derivatives would lose value.

The film cleverly solved the problem of representing complex issues in ways easy to understand. "Mortgage-backed securities, subprime loans, tranches—it's pretty confusing, right?" asks the actor Ryan Gosling, portraying a Deutsche Bank bond trader. "I reap tremendous financial rewards," he continues. "Does it make you feel bored or stupid? Well, it's supposed to. Wall Street loves to use confusing terms to make you think only they can do what they can do or even better for you to just leave them the fuck alone."

The director Adam McKay cleverly solved the representational problem by breaking through the proverbial fourth wall that normally separates actors from audiences. He did so by creating cleverly crafted moments dramatizing what had happened in the worlds of finance. Early on, Margot Robbie talks directly to viewers while taking a luxurious bubble bath as a butler fills and refills her glass of Champagne. She explains how "amazingly profitable" it was for banks to fill bond funds with more and more risky mortgages. Later on, the chef Anthony Bourdain, playing himself, looks out at the viewer and explains how he throws fish that is going bad into a pot and repurposes it into a stew. The movie's narrative underscores how the same thing happened when bankers repurposed toxic mortgages and placed them in a financial stew.

Then Richard Thaler and Selena Gomez, portraying themselves, describe leverage while sitting at a blackjack table. The behavioral economist who in 2017 would win the Nobel Prize in Economics and the popular entertainer look out at audience and relate how the "hot hand fallacy" explains the assumption that if a basketball player makes several baskets in a row, more are certain to follow. This is what casino gamblers might assume about the next hand in poker or the next spin of the roulette wheel. Thaler and Gomez mention the parallel assumption by real estate investors: that with markets continually going up, they would continue to do so—something that often happened in the short term but obviously could not go on forever. Standing behind Thaler and Gomez are several couples, each one making bets that carry greater odds. Eventually, we learn from Thaler and Gomez, relatively small wagers would turn into bets worth (or not worth) billions.

Later, the scene shifts to Las Vegas, the center of American casino gambling, which is also ground zero for bets on the housing market. With his colleagues, Steve Carell playing Mark Baum (Steve Eisman in the book) goes to Las Vegas to attend the meeting of the American Securitization Forum in early January 2007. Lewis described Eisman as having "a special talent for making noise and breaking with consensus opinions."[8] In a penetrating essay on behavioral economics and masculinity in which the work of Lewis figures prominently, the literary scholar Michelle Chihara calls Eisman one in a series of Lewis's "scrappy heroes [who] demonstrate a fierce sense of individuality as they determine their own moral compasses."[9] Long skeptical about the fragility of the house of cards the mortgage market built on CDOs, Baum stands up at a presentation at which the speaker brags that "the mortgage continues to be the bedrock on which this economy is built." Baum asks the speaker whether it is "a possibility or probability that subprime losses stop at five percent." In response to a confident reassurance, Baum, forming a circle with his thumb and index finger, emphatically insists that there was zero chance they would stop there.

Although the book does not dramatize what happened on the ground in the residential real estate market, the movie does. Throughout the film, viewers catch glimpses of unemployed and homeless people. About one-third of the way through come compelling glimpses of the tragic results of financialization when the scene shifts to visit to a Miami suburb, a trip Lewis described in just two sentences. Baum and his colleagues drive through a neighborhood where housing prices have skyrocketed but is now filled with "For Sale" signs. A real estate broker reassuringly insists that the market is in "an itsy-bitsy little gully right now." Well, that "little gully" soon turned into a Grand Canyon as deep and as dangerous to navigate as the one a few hundred miles east of the gambling capital. The three short-sellers, suspecting that financial institutions have hidden troubled assets, go to an upscale housing development marked by signs of distress.[10] They knock on the door of one residence and learn from the man renting the home that the landlord filled out the mortgage application using his dog's name. The scruffy, tattooed working-class occupant fears he is going to have to leave, just when his kids had settled in school. "Seriously, man, is everything going to be OK?" he asks. Then they enter an abandoned house nearby, with mail piled up at the entrance and an alligator in the swimming pool, an image that evokes the theme of zombies taking over a world during an economic crisis. "It's like Chernobyl," one of them comments, using another frightening metaphor. "There's a hundred houses. There can't be four people living here."[11] Suspicious, they ask to meet with

A still from *The Big Short* (2015). When this Las Vegas stripper mentions "all my loans" to Mark Baum (Steve Carell), he responds by asking, "What do you mean all your loans?"—thereby learning how recklessly lenders have written mortgages.

local mortgage brokers. Slick, fast-talking men, the brokers brag that they can make $2,000 writing a fixed-rate prime mortgage but five times that amount for an adjustable-rate subprime one. They laugh when asked if applicants ever get rejected. Of course not, they boast; they write NINJA loans—no income, no jobs, no assets—and leave the income section blank since "corporate doesn't care." One broker says he focuses on immigrants, because as "fucking idiots" they just sign, as they assume they are getting a home. Then they interview a stripper who told the mortgage company she was a therapist, made a down payment of only 5 percent, has five homes and a condo, and does not understand that her monthly payments can go up dramatically. This is when Baum and his colleagues, realizing there is a bubble, decide to short the market.

Both the book and the movie capture some but hardly all of the major changes that connected residential real estate, the worlds of finance, and the Great Recession. The film includes a brief clip of Cramer on CNBC. Both film and book go briefly back—the former to the 1970s and the latter to the 1980s, with attention paid to the invention of mortgage-backed securities, but focused principally on what happened in the early twenty-first century. Neither book nor film place the story in a global context, pay more than cursory attention to government policy, or more than briefly (and often elliptically) refer to how Alan Greenspan, Henry Paulson, and Ben Bernanke offered what turned out to be hollow and dangerous reassurances. Instead, they focus on the corruption and blindness to risk at major Wall Street financial institutions and the quirky outsiders who dissented and bet against them. At the heart of the film (but not the book) are especially vivid pictures of the consequences of financialization. The book and film make clear how over time CDOs and CDSs became essential components of bets upon bets upon bets—what the *Financial Times* journalist Gillian Tett called "derivatives of credit derivatives, or even 'derivatives cubed,'" as well as what Thaler and Gomez compared to repurposed rotting fish: holdings that derived their value from an invisible, toxic, and underlying asset usually at several removes.[12] The situation grew more complicated and difficult for regulators and ordinary citizen investors to understand when financiers developed contractual derivatives through which one investor guarantees another against default, in an ideal world involving payment of a premium in exchange for risk reduction or prevention.

Lewis makes clear that the stories he tells are tragic, even though whatever moral judgment he has remains implicit, conveyed principally through stories and characters. In contrast, the film more forcefully and explicitly deploys figures who represent its moral center. Baum, his outlook shaped by his brother's suicide, believes that the "whole system [is] a lie." "CDOs," he remarks at one point, "are dog shit wrapped in cat shit." He realizes that what is at stake is that the "whole world economy might collapse." He understands that Wall Street took the idea behind mortgage-backed securities and then

> turned it into an atomic bomb of fraud and stupidity that's on its way to decimating the world economy.... We live in an era of fraud in America, not just in banking, but in government, education, religion, food, even baseball.... The fact that we're not better than this does not make me feel all right and superior; it makes me feel sad.... I just know that at the end of the day average people are going to be the ones that are going to have to pay for all of this because they always, always do.

Then there is Ben Rickert (in real life, Ben Hockett, played here by Brad Pitt) a bond trader at Deutsche Bank who, impelled by an apocalyptic streak, had left his Wall Street life behind. When one of the short-sellers is self-congratulatory about what he is doing, Ben looks into the camera and says, "You just bet against the American economy," to which they respond, "Fuck yeah, we did." Ben emphasizes the disastrous impact a financial crisis has on ordinary people: "People lose homes. People lose jobs. People lose retirement savings. People lose pensions." If Lewis mentions unemployment only once, in the film Ben asks his colleagues and the audience whether they realize that every 1 percent increase in unemployment results in the deaths of 40,000 people.

Near the end, the film drives home the consequences of Wall Street's misdeeds. We see the family of renters from Miami living in a car and the boastful loan originators wandering around at a job exposition looking for employment. Soon after, the omniscient narrator claims that bankers went to jail, the SEC was overhauled, and Congress broke up big banks. "Just kidding," he says: the banks used the people's money, paid themselves handsomely, and helped kill reform. "And then they blamed immigrants and poor people." On-screen roll statements that $5 trillion in assets were gone in real estate, pensions, and savings; 8 million people lost their jobs and 6 million families their homes. "And that was just in the USA," we learn in one of the film's few references connecting Wall Street and the global economy. "This is like the end of capitalism," one of the short-sellers had earlier remarked, but in the end the film drives home the conclusion that the more accurate story is about the restoration and strengthening of the U.S. financial sector.

The book and film reveal the role of women in chronicling the crisis in complex and contradictory ways and underscore that some masculinist renderings of the events paid too little attention to what some prescient women wrote and mirrored instead of analyzing the boom-and-bust nature of financial capitalism. Meredith Whitney was present in the book by Lewis but missing from the movie, highlighting the tendency in many media depictions of the crisis to focus on the destructive behavior of some men while remaining, as two critics observed, "unwilling to cede positions of authority to women."[13] Her warnings in 2007 and 2008—about Citigroup and IndyMac, respectively—earned her a prominent place at the beginning of the book *The Big Short*. "It's hardly shocking that a bunch of middle-aged male bank executives would spare time for a glamorous analyst with a megawatt personality and a jock-celebrity husband [the WWE wrestler John Layfield]," a journalist noted in 2008 as he pointed out the gendered dynamics overlooked by the film.[14] Issued when she worked at the Wall Street firm Oppenheimer, Whitney's admonitions played a pivotal role in enabling Michael Lewis to drive the narrative of his book. In the late 1980s, Lewis had worked as a bond salesman at Salomon Brothers. In *Liar's Poker: Rising through the Wreckage on Wall Street* (1989), he had captured the risky game of trading mortgage bonds. When he left Salomon Brothers a year before that book's publication, he was convinced that, sooner rather than later, a "Great Reckoning" would make clear that Wall Street had embarked on a reckless and unsustainable course. Lewis waited and waited and waited, longer than he had expected, until he stopped waiting. Then, on the last day of October 2007, Whitney came along—"an obscure analyst of financial firms," he called her. She told readers of *Fortune* "that Citigroup had so mismanaged its affairs that it would need to slash its dividend or go bust." Financial stocks crashed. The company's CEO resigned four days later. Soon after, Citigroup cut its dividend. In the ensuing months, Whitney made clear the extent to which the financial world was built on a house of little-understood cards. In March 2008, just before the collapse of Bear Stearns, Lewis called Whitney—and she provided the leads that were among those that made it possible for him to write *The Big Short*.[15]

Whitney played such a significant role in *The Big Short* as a book but disappeared when it came to the movie. The film's producers failed to give her even a cameo appearance, instead featuring a series of men. Moreover, virtually none of the women in the movie, including Margot Robbie, were virtuous or heroic: not the Goldman Sachs banker who laughed off the short-sellers' scheme; the Miami real estate agent who spoke of "an itsy-bitsy little gully"; the woman at a rating agency who briefly admitted how corrupt it was to sell favorable evaluations for robust fees; or the SEC official who falsely claimed that there was nothing wrong or illegal about failing to police financial firms at the same time that she was angling for a job at an investment bank.[16]

Had the movie featured Whitney, audiences would have learned that, better than most male writers, there was at least one woman who early on best understood the dangers of securitization. Indeed, along with Gretchen Morgenson, Bethany McLean, and Gillian Tett, Whitney was one of four women who in the most critically intense years of the meltdown underscored the dangers posed by the nexus between residential real estate and new financial instruments. In different combinations, these women, whose warnings we see later in this chapter and earlier in the previous one, wrote books and figured in several movies about the global financial crisis. Most journalists who were meeting daily or monthly deadlines, and were obligated to their sources, could not figure out how to devise stories that presciently or even somewhat accurately captured the unfolding global crisis. In contrast, those who worked on movies or books could do so since as outsiders they were less reliant on their sources, freer to speak their minds, and more committed to developing critical perspectives in extended narratives offered in a medium different from what most business journalists wrote.[17]

Morgenson made many TV appearances as a talking head, but never appeared in a movie. However, in addition to her award-winning reporting for the *New York Times*, she did produce a book. When the dust had settled, along with Joshua Rosner she wrote *Reckless Endangerment: How*

Outsized Ambition, Greed, and Corruption Led to Economic Armageddon.[18] Published in the spring of 2011, *Reckless Endangerment* was in some ways remarkable in its scope, its ability to combine finely grained and detailed reporting of often arcane incidents with a dramatic narrative driven by stories of major figures and institutions in New York and the nation's capital, and its power to explain what had happened so soon after it did.

Though Morgenson's articles in the *New York Times* focused mainly on Wall Street and securitization, the book was more Washington, D.C.-centered, possibly because of Rosner's role in shaping its narrative, but more likely because of how the coauthors structured their story. As "an economic whodunit," the book's central narrative began and ended with James A. Johnson, the chair and CEO of Fannie Mae from 1991 to 1998. They offered a drama that was global in nature, but, with the focus on Johnson, theirs was really a national tale. Men dominated the world they described, and among the few women they mentioned were two to whom they gave more than cursory attention. Anne Canfield published *The GSE Report*, which, they noted, "became a crucial resource" for who those worried about the threat that Fannie Mae and Freddie Mac "posed to the taxpayers." Then there was June O'Neill, the director of the Congressional Budget Office, who struggled mightily against the powerful men at the GSEs (government-sponsored enterprises), Johnson included.[19]

However, *Reckless Endangerment* was much broader in its scope than a focus on Johnson suggested. Under his leadership at Fannie Mae, the book's authors claimed, he built the government-sponsored but publicly traded corporation into a financial behemoth that underwrote a huge percentage of the nation's mortgages, set the standard for how others operated, and fundamentally reshaped the financial and political systems. Johnson proved to be a model that others followed. Morgenson and Rosner offered stories of regulators being captured by the financial institutions they were supposed to regulate. Johnson was among those who led the way in having the federal government decide, "in its infinite wisdom, that every living, breathing citizen should own a home."[20] With Johnson in command, Fannie Mae fought against being privatized, deployed patronage lavishly, acted corruptly, built connections with members of Congress and federal agencies, supported and took advantage of deregulation, silenced critics, sponsored research by academics, and advocated for affordability that turned out to be toxic to homeowners and the economy. His "manipulation of his company's regulators provided a blueprint for the financial industry, showing them how to control their controllers," they wrote, in ways that freed financial institutions from regulation and enabled them to reap personal wealth and institutional power.²¹ To show the spreading influence of these tactics, Morgenson and Rosner also explored how others operated, paying special attention to Countrywide Financial, which, under the leadership of Angelo Mozilo, ruthlessly operated as one of the nation's largest and most aggressive mortgage lenders.

Morgenson and Rosner might have given Wall Street—or even federal policy—more attention than they did, instead of Johnson and Fannie Mae, which played the major role in creating the arc of their dramatic story. And it was not until near the end of the book that they declared that, "of all the partners in the homeownership push, no industry contributed more to the corruption of the lending process than Wall Street." Manhattan's outsized financial institutions played a major role in the book's plotline—by generating innovative but highly leveraged financial instruments and, especially in the case of Goldman Sachs, by providing the key connections between Wall Street and the levers of power in the nation's capital. Although Johnson, Fannie Mae, and weakened or inept government entities drove much of the book's narrative, "Wall Street and its securitization machine" were never out of sight or out of power.²²

The stories Morgenson and Rosner tell focus on the power of elites. The authors are critical of the drive to increase rates of homeownership, what they called "the potent combination" of "unfettered capitalism coupled with the ownership society."²³ They thus saw this as stemming from Wall Street and the nation's capital rather than the stoking of the yearnings of ordinary people pursuing the American dream. Indeed, though they offered statistical evidence of the damage, flesh and blood was given to people at the top and not those below, since virtually no ordinary citizens or struggling homeowners made appearances in print.²⁴ As a result, they revealed remarkably little of the impact of events in the Washington–New York axis on lives of Americans outside that corridor. Moreover, although they never labeled what they described, theirs was the drama, reaching back to the presidency of Bill Clinton, of bold entrepreneurship significantly weakening government in ways that enriched the powerful at the expense of vulnerable homeowners and taxpayers. Carefully researched, meticulously detailed, and passionately written, their book highlights an epic tragedy. This was what happened, the authors insist, "when unfettered risk taking, with an eye to personal paydays, gains the upper hand in corporate executive suites and on Wall Street trading floors."²⁵

In this case and other examples of narrative nonfiction, a focus on stories and key figures kept any sustained exploration of the economic system's systemic problems largely out of sight. Yet, based on a decade and a half of reporting, Morgenson and Rosner revealed how access, even to the powerful, could lead to an emphasis on accountability. Virtually every word in the book's title and subtitle—reckless, endangerment, outsized, ambition, greed, corruption, Armageddon—underscored the force of the authors' judgment. This was, they similarly insisted, the story of "reckless endangerment of the entire nation by people at the highest levels of Washington and corporate America." They felt "compelled to write this book," they explained, "because we are angry that the American economy was almost wrecked by a crowd of self-interested, politically influential, and arrogant people who have not been held accountable for their actions." The financial crisis, they insisted, "was the result of actions taken by people at the height of power in both the public and private sectors, people who continue, even now, to hold sway in the corridors of Washington and Wall Street."[26]

While Whitney reported on the financial crisis in a way that sparked a book and a movie, and Morgenson reported and wrote a book, Bethany McLean warned of the dangers of financialization as a reporter, was involved in several documentaries on the same topic, and wrote three related books. Her March 5, 2001, article in *Fortune*, "Is Enron Overpriced?," helped launch her career as an astute financial reporter. Anyone taking seriously what she wrote would not have been surprised by the corporation's collapse almost exactly ten months later. She followed that with her 2003 book, written with Peter Elkind, *The Smartest Guys in the Room: The Amazing Rise and Scandalous Fall of Enron*. Based on investigative reporting, McLean and Elkind told the dramatic story of the rise and fall of Enron. The figures in the books may have been uniquely smart, but, epitomizing the connections between systematic corruption and wildly excessive risk-taking in a macho world, they relied on deregulation, arrogance, and greed as they transformed an unexceptional energy corporation into an exceptionally fraudulent trading firm.[27] The authors characterized the behavior they reported on as "scandalous," a word echoed in the book's subtitle. However, the evidence they presented demanded stronger words, like "immoral" or "disastrous." Near the book's end, they edged toward an even harsher conclusion. They noted the accounting firm Arthur Andersen's comment that the mid-2002 conviction of the company executives for destruction of evidence "represents only a technical conviction." This was, the authors responded, "an astonishing comment on the mores of American life at the dawn of a new century. In the aftermath of one of the largest corporate scandals in American history, precious few were willing to concede that they had done anything wrong. Wasn't anybody sorry?"[28]

Almost all of the story took place in Houston, with the authors paying minimal attention to the role of the federal government as a causal factor and a fair amount of attention to the complicity of Wall Street investment banks, "without whose zealous participation," they observed, "Enron's financial shenanigans would simply not have been possible." Of the well over one hundred people listed in the "cast of characters," there was not one who suffered down below, from the predatory behavior of those on high—not one small-scale customer or investor made an appearance.[29]

The authors did highlight the activities of many women in the hypermasculine world their book described. Among the heroic ones were investigative reporters and whistleblowers who uncovered corporate malpractice. In contrast, there were a fair number of women whose behavior was troublesome, prominent among them the highly placed corporate executive Rebecca Mark. In explaining her rise, McLean and Elkind deployed a gendered analysis. Even though she was CEO of the corporation's major subsidiary, Enron Power, another highly placed executive, who was also her lover, "sometimes treated her like a secretary, ordering her to fetch his coffee or type his letters." The authors also began a chapter titled "The Empress of Energy" by saying that in the mid-1990s Mark was, "to the outside world, the person who *was* Enron, who had a reputation for turning impossible concepts into glittering realities." They went on to portray her as someone who intensified the corporation's macho culture. Enron Development, which focused on energy in emerging markets and that she headed at one point, they observed, "had its own culture, where the ex-military guys she liked to hire sought to outdo each other at parties featuring elephants, motorcades, and belly dancers, and where Mark herself once came roaring in on the back of a Harley to the beat of 'Eye of the Tiger.'" Even though, as they noted, she was optimistic and hardworking, people initially mentioned her glamorous looks "partly because she operated in the all-male energy industry and partly because the world can still be a sexist place." So she "unapologetically viewed being a woman—a smart, charismatic woman—as a way to 'get privileges that other people don't get, and . . . audiences that others can never hope to achieve,' as she told one reporter. Her gender was not an obstacle to be overcome but an advantage. As she liked to put it, 'I'll take all the advantages I can get.'"[30]

Mark's downfall, which the authors did not explain in gendered terms, was not long in coming. Best at marketing herself and her enterprises, if Mark rose because of her skill as a salesperson, she was not good at managing, suffering from the excessive risk-taking and compensation incentives that eventually brought down others at Enron. Compared in *Fortune* to "a character in an Ayn Rand novel," when she was eventually forced to resign from her new post at one of Enron's subsidiaries, her "failings were on vivid display, for anyone to see." It was clear that she had taken a "bad situation and made it even worse at every turn." Even though she benefited from selling $80 million of Enron stock near its highest price, "she continued to boil over about what Skilling and Lay," the two men in charge of Enron, "had done to her" and "never stopped believing that success was just around the corner."[31]

That book's title had another life as that of the award-winning 2005 documentary film *Enron: The Smartest Guys in the Room*, in which McLean appeared on-screen while also serving as one of the screenwriters. The movie, like the book, told the story of the transformation of Enron from a small, regional energy company into an international, technologically crafty energy and financial services corporation that deployed dishonest and opaque methods of securitization driven by testosterone-fueled masculinity. Hailed by *Fortune* for six consecutive years as the nation's most innovative company, Enron relied on greed, fraud, political shenanigans, and deregulation, which drove it into bankruptcy, with its stock price going from ninety dollars per share in late 2000 to less than a dollar by the end of 2001.

The book and film handled gender differently, though both of them highlighted a Darwinian world, what Eklind as a talking head labeled a "macho culture." While McLean and Elkind's book prominently featured Rebecca Mark, she made no appearance on-screen, perhaps because she somehow blocked cooperation. Moreover, there was no other woman portrayed who was culpable of wrongdoing and several who were heroic, especially McLean—not so much in her role as a calm and largely nonjudgmental talking head, but as the author of the 2001 *Fortune* article "Is Enron Overpriced?" In an extensive sequence, the film highlighted how Jeffrey Skilling, Enron's mastermind, struggled to respond convincingly to questions at a congressional hearing about her dynamite reporting. In addition, more than in the book, the film prominently featured Sherron Watkins as a whistleblower, and Mimi Swartz, with whom she wrote *Power Failure: The Inside Story of the Collapse of Enron* (2002). The filmmakers gave Swartz plenty of screen time, but McLean and Elkind had only briefly referenced her.[32]

If understated judgments were common to the narratives in major books, documentary films demanded something else that made them better able to shift responsibility from individuals to systems. Consequently, just as the movie *Inside Job* was more hard hitting than the book *Fool's Gold*, the same was true of the comparable versions of *The Smartest Guys in the Room*. Both emphasized the importance of deregulation, but the striking difference in the coverage of the role of politics in Enron's rise is the film's considerable attention to the intertwined and corrupt relationship between Enron and the presidents Bush, especially "W," a relationship the book mentioned only briefly and with less conspiratorial overtones.

Moreover, while McLean and Elkind paid virtually no attention to ordinary Americans whose lives Enron upended, the same was hardly true of the movie. Initially, we watch as Enron executives tell employees to fill their retirement funds with Enron stock, even as they are selling theirs. Later, we hear of the destruction of the livelihoods, pensions, and health insurance of tens of thousands of employees even as their bosses were relying on inside information to unload their holdings. We watch as the film weaves together the stories of the devastation (represented by wildfires, traffic accidents, and budget crises) unleashed by manipulation of California's electrical grid, pictures from Stanley Milgram's experiments on the way respectable Americans would administer pain when an authority figure reassured them it was OK to do so, and recently uncovered tape recordings of Enron's smartest guys gloating over what they had wrought. The film also presents original footage of the story of a lineman at an Enron subsidiary, Portland General Electric, who saw the value of the Enron stock in his portfolio go from $348,000 to a mere $1,200.

The book's moral judgments remained muted, but in contrast the movie powerfully drove home tough-minded conclusions. The film effectively used footage in which members of Congress relentlessly exposed the predatory behavior of Enron officials. It featured several prominent figures central to the corporation's rise and fall who either fessed up or doubled down on their negative assessments. Then Swartz said that the Milgram experiment revealed that "people lost their sense of morality." Or, as the poster held up by a California protestor read, "Greed Sucks!!" Then, in a rare on-screen judgmental moment, McLean remarked that while Enron's commanders thought they "were changing the world . . . they became victims of their own hubris, victims of their own greed." Finally, the film ended with news of the consequences of Enron's wrongdoing. Flashing across the screen was information on jobs and pensions lost. If we learn that the average severance pay for Enron's employees was $6,850, the top executives exited with bonuses worth $744 million in stocks and cash.[33]

The film was nominated for but did not win an Oscar for Best Documentary Feature. The *Guardian*'s film critic Peter Bradshaw, however, perceptively insisted that there should be a gold statue "outside every journalism school in the world" honoring McLean as "the magnificently persistent reporter who" did not give up despite the "sneering from the American business boys' club." The movie, he went on to say, "has disquieting resonances about our own Enronised prosperity" built on the way middle-class homeowners in Britain were "borrowing more, spending more and unconcerned about the future because ever-increasing property prices will buy us out of trouble."[34]

"Just as McLean's *The Smartest Guys in the Room* was hailed as the best Enron book on a crowded shelf, so will *All the Devils Are Here* be remembered for finally making sense of the meltdown and its consequences," asserted the jacket copy of McLean's next book. McLean's coauthor was Joe Nocera, another skilled writer and business journalist. Carrying the subtitle *The Hidden History of the Financial Crisis* and appearing in late 2010, months before *Reckless Endangerment*, *All the Devils Are Here* extended what McLean learned about securitization, risk, deregulation, corruption, and avariciousness from covering Enron.[35] Of the books by journalists under consideration here, *All the Devils Are Here* (2010) strikes me as the most probing and comprehensive.

McLean and Nocera organized their book around a series of stories about powerful and colorful personalities whose actions represented major changes driven by the interactions of policies and elite figures in government and financial institutions. With relatively few exceptions, they unselfconsciously described the world composed as a series of men's clubs to which few women, as either heroes or villains, gained entrance.[36] McLean and Nocera did, however, honor the work of Sheila Bair and Donna Tanoue and, more extensively, Brooksley Born for warning about dangers ahead. Unlike *The Big Short* as a movie, the book by McLean and Nocera paid minimal attention to events in the United States beyond those that unwound in Manhattan and Washington. As a result, they did little to explore how ordinary people suffered because of the actions of extraordinarily powerful people. *The Big Short* as both a book and film, *Reckless Endangerment*, and *All the Devils Are Here* were similarly focused on the United States in ways that minimized the global dimensions of the evolving crisis. More so than Morgenson and Rosner, McLean and Nocera emphasized the connections among what went on in the nation's capital, Wall Street, and local mortgage originators. More so than Morgenson and Rosner, they captured the complicated but vitally important relationships between public and private spheres—represented not only by the hybrid nature of Fannie Mae but also by the interactions between investment banks, mortgage companies, rating agencies, deregulation, low interest rates, the Federal Reserve, subprime lending, congressional legislation, party politics, and presidential leadership. All four writers captured dramas driven by outsized personalities whose complacency, greed, recklessness, arrogance, and ambition knew few limits and ultimately were responsible for tragic consequences. Both sets of authors paid attention to affordable homeownership, though Morgenson and Rosner laid more blame on this as a driving force that brought adverse consequences.

Above all, Nocera and McLean, like Morgenson and Rosner, were journalists who told stories that made people and their institutions more responsible for the Great Recession than the economic system itself.[37] Unlike social scientists, especially radicals among them, McLean and Nocera did not see a long-term crisis having to do with the nexus of globalization, technology, precarious work, inequality, and public policy. Their commitment to a narrative driven by capsule portraits meant the focus was on people, stories, incidents, and organizations rather than persistent and powerful underlying forces.[38]

Yet there were more than enough "devils" who seemed to share, in roughly equal portions, the abundant blame for what happened. "In truth, they were all taking on huge risks in granting these terrible loans," McLean and Nocera remarked of the period when the subprime mortgage market was on the verge of collapsing. "But they were all making too much money to see it. Everyone assumed that someone else would be left holding the bag."[39] Understandably, but at some cost, it is easier to capture and sustain the attention of well-informed and generally well-educated readers with dramatic renderings than with systematic, more theoretical analyses.

Yet McLean and Nocera offered stories that often accurately captured a reasonably capacious picture of what led to the Great Recession. They reached back further into the past than did Morgenson and Rosner, including into the long-term leadership of Fannie Mae. More than Morgenson and Rosner, McLean and Nocera seemed to connect most of the dots. They explained the importance of crucial changes in government-mandated levels of capital reserves. They patiently told readers how academically trained quants helped make risk assessment a more powerful tool that drove the way investment banks operated. And, rather than using one person to undergird the book's arc, Nocera and McLean focused on the nation's political capital rather than its financial capital, developing a more complicated narrative that moved easily between Washington, D.C., and Wall Street and capturing the often-tense connections between people in the two centers. Their command of the intricacies of alphabetical acronyms and of the economics of securitization strikes me as impressive. That approach, as well as a more comprehensive cast of characters, may have come at the expense of readability, for theirs is a story that at times is difficult to follow.[40]

As evidence of their reach, in approaching the end of their book they turned first to "The Volcano Erupts," with the onset of the financial crisis, and then to "Rage at the Machine," as citizens expressed "populist fury" for having to foot the bill for all the damage Wall Street had done. "All people could really know for sure," they insisted, even as they focused more on those who expressed populist fury than on the homeowning victims absent from the book, "was that taxpayers' money was going to prop up the very firms whose greed and mistakes had helped cause the crisis." After all, the federal government had rescued corporations that, though they were supposed to finance national well-being, "had turned out to make gargantuan side bets that served no purpose other than lining their own pockets" while ordinary Americans paid for bailouts but received no help for what they had lost—crimes without punishments. At the very end of their book, Nocera and McLean offered the vaguely articulated and faint hope that in the future the nation would solve the problems the financial crisis revealed, including the "unfairness" of the broader impact of financial innovation, protection "against the worst of the abuses that took place during the bubble," and Wall Street's lack of "a sense of moral purpose." "Maybe, thirty-plus years after the creations of mortgage-backed securities," they hoped, "we can get it right this time."[41]

Eight years later, in 2018, McLean appeared as a talking head in the documentary *Panic: The Untold Story of the 2008 Financial Crisis*.[42] In the early scenes, which covered the previously told stories familiar to those who had read *All the Devils Are Here*, viewers could watch as she talked about the origins of the financial crisis. In relatively brief talking-head sequences, she explains how what had begun as a good idea to increase homeownership among people with low incomes ended up badly. People could take out "liar loans" by misrepresenting their incomes and having no one check for accuracy.

Yet McLean was hardly responsible for the film's focus on the crisis as an inside job featuring insiders. The filmmakers had the full cooperation of key figures, whom we watch talking on-screen, including Henry Paulson, Ben Bernanke, Timothy Geithner, and George W. Bush, as well as financial titans Jamie Dimon, Warren Buffett, and John Mack. At the start and end, we witness a "financial crisis dinner" in a Washington hotel held on September 11, 2018—appropriately enough, the anniversary of another devastating crisis—where major Wall Street and Washington figures chat over cocktails

A still from the documentary *Panic: The Untold Story of the 2008 Financial Crisis* (2018) showing protestors against "Wall Street crooks." Because the film focused on insiders as saviors of the economy, it might well have been titled *Inside Job*. Only momentarily did it suggest the impact on and responses of outsiders.

and then listen at the end when Paulson, Bernanke, and Geithner look back and justify what they did.

With both the nation's capital and Wall Street in focus, but global perspectives out of sight, the documentary concentrated on the role of heroic and not-so-heroic men (and one heroic woman, Nancy Pelosi). *Panic* made it clear, albeit briefly, what it meant for people to lose their homes to foreclosure because of dangerous levels of borrowing and lending. At several points we see suburban homes from the air and can read newspaper headlines about difficulties people face on the ground. Threaded throughout are images of unemployment, foreclosures, and homelessness, but at only one brief moment do we encounter the voices of those so adversely affected—when a woman notes that she lost her job, but the government rescued banks.

With Secretary of the Treasury Henry Paulson as the central figure, the main narrative begins with the collapse of Bear Stearns in mid-March 2008 and tells the story of how so many major figures who believed in free markets, such as Paulson and Bush, came to embrace government intervention on a massive scale. The more original section, in which neither McLean's writing nor her on-screen appearance played a role, focused on the dramatically revealing moments from September and early November 2008. Among them were a meeting in the White House on September 25; the

October 3 passage of the Troubled Asset Relief Program (TARP); a suggestion by Warren Buffett that the government infuse a massive amount of capital into banks; an October 13 meeting in Washington of Treasury officials and Wall Street bankers; and the election of Barack Obama as president on November 4.

The populist response to the collusion between elites in the nation's capital and on Wall Street is a theme made by many of the post-2008 treatments of the global financial crisis, *Panic* included. *All the Devils Are Here* referred to "populist fury" that ensued with the passage of TARP, just as Nina Easton had talked of it in a September 28, 2018, *Fortune* story under the title "Main Street Turns against Wall Street: A Populist Backlash Is Changing the Country's Political Climate."[43] Much of the last fifteen minutes of *Panic*, which had the advantage of being produced after the election of Donald Trump, explored how the events that culminated in the fall of 2008 produced highly consequential populist fury. On the left, Occupy Wall Street attacked the way financiers lined their own pockets but the powerful among elites refused to offer help to those who suffered. More sustained and prominent was what happened on the right, where insurgent members of the Tea Party, their anger stoked by Sarah Palin, railed against the ways the federal government bailed out corporations responsible for the crisis in the first place and also rewarded undeserving deadbeats. As Steve Bannon insists near the film's end, "The fuse was lit in 2008 and Donald Trump was the explosion." And, as Trump himself said at his inauguration, "American carnage stops right here and stops right now." Then, at a rally in 2017, we listen as he insists, "This is a sick system from the inside." The filmmakers also present Obama's response when he attacks "irresponsible politicians" who offer conspiracy theories "scapegoating people who don't look like you."[44]

Nonetheless, *Panic* tries its best to be reassuring by offering a heroic narrative that focuses on miscalculations about risk rather than the prevalence of corruption. To be sure, viewers witness dissenters. At one point we see Rick Santelli's infamous outburst on the floor of the Chicago Mercantile Exchange that helped lead to the creation of the Tea Party. The strongest contrasting moral perspective comes from Rahm Emmanuel, President Barack Obama's chief of staff. Invoking Old Testament values of justice and responsibility, he insists that Wall Street titans should acknowledge that they messed up rather than be allowed to keep their bonuses. There are, he notes, two rule books, one for elites and another for all others. Yet, although Geithner remarks that the crisis raised issues of fairness and morality, he stops short of offering specificity or elaboration. And, in a rare moment, Bernanke hints at systemic risk and "some underlying tensions" such as stagnant wages and limits to upward mobility. Yet the general impression, as rendered in appearances by Paulson, Bernanke, Geithner, and Bush, reassuringly avoids moral judgment or condemnation. Despite their reluctance to rely on massive interventions by the federal government, under emergency conditions they made tough decisions—or in Paulson's words, did "some pretty repugnant things"—that saved the nation from a depression. At the end, Bernanke insists "that was the best we could do." The last word comes from Geithner, who, standing before the crowd after the dinner, says, "It's really fun to see you all again, though it's really kind of painful, too." Full access, limited accountability.

Gillian Tett is a key figure in the story of multiple renditions of the financial crisis. Working for almost thirty years as a reporter for the *Financial Times*, she also authored four influential books and participated in TV shows and documentaries. Her deployment of what she learned as an anthropologist both enriched what she wrote and attracted the attention of professors of anthropology interested in using the field's analytic tools to understand the global financial system.

In 1994, after she had become a correspondent for the *Financial Times*, Tett published a scholarly article based on her Cambridge dissertation in anthropology, "'Guardians of the Faith'? Gender and Religion in an (Ex) Soviet Tajik Village," in an edited scholarly book, *Muslim Women's Choices: Religious Belief and Social Reality*. She had carried out her fieldwork for about a year beginning in July 1990—that is, just before the collapse of the USSR that started with the failed August 1991 coup.

She worked as an ethnographer in a place she called Obi-Safed, a small rural village in Tajikistan located near the Soviet-Afghan border. She explored how the "woman question" played out, in terms of the tensions between the Soviet commitment to liberate women and more traditional Islamic imperatives. Relying on a feminist perspective, she sought to counter "the prevailing perception that what women do in Islam is often less 'orthodox,' less visible and less prestigious, and thus, by inference, less vital to the religious well-being of their communities." In contrast, she argued that "during the Soviet period, rural Tajik women were a key focus for their community's religious life and Muslim identity." Village residents, even under the repressive conditions the Soviets imposed, understood that women were central to the village's "traditional values," since they were "not simply at the 'hearth' of the house, but at the very heart of the most 'traditional,' and most 'Islamic' side of village life." Although in public they might be modern Soviet citizens, in private they played key roles in the community's vitality; women, rather than men, she concluded, were "the main 'guardians' of Islam in the community." When Tett returned for brief visits in 1991 and 1992, she noticed—perhaps with a touch of feminist regret—that in a local countercoup it was men who were now "dominating the on-going revival of the village's Islamic identity."[45] As she wrote later, "The villagers maintained their Muslim identity in a supposedly atheist communist system by juggling these marriage rituals and symbols, subdividing their space and using marriage ties to define their social group."[46]

In her books, Tett wrote about economics as she relied on her formal education as an anthropologist and her on-the-job training as a journalist. Her first book was 2003's *Saving the Sun: A Wall Street Gamble to Rescue Japan from Its Trillion-Dollar Meltdown*. As a journalist for the *Financial Times*, she had arrived in Tokyo in 1997, well into Japan's Lost Decade, which had begun in late 1991 with the collapse of asset prices. She told the story of the attempt to transform one of that nation's leading financial institutions, the Long Term Credit Bank (LTCB), into an American-style corporation. She did so by focusing on three principal figures: Katsunobu Onogi, the bank's final president; Tim Collins, who orchestrated the takeover of LTCB in 1999 and then "introduced a distinctly alien Wall Street philosophy into Japan"; and Masamoto Yashiro, who headed Shinsei, the new and renamed entity, as he worked to "blend the contrasting Japanese and American approaches" to running a business.[47]

Tett claimed her approach was distinctive. She mentioned "many admirable macroeconomic analyses of Japan's problems. . . . 'top-down' discussions" that did not rely on "any sense of the cultural context and political pressures" involved, written as they were "from 30,000 feet." Instead, she remarked, she wrote "by telling the banking tale from a deliberately 'bottom-up' perspective." What she deployed, she insisted, was not macroeconomic analysis carried out by academic economists but a narrative that focused on "the *people* behind the financial woes [who] have often been forgotten" as she drew on both her own "experience in financial journalism and an earlier academic background in social anthropology."[48] Yet her approach strikes me as the opposite of what we usually consider bottom-up. The names she named were leading American and Japanese bankers and politicians; those who received little attention were unnamed and presumably male borrowers, bureaucrats, junior bankers, tabloid journalists, and gangsters while the only women mentioned were the bankers' wives and unnamed female sex workers. Thus, *Saving the Sun* was not like the ethnography she carried out and wrote about for Tajikistan, but investigative reporting that drew on more than 200 interviews and what journalists, bankers, and scholars had written.

To be sure, Tett did deploy what she learned as an anthropologist, since central to her book was the tension between Japanese and Western cultures, especially in divergent business and financial worlds. In most cases the nature of their relationships was more stated than fully explored. Yet there were times when she was more expansive. For example, she explained *nemawashi*, "the traditional Japanese process whereby a middle manager would create a consensus in an organization *before* implementing any action." In contrast stood "the dogged optimism, opportunism, self-confidence—and sheer entrepreneurial energy—that had historically made America's brand of capitalism so extraordinarily vibrant" but in the end turned out to be less successful. As she wrote of American financiers in the book's final sentence, "Like generations of foreigners before them—and to come—they are still convinced that Japan is a baffling place."[49]

In a way more directly related to what caused the Great Recession, Tett also transformed and expanded upon what she had learned from writing nine-hundred-word articles for the *Financial Times* about the crisis that caused the Great Recession into a timely, award-winning and best-selling book: *Fool's Gold: How the Bold Dream of a Small Tribe at J. P. Morgan Was Corrupted by Wall Street Greed and Unleashed a Catastrophe* (2009). Although at one point she drew implicitly on the ethnographic work she had carried out several years earlier in the South of France, the book drew principally on written documents and extensive interviews with bankers, especially those at J. P. Morgan Chase, all the way to CEO Jamie Dimon at the top (to whom the dust jacket said she had "exclusive access"), as well as with representatives from rating agencies such as Moody's, and with government officials such as Timothy Geithner, head of the New York Federal Reserve Bank.

In important ways, what Tett accomplished was not very different from what McLean and Nocera had achieved in 2010 with *All the Devils Are Here* and Morgenson and Rosner in *Reckless Endangerment* a year later. In a microhistory with macroconsequences, she explored how securitization eventually threatened to bring down the global economy. Combining well-informed financial analysis, a focus on key players, and dramatic narratives, Tett told the story of the development of derivatives squared and cubed on a grand scale that their creators hoped (incorrectly, it turned out) would provide successful hedges against risk. Like her book-writing peers, she made the arcane world of financial derivatives understandable by telling stories driven by depictions of colorful and powerful characters who inhabited the upper reaches of the financial world. To be sure, there were important differences. Even though the focus was on what the title announced as the "Small Tribe at J. P. Morgan," her perspective was more global than that of others, principally because she focused not only on Manhattan but also on events in the City of London, Tokyo, and at the offices of the European Central Bank. Yet, if McLean, Nocera, Rosner, and Morgenson connected what happened on Wall Street and in Washington, D.C., Tett paid relatively little attention what was going on in the nation's capital.

While the book's subtitle stressed how a "Small Tribe at J. P. Morgan Was Corrupted by Wall Street Greed and Unleashed a Catastrophe," in the preface Tett was both more tentatively cautious and more wide ranging. "The story of the great credit boom and bust," she noted, "is not a saga that can be neatly blamed on a few greedy or evil individuals." Rather, it was one of "how an entire financial *system* went wrong" due to "flawed incentives" that governed banks and rating agencies as well as regulation whose structures were "warped" and oversight lacking. Then she seemed to step back, as she emphasized "human foibles" and how "greedy bankers—and perhaps a few mad, or evil, ones, . . . were not acting out of deliberately bad motives." Indeed, she noted, they developed derivatives "in the hope that they would be *good* for the financial system," and some of them "should be seen as potentially valuable for twenty-first-century finance."[50] The corruption and greed of evil individuals who intended no harm, or an entire system based on financial instruments that caused a catastrophe but remained useful?

In Tett's rendition, what characterized the financial world were testosterone-driven men, even though she also identified some powerful women. "Surprisingly for an account of the masculine world of finance," remarked Ruth Sunderland in a review of the book in the *Guardian*, it was full of women: not only Tett herself, "the most prescient British financial journalist on the credit crunch," but also Blythe Masters, "a blonde, porcelain-faced Tilda Swinton lookalike who has the dubious distinction of having devised the credit default swap," and Terri Duhon, "a Harley-Davidson riding maths whiz from rural Louisiana whose talent for numbers catapulted her into the rarefied world of finance," who, it should be said, graduated from MIT.[51] Masters was unusual as a woman who not only played a major role in developing complicated financial instruments but also gave birth to a child while working at Morgan, as Tett had done while working at the *Financial Times*. "Nobody ever asks *men* about their families or their decision to have children!" Tett reported Masters saying. "Why should anyone care about mine?" After all, like Tett, who combined a high-powered career with motherhood, Masters "knew only too well, though, that she would need to demonstrate extraordinary devotion to her job if she were to be taken seriously." Yet in other ways Masters was someone many would consider more villainous than heroic. After all, she had played a key role in mastering the development of credit default swaps and then persuading federal regulators to pay less attention to them than they should have. Indeed, in late 2008, Masters referred to herself—with some regret—as "the woman who built financial weapons of mass destruction."[52]

However, if *Fool's Gold* was a book written by a woman who placed other women in central positions in a world that sometimes resembled *Animal House*, in Tett's hands it was also a book informed by her education as an anthropologist.[53] Usually what she offered was implicit, especially when she described tribes, each with their own customs and rituals. On relatively rare occasions she was more explicit. "Like priests in the medieval church," she noted, "ratings agency representatives spoke the equivalent of financial Latin, which few in their investor congregation actually understood. Nevertheless, the congregation was comforted by the fact that the priests appeared able to confer guidance and blessings." Moreover, even when she used her ethnographic skills to do investigative reporting for the *Financial Times*, as when, in 2005, she attended a conference of investment bankers in Nice, in the book she relied on her authoritative, impersonal third-person voice.[54]

However, in a three-page section at the very end of *Fool's Gold*, Tett did step back. She wrote about the benefits of her earlier training as an anthropologist, a perspective worthy of a hippie, "as one banker caustically observed." In doing so, she deployed several concepts. To begin with, she emphasized that anthropologists could muster "a sense of skepticism about official rhetoric" and "mainstream ideologies" that elites mobilized to "maintain power structures" by promoting "social 'silences.'" In turn this undermined a "holistic analysis," which prevented those in the world of finance from having an "interest in wider social matters" that "cuts to the very heart of what has gone wrong." Such a comprehensive and interrelated approach would connect "different parts of a social structure," whether in the case of ritual in Tajikistan or in the world of high finance. "To our collective cost," she insisted, "bankers, politicians, investors, and journalists have all failed to employ truly holistic thought." Central to such a failure, she continued, was the third concept she deployed—"a 'silo' mentality" that prevented people from understanding relationships within and between key business and governmental institutions. "Most pernicious of all," she asserted, "financiers have come to regard banking as a silo in its own right, detached from the rest of society."[55]

Though in the main portion of her book she had ignored those who inhabited "the rest of society," she now made a brief reference to the

"What can we believe in? There's nothing we can trust anymore," remarks Gillian Tett, the anthropologist turned journalist, in an interview for *Inside Job* (2010).

"millions of ordinary families, who never knew that CDOs existed" but had now "suffered shattering financial blows." Their understandable anger, and hers, reflected an awareness of a "damning indictment of how twenty-first-century Western society works"—one that strikes me at odds with what I see as equivocation in her preface. "A wider rethinking of the culture of finance," a restoration of "sanity to banking," and "a more *holistic* vision of finance" would bring "a return to the seemingly dull virtues of prudence, moderation, balance, and common sense." She called for this even as she acknowledged the importance of unspecified "tangible macroeconomic issues." Yet Tett fell far short of recognizing the benefits of a fuller application of anthropology that could have revealed the nature of power relationships undergirding the devastating impact of what inhabitants of Wall Street (and their allies in government) did and failed to do. After all, the impact of finance on what she called "our fragile, interconnected world" extended far beyond the elite quarters her book explored.[56]

Tett's articles and book led to her making several appearances as a talking head in *Inside Job*, which won the Academy Award for the best documentary of 2010.[57] The movie offered a scathing picture of the financial wrongdoing that led to the Great Recession and left in its wake jobs lost, homes foreclosed, and lives destroyed. To drive home its conclusions, it focused on the interrelated processes of deregulation and securitization. Believing that what they did made the economy more efficient and less risky, as well as their companies more profitable, financiers and their supporters in universities and politics were nonetheless sacrificing long-term economic well-being for short-term gains, in the form of profits, year-end bonuses, consulting fees, and campaign contributions.

If the truly inside job of *Panic* relied on a morally evasive narrative where insiders did their jobs heroically under challenging circumstances, *Inside Job* offered critically persuasive tales of insiders acting corruptly. If the books by journalists depended on access to major figures and *Panic* on prominently extensive interviews with them, Paulson refused to be interviewed for *Inside Job*, as did Larry Summers, Timothy Geithner, and representatives from the rating agencies. More critical than other films and the books under discussion, this documentary was also more global—beginning as it did with a long sequence on the tragic impact of financialization on Iceland and then later making reference to its impact around the world. It offered an accessible and comprehensive analysis of the origins and outcomes of the global financial crisis. It dramatized the consequences of deregulation and the "securitization food chain" of the global economy driven by investment bankers, with the help of politicians of both parties and professors of economics.

Almost all of the evildoers were men, including academics Glenn Hubbard, Frederic Mishkin, and Martin Feldstein, as well as Obama, whom the film criticizes for relying on the advice of Summers and Goldman Sachs bankers. To be sure, there were also men who were either heroic or prescient, or both: among them billionaire George Soros, New York State attorney general Eliot Spitzer, social justice lawyer Robert Gnaizda, economist Nouriel Roubini, International Monetary Fund economist Raghuram Rajan, Wall Street trader turned truth teller Satyajit Das, and authors such as Robert Morris. Except for Laura Tyson, an economist who had chaired the president's Council of Economic Advisers under Clinton and served as the director of the National Economic Council under George W. Bush, there were no women cast in significant negative roles, but several made important on-screen appearances to bolster the filmmakers' assertions: central banker Christine Lagarde, who warned her American counterparts of the dangers ahead; Wall Street madam Kristin Davis, who provided financiers with prostitutes; and Brooksley Born, who unsuccessfully lobbied for federal oversight of derivatives.[58]

The documentary paid abundant attention to the impact of the crisis on ordinary people. It did so by emphasizing the growth in inequality and, especially, by focusing on interviews with migrant workers in China, a Spanish-speaking woman in California whose family had been defrauded by predatory lending, and an unemployed truck driver living in a tent city in Florida who was struggling to find employment as a construction worker. At another moment, the film suggested that the global financial crisis was one of a series of lesser crises, going back at least to the 1970s, that stemmed

Documentaries used pictures such as these to illustrate the housing crisis, in this case in the Miami, Florida, area for *Inside Job*.

from a combination of excessive deregulation, faulty oversight in the public realm, and unbounded greed and underestimation of risk in the financial sector. It contrasted the average pension of $18,700 of state employees in Mississippi devastated by investments in derivatives with the $31 million that Paulson earned in one year. More broadly, the film highlighted increasing inequality as it emphasized the adverse impact on American workers of jobs moved overseas; the escalating costs of higher education, which limited the possibilities of social mobility; and the ways American families coped by working harder and taking on more debt to pay for homes, health care, education, cars, and daily expenses. Unlike them, narrator Matt Damon observed, "men who destroyed their own companies and plunged the world into crisis walked away from the wreckage with their fortunes intact." Contrast this with remarks by Countrywide Financial's head Angelo Mozilo: "If they lose, we lose," he insisted. However, the film noted that Mozilo made almost $500 million in these years, much of it from dumping his company's stock before it collapsed. "The financial industry turned its back on society, corrupted our political system and plunged the world economy into crisis," we hear, even as most of the men who caused all this remained in power.

What was especially striking was the gendered contrast *Inside Job* offered up of two journalists for financial publications. On the one hand, the documentary prominently featured Allan Sloan of *Fortune*.[59] The press kit prepared for the film described him as "the journalist who wrote for *Fortune* magazine about the market, the crisis, and the wrongdoing that led to the financial crisis." The documentary showed him talking about his investigative reporting, accompanied by an on-screen picture of "House of Junk," his 2007 prize-winning article. The press kit described Tett as "the award-winning journalist at the *Financial Times* [and] the author of *Fool's Gold*, which traced the development of the CDO market and its role in the financial crisis." On-screen, Tett made a handful of brief appearances in which she described the crash retrospectively, her comments usually more observational than judgmental. Sloan's 2007 article had focused primarily on the riskiness of subprime mortgages for borrowers, lenders, and investors. However, when the movie turned its attention to Tett, there was no mention of her transformative anthropological perspectives or the articles she had written for the *Financial Times* that, early on and with stylistic wit, described key aspects of securitization and offered timely warnings about risk to the shaky architecture of the global financial system.[60]

For someone like me who naively wants to believe in progress, the trajectory from McLean's prominence in *Enron* to Tett's sidelining in *Inside Job* and then to Whitney's absence from *The Big Short* is not encouraging. It is as if the films replicate the gendered power relationships in the world of finance itself—what one scholar in a different context described as "a mainly masculine focus, with women largely sidelined as voices of reason."[61] Or, as the film scholar April Miller noted in a different context in a comment that may well apply to the work of McLean, Tett, and Whitney, it is possible to imagine "a feminist vision of the financial industry, linking the fallout from the subprime mortgage crisis to greedy men and their testosterone-laden pronouncements, and presenting women as more thoughtful and sympathetic arbiters of finance."[62]

In the first of her two more ambitious and intriguing books, *The Silo Effect: The Peril of Expertise and the Promise of Breaking Down Barriers* (2015), Tett successfully integrated her skills as an anthropologist and financial reporter. Expanding well beyond what she had learned about the danger of worlds divided into tribes and living in silos when she reported on the Morgan Mafia, she now explored how societies developed epistemological and organizational boundaries that separated people from one another—usually in seemingly unexamined, natural, and unselfconscious ways. She examined the "peril" referred to in the book's title by focusing on Sony, the Swiss bank UBS, and economists at central banks in Great Britain and the United States. On the other hand, she reported on the "promise" of the "silo busters" at the Chicago Police Department, Facebook, the Cleveland Clinic, and the hedge fund BlueMountain Capital Management.

After introducing the book, Tett turned to eminent French cultural analyst Pierre Bourdieu. She told the story of his witnessing a dance in 1959 as an "insider-outsider" in a valley in southwest France, where he had grown up—not unlike, by implication, how she witnessed the global financial crisis as both an insider and an outsider. Bourdieu had noticed the differences between marriageable men who were dancing and unmarriageable men silently watching from the sidelines. What this division reflected were the consequences of a fundamental economic change: one group that had embraced modern urban living and another that was suffering not only social marginalization at the dance but also the economic and cultural consequences of an endangered agricultural way of life. The task of the anthropologist, Tett stated, drawing on Bourdieu's work, was to understand both groups, their cultures, and the relationships between them. Over the course of his career, during which he studied the cultures of Algeria, France, and the United States, Bourdieu, Tett observed, "tried to turn his analytical lens back and forth from insider to outsider, seeking to uncover patterns that people inside could not always see." In the process he focused especially on "the patterns of thought and classifications systems" that helped "to reproduce the status of the elite." At the same time, these patterns enabled others to challenge the status quo dominated by elites by imagining "a different way of organizing our world—particularly if they—like Bourdieu—have become an insider-outsider by jumping across boundaries."[63]

In earlier writings, Tett had already made clear how Bourdieu's writing helped explain the financial crisis. She acknowledged the accuracy of the commonly accepted explanations for the crisis, not only the failures of rating agencies, government regulation, and the fervid belief in free efficient markets, but also the avarice and ambition of bankers. However, to these she added the business media's failure to focus on the explosive growth of derivatives, which left financiers "able to operate free from external scrutiny in a manner that fueled the bubble" in ways "that suited the banking industry extremely well."[64] The cognitive and structural power of silos "made it hard for both insiders and outsiders alike to take a holistic vision of how credit was developing"—the relationship between dancers and nondancers. Bourdieu's notion of social silences made it possible to understand "that the operations of complex credit were deemed too dull, irrelevant or technical to attract interest from outsiders, such as journalists or politicians." This enabled elites to remain in power "not simply by controlling the means of production (i.e. wealth), but by shaping the discourse (or the cognitive map that a society uses to describe the world around it)." As Bourdieu had written, she said, "the most successful ideological effects are those which have no need of words, but ask no more than a complicitous silence." Combined, these silos and social silences, Tett wrote, "made it hard to 'join up the dots' about the dangers in the credit world, until it was too late."[65]

As what she called a cultural "anthropologist-cum-journalist," Tett wrote in *The Silo Effect* that she had learned to understand not only remote places like Tajikistan but also highly developed societies. What people considered natural, she explained, was actually historical and contingent. In a world both more highly integrated and exceptionally fragmented, anthropologists could help people—inside and outside the silos they inhabited—understand the importance of systems of classification and order based on customs, rituals, traditions, conventions, and rules. As was true in *Fool's Gold*, as an anthropologist she could not stop "asking questions about how different elements of a society interact, looking at the gap between rhetoric and reality, noting the concealed functions of rituals and symbols, and hunting our social silences."[66]

In a world she reported on as dominated by men, Tett also focused at a few moments on women who were closer to the center than the periphery—dancers rather than nondancers. She talked of how, on November 4, 2008, a few short weeks after the collapse of Lehman Brothers and AIG, Queen Elizabeth II broke protocol and asked an embarrassing question. Speaking at an event at London School of Economics that was supposed to celebrate the wisdom of academics, she wondered aloud, "Why did nobody see the crisis coming?" Then there was Jocelyn Goldfein at Facebook, who took a leadership role in creating a corporate culture that broke down barriers between silos. Playing an even more prominent but nonetheless secondary role was Kara Medoff Barnett. As a student at Harvard Business School, she asked Toby Cosgrove, a doctor visiting from the Cleveland Clinic, a question that later helped inspire him to transform the institution he headed: "Dr. Cosgrove, do you teach empathy at Cleveland Clinic?"[67]

However, as with the authors of *All the Devils Are Here* and *Reckless Endangerment*, and even as was true of her own work in *Fool's Gold*, there were limits to how capaciously Tett understood the modern equivalents of dancers and nondancers. She did jump across some boundaries that divided the worlds of finance and anthropology, but not others. "Like the villagers in Bourdieu's dancehall," she had written, unintentionally reflecting how she usually limited her work by focusing principally on the dancers, "economists were so busy watching the 'dancers' (or the pieces of the economic picture that everyone was expected to watch), that they ignored the 'nondancers' (or the parts of the picture shrouded in social silence)."[68] Also in *The Silo Effect*, she mentioned "a bottom-up view of life" in which anthropologists "get out of their offices and experience life on the ground, trying to understand micro-level patterns to make sense of the macro picture." She admired those who "try to see how all the different pieces of a social group or system interconnect," who "try to look at the totality of what they see" and thus "end up examining the parts of life that people do not want to talk about, because they are considered taboo, dull, or boring."[69] Much as I admire what Tett accomplished, I also need to note that even though she mentioned the importance of taking a bottom-up view, like many others under consideration here she failed to focus more than minimally and sometimes not at all on the Americans and others around the world whose lives were so tragically affected by elites on Wall Street and in the nation's capital—even though she seemed to know better than to narrow her focus.

The second of Tett's expansive books was *Anthro-Vision: A New Way to See in Business and Life* (2021). As she had done in *The Silo Effect*, here she showed how useful it was to deploy anthropology to understand a wide range of situations—from the way major corporations responded to globalization to the failure of normally astute political observers to understand Donald J. Trump's rise to power—and in between she returned to her coverage of the financial crisis.[70] She focused on three approaches offered by the field in which she had trained. First was how participant observation helped make the seemingly strange familiar, how "in an era of global contagion, we urgently need to cultivate a mindset of empathy for strangers and value diversity." Next was the flipside: by understanding the apparently strange we actually can better comprehend ourselves. Finally, there was listening out for social silences, what was sitting there before but that we often too easily overlooked, "to see blind spots in others and ourselves."[71] In short, *Anthro-Vision* involved avoiding tunnel vision and unquestioned assumptions and instead benefiting from childlike wonderment, curiosity, and the maneuvering between top-down and bottom-up perspectives.

If we move beyond the films and books involving Bethany McLean, Gretchen Morgenson, Gillian Tett, and Meredith Whitney, we can see a wider range of approaches and ideologies that help us understand key issues. At one end stands Andrew Ross Sorkin's *Too Big to Fail: Inside the Battle to Save Wall Street* (2009). Written by the *New York Times* reporter who focused on mergers and acquisitions, it was the consummate book of insider knowledge based on robust access. Like many other renditions, this was a narrative driven by a focus on key figures and events played out along the Wall Street–Washington axis. Compared with other books or documentaries, it barely referenced events outside the United States, heroic women, or the adverse effects of the crisis on ordinary people. At the beginning, Sorkin noted that his book was "the product of more than five hundred hours of interviews with more than two hundred individuals who participated directly in the events surrounding the financial crisis." Almost 550 pages later, he seemed to suspend judgment. Referring to "Paulson, Geithner, Bernanke, and the dozens of public- and private-sector figures who populate this book," the best he could muster in the very last sentence was "It will be left to history to judge how they fared in their own time."[72] Unlike most films and books on the subject, Sorkin's suspended moral judgments, left implicit or ambiguous whether there were evildoers, and offered no suggestions as to whether or how the problems the crisis revealed were solvable in the future.

There was no such suspension of judgment, moral ambiguity, or absence of a road forward in Michael Moore's *Capitalism: A Love Story* (2009).[73] With wit and passion, he assailed the way capitalism had triumphed over democracy. With a more ample historical sense than almost all others, he connected the Great Depression and the Great Recession. The parallels were clear: between the promise of a Second Bill of Rights FDR articulated in 1944 and what Obama promised during the 2008 campaign; in his hometown of Flint, Michigan, between the 1936 sit-down strike and his father's employment at General Motors for thirty-three years, on the one hand, to standing in 2009 with his dad on the edge of the vacant property where that factory once stood, on the other. In between these two eras were the 1950s, when men with powerful megaphones celebrated free enterprise. Yet Moore also pictured the immediate postwar period as a time when families could rely on a male breadwinner while living in a home they actually owned. Then, in the late 1970s, he insisted, paradise began to turn into purgatory—characterized by competition from abroad, deregulation, union busting, factory closings, and a capitalist conspiracy to stoke both hopes and fears. The results were high levels of personal debt, out-of-reach costs for medical care and higher education, mass incarceration, the privatization of public institutions, a hollowing out of the middle class, and a yawning gap between the very rich and everyone else. Eventually financialization took hold, teaching people how to treat their homes as cash cows and developing derivatives, which neither a vice president from Lehman Brothers nor a Harvard economist seemed able to explain on-screen.

Denied access to Paulson and to the CEO of General Motors, Moore stood outside Wall Street buildings and used a bullhorn to announce a citizen's arrest of Wall Street titans. In insistent and powerful contrast to the familiar narrative of wrongdoing in high places on which most depictions focused, Moore concentrated on the human costs of fraud, greed, and corruption, especially how evictions and foreclosures ripped people from their homes, often ones where they had lived for decades. At one point, we see Condo Vultures, a firm that searches databases for foreclosed properties, swooping

In this still from *Capitalism: A Love Story* (2009), documentary filmmaker Michael Moore stands in front of a Wall Street building, its entry guarded by three men. "We're going to get the money back for the American people," he says. "I've got more bags. The ten billion probably won't fit in here."

in and buying up homes and apartments. Throughout the film bankers relied on police to create what Karl Marx might have called a reserve army of unemployed homeless people. If bankers and government officials, both locally and nationally, served as the villains, among the film's many heroes several stood out. Especially notable, given how other texts focus not at all on religious leaders, were Roman Catholic priests from Flint who insisted that capitalism was evil and that the rich had hijacked Christ. Also heroic were noble workers and community activists who resisted corporate power from below by taking over abandoned factories and restoring people to the homes ripped away from them. Although he paid little attention to Tea Party populism, Moore lavished praise on its left-wing counterparts. In the end, he insisted, the long history since the 1930s reveals a fierce battle between capitalism and democracy, or we might say between 1950s democratic capitalism and early twenty-first-century democratic socialism. Which side he was on remains abundantly clear.

All these books and films, produced soon after the heights or depths of the global financial crisis, offer important if sometimes dubious treatments of what had happened. In various combinations they laid the blame at the feet of low interest rates and the resulting bubble in housing prices; decades of deregulation; dangerous incentives at banks and rating and governmental agencies; complex new financial instruments, derivatives especially, that exacerbated risk rather than reducing it; and the toxic combination of lenders driven by greed and borrowers motivated by aspirations they could ill afford to pay for. There was more than enough blame to go around, combining as they did corruption and poor judgment about risk. Some authors and directors were better than others at offering clear and convincing moral evaluations. To varying extents, they all solved the representational challenge of explaining the almost incomprehensible comprehensibly. However, rare was the book or film that probed more deeply in order to explain the historical and systemic forces that undergirded the crisis—the decades-long power of globalization, technological transformation, and dramatically growing inequalities of wealth and income that hollowed out the middle class and drove those below into ever more precarious situations. In the hands of skilled writers and directors, narratives driven by interweaving people and events can be powerful. Yet a focus on Moore's film underscores that if narrative nonfiction featuring elite movers and shakers makes it possible to see what happened, in order to explain why usually required going deeper into systematic issues and longer into history.[74]

Not long before I sent the manuscript of this book off to the University of North Carolina Press, I discovered the rigorous, carefully argued, and data-driven work of a group of well-respected economists. Their scholarship counters the narratives and explanations that journalists and documentary filmmakers offer and that I report on in this and the previous chapter. Among other sources, they drew on the behavioral economics of Daniel Kahneman and Amos Tversky; the earlier work by the economic historian Charles P. Kindleberger; and the emphasis of Robert J. Shiller on narratives that go viral, including his own focus on irrational exuberance. They stood in opposition to widely accepted explanations that blamed highly placed people and institutions for the global financial crisis. The "insider-outsider interpretation of the crisis has inspired an Academy Award–winning documentary, appropriately titled *Inside Job*," noted Christopher L. Foote, Kristopher S. Gerardi, and Paul S. Willen—and I hasten to add, as they surely would, this outlook also shaped the work of so many other observers.[75]

As early as 2008, these three economists and others noted that the inside job approach emphasized how the rise in housing prices relied on the spread of subprime loans that promised to extend homeownership to people whom the mortgage market had not previously or extensively reached. Rather, they insisted, their explanation of the bubble reversed cause and effect by showing, instead of looser credit leading to higher prices for homes, the expectation that housing prices would increase caused looser credit. Moreover, they stressed that because wealthier people took out larger mortgages, it was they and not the previously underserved who accounted for most of the dollar value of mortgage indebtedness. They concentrated more on the bubble than its bursting. They did not blame, as did so many journalists and filmmakers, the way financial institutions deceived naive or ill-informed investors and borrowers, the proliferation of newfangled financial instruments, or the events that took place on Wall Street and in the nation's capital. Rather, they focused on intensified optimism concerning the expectations about the future of housing prices shared by borrowers and major banks. Both parties, they insist, "made decisions that were rational and logical given their ex post overly optimistic beliefs about housing prices."[76] Yet this historian has to wonder what would it mean to shift from economic explanations of robust expectations to the harder-to-pin-down cultural, social, and political and socioeconomic ones. This might involve an exploration of the roles played by the stoking of expectations by traditional media such as HGTV shows; by the way social media made it possible for dreams to circulate so virally; and by major shifts in technology, globalization, labor markets, and the increasingly unequal distribution of wealth and income.

Reaching back to Ida Tarbell's *The History of the Standard Oil Company* (1904), we see that as investigative journalists women have often done pathbreaking reporting holding the rich and powerful accountable for their misdeeds. Before she emerged as a major feminist author, Susan Faludi won a Pulitzer Price for her 1990 "The Reckoning: Safeway LBO Yields Vast Profits but Exacts a Heavy Human Toll," which Dean Starkman called "perhaps the high-water mark of the business investigation into Wall Street."[77] In the next decade McLean, Morgenson, Tett, and Whitney produced other high-water marks. These six women shared much in common, aside from their skills as researchers and writers. Their collegiate education was in the liberal arts rather than business. As women, they were outsiders, nondancers who could stand aside skeptically from the macho worlds they described. Often more implicitly than explicitly, they resembled how the anthropologist Melissa Fisher in *Wall Street Women* (2012) characterizes the first generation of women who entered the financial world in the 1960s and 1970s, when they began working in investment banks. They "articulated," she notes, "a divide between masculine, greedy, risk-taking actors and behaviors, probably leading to the crisis, and a more feminine, conservative, long-term approach to financial practice that could possibly help the economy or could fix it."[78]

Then there is the issue of how these books and films handled the relationship between access and accountability, with each of them occupying a different point on the spectrum from one to another and both of them profoundly shaped by structural forces, especially the availability of funding. With at-the-moment reporting in print media, the distinctions and tensions between the two were clear. Access reporting was immediate, relied on elite sources, and addressed investors. In contrast, its opposite was long term, drew on dissidents, and treated readers as citizens.[79] With the retrospective books and films we see a range of relationships between the two approaches. At one end was Sorkin's book, based on abundant access and offering few judgments about who was accountable. Along with Morgenson and McLean, at the other end was Moore, whose filmmaking, denied access, was powerfully accountable. If those involved in the production of *Inside Job* were denied access and felt freer to hold insiders accountable, the ample access that their counterparts who produced *Panic* had meant that they treated those in power in Washington and Manhattan as heroically responsible figures who did the best job they could. Many were those who created narratives that revealed that access and accountability could go hand in hand. While the book and movie *The Big Short* confirmed the benefit of a connection between access to outsider dissidents and critical accountability, Tett's *Fool's Gold* revealed that an exceptionally skilled reporter/writer could rely on access to drive stories that insisted on responsibility. A clearer division between access and accountability appeared in the respective roles of Jim Cramer of CNBC and Jon Stewart on Comedy Central.

The Cramer/Stewart exchange also reminds us of the tension in treatments of the global financial crisis between perpetrators and victims, those on high and those below. Stewart trenchantly captured both ends when he talked of men "on a Sherman's March" who were burning "the fucking house down." For most others, the focus was on either the oppressors or the oppressed. Again, at one extreme stood Sorkin, who trolled the halls of Wall Street but never interviewed those who were victims of dangerous financing that led to foreclosures or evictions. The opposite was Moore, whose *Capitalism: A Love Story* gave the powerful little space except as villains but instead placed at the very center of his film the struggles of workers and homeowners to live decent lives against great odds. In between, despite visits to homeless encampments or devastated neighborhoods, as well as clips of unemployment lines and boarded-up houses, many treatments in books and on film did not fully connect the high and low.

CHAPTER 5

LOOKING UP AND DOWN

ANTHROPOLOGY, HORROR FILMS,
AND THE FINANCIAL CRISIS

The 1979 movie *Kramer vs. Kramer* depicted husband and wife engaged in a bitter struggle over custody of their son. Thirty years later, Cramer vs. Stewart highlighted the ideological and social dimensions of a fight over the causes and consequences of the Great Recession, with Stewart connecting the perpetrators and victims. While Cramer vs. Stewart involved two guys arguing, the work of journalists, anthropologists, and filmmakers reveals more nuanced gender relationships. Most book authors and movie directors did not adequately focus on both ends of the socioeconomic spectrum: those engaged in the world of high finance, and the victims of what they and their political allies had wrought. A more complicated picture emerges if we turn our attention to the work of anthropologists—especially Melissa Fisher, Karen Ho, Noelle Stout, and Gillian Tett—as well as to three horror films, *Get Out* (2017), *Home* (2016), and *Parasite* (2019). As is true of what journalists wrote in short articles and long books and what documentary filmmakers created on-screen, what anthropologists and directors of horror films presented was richly suggestive and sometimes incomplete. To be sure, all of these texts emerged at different times and under different circumstances. Yet juxtaposing them enriches what we can learn from such varied takes on housing during the Great Recession.

To begin this story, we can usefully return to the work of Gillian Tett. Her relationship to the worlds academic anthropologists inhabited was that of an insider/outsider—or, as Pierre Bourdieu would have put it, a dancer and a nondancer. In *The Silo Effect*, Tett mentioned that she "became frustrated with what I saw of the world of academic anthropology," given how "university departments of anthropology can be surprisingly introverted and detached from the world . . . partly because the discipline tends to attract people who are better at listening and observing than thrusting themselves into the limelight. Its adherents also tend to be antiestablishment, and wary of dealing with the institutions of power."[1] This detachment may have been true of Cambridge, England, when Tett studied there in the late 1980s. Yet Erving Goffman's *Asylums: Essays on the Social Situation of Mental Patients and Other Inmates* (1961), Elliot Liebow's *Tally Corner: A Study of Negro Streetcorner Men* (1967), and the work of generations of scholars trained as anthropologists in the last half century underscore how engaged in the world so many of them were. Writing in an article titled "Anthropology and 1968"—which, coincidentally, was the year after Tett's birth—two Norwegian anthropologists noted "the intensity and politicization of anthropological engagements at the time" that transformed the field in ways that hardly left practitioners detached, as Tett had claimed.[2] Indeed, as we shall soon see, in the early twenty-first century American anthropologists were not "introverted and detached from the world," nor were they "wary of dealing with the institutions of power."

On several occasions, Tett addressed the issue of the relationships between her training as an anthropologist and her work as a journalist.[3] One revealing example occurred in mid-November 2009 when she gave a talk, "Silence and Silos: The Problems of Fractured Thought in Finance," at the annual meeting of the American Anthropological Association (AAA). Well prepared but speaking without reading from a paper or even, apparently, from notes, she talked compellingly about what it meant to deploy in her final reporting what she learned as an anthropologist. She pictured herself, at least early in her career, as someone caught between two worlds: on the one hand, feeling "a bit of an impostor" among anthropologists, but on the other, hiding her professional training because bankers "did not like touchy-feely cultural studies." Though she continued to feel like an amateur, when the financial crisis hit people in the world of finance came to respect and listen to her more than they had done before. She also mentioned the compromises she had to make as an author, especially developing a narrative peopled with colorful figures and keeping theory implicit and under wraps. Although she acknowledged that her work resembled that of a reporter more than an ethnographer, she nonetheless made clear how central to her journalism were key approaches of the field in which she earned her doctorate—analyzing rituals, underscoring the danger of silos and social silences, understanding a situation holistically, looking at the world from the bottom up, paying attention to power structures, and distinguishing between the seen and unseen. She criticized bankers who lived in silos and "almost never actually encountered a real live subprime borrower in the flesh." So it should come as no surprise that she called on those in her audience to break out of their "geeky" world, to "bust out of their own little" silos.

During the Q and A period, a woman from the audience asked about gender: after all, Tett was a woman in a man's world, a widow raising two children even while holding an exacting full-time job at the *Financial Times*. She replied that people constantly inquired about the role of gender in her life and career, but she did not want to reduce her situation to the impact of biology—an odd statement coming from a cultural anthropologist. She nonetheless said that women had to learn how to navigate structures, a process for which anthropology, with its emphasis on the role of an outsider, was vitally useful. She deflected attention from gender by insisting that it was part of a larger issue of diversity. She continued by noting that she had spent her whole life being "weird," and that being a pregnant woman in the financial world gave her the status of an insider/outsider. Acknowledging how much the field had changed, she observed that earlier, when she left the world of academic anthropology, she was frustrated with how "abstract" it was, and she feared committing "intellectual suicide." Yet when Louise Lamphere, formerly president of the AAA and herself famously subjected to discrimination early in her career, told Tett what a wonderful ethnographer and writer she was, Tett demurred, saying she was "embarrassed" to call either of her first two books an ethnography.[4]

Tett's training as an anthropologist, her deployment of its explanatory concepts, and her prominence in print and on screen continued to catch the attention of academic anthropologists. In 2011, writing in the house organ of the Society for Applied Anthropology, Brian McKenna, a professor at the University of Michigan–Dearborn, explored the relationships between the work of Tett as an anthropologist turned journalist and that of many academics who used ethnography to study the worlds of finance. He described her as "on the move," now a "movie star" because of her "significant role" in the film *Inside Job*, which he called "the counter-curriculum to neoliberal deceptions." Now heading the American operations of the *Financial Times*, and "one of the most powerful women in the media," she was, he reported, "prepared to take the country by storm." Referring to Tett's visit to Goldman Sachs followed by dinner with George Soros; Gerry Corrigan, a former head of the New York Fed and currently a partner at Goldman Sachs; and Andy Salmon, a one-time Commandant General of the British Royal Marines, McKenna insisted that she "hobnobs with the ruling class and reports on their activities as a kind of cultural pedagogue or public anthropologist." He seemed to take offense at Tett's assertion that, with her PhD in hand, she did not aspire to become a professor because she felt academic anthropologists were committing "intellectual suicide." He noted that in her talk at the AAA she mentioned a "rude email" from an academic anthropologist who told her, in McKenna's words, to "Stop Calling herself an Anthropologist."[5]

Yet he honored "Tett's greatest anthropological achievement." That came when studying the J. P. Morgan tribe, as "she sleuthed how a group of Gordon Gekko-type hot-shots brought capitalism to its knees." He asserted that Tett had "much to teach applied anthropologists," with *Fool's Gold* as "exhibit number one." As "an anthropologist immersed in high stakes power politics," she offered "a powerful antidote to the tired rituals of a cloistered academic in the knowledge factory." She did so by highlighting the limits to a broad awareness due to what she called "incredibly tribal" people living in separated silos and keeping specialized information to themselves, so much so that only a few people were in a position to develop a comprehensive understanding. Whatever reservations he had about her and her work, McKenna hailed Tett as someone whose articles were "fieldnotes from the front, read by scholars of all orientations, from Left to Right." Nonetheless, he criticized her for using the word "capitalism" in *Fool's Gold* only once and for never mentioning neoliberalism, Karl Marx, or the relevant work of anthropologists such as the Marxist David Harvey. To have done so would have "offered a different perspective on the causes and cures of the Meltdown than Tett."[6]

McKenna (or the headline writer for his essay) put the word "predicted" in the title in quotation marks when describing what Tett had written about the financial crisis. It is true that some radical social scientists had for a long time offered analyses that made it possible to explain, if not precisely predict, cataclysmic financial crashes. Moreover, what academic anthropologists did do, often earlier and sometime in more sophisticated ways than Tett, was use ethnographic studies to explore the culture of finance capitalism.

Karen Ho's work was among that which Tett mentioned when she gave her talk at the meeting of the AAA. Indeed, she had reviewed Ho's book *Liquidated: An Ethnography of Wall Street* in the *Financial Times* when it appeared a year earlier. Ho, Tett remarked, "had picked an excellent time to publish her fascinating new study," with her "patient ethnographic analysis" producing "a fascinating portrait that will be refreshingly novel to most bankers." To be sure, Tett felt that, given how she found some of Ho's language "off-puttingly academic," some bankers might call Ho's approach "hippy." However, she insisted that if more of them "had been willing to analyse their sector's cultural foibles, the financial world might not be quite in the mess it is today." Consequently, she paid Ho the compliment of recommending that her book become "mandatory reading on any MBA (or investment banking course); if nothing else, it might be more entertaining than the other texts that bankers swallow so uncritically."[7]

Tett successfully captured what Ho had accomplished. She had, Tett noted, deployed Bourdieu's notion of "habitus" to reveal that "modern financiers live in a world where jobs are insecure, and where bankers are paid by trading things or cutting deals." Moreover, they "tend to project their experience on to the economy by aspiring to make everything 'liquid,' or tradable, including jobs and people. These projections," Tett observed, "are typically couched in the rhetoric of 'shareholder values' or abstract concepts of 'free-market capitalism'—presented as absolute 'truths.'" Tett proceeded to note that Ho found that many of the so-called truths were "riddled with contradictions that bankers ignore because they are seduced by their own rhetoric." Then, without acknowledging how Ho's analysis of the origins of the financial crisis might differ from her own, she reported that Ho argued that "massive corporate restructurings are not caused so much by abstract financial models as by the local, cultural habitus of investment bankers, the mission-driven narratives of shareholder value and the institutional culture of Wall Street."[8]

Watching the restructuring of AT&T in 1995 had started Ho on the path to what she accomplished in *Liquidated*. What struck her then was the contrast between the company laying off 40,000 employees on the one hand, and both its stock rising and the flourishing of the investment bank that arranged the deal on the other. For 1996–97, she took a year off from her graduate studies in anthropology at Princeton to work on Wall Street, initially for the Management Consulting Group at Bankers Trust for three times her school stipend. Back at Princeton in the fall of 1997, she conducted one hundred interviews to better understand the culture of finance—and did so as the stock market was booming in the midst of the dot-com bubble.[9]

Ho's dissertation, copyrighted in 2002 but dated January 2003, explored how the power and values of finance capitalism, best represented by major investment banks, were responsible for the "severe social dislocations" of global capitalism. She asserted that it was "precisely the expansion and prominence of financial and stock market values that have strongly contributed to the severe social dislocations social scientists have attributed to global capitalism at large: the dismantling of corporate and governmental safety nets, the wave of corporate downsizings and restructurings, the reinscribing of hierarchical urban and global spaces." Since the mid-1970s, this new social and economic order, part of what she saw as a broader neoliberal project, had "triumphed" over "paternalistic welfare capitalism." Central to this transformation were the ways in which what she called "late capitalist social relations in the United States" had placed shareholder value in a commanding position—claims, she noted in passing, that Jesse Jackson's Rainbow PUSH Wall Street Project was challenging. Though invoking democratic values of an ownership society, investment banks nonetheless represented the specific location of elite power—distinct from the corporate America of the industrial, consumer-goods, and agricultural sectors and from the lives of most Americans. Yet, however powerful they seemed, investment bankers were insecure; with their focus on the short term, she noted the uncertainty of their continued employment, as well as their more than ample compensation. The "organizational culture of Wall Street firms," she revealed, relied on quotidian strategic practices that laid "the foundation for market crashes" and reflected cycles of boom and bust.[10]

Yet, by and large, Ho paid relatively little attention to the specific forms liquefying took because, as Tett noted in her review of the book, the central focus of Ho's work was the cultural habitus of the people who occupied the financial world and not what would turn out to be the dangerous derivatives that as a reporter Tett had done so much to expose. Ho did not mention CDOs, subprime mortgages, or mortgage-backed securities at all, and she named the process of securitization only twice. The only reference to a recession was to an event in the past, not to one that was possible in the future. The centrality of residential mortgages, especially risky ones, to global capitalism was not very much on her mind. After all, the ideology of investment bankers left little room for the ordinary home borrower and lender.[11] However, Ho amply demonstrated that gender was part of the habitus of the corporate world. She mentioned how men on Wall Street appropriated the language of the feminist movement and in multiple ways did their best to minimize or disparage its legitimacy. She noted the pressure women were under to flaunt their femininity and minimize their feminism. She emphasized "the extent to which women need to conform to men's comfort zones and imaginations of 'femininity' and of how 'women' should behave in order to succeed, as not surprisingly, almost all of women's bosses and coworkers on Wall Street (as well as in corporate America) are men." More generally, she pointed out how "the invidious distinctions of race, gender, and class deeply structure bankers' experiences at work and their opportunities for success."[12]

After completing the dissertation and taking a job in the Department of Anthropology at the University of Minnesota, Ho transformed the dissertation into a compelling and sophisticated 2009 book—*Liquidated: An*

Ethnography of Wall Street—that was informed by her own ethnographic work and by social science theory, especially Bourdieu's. In important ways she expanded, deepened, and transformed her analysis, although it strikes me that her emphasis on gender is more implicit in the book than it was in her dissertation. The word "feminism" does not appear in the index. In the central argument of her book, foretold somewhat in her dissertation but now amplified, Ho focused on the relationships between the habitus of investment bankers and the headwinds the global economy continually faced. She talked of "the daily practices and corporate cultural values of investment bankers in the workplace," which included an emphasis on smartness, hubris, elitism, risk, liquidity, "strategy of no-strategy," insecurity, and the ideology of shareholder value. Yet she pressed on to explore the connection between these aspects of how bankers worked on the "broader U.S. corporate restructuring *and* the construction of financial markets booms and busts." She thus emphasized the powerful, and ultimately problematic, impact of the way the quotidian culture of Wall Street "continually lays the foundation for the construction *and* the bursting of financial market bubbles." This helped explain how bankers' cultural values and practices engendered abundant profits, "but also financial crises that can have a domino effect globally, and in some instances, threaten the very existence of Wall Street itself."[13]

Appropriately so, since Ho focused on events in the 1990s, there was little in her book, published in late June 2009, several weeks after Tett's *Fool's Gold*, on the financial crisis that had reached a crescendo nine months earlier, with the collapse of Lehman Brothers and AIG. She did mention "what is currently being dubbed the worst financial crisis since the Great Depression . . . brought on by investment banks' engendering of the subprime debacle, which has in turn caused a global credit panic." And at the very end of *Liquidated*, she added a six-page section titled "Subprime Coda." There she emphasized what stood at the center of the body of the book: "Wall Street's institutional culture," which relied on expanding outward from the "very privileged subjectivities" of investment bankers. Among the key components of their dispositions were "the milking of the present and a strategy of no strategy," "shareholder value ideology," and global-transforming ambitions. She paid abundant attention to how "expansions into mortgage lending proved disastrous for Wall Street," but barely mentioned how disastrous the crisis was for people who saw their homes or pensions lose value, if not actually disappear. In the end, she insisted, "Wall Street-led financial booms are made possible by the very financial ideologies and transactions which eventually implode under the accumulated weight of broken promises, failed shareholder values, and the mining of capital without replenishing it."[14]

Early in her book, Ho remarked that it was "beyond the scope" of her work "to document all the myriad and complex conditions and practices that have enabled financial market values and actors to consolidate their influence over corporate America." Notably, she did mention what her journalist peers usually did not, especially "the compromising of labor movements punctuated by racialized and gendered inequalities." In contrast, she did list some of what books like *Fool's Gold*, *All the Devils Are Here*, and *Reckless Endangerment* emphasized: federal policies, decisions made by leaders of corporations, and "the invention and popularity of new financial instruments." Yet when she described what these innovations were, at times she seemed more oriented to the past than the present, since she mentioned mutual funds (by 2009, available for decades), junk bonds (which had grown dramatically in the 1980s), and credit default swaps, which, she said, had "recently come to light" (but which had come into existence in the 1990s and whose dangers Tett had underscored in April 2005 in the pages of the *Financial Times*).[15]

Several times after her book's publication, Ho focused on an issue that she had not significantly covered in her dissertation: whether what she described provided an adequate basis for readers to understand the forces that caused the Great Recession. Writing in 2010, she asserted that many of those she interviewed "actually sensed the impending bubble burst," since, "through their daily practices, they often recognized that they had pushed as many financial transactions as the markets could bear." Many of her informants "anticipated not only a crash, but also an *eventual bailout*," because the institutions for which they worked were too big to fail. This underscored that, in the end, despite their free-market ideology, they relied on the government to underwrite risk. This meant that globalization and securitization "both generated the crisis and assured its rescue."[16] Then, in an article published in 2012, Ho responded to a question she was frequently asked: What had her research foreseen "in the wake of the most devastating global financial crisis since the Great Depression"? She responded that she "was able to get at and portray Wall Street's specific culture of liquidity and crisis through tracking" what bankers and financial institutions did and believed, "which in turn created the conditions of unsustainability in corporate America that led to financial crises."[17]

In addition to Ho's scholarship, McKenna had referenced a number of works by social scientists, including those by anthropologists, that Tett should have paid attention to.[18] Citing the work of David Harvey and Richard

Robbins, he said he wished Tett had taken into account what radical critics of neoliberalism had written.[19]

In addition, he highlighted the work of anthropologists who focused on financialization and the powerful institutions driving it. "Indeed there is a wealth of books on the crisis by what might be called 'finance anthropologists,'" he wrote, before going on to point out that Tett had failed to reference some of them available when she wrote *Fool's Gold*.[20] He credited the economist Michael Perelman's *The Confiscation of American Prosperity: From Right-Wing Extremism to the Next Great Depression* (2007) for the predictive power suggested by the book's subtitle. Although that referred to the "Next Great Depression," Perelman did not focus on derivatives. McKenna also mentioned Edward LiPuma and Benjamin Lee's *Financial Derivatives and the Globalization of Risk* (2004). More than many anthropologists, they focused on derivatives, but their principal concern was not on the nexus between Wall Street and residential real estate; rather, it was on the connections between the financial center in the Metropole and developing nations in terms of risky current bets. He also called attention to Alexandra Ouroussoff's *Wall Street at War: The Secret Struggle for the Global Economy* (2010) and Caitlin Zaloom's *Out of the Pits: Traders and Technology from Chicago to London* (2007). Yet a careful reading of these sources, and others he mentioned, makes clear that though these authors understood that financialization was likely to lead to an economic meltdown, they did not understand as well as Tett did exactly what might be the cause, especially the role of the kind of derivatives she focused on.

By and large, these works by social scientists paid little or no attention to gender, even though, more implicitly than explicitly, they pictured a macho-driven world. In contrast, Melissa S. Fisher's *Wall Street Women* (2012), even more so than Karen Ho's work, placed gender at the center of her ethnography of the first generation of women who entered the upper reaches of the financial world in the 1960s and 1970s. These pioneers in investment banking, Fisher showed, saw the origins and impact of the Great Recession in gendered terms, "identifying women's feminine qualities," such as risk aversion, an antipathy to greed, and a preference for long-term considerations, "as uniquely suited to lead—even repair—the financial debacle."[21]

One of the central figures among anthropologists who explored how ethnography illuminated the roles of women in finance, Fisher offered an appropriately complex gendered analysis. Women who entered the worlds of finance early, she emphasized, "were forced to keep their sense of themselves as professional women in finance separate and apart from their identification with and identity as feminists." Moreover, she made it clear that though women involved in research were cautious, those close to the highest reaches of investment banks were seen as monster mothers, as products of the "masculinization of powerful Wall Street women in the nineties," who more fully embraced risk than did their researcher counterparts. Consequently, although they deployed important concepts of a gendered discourse, they also embraced the celebration of the American dream of success, as well as commitments to hard work, merit, and the power of markets. Ironically, when the derivatives dregs hit the proverbial fan, Fisher noted, as she used the words from Michael Lewis's *The Big Short*, those in power "purged women from senior Wall Street roles" even as, she noted, observers who looked at the crisis blamed "the greedy, risk-taking behavior of men." Thus, at a December 2008 conference, women from the financial world talked of being "possible saviors" as they doubled down on the gendered description of the financial crisis and "articulated a divide between masculine, greedy, risk-taking actors and behaviors, probably leading to the crisis, and a more feminine, conservative, long-term approach to financial practice that could possibly help the economy or could fix it." Precisely when women, voluntarily or involuntarily, were leaving the world of high finance in droves, some of them "drew on historical discourses about corporate domesticity, motherhood, and women's innate care-taking qualities" as they articulated a vision in which they saw the financial crisis "as a window of opportunity for a new kind of more 'caring' and 'softer' capitalism" in ways that "are amplifying gendered differences (biological and otherwise) and the value of a certain kind of feminized mode of being (risk awareness)."[22]

Like the books by Meredith Whitney, Bethany McLean/Joe Nocera, Gretchen Morgenson/Joshua Rosner, and Gillian Tett, most of the ethnographies of the world of high finance focused principally on what elites did and paid relatively little attention to how Americans suffered as a result. There is at least one exception: a notably elegant and compelling book, published with the benefit of the ten years that had occurred after *Liquidated*. In *Dispossessed: How Predatory Bureaucracy Foreclosed on the American Middle Class* (2019), the anthropologist Noelle Stout combined attention to both those in powerful positions and those below their ranks who suffered as a result of how elites abused their power. With class, race, ethnicity, and generations as her primary categories, she paid relatively little explicit attention to gender, even though in her book there was abundant evidence of men in positions of power making the situations women faced more precarious. For twenty-six months, beginning in 2012 and continuing more episodically later, Stout returned to the areas of California where she lived early in her life in order to study the painful results of the collapse of the housing market. Having grown up in a blue-collar family and then earning degrees at Stanford and Harvard, she intensely felt her status as an insider and an outsider. As a researcher, she focused on twelve families living in neighborhoods differentiated by class and ethnicity, as well as activists who later worked tirelessly to help them recover what they had lost. She also interviewed people ranging from the former secretary of the treasury Timothy Geithner to low-level operatives in the offices of mortgage originators and loan servicers—and, in between, influential lobbyists and executives. The inland area in Northern California, among the places hardest hit by the market crashes, was the setting for Stout's exploration of the way predatory actions by bankers and failures of federal policies undermined the struggles of residents to gain secure footholds in the middle class. To enhance corporate profits, bankers denied 70 percent of the requests under the Home Affordable Modification Program (HAMP), a federal program funded by $300 billion and designed to keep families in their homes; thus the funds remained largely unspent.

Stout wrote both like a novelist and a social scientist, telling dramatically tragic stories and analyzing what she discovered with keen, analytic skill. If most others confined themselves to the last quarter of the twentieth century and the first decade of the twenty-first, Stout linked the predatory and racist forces of the more distant past with those in the present. In movingly revealing ways, she also connected the story of her own working-poor family's struggle to gain a hold on the middle class with what happened to those who peopled her book. Stout was able to help readers feel the pain that struggling family members experienced in the Kafkaesque worlds she explored. Though the main focus of her ethnography was the impact of the Great Recession on ordinary citizens in California's Sacramento Valley, she also looked outside that silo by focusing on the actions of people on Wall Street and in the nation's capital. There were more than enough villains and heroes to drive the narrative whose larger scope was people in the 9 million households who lost their homes to foreclosure. Those among the former ranged from Wall Street bankers to local mortgage originators, some of whom later became bureaucrats who facilitated foreclosures. Among the latter were African Americans, Latinx, and others who lost their homes and their footholds on middle-class life. In between were more sympathetic employees working at call centers, many of them with the same precarious backgrounds as the struggling petitioners on the other end of the telephone line.[23]

What Stout dramatized stood in sharp contrast with what HGTV's residential real estate shows offered and what Robert Kiyosaki and Than Merrill's workshops promised. Stout emphasized the plight of people who had to rely on burdensome consumer debt rather than good jobs as the ladder to a more secure life. Homeownership, she observed, had "come to replace the social benefits once provided by employers and the government." Theirs were uphill battles, confronted as they were not only by failed government policies and deleterious corporate power but also by insecure employment caused by globalization, escalating health care costs, a recession, and deindustrialization when the housing bubble burst in 2008. She assigned blame not to immoral consumers compromised by moral hazard but to powerful people, including distant investment bankers who created the disaster and then profited from it, officials in rating and government agencies who failed to do their jobs, and predatory mortgage originators who later worked at call centers and customer service offices. Faced with lost paperwork, hours-long waits on the telephone, and failed computer systems, people struggling to recoup their losses and their lives entered "a world of privatized government assistance, mismanaged corporate bureaucracy, and failed mortgage modification programs, an administrative universe that absconds with our time and energy but rarely sees the light of public exposure." In addition, Stout revealed that "racial and economic inequalities endemic to American late-liberal capitalism spawned the housing crash" and then exacerbated its consequences.[24]

Once shaped by a sense of mutuality between lenders and borrowers, homeowners now faced loss of their homes. Along with the rupture of the social contract, this threatened the moral vision that had undergirded their personal pride and social dreams. Encountering the forces arrayed against them engendered complex reactions, including a sense of abandonment and moral outrage. They also deployed tactics of resistance such as squatting, community activism, and the transformation of "their feelings toward the U.S. government and mainstream financial institutions, shifting dominant American moral economies in the process."[25]

Though Stout studied the financial crisis largely from the bottom up, not only Lewis, Whitney, McLean/Nocera, Morgenson/Rosner, but also Ho, Lee, LiPuma, Ouroussoff, Perelman, Tett, and Zaloom did so mostly from the top down. Such decisions were consequential. Ho acknowledged that in doing so she was following what anthropologist Laura Nader at the University of California, Berkeley, had suggested in an influential 1972 article. As Ho observed in a footnote, Nader "first issued her call for anthropologists to 'study up,' to analyze 'the colonizers rather than the colonized, the culture of power rather than the culture of the powerless, the culture of affluence rather than the culture of poverty.'"[26] What Tett may have meant when she used the term "bottom up" was an emphasis on firsthand observation rather than reliance on public relations offerings and talks only with those at the very top of the financial world. In a somewhat similar vein, Ho noted that she wanted anthropologists to see things not through abstract terms like "markets," "capitalism," and "globalization," but "as a set of daily, embodied practices and models." Nader's move was important, but what resulted—in the work of anthropologists and, for different reasons, of journalists—were views from silos of elites in Manhattan and the District of Columbia with only minimal attention to the impact of what they did on those well below. This top-down approach had its costs. Laura Nader and others might have been following the lead of her brother Ralph Nader, who in *Unsafe at Any Speed* (1963) focused mainly on corporate executives, engineers, and stylists, as well as government officials, but asserted that they were responsible for dangerous and smog-producing automobiles that affected tens of millions of Americans.

"A reviewer in the FT noted," remarked an anthropologist using a common shorthand for the *Financial Times* as he referred to Ho's *Liquidated* and Tett's *Fool's Gold*, as well as Ouroussoff's *Wall Street at War*, "that books like these suggest a new synthesis of anthropology, economics and history may be round the corner."[27] On a related but somewhat different note, a blogger in 2019 stated that "neither economists nor business analysts, both specialists in the field of finance, saw it coming, while journalists such as Gillian Tett did."[28] If it was difficult for most journalists who had to meet short-term deadlines and were beholden to their sources to put together the pieces of the puzzle that explained the global financial meltdown, documentary filmmakers, anthropologists, and journalists who authored books could do so—sometimes during but more typically after the onset of the Great Recession. Yet, although they covered much of the same territory and asked similar questions, it is striking how much anthropologists and journalists remained in their own silos. Gretchen Morgenson/Joshua Rosner and Bethany McLean/Joe Nocera, the authors of *Reckless Endangerment* and *All the Devils Are Here*, paid no attention to the relevant work of anthropologists, including Tett's crossover efforts. To be sure, in writing *The Big Short* Michael Lewis credited Tett for "painstakingly" telling the story of the invention of credit default swaps.[29] However, by writing about the relationship between anthropology and journalism, addressing academics on their own turf, and recognizing some of the work academic anthropologists did,

Tett was more successful in bursting through the walls of silos than either fellow journalists or academic anthropologists when she acknowledged the work of some of the anthropologists discussed: not only Ho but also Zaloom.[30]

In contrast, by and large anthropologists did not adequately recognize what Tett did—neither in her articles written in the midst of the crisis in the *Financial Times*, nor in her books. There were places in books by academics where they might have but did not engage the work of Tett and other journalists, such as in their discussions of Pierre Bourdieu, the collapse of Long Term Capital Management and Enron, the way the business press covered finance, and what elites failed to understand.[31] Those who wrote for major journals in anthropology paid remarkably little attention to Tett's work, apparently with no review of any of her books making an appearance.[32]

Yet in the field's flagship journal, *American Anthropologist*, in addition to a handful of citations to her work, *Fool's Gold* especially, there was one major article that paid significant attention to her crossover contributions. In the March 2010 issue, Michael G. Powell, an anthropologist who worked in architectural firms, congratulated Tett for predicting the financial crisis but called into question how well she applied anthropology in what she wrote. He noted that what she offered did "not seem to engage with or benefit from more contemporary anthropological currents." In her articles, he insisted, partly because journalists are separated into different silos (a word he did not use) "by concentrating almost solely on the credit-derivative market and the world of high finance, she never follows the story into the subprime housing industry and the culture of excessive lending in the everyday world of personal finance." He noted that, with *Fool's Gold*, "Tett corrects this, but she still never provides a 'more on the ground' ethnographic account that might help readers understand the complex social relationship between the overleveraged credit frenzy among middle-class U.S. citizens and the overleveraged credit party on Wall Street. There is never a full sense of how the everyday culture of these financial tribes ends up impacting bigger economic issues for regular people around the world." Yet, though he had these reservations, he ended on a positive note. He noted the disadvantages and advantages of journalists with tight deadlines and anthropologists who had the benefit of taking the longer view. Then, in the final sentence, he said, "Although we might debate which form is preferable, Tett shows that journalists with an anthropological sensibility have the ability to provide far-reaching, insightful, and critical analyses of contemporary social currents."[33]

And then, in addition to the work of anthropologists, there were revelations in housing nightmares caused by crises of capitalism, like the ones Stout explored in *Dispossessed*, though even more horror filled. In the wake of the Great Recession, three award-winning films pictured dangerous and tense residences. To be sure, combination is not causation, given the complicated relationship between these cultural productions and a global financial crisis that made it difficult for millions of people to hold on to their homes. Nonetheless, *Room* (2015), *Get Out* (2017), and *Parasite* (2019) may well have resonated with American audiences by making it possible for viewers to experience the terrors of domesticity.[34] Better than the work of most anthropologists, they also enabled this historian to explore the compelling evocations of homes as socially and psychologically toxic sites in ways that reveal the complicated relationships between men and women, as well as the dispossessed and the dispossessors. The media scholar Tim Snelson has noted of other cultural productions that "the morbid fascination—of both industry and audiences—with disruption, takeover, and abandonment resonates with the reality of many recession-era households and particularly the gendered power relations therein" as they "work to reveal the fragility of the wider economic system."[35]

Room, directed by Lenny Abrahamson, tells the story of a mother, Ma (played by Brie Larson) and her five-year-old son, Jack (played by Jacob Tremblay), born in captivity as a result of the rape of Ma. The rapist and the boy's biological father, Old Nick (played by Sean Bridgers), hold Ma and Jack captive in a tiny shack, and Jack is unable to imagine there is anything real aside from the Room and what he sees on the TV screen. "Do you remember how Alice wasn't always in Wonderland?" Ma asks Jack as a way of trying to teach him that there is a real world outside. To illustrate this, she tells him of the house where she grew up. "A TV house?" he asks, and Ma tells him it is a real house. *Room*, as Jack calls where he lives, takes place in Akron, Ohio, where Old Nick kidnapped and raped Ma when she was still in her teens. Located in the rust belt of northern Ohio, it is a city hard hit by the Great Recession, from which it never fully recovered. Old Nick has recently lost his job and despairs about ever getting another one. "There's no fucking jobs!" he screams. In the novel on which the movie is based, he says, "Six months I've been laid off," while later on Ma tells Jack, "Old Nick doesn't really own his house, the bank does. And if he's lost his job and he doesn't have any money left and he stops paying them, the bank—they'll get mad and they might try and take his house away."[36]

After they escape thanks to a ruse Ma devises, Jack experiences the outside world for the first time, overwhelmed and responding with disbelief

This view of the sky is the only glimpse of the outside world available to five-year-old Jack (Jacob Tremblay) in *Room* (2015).

at all that he sees. "Are we on another planet?" he asks. "No," Ma declares. "Same one, just a different spot." The police rescue Ma and arrest Old Nick. After a brief stay in a psychiatric hospital, Jack and Ma (whose name, we now learn, is Joy) move into the home where she grew up—peopled initially by her mother and father, as well as her mother's new boyfriend. Her childhood home is very different from Room in so many ways: ample and stylishly furnished, it is located in a leafy suburban neighborhood. So, what we come to understand are the contrasts between life in Room and in Joy's childhood home. Though in the former Ma experienced sexual assaults and, along with Jack, lived under harsh conditions, with inventiveness and abundant love she created a wonderful environment there for her son. In ironic contrast, what characterizes life in her childhood home, to which she has returned, reminds us that psychological problems plague even those in contemporary suburban homes. Ma fights with Jack as she urges him to spend less time watching cartoons on a smartphone, insisting it would be better for "him to connect with something." Joy and her mother disagree over who is responsible for raising Jack and who was responsible for Joy's abduction. During a TV interview, Joy faces questions about why she did not give Jack up for adoption when he was born and whether as the biological father Old Nick has any rightful claim about how to raise Jack.

Thrown by prying inquiries that evoked what she had been through, and of course by how they call her mothering into question, Ma attempts to kill herself. Soon after, we listen as Jack delivers a soliloquy about how life away from Room is problematic, with people so busy and aliens having broken his mother's spirit. Then, with his mother still hospitalized, Jack's grandmother makes cupcakes with him, while he says that sometimes he misses Room—it was not too small, and Ma was always there. Mother and son are soon reconciled. As the film nears its end, Jack asks, "Can we go back to Room? . . . Just for a visit?" Escorted by a police officer, they return. Jack says goodbye affectionately to objects within. As music plays, we see mother and son walk away, holding hands, leaving what is clearly a lower-middle-class or working-class neighborhood that stands in sharp contrast to where Ma grew up and where she has returned with Jack. What we have learned is that both the working-class Room (its troubles explicitly linked to the Great Recession) and the middle-class suburban house (its problems psychosocial) have their own distinctive traps and dysfunctional families. In turn, this raises questions about whether one reality is obviously worse than the other.

Room juxtaposes a residence in a working-class neighborhood with one more favorably situated. On the other hand, *Parasite* does so through vivid, inventively crafted, and often violent interactions between a working-class family living precariously and a wealthy one headed by a CEO of a high-tech firm. Set in Seoul, South Korea, and directed by Bong Joon-ho, the film nonetheless attracted audiences and earned accolades in the United States. It garnered four Oscars, including Best Picture—the first non-English-language film to win that award.

The basic plot revolves around two families: the wealthy Parks, who live in a luxurious multilevel modern house, and the Kims, who reside in a cramped apartment located in a dense urban neighborhood. Through a series of ruses, the Kims insinuate themselves into the Parks' lives and home. While the Parks are away on a vacation, the Kims take over their house, performing what it means to live in the lap of luxury. After the Parks return unexpectedly, the Kims return to their low-lying apartment, which is inundated with sewage. Forced out of their home, they end up in a third home: a gym, where they find themselves among other homeless people. The film ends with a series of intricate twists in the plot that underscore the violence of class conflicts.

Throughout, Joon-ho inventively deploys a series of residences, the principal two of them vertically layered in ways that underscore social hierarchies. *Parasite* vividly dramatizes the relationships between homes and class conflicts that result from the yawning gaps between the extremely wealthy and the embattled poor. We see members of the Kim family going from the leafy heights where the Parks live down to the cramped neighborhood and quarters where they reside. The film also accentuates the vertical nature of class relations by revealing that the husband of the Parks' original housekeeper has been living for four years in a subterranean location below their house, hiding out from debt collectors after he lost his job.

Parasite (2019) emphasizes the contrasting levels inhabited by families from different social classes. These pictures capture the contrast between the view from the lowly apartment where the Kims reside and the luxurious, more elevated setting where the Parks live.

For our purposes, the complicated twists in the plot are less important than the themes they reveal: the parasitical and violent relationships between the rich and the poor, of course, as well as how intraclass warfare makes it impossible for members of the underclass to cooperate with each other. We learn from the way members of the Kim family operate that social class is a cultural construction that can be imitated and performed, even by people from the underclass who lack formal education and social status. Echoing the problematic distribution of resources, while the Parks live in the lap of luxury, both working-class families, the Kims as well as the housekeeper and her husband, struggle to subsist, plagued as they are by debt, poorly compensated employment, or no employment at all, and the lack of a social safety net. Yet, like Ma and her middle-class family of origin in *Room*, but even more so here, the upper-class family in *Parasite* suffers from psychological trauma, not economic adversity. As a writer later noted in ways that helps us ponder the Kims' fate, "for those familiar with a typical career trajectory in South Korea," the film referenced symbols of "a whole world of middle-class failure—reflecting economic hopes and tragedies that still resonate throughout the country."[37] American audiences may not have caught the specific references, but, like their Korean counterparts, they could well understand how corporate downsizing, crushing debt, precarious employment, the hollowing-out of the middle class, and financial crises impelled middle-class families physically and economically downward. Although the Great Recession garners no direct mention, evidence of its sources and costs do—problematic jobs, life-altering debt, and traumatic experiences dramatized by the widest variety of residential locations. In both *Room* and *Parasite*, folks are trapped in confined and compromised residences while the homes of the middle class and wealthy are traps in psychological rather than economic ways.

Although it contains no hint of the Great Recession, *Get Out* accomplishes for race what *Room* and *Parasite* did for social class, providing as it does a picture of the home as a place of horrifying danger. As Jordan Peele's first film, *Get Out* echoes and complicates the hypocrisy of the 1967 *Guess Who's Coming to Dinner?* but with the terrifying twists of a horror film. *Get Out* tells the story of Chris Washington (played by Daniel Kaluuya), a young African American photographer from a humble background who travels to a rural location in upstate New York to meet the family of his white girlfriend, Rose Armitage (played by Allison Williams).

Before they get there, we see the contrast between an opening scene in which another African American man is kidnapped while finding his way through a "creepy" suburban neighborhood where he feels "like a sore thumb out here" and reassuring images of a predominantly Black urban neighborhood. Then, without making an explicit connection between these two locations, we encounter the young couple discussing an upcoming trip as they pack to leave what seems like a modest but tastefully furnished urban apartment. Chris tells Rose he does not want to be chased off the lawn with a shotgun. Rose reassures him—after all, she remarks, her dad would have voted for Obama a third time, the first hint we have of the problem with racial liberalism. Despite what we initially see as the young couple's loving relationship, we later discover Rose's complicity in what takes place in her family's upper-middle-class home. Its garden and aboveground floors are sites of not-so-subtle white racism, while its basement is the location of dramatic and potentially gruesome psychological terror that references the cultural dynamics of racism. Initially handcuffed into a chair where he is to be operated on, he frees himself.

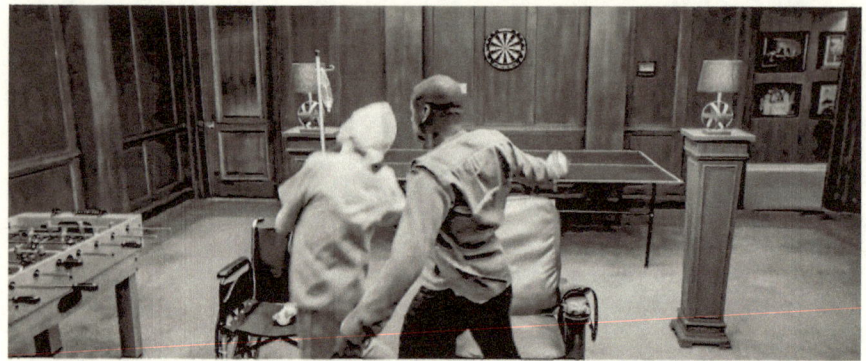

In *Get Out* (2017), Chris Washington (Daniel Kaluuya) liberates himself from the chair in which his white hosts/captors have placed him so they can perform an operation that will deracinate Chris but empower whites.

In *Get Out* we again encounter many of themes evoked in *Room* and *Parasite*. If *Room* involves confinement in a working-class neighborhood, both *Parasite* and *Get Out* use underground locations as metaphorical suggestions that the lower you go the greater the danger, in this movie reiterated by images of Chris floating down as he reexperiences a childhood trauma. The well-appointed and commodious home of Rose's parents turns out to be the site of psychologically driven traps and confinement, this time compellingly marked by deep-seated racism rather than the psychosocial tensions in *Room* or the class conflict in *Parasite*. Above all, the three movies reveal in psychological and social terms that residences are dangerous places to live in the early twenty-first century—here more intensely portrayed than in major books, documentary films, or ethnographic studies.

All three films highlight gender relationships. *Room* contrasts an evil father with a nurturing and clever mother as well as a loving grandmother. *Get Out* juxtaposes two heroic Black men (Chris and his friend Rod Williams, who comes from the city to rescue him) with two evil white women (the deceiving Rose Armitage and hypnotizing mother, Missy, who uses her skills as a professional healer in insidiously destructive ways). *Parasite* offers up no truly heroic woman, with mothers unable to protect their sons. In contrast, if both the Kim and Park dads are violently evil, as in *Room*, it is the young boy who is both victimized and full of understanding.

All three movies play in complicated ways with social and racial hierarchies as they reveal the connections between high and low. *Room* contrasts captivity in a working-class neighborhood with the more comfortable and much larger suburban home, albeit not one that is problem-free. *Get Out* explores the storied levels in an exurban home—with its white, liberal racism upstairs and down below, in the basement, a place of racist torture. *Parasite* continually plays with residential levels: the lower the level, the lower the class and the more dangerous the situation, at least initially. The Parks reside high up, spatially and socially. The Kims, as well as the housekeeper and her husband, live below in both senses. Near the end, we learn that the Kim son is the redeeming man, determined to earn enough money to place his family upstairs in the house the Parks once occupied.

Jon Stewart dramatically but briefly connected the dots between perpetrators and victims. To varying degrees, so too did authors of important books and movie directors. Among the retrospective texts some were notably successful in keeping an eye on the high and low. Among the most exemplary are Michael G. Hudson's *The Monster: How a Gang of Predatory Lenders and Wall Street Bankers Fleeced America—and Spawned a Global Crisis* and Noelle Stout's *Dispossessed: How Predatory Bureaucracy Foreclosed on the American Middle Class* as well as the films *Inside Job*, *Parasite*, and *Capitalism: A Love Story*. Then there is *The Big Short*, in which the actor Brad Pitt, who supposedly ventriloquized Ben Hockett, the former bond trader at Deutsche Bank, elaborated what on Stewart had said. He was responding to a short-seller who was gloating over the rewards reaped from his foresighted success. "You just bet against the American economy," he insisted, and "if we're right, people lose homes. People lose jobs. People lose retirement savings. People lose pensions. You know what I hate about fucking banking? It reduces people to numbers. Here's a number—every 1 percent unemployment goes up, 40,000 people die, did you know that?" Presenting a comprehensive and accurate picture of the origins and impact of the Great Recession is not easy, but it is both possible and worth the effort.

CHAPTER 6

NEW MEDIA AND RESIDENTIAL REAL ESTATE

If to varying degrees writers for well-established print media understood how securitization was significantly changing the housing market, at the same time new media was threatening or promising to transform housing in fundamental ways. In the years around the Great Recession, such disruption seemed to be everywhere—websites such as Trulia, Zillow, and Redfin upended the business of acquiring a home; Airbnb challenged the way people found short-term rentals; FlexJobs enabled remote work; Google made information-gathering easier; Amazon provided the option of shopping remotely; Skype and Zoom made it possible to sit at your laptop and meet with virtually anyone who also had a computer; Netflix, Wayfair, Grubhub, Plated, and OpenTable facilitated finding entertainment, decorating a home, and eating meals without going to a movie theater, furniture store, supermarket, or restaurant.

During and after the Great Recession, these technologies and media shaped residential and commercial real estate and in the process disrupted long-established relationships between work, consumption, and ownership. Perhaps it is too early to gauge the impact of these forces on home buying and living, but the scale and direction of shifts are clear. New media have fostered major changes in the allocation of time, space, and financial resources. They have helped redefine work, leisure, personal relationships, and entrepreneurship. Emphasizing as they do the goal of self-governance, they have accentuated the power of individualism and eroded the roles of or support for governments, as well as of well-established social organizations and public life. Yet disruptive technologies have also fostered the creation of new communities and new ways to organize social life. In addition, the changes brought by new technologies have dramatically and significantly shifted the balance between private and public as they strengthened the former and weakened the latter.[1] They also provided the technology, employment, and fortunes that caused tectonic shifts along generational, regional, and class lines and shifted locations of where and how people lived, worked, and played.

All this happened in part because of changes in technologies, labor practices, and marketing strategies. They have enabled a wide range of enterprises involved in residential real estate and other fields to exploit market inefficiencies such as high transaction costs by appealing to consumers who seek lower costs and greater convenience. Those who launched Uber in 2009 and Lyft three years later understood that highly regulated taxi companies benefited from monopolistic conditions that limited the number of cabs and prevented them from picking up passengers in locations where they were not licensed to do so. They realized that temporary or contingent labor made more economic sense than having a driver sit for hours at a taxi stand, and that it was possible to run a transportation company without owning any vehicles or employing any drivers. The founders of Dollar Shave Club and Harry's Razors surely knew that the business model of Gillette (founded more than a century earlier) relied too heavily on high prices and boring—if not seemingly invisible—marketing strategies rather than more reasonable prices and the ostensible exclusivity of a club. More and more millennials and their even younger counterparts turned away from brick-and-mortar financial institutions. Instead, convenience and lower costs tempted them to use internet-enabled enterprises and digital-only businesses such as GoBank, peer-to-peer lender Prosper, peer-to-peer investor Kickstarter, cryptocurrency exchange Coinbase, and robo-advisor Betterment. The problematic coworking company WeWork provides more flexible and less expensive office space than do commercial real estate firms that write long-term, inflexible leases for large corporations.[2] Oscar Health deploys new technologies such as telemedicine and remote ways of measuring health conditions as it promises more consumer-friendly medical services than traditional companies such as BlueCross/BlueShield or United Health Care. These examples underscore what makes disruptive innovation possible, especially venture capital and private equity funding, new technologies, complacent legacy corporations, lower capital requirements, visionary entrepreneurs, flexible or contingent labor, and customers who lack loyalty to established offerings.[3]

Observers deploy several terms for what I am describing: the "gig economy" (which refers to contingent or short-term labor), the "sharing economy," the "platform economy," and "disruption." The sharing (or peer-to-peer) economy involves the ways that an internet-based corporation enables two people or organizations to come together, often briefly and/or for one time only, in order to take advantage of services or items that might otherwise go unused or underutilized—or, as professors in business schools and departments of economics would say, "idle resources." People can monetize what they have by selling or renting clothing they no longer use; renting out rooms that are temporarily available; or driving cars that would otherwise sit idle. Freelance workers can take advantage of temporary workspaces that provide access to facilities and fellow workers. Borrowers and lenders can meet online in order to exchange funds, whether for charitable or entrepreneurial purposes. Employers can connect with employees so that short-term needs can be taken care of. Yet I find the word "sharing" problematic because it seems to assume that parity is in play, that participants operate in the marketplace on equal terms. An Uber driver and passenger, two women who exchange a dress on Poshmark, or people who find each other on any of the many dating apps may indeed come together as equals, but what stands between them is a platform—an often invisible corporation with hundreds or thousands of employees and a market capitalization in some cases of more than $1 billion.[4]

Over time the platform economy emerged as a more useful and commonly used concept. A platform refers to a company that generates revenues and perhaps even profits by using technologically enabled, interactive networks that at their best rely on trust to connect buyers and sellers of goods or services.[5] Rather than owning the means of production, to borrow a Marxist term, matchmaker platforms own the means of connecting people with people through a command of data. Google and Facebook led the way, offering individuals free access to information and other people, respectively, in exchange for accumulating information from them that was valuable to advertisers and others. Thus, Uber does not own any of the cars its drivers and customers use; Airbnb, any residences rented; WeWork, any of the offices offered to coworkers; or Etsy or eBay, any of the goods traded. Rather, these companies rely on sophisticated data, the World Wide Web, cloud technology, and computer or smartphone connections that foster social networks to bring people together so they can complete transactions. Platform enterprises, which come in many different sizes and types, benefit from reliance on network effects, the cascading intensification of personal connections that empowers an enterprise; on the availability of cheap and abundant capital, when available; on the weakness of governmental regulations; on the power of monopolistic or winner-take-all situations; on reservoirs of inexpensive workers who lack the power to bargain effectively; on access to information for both buyers and sellers; on the availability of data and the technological ability to exploit it; on efficiency that results from the elimination of the need for gatekeepers and inventory; and on the enhancement of values that results from new and more efficient business models.

"Today's platforms," claim the three enthusiastic authors of *Platform Revolution: How Networked Markets Are Transforming the Economy—and How to Make Them Work for You* (2016), "empowered by digital technology that annihilates barriers of space and time, and employing smart, sophisticated software tools that connect producers and consumers more precisely, speedily, and easily than ever before, are producing results that are little short of miraculous."[6] In contrast stands the more critical assessment of the professor Nick Srnicek of King's College, London. When capitalism faces a crisis, he has noted, restructuring is necessary. "New technologies, new organizational forms, new modes of exploitation, new types of jobs, and new markets all emerge to create new ways of accumulating capital," as happened with platform capitalism in the wake of a series of crises in the late twentieth and early twenty-first centuries.[7]

Platform corporations promise or threaten the third process: disruption. The intellectual godfather of that process was the economist Joseph Schumpeter. Writing in 1942, he described "a gale of creative destruction" as the "essential fact about capitalism," epitomized by an enterprise that "incessantly revolutionizes the economic structure from within, incessantly destroying the old one, incessantly creating a new one."[8] Think about what Amazon did to shopping centers or bookstores, Google to newspapers, Netflix to video stores like Blockbuster and to Hollywood studios, Microsoft Word to typewriters and typists, or Apple Music and Spotify to CDs.

Together, sharing, platforms, and disruption promise to make the economy more efficient, shift power relationships, and change how we work. "Its boosters," write Martin Kenney and John Zysman, two scholars who in 2016 surveyed the field, "have called it the Creative Economy or the Sharing Economy, whereas those less convinced of its beneficence have dubbed it the Gig Economy, the Precariat, or the 1099 Economy, focusing on its impact on workers and how they are compensated." They rely on powerful technological changes, including the internet; the development and application of algorithms to a wide and growing range of activities; and then their placement on the cloud, which makes it possible to draw on them easily and remotely. Kenney and Zysman assert that the choices societies make will shape their impact, even if it is already clear that, driven by globalization and new technologies, we have already entered a period of fundamental change worldwide equal if not greater than the industrial revolution.[9] "Traditional manufacturing businesses, for instance," write two MIT economists who have worked with platform enterprises, "buy raw materials, make stuff, and sell that stuff to customers. But matchmakers' raw materials are the different groups of customers that they help bring together, not anything that they buy at all. And part of the stuff they sell to members of each group is access to members of the other group"—thus, Uber or Lyft connecting riders and drivers.[10]

The force of the sharing economy, platforms, and disruption played out in the world of residential real estate during and following the Great Recession. Enterprises, many of them launched in the new century's first decade, often exacerbated the effects of the global economic crisis that began and then reverberated afterward. Prospective homeowners could look at online sites that relied on detailed and easily accessible digital information to help them make decisions about where they might live. Such sites also provided millions of people the ability to dream of residing elsewhere and living differently. As they were thinking of actually moving, at least initially and maybe longer, they could bypass realtors, who, through their control of access to listings on the Multiple Listing Service (MLS), steer prospective homeowners in one direction or another in exchange for a commission of 5 percent or higher. Founders of three internet-based firms—Redfin, Zillow, and Trulia—set out to disrupt the business of residential real estate by providing prospective homeowners with easy access to robust packets of data. They hoped that a corporation that benefited from the use of internet-based data analytics might be more efficient and profitable than one based on an older business model that relied on renting expensive office space from which real estate agents would go out and spend hours and hours painstakingly showing multiple properties to potential buyers. Initially what drove the revenues of these companies were payments that a wide range of real estate–related companies made to secure advertisements and facilitate connections on their websites. Though perhaps at the outset they did not intend (or more likely announce an intention) to intrude in the relationships between buyer, agent, and seller, ultimately the financial rewards for doing so were too tempting.

An examination of Zillow's business model enables us to understand the dynamics of disruption in the buying and selling of houses.[11] Through advertising and a series of strategic partnerships, the company derives revenue from referrals to realtors and mortgage lenders, as well as relationships with landlords, property managers, and newspapers. Online for all to see are aerial views, continually updated evaluations, comparable prices, market reports, and data on mortgages and schools. You can calculate whether you can afford a home, explore current market trends, figure out how to carry out home improvements, get in touch with a realtor, post a "for sale by owner" notice, design a flyer before placing your house or apartment on the market, and find someone to repair or inspect a property. Relying on a wide range of publicly available data and its proprietary algorithms, based on the daily processing of 3.2 terabytes, Zillow provides an ever-changing Zestimate, a judgment of the property's value. This saves an interested home buyer the time and money involved in hiring an appraiser.[12]

Those who funded and led Zillow well understood that the field of buying and selling homes was ripe for fundamental disruption. Writing in the *Economist* in mid-February 2020 under the headline "The Real-Estate Racket: Property Brokers Get a Bad Rap All over the World. In America They Deserve It," a journalist made clear what was at stake. The nation's homes were worth more than the sum of all of America's publicly traded stock. Fees earned on $1.5 trillion in annual sales could be there for the picking. Not to mention other transaction costs, commissions as high as 6 percent, dramatically greater than those elsewhere, brought income of $75 billion to the nation's 2 million realtors. Compared with what went on in many other nations, home purchasing in the United States was both cumbersome and expensive. "In an industry crying out for technological disruption," the author wrote colorfully, in a way that connected the story to HGTV's offerings, "the only revolutionary change over the past decade has been the rise of . . . reality TV shows including *Flip or Flop*." At just over 1 percent of the nation's workforce, the number of realtors represents an astounding figure, although a significant percentage of agents work part time and sell only a few houses a year.

The *Economist*'s writer noted that, though Zillow, like similar platforms, had made some inroads into sales, the National Association of Realtors (NAR) insisted on justifying the benefits of its powerful and borderline monopolistic hold through MLS. But change was in the air. The Department of Justice was pursuing trust busting and class action lawsuits against high fixed fees. In 2019 venture capitalists had poured $6 billion "into 'prop tech' firms." Perhaps "competition can make America's property market work better," the author wrote, allowing people to gain the knowledge that might allow them to enter through "an open door."[13]

Eventually Zillow moved from providing information to competing directly with NAR members, even though it relied on advertisements from the industry's association and its agents for revenue. "Zillow Plans to Do to Real Estate What Amazon Did to Retailing," read a late 2019 headline from the *Motley Fool*, the sassy online source of financial news. As "part of its new strategy of flipping real estate," with Zillow 2.0 the company was "taking on the neighborhood real estate broker"—but was doing so as part of a "replatforming" of the industry with a combination of data-driven analytics, enhanced convenience, and quick financing. Zillow Offers, its home-purchasing program, enables homeowners to go online and within a day or so be able to sell their house, without the inconveniences of staging open houses and at a price that relied on the company's analytic tools. Zillow took a service fee from the seller, fixed up the house, for a brief period kept the property on its books, and then sold it using efficient and convenient methods similar to the ones used to purchase it. Then, in late December 2020, a brochure arrived in my mail, promoting Zillow Rental Manager. "List Your Rental. Screen Tenants," it urged me. "Sign a Lease. Get Paid. All in One Place with Zillow Rental Manager," and I could post my first listing for free.

Given the immense size of the market for residential real estate, a *Motley Fool* reporter noted, if Zillow could sell even a tiny percentage of homes on the market in a given year, this would bring in billions of dollars in revenues and hundreds of millions in profits—obviously a strategy with tremendous potential rewards.[14] Yet surely it also held equivalent risks. "Houses are not taxicabs," remarked two reporters for the *New York Times*. "A bad Uber ride might set a user back $20 and make her late for a meeting," but it was something else to take on risk with a decision that affected a family's financial and residential well-being. There were also clouds over yet another of Silicon Valley's roll of the dice. Initial indications were that instant buying or iBuying was catching on in places like Phoenix and Las Vegas but had yet to successfully counter the complications of more quirky real estate markets, let alone the challenges of unpredictable costs and fluctuating interest rates in a capital-intensive field.[15]

In expanding well beyond collecting data and revenues from advertisements, Zillow was hardly alone in trying to compete with traditional realtors in order to reap the rewards of a business model that relied on high commissions. In the new world of technology-driven disrupters, other companies entered the fray with a range of different and somewhat distinctive models. All of them used what the author of the article in the *Economist* called "vast quantities of data and whizzy machine-learning algorithms to appraise homes" and then consummated deals as quickly as possible.[16] Compass is an example of a somewhat traditional real estate firm that combines physical offices and knowledgeable agents with abundant technological savvy. Redfin works to upend the traditional fee structure. Open Door, Offerpad, and other iBuying enterprises such as Zillow Offer emphasize speed, transparency, certainty, and convenience. REX relies on buyer's agents who work on commission and draws on its own analytics instead of MLS listings. Knock modifies the iBuying approach by deploying a trade-in model that promises to simplify a change in residence by facilitating selling, buying, and financing. In mid-2019 Amazon, never shy about expanding into new markets, partnered with Realogy, America's largest brokerage conglomerate, to develop TurnKey. By using a broker you found through Amazon's portal, you'd get as much as $5,000 in Amazon's services and products.[17] And, of course, because the iBuying might become such a significant force, noted the reporters for the *New York Times* in May 2019, legacy real estate firms such as Keller Williams developed their own online projects, since they felt "if it is going to happen regardless, they would rather get a piece of the action."[18]

Not surprisingly, the NAR also had to protect its flank, its institutional self-interest. Providing "Answers to Zillow's 'Instant Offers'" in a May 2017 issue of *Realtor Magazine*, a writer was sure many real estate agents would readily "relish the opportunity to compete and communicate their value as a real estate professional." After all, they could emphasize to their clients that they were more familiar with their community than was any website; they best understood how to stage a house for sale; unlike profit-seeking investors, they would seek buyers "who will love your home the way you do"; they knew how to generate the best offers and then negotiate the sale's terms; and a REALTOR followed "A Code of Ethics" that included a pledge to "protect and promote the interests of [my] client," while "online companies may facilitate your transaction, but not necessarily with your interests in mind."[19]

It is still too early to know how significantly disruptive new models of home buying and selling will be. The vast majority of home buyers, well in excess of 90 percent, begin their searches by going online. Yet, so far, the impact of iBuying has been limited. To date, many such firms spend more than they earn in profits and nationally have captured a small percentage of the market for residential real estate. This is so even though the figures are much higher in some communities where there is a plethora of cookie-cutter homes. Moreover, these approaches may be more likely to tempt institutional investors who seek to buy multiple properties rather than families who, eager to find that special and unique home, prefer to rely on the personal relationships and reassurances that a local realtor offers.[20]

If creative destruction of long-established patterns and the undermining of powerful interests is difficult, changing the experience of house hunting is easier. New technology-based enterprises have the potential to transform the pursuit of homeownership and influence aspirations. Having cruised sites such as Realtor.com or Zillow and even gone on virtual tours of homes, aspiring buyers or mere lookie-loos can approach the market with more knowledge than before. This is part of a widespread pattern of the way the internet enabled nonprofessionals to crack professional codes and develop expertise on their own. While real estate websites have the potential to challenge (or at least complicate) the expertise of realtors, there are limits to how well they empower home buyers by giving them more responsibility and knowledge.[21]

If it is difficult to determine the impact of new media on the economics of buying and selling homes, it is already clear that the rise of virtual real estate, like the power of HGTV, has created millions of voyeurs who shop in the private comfort of their homes. "In the same way society has wholeheartedly embraced using the internet to peruse potential mates, weighing up his or her smile, body and back story," quipped an observer in 2018, "we're now also spending time online swooning for wraparound porches, swimming pools and finished basements."[22] Spectatorship, or what clever observers call the pleasures of housing porn, now suffuses the culture. After you have checked the house where you grew up and the one where your boss lives, suggested a writer for *Fortune* in 2007, "your spouse calls out from the bedroom, wanting to know what the hell you've been doing for the past two hours. 'Nothing honey,' you say, shutting the laptop and trudging off to bed caught red-handed in a loop of real estate yuppie porn."[23] Remarked two top executives at Zillow, "We now fantasize about upsizing our houses by viewing 'real estate porn' online and on dozens of home-related TV shows," many of them broadcast on HGTV.[24] However, watching a professional football game or an election result on television was nowhere near the more personal and even secretive results of eyeing potential houses online whether or not one actually entered a real marketplace, intending to buy, or even living within thousands of miles of what is on view. In transforming the relationships between buyers and real estate agents, surfing these residential real estate sites may change aspirations. After all, twenty years ago, how many Americans had heard of crown moldings, or insisted on open-concept kitchens or free-standing soaking tubs?

Nor should it be surprising that Zillow provides the curious with the results of its own research. What appears to be a considerable team of investigators uses data from searches on Zillow.com plus other sources to track residential real estate markets—which cities are hot and which are not; price trends for renters and buyers; fluctuations in mortgage rates; and the impact of exogenous factors, such as major political, social, and economic forces. Moreover, the company provides the results of its own analysis of voyeurism. For example, a fall 2016 posting announced the findings of a survey of "Coming and Going: What Home Views Do, and Don't, Reveal about Our Potential Moves." Among the key revelations: more than elsewhere, people in Austin, Texas, and San Francisco, California, were wondering about moving to less expensive cities; most people looked at properties in warm locations; and yet in general people tended to cruise locations near their own. But the writer for Zillow had to issue a caveat. How some people use the website, Lauren Bretz remarked, "may reveal more about their housing fantasies or just plain voyeurism than any actual intent to move near or far." Since most people cannot easily pick up and move, while others troll in order "simply to revisit their childhood home or ogle celebrity mansions," data tracking what they look for doesn't "necessarily predict broad national migration patterns."[25]

Nonetheless, voyeurism continues. "This Is Awkward, but I Know How Much Your House Cost," wrote Megan Garber in the *Atlantic* in mid-2014. Supposedly looking for directions so she could visit a friend, she googled the address and then clicked on a link on Zillow.com, one of several "Real Estate CyberStalker Sites." She had not wanted to become "a shameless real estate voyeur," but there she was. She had invaded a friend's privacy, but, after all, that was because Zillow was "doing what Mark Zuckerberg has claimed he wants to do with Facebook on a broad cultural level: to make us all more comfortable with sharing," even if that eroded taboos. Yet, in the end, she insisted, "it's hard to talk about voyeurism, after all, when everyone is looking at the same thing."[26]

That said, the erosion of privacy and the growth of voyeurism may well not be among the most problematic consequences of the connections between the Great Recession, residential real estate, and social change. After all, another report from Zillow's researchers, this one posted in the fall of 2018, announced in its title that "The Housing Bust Widened the Wealth Gap." It turns out that while the less financially fortunate suffered disproportionately from foreclosures, over the longer term affluent folks who held on to their homes experienced increases in the values of their holdings. Writing a little more than ten years after the collapse of Lehman Brothers and AIG, the writer talked of one way that "the Great Recession helped widen the already yawning gap between the nation's rich and poor."[27]

If internet sites like Zillow have begun to transform the market for buying and selling homes, as well as renting on a long-term basis, Airbnb has already had a tremendous impact not only on how owners and renters come together for the short term but also on the hospitality industry and residential real estate in popular destinations over a longer haul. Offering accommodations from yurts and treehouses to castles and everything in between, the company has experienced unusually rapid growth, to the point where it now offers more rooms than do the five largest hotel chains.

It used to be that to find a vacation home or short-term rental you relied on word-of-mouth, classified advertisements, a local realtor, or an American Automobile Association Tour Book. Websites for short-term rentals changed all that—and other things as well. VRBO (Vacation Rentals by Owner) was founded in 1995 as a company that made it possible for homeowners and renters, mainly vacationers, to come together. Airbnb came on the scene in 2008 and, with its more robust business model and capitalization, soon outdid VRBO, owned after 2015 by the online travel conglomerate Expedia. VRBO upset some traditional patterns, but Airbnb had an even more disruptive impact. The Great Recession provided fertile ground for corporations like Airbnb to provide opportunities for both voyeurism and convenience at the same time that it intensified the problems the global economic crisis brought in its wake.

While Airbnb made lives easier and more pleasurable for millions of those who travel for business and pleasure, it made life more difficult for others by undermining traditional patterns of where and how people lived. There is some evidence that exploding markets for short-term rentals helped drive up the cost of renting an apartment and intensified disparities of wealth and income by benefiting landlords with multiple properties, ordinary residential property owners, and even some renters. The availability of alternatives to hotels exacerbated problems with occupancy rates. Major shifts in the world of short-term rentals created ancillary businesses even as they intensified problems for increasing numbers of contingent workers. Along with internet sites for employment or used cars specifically, Craigslist and Facebook all but ended classified ads and thus, along with other forces, jeopardized the future of print journalism. They created additional businesses, from home-based part-timers and emerging companies who for a modest rate wrote copy describing apartments, to private equity and venture capital executives who invested hundreds of millions or more in residential real estate in the hope of enhancing their fortunes. They heightened changing patterns of labor relationships, including for those who, as part of a contingent labor force, cleaned up a residence after one tenant left and made it ready for another. Along with other forces, they intensified the precarious situations that African Americans and Latinx faced. They had the potential to change the business models of hotel owners. Above all, while they helped owners or even some renters increase their income in tough times, they also brought in more powerful and disruptive forces that exacerbated many ill effects of Great Recession by monetizing and making residential real estate flexibly fluid.[28]

If what inspired the founders of Zillow was their work for major high-tech corporations, the origin of Airbnb points to more humble inspiration. In the fall of 2007, Brian Chesky and Joe Gebbia, who had moved to San Francisco soon after graduating from the Rhode Island School of Design, realized they could offset the high cost of renting their apartment by finding people who would pay to sleep in their living room on an air mattress instead of paying for a high-priced hotel room. Thus, the original name of the company they founded in 2008: AirBed&Breakfast.com. One of the reasons why it took off when it did, writes its chronicler, "was economic: coming as it did right out of the Great Recession, it offered a way for everyday people to make money off of their homes and a much more affordable way to travel."[29]

Airbnb.com is easy to use, stunning in its design, and comprehensive. Early on the company learned the importance of making payments easy to execute and of paying for professional photographers who could highlight distinctive features that made the property look tempting. As is true of Zillow, Airbnb's website makes dreaming and voyeurism possible.[30] I look at it for Shreveport, Louisiana—not the place where that many people seek a short-term rental for business or pleasure. But I pick it because I know it fairly well: as the city where my wife grew up, where we were wed in the summer of 1963, where we returned to see her parents, and where even later on I thought of carrying out research for this project, something the pandemic prevented me from doing. I enter some random dates I hope to be there and a fictive figure for how many people will accompany me. To the right is a Google map that takes up almost half the screen. I can see highways and lakes. I see the Red River, with which, in the 1830s, Captain Henry Miller Shreve, by clearing a massive cluster of logs called the Great Raft, helped build the basis for the city's future. I see the outline of the city limits and beyond them other areas, including Bossier City's Barksdale Air Force Base, to which President George W. Bush flew for safety right after the attacks of 9/11 and from which pilots flew massive B-52s as part of the ensuing global war on terror.

I can easily zoom in or out on the map and click on a small icon with its location and nightly price. On the top of the left side of the screen there is a series of boxes that I can click on to find the cancellation policy, to choose between a place all to our own or a room along with some shared facilities, to use a graph and some boxes that help me figure out how much I will spend, and additional filters to specify my choices—the number of rooms and bathrooms; amenities and facilities; whether smoking and pets are allowed; what languages the hosts speak; and, most temptingly, if I want to find "Superhosts," which, another website tells me, "provide a shining example for other hosts, and extraordinary experiences for their guests." Then I can scroll down to decide among the almost one hundred choices. When I click on a particular offering, up comes a site complete with pictures, more information including evaluations by recent guests, and instructions on how to contact my hosts. Am I tempted by the "Barn-apartment @ Jardin de LaRue—historic!" for a mere forty-five dollars a night plus fees? Its modest price underscores for me that we're not in Manhattan or San Francisco anymore, but I can easily travel to "all that Shreveport/Bossier has to offer," including the Louisiana Boardwalk Outlet Mall and one of five gambling casinos. These are all short drives from where I can stay, an "Entire Guesthouse.... Located on just over an acre of a historic 1903 Foursquare Craftsman remodel.... appointed in a subtle and tasteful mid-century aesthetic—stocked with all the amenities you'll need, and even some you may never have thought of!"

Part travel agent and part property manager, like many tech companies Airbnb operates in distinctive ways. With a dedication to develop a kinder and gentler capitalism, it is an example of the commitment culture found elsewhere in Silicon Valley corporations.[31] It relies on a relatively simple business model, even though the company requires property owners to sign a lengthy and complicated legal agreement. The host pays the corporation an Airbnb service fee, in the United States 3 percent, levied not only on the nightly fee but also on additional charges such as the expenses for cleaning. In exchange, the host benefits from the business that Airbnb drives its way, the rent collected, and a convenient system of booking and paying. The guest, who pays Airbnb a fee that ranges from 6 to 12 percent of total costs, might enjoy lower costs than would be charged by a hotel, as well as household amenities and the promise of greater charm and authentic personal interactions. By offering hosts and guests the ability to review each other, it promises to enhance a sense of trust. To be sure, as with most platform enterprises handling residential real estate, increased automation hardly promotes fairness. For example, renting via Airbnb is not without its downsides, with people reporting racial discrimination, unreliable and even dangerous hosts, safety issues, and deceptive advertising.[32] As is true with most platform corporations, for Airbnb there is a website, Airbnbhell.com, that features everything that can possibly go wrong for customers. Like most platform companies, Airbnb generates revenues and profits without the costs of owning and maintaining what it is selling. With 4 million places on offer in tens of thousands of cities within almost 200 nations, since its founding it has helped host over 400 million guests.[33] When I first drafted this chapter before the pandemic, it had over 6000 employees and a market capitalization just below $40 billion. Chesky and Gebbia were then reportedly each worth as much as $3 billion.

Even more widely than is true with Zillow, Airbnb's powerful impact has generated considerable controversy, given the ample extent to which it has powerfully disrupted residential real estate and the hospitality industry during and after the Great Recession.[34] Reducing a city's stock of rental properties raises rents and intensifies problems of affordability. Thus, if, along with its competitors such as Tripping.com, HomeToGo.com, Homestay.com, and FlipKey.com, Airbnb makes it possible for current homeowners to make more money and for others to become homeowners, it also makes it more difficult for prospective ones to turn an aspiration into reality and for long-term renters to find a reasonably priced place to live. Nor is the impact of platform enterprises in residential real estate confined to cities. Those who own vacation properties have benefited from the more frequent rentals that enhanced visibility brings, even though the adverse consequences are less serious in vacationland than in popular cities. Especially with properties in vacation spots and urban areas with high rents, what may have started with air mattresses and couch surfing eventually attracted institutional investors seeking ample returns on their investments by buying up multiple locations.

Indeed, to some extent what has amplified the power of Airbnb along with the problems that ensued is the power of institutional investors in the short-term rental market. The company started in late 2007 with an air mattress blown up in a living room and then in early 2009 secured as its first institutional funder a mere but highly significant $20,000 from the legendary Paul Graham's transformative startup accelerator Y Combinator. While Airbnb may have initially relied on individual homeowners hoping to make a few bucks by renting out a spare room, eventually private parties and institutional investors jumped it, albeit because regulation is so complicated and its impact uncertain.[35]

The term "sharing economy" may not properly describe what Airbnb involves because the word "sharing" implies an egalitarian relationship that rarely exists between a major corporation and owners and occupants of a spare room in a house. On the other hand, "disruption" is a more apt term to describe what Airbnb has done. One affected area is the hotel world. A growing and significant number of people prefer what Airbnb may provide: convenience, amenities, cost, distinctive and serendipitous experiences, authenticity, and personal connections. "Airbnb tapped into something greater than low prices and an abundance of available inventory," explains a writer for *Fortune* who has closely tracked the company's fortunes. "It offered an experience that was special and different. . . . that felt a little smaller-scale and more 'artisanal' than staying at a standard hotel. It also opened up access to different kinds of neighborhoods than traditional tourist zones, so you could have an experience that felt more local." Over time, the company expanded what it offered as it added ways to reserve tables at restaurants as well as distinctive activities through Airbnb Experiences. It curated arrangements like specialized tours and cooking classes, "hyperlocal activities like training with ultramarathoners in Kenya, or trimming Bonsai trees with like-minded enthusiasts." In some quarters, Airbnb represents cult-like promises of counterculture that celebrate belongingness, antipathy to commodification, and communitarian values. "The surge of millennials and their dramatically different value systems," writes the company's chronicler Leigh Gallagher appreciatively, "represented a fertile consumer base, with their preference for authentic experiences over things, their anticorporate and antiestablishment leanings, their hunger for anything that claimed to have a purpose or mission, and their desire to seek out community wherever they could find it."[36]

Nonetheless, whatever near-utopian dreams Airbnb inspired, it remains deeply integrated into the commodified worlds of capitalism. As is true to a lesser extent than with other high-tech behemoths, Airbnb spawned a host of independent but related enterprises, what a knowledgeable observer called "a robust cottage industry of start-ups offering services to support them, everything from pillow fluffing, turndown service, key exchanges, property management, minibar services, tax compliance, data analytics, and more."[37] There is some evidence that tourists are more likely than business travelers to rely on Airbnb, and that the use of short-term rentals competes more significantly with mid-priced and independent hotels than with those at either end of the price scale and those run by corporations such as Westin or Hilton.[38] Initially operators of hotel chains minimized the threat posed by sites such as Airbnb.com. Though the long-term challenge is too early to assess, there is some evidence that legacy accommodation providers such as executives at well-established hotel chains correctly feared how lower prices and occupancy threaten profitability.

Just as real estate giant Keller Williams decided to get a piece of the action that Zillow was stealing, so, too, did hotel giant Marriott enter the competitive fray. In 2014 it launched its Moxy brand, a line of hip hotels. "At Moxy hotels," its website reads, "we don't take ourselves too seriously. But we're seriously into showing you a good time with small but smart rooms, stylish communal spaces, and bars you'll love." Moreover, Marriott moved to compete directly with Airbnb's hold on vacation rentals. In April 2019, a reporter for the *New York Times* announced that "with hotel companies feeling the competition from the surging home-share industry led by Airbnb, Marriott International had decided if you can't beat them, join them" by offering comparable choices. Yet the impact of Airbnb on the hospitality industry remains to be seen: Marriott was dipping the traveler's proverbial foot in the swimming pool or ocean only by focusing on luxury rentals abroad.[39]

In contrast to what has happened to the hospitality industry, the disruptive impact of Airbnb on residential real estate, especially in popular, already-high-priced urban destinations, was clearly more momentous. Airbnb did indeed involve disruptive innovation based on new technologies through the process of what the scholar Daniel Guttentag calls the "touristification of residential areas."[40] Like enterprises such as Uber, it took advantage of rapid and low barrier entry, a lack of regulations, and complacent legacy competitors to achieve remarkable growth. Yet eventually the price of disruption became abundantly clear. Especially in fashionable and gentrifying areas of major cities, it drove up prices of residential real estate. Though Airbnb began with roommates making a couch available for surfing, eventually major investors saw money to be made. "The so-called sharing economy," wrote William Alden in the *New York Times* in late 2014, was supposed to be "one where regular folks" could deploy platforms to "turn their fallow assets into cash machines." The result would be abundant efficiency and low-cost entrepreneurship. The truth was, he continued, pointing to a New York City operation whose almost 300 listings brought in almost $7 million in four and a half years, "that these markets also tend to attract a class of well-heeled professional operators."[41]

Local governments began to regulate the real estate sector Airbnb represented in response to pressure from labor unions, advocates of affordable housing, and representatives of hotel owners.[42] One example is the city of Cambridge, Massachusetts, which has faced a crisis of housing affordability that Shreveport seems to have avoided. Renting a studio apartment smaller than 400 square feet for $2,500 per month would stretch the budget of someone who earned as much as $100,000 working for local high-tech firms. Travelers to Shreveport could pick among a small number of relatively inexpensive properties, while those coming to Cambridge faced more choices and higher prices. At the higher end, they could stay in a "Newly Renovated & Oh-So-Convenient!" one-bedroom apartment for just under $250 per night. Located in East Cambridge, it was convenient to

MIT and to one of the hundreds of small, medium, and huge life sciences companies and institutes. An August 2017 municipal ordinance set out to regulate Airbnb and its less powerful competitors. The city required landlords who rented a property on a short-term basis to register with the city's Inspectional Service Department, which would examine the property to make sure it complied with local ordinances governing health and safety. The operator of an Airbnb offering had to live in or adjacent to the rental unit. In addition to the state's room occupancy tax of 5.7 percent, the city levied both one of 6 percent and a 3 percent short-term rental community impact fee. Companies like Uber took a preemptive and adversarial stance to governments. Airbnb, though arguably as disruptive as any platform corporation, engaged in regulator management by negotiating deals on issues such as taxes and regulations.

Compared with what happened in cities, Airbnb caused less disruption in vacationland, though the impact on resort hotels and vacation homes was significant. "How Vacation Homes Went from Private Escape to Investment Opportunities" ran the lead to a fall 2018 posting of Curbed, a real estate blog network created in 2006. "Rural areas, beach communities, and ski towns," noted reporter Patrick Sisson, "have seen their hospitality and hotel markets shift as second homes increasingly become second sources of income—and targets of speculation." Of course, owners of second homes have long relied on income from rentals, but Airbnb made the process simpler and more lucrative. According to one report, as recently as the beginning of the new century, 80 percent of owners of second homes had never put them on the rental market. However, the Great Recession, along with new business models build on transformative technologies, shifted the incentives for owners and renters and reduced the costs, hassles, and concerns about safety. A weakened economy made additional income tempting and often necessary at a time when it was difficult to unload a second home in a depressed real estate market, while tighter vacation budgets drove people to seek geographically convenient bargains rather than expensive, distant, and exotic locations. During challenging economic times, remarked the CEO of Rented.com, one of Airbnb's competitors, "when purse strings are pulled tighter, people aren't looking for Bali."[43]

Less than in popular urban destinations but nonetheless significantly, platform-based companies like Airbnb could be disruptive to communities in rural areas and small towns. Short-term renters might make these locales more vibrant and enhance the income of locals who had spare rooms and empty houses to rent, store inventory to sell, and restaurants to fill. Yet many long-term residents of ski and beach communities, like some of their urban counterparts, felt that Airbnb threatened their sense of community and their economic well-being. Replacing neighbors with tourists meant that a souvenir shop might take the place of a local butcher and increase the annoyance of late-night partying. So, as happened in cities, homeowners in vacation communities moved to regulate and benefit from the arrival of people whom Airbnb made possible. "The debate in these vacation communities about the impact of short-term [rentals]," wrote Sisson, "quickly begins to resemble the conversation taking place at a large scale in cities, a conversation that hinges on issues of displacement, housing supply, and the freedom of property owners to do as they please. . . . when homeownership has become more difficult for many Americans, second-home speculation showcases" one "impact of the Great Recession: the widening growth of inequality."[44]

If we return our attention to primary residences, we see that for many families in the early twenty-first century, new technologies promised to transform the home into a secular, somewhat self-contained sanctuary. What the emerging technologies of the early twenty-first century also seemed to make possible was a domestic world in which men and women could be equal, and in which the home's relationship to the outside world was reconfigured. Especially under the impact of the Great Recession, new technologies and media enabled people to arrange so much of their lives while at home.[45] Early on Amazon led the way in enabling people to avoid the inconvenience of going to a brick-and-mortar store in search of almost anything. Eventually people could go to a seemingly infinite variety of websites to select items to bring into the home with the click of a mouse on a computer or touch on a smartphone screen and then pay remotely by credit card. Following a year after Amazon's founding in 1994 came eBay, a platform company that connects buyers with sellers. Its website mentions "Electronics, Cars, Fashion, Collectibles & More," with that last word referring to the widest possible range of goods. Behemoths like Walmart and Target played catch-up by launching websites in the hopes of competing with Amazon, while Sears, Kmart, and Borders Books faltered or failed in part because they were slow to do so. Then there were ambitious but more specialized e-commerce enterprises. Etsy offers vintage and handmade items in abundance, while Poshmark does the same for used clothing and accessories. Wayfair presents "A Zillion Things Home": in addition to furniture and home decor items delivered with the now-obligatory promise of free shipping and easy returns, it offers the service "Remodel and Recreate with Wayfair." More difficult to crack is the hold of car dealerships, at least for new cars. But among those making headway in the used car markets were CarMax and Carvana, the latter with its clever multistory automobile vending machines, easy-to-use website, and delivery to your home.[46]

So much for accumulation of possessions. For disaccumulation, choices are also multiplying. With friends, I have jokingly dreamed of creating The Museum of Things Your Children Don't Want—tongue-in-cheek funded by the Sackler Foundation, which, given its riches from peddling opioids, makes real museums reluctant to receive or acknowledge support. Located in a difficult-to-travel-to town where real estate is inexpensive, it will have a China Room, Crystal Room, Silver Room, Linen Room, and even a Memento Room. But we've been beaten to the punch by internet-enabled sites, including Everything but the House (EBTH), which seeks to replace the physicality of the estate sale with its virtual equivalent. "As much as we love our childhood home," remarked a writer for *Forbes* in 2016, "we don't necessarily want all the items that have accumulated in it over the years." So in stepped EBTH, which was "betting that they can find buyers for not just some, but *all* of the contents of your home." As their name suggests, they liquidate everything but the house—after photographing it, cataloging it, auctioning it off online, and then arranging to have it shipped to its new owners.[47] At the other end of the possession disposal chain are Craigslist and 1-800-GOT-JUNK? Then there are the nonprofits that facilitate local exchanges, such as the FreeCycle Network, receptacle bins provided by American Red Cross or Goodwill Industries, or the simple leaving of items on the sidewalk with a note indicating they're for the taking.

If we shift from goods to services, a similarly ample range of internet-enabled enterprises make it possible for people throughout the life cycle to carry on their lives while remaining at home. For a home birth, which about 1 percent of parents prefer, you can go online to find a midwife. Homeschooling, in some ways a return to patterns upended in the nineteenth century by state-mandated compulsory school attendance laws, returned with the 1960s counterculture and then gained ground with families that preferred to educate their children at home because of issues involving religion, ideology, or quality—or simply because they wanted to be closely involved in their children's education. With about 2 million (or well over 3 percent of) children learning at home, an infrastructure has emerged, much of it technologically enabled. Going online, parents can use sites like Time4Learning to explore curricular options, locate standardized tests, find out how to secure accreditation, obtain a high school diploma, and identify homeschooling-friendly colleges. Facebook and other sites provide access to networks of other homeschooling families and institutions, a veritable cornucopia that has on offer a range of secular and religious choices. Later on, Junior can find their perfect mate on any one of a proliferating number of online dating sites and then, if so inclined, turn to an officiant on a site such as American Marriage Ministries (AMM, 2009). "Unlike other religious institutions that require years of seminary study and many thousands of dollars," its website says reassuringly, "ordination through AMM is free and takes only minutes." It enables you to have the "full legal authority to conduct marriage ceremonies all across the US!" and in doing so you join the more than 700,000 already ordained. And folks can also use the website The Knot as their bridal registry.

Once married or partnered, the couple can find an apartment to rent or a home to buy on Zillow and finance a purchase on LendingTree, one of many online sites rather than an actual bank. They can fill their home using websites discussed above. But before doing so they face seemingly infinite choices as they decide on home design, something that gives the illusion of easy work and freedom. "'Power to the people' (or power to Apple and its codependents)—house design apps are 'applications,'" notes one observer wittily, "usually on an iPhone or Android that allow you to foresee how your house will look after renovations, an interior-rejig or simply, a new paint job."[48] For example, claims another observer at SketchUp.com, "the most comprehensive free 3D design software you'll find on the web. . . . Immersive enough to make it seem like you are moving through your future home, while being flexible enough to make it feel as if you're working with paper and pen."[49] The website of the immensely popular organizing and simplifying guru Marie Kondo can help you "live a life that sparks joy." And the magazine *Real Simple*'s website may put you on the road to simplicity—though I always find that its recommendations might just as easily lead you to a consumption-complicated life. Influencers on Instagram offer widely followed advice about what home design fashions to follow. For example, there is Inspire Me! Home Decor, with its almost 6 million followers. "Let's Be Friends!" its host Farah Merhi says to me. "It's all about making your house your home" and "your sanctuary."

Once settled, you can use the internet to bring the world out there into your domicile. Instacart will pick up your groceries in a supermarket and deliver them to your home. Grubhub brings restaurant food to your front door, while Plated or Blue Apron deliver ready-to-prepare meals. Angi (formerly Angie's List) and its subsidiary Home Advisor connect you with vetted professionals who will remodel or repair your residence. TaskRabbit can help you connect with an even wider range of helpers, including those who can run errands or help move furniture. Tasks accomplished and perhaps exhausted by all that free labor you devoted to the internet, it is time to sit back and relax—and this is an area where home dwellers can experience the results of the most dramatic changes and abundant opportunities. Online music streaming services from Apple, Amazon, and Spotify confined collections of CDs to the dustbin of history by offering a virtually unlimited selection of music that you could access on a smartphone, computer, or home music system in exchange for a modest monthly fee.

However, for the time being the award for disruptive innovation in entertainment, one whose impact reverberated well beyond that sphere, surely goes to Netflix. Along with Amazon Prime Video, Hulu, iTunes, Google Play, and Vudu, among others, Netflix brings robust entertainment choices into the home at the same time that it has weakened public entertainment venues. Ten years after its founding in 1997, it shifted from selling and renting movies to streaming them, thus bringing entertainment into your home almost immediately. Debt-laden and only recently profitable, it is now available in almost 200 nations worldwide and to 70 million customers in the United States alone. Building on both a platform and linear supply chain model, Netflix offers previously produced and original in-house offerings, for the latter of which it spends well in excess of $10 billion annually. With a market capitalization of $300 million when it went public in 2002, that figure now hovers around $200 billion. The disruptive power of Netflix is enormous. It helped close down stores that rented movie videos, most notably Blockbuster, which went from 4,500 outlets in the United States at its height in 2004 to close to zero now. It upended the business of movie theaters, driving ticket sales from 1.5 million in 2002 down to 223,000 in 2020. Its algorithm-driven recommendation system—the envy of less sophisticated enterprises—divides people into several thousand "taste groups" in order to figure out what you might enjoy watching next.[50] It taught viewers that they could watch movies and TV shows without being bombarded by advertisements. As the world's largest user of bandwidth, it tests the limits of technology. Challenging Hollywood's power, it transformed the markets for talent and audiences as well as entertainment's awards systems.

Before you sink too deeply into the pleasures of what disruptive enterprises bring, you might encounter the challenges of health and aging. First you can use new technologies to monitor your own health at home and have it reported to your doctor but hope no one steals your data and privacy. Then you can turn to telemedicine, which, though still in its infancy prepandemic, brings doctors and patients together over the internet. Data sharing between doctors across specialties and geographical boundaries, remote monitoring of patients, disease and medicine management—all these can increase convenience and mitigate problems of mobility, disease spread, work schedules, and home care. "You're in good hands," the website of Teladoc remarks reassuringly, because it provides "Care that's about you. Always," by facilitating "access to board-certified doctors, licensed nurses, and world-renowned specialists." Or you can turn to Doctor on Demand, launched by reality TV star Dr. Phil and his son Jay. Then when aging begins to take its toll on you or your loved one, you can turn to a site like a Place for Mom for help in sorting out options for senior care. If you prefer a noninstitutional option for yourself or your parents, turn to a company like Home Instead Senior Care, a franchise-based, internet-enabled service that makes aging in place more feasible for those who prefer it and can afford it. For better or worse, though burial on a family's land was popular when great numbers of Americans lived on farms, now zoning and other laws, along with the issue of the future of the value of your property, makes burial at home difficult. Even more daunting and impossible is cremating a body at home. There are simply some opportunities new technologies have yet to exploit. A number of factors both complicate and amplify the notion of the home as a somewhat self-contained sanctuary from a troubled world. Given the power of corporations, internet-enabled homes are hardly isolated from the world, but these powerful forces nonetheless help erode the important benefits of face-to-face personal encounters.

In addition to how significantly new technologies have transformed the dynamics of domestic consumer culture, there are the ways the internet is transforming the home as a site of work. Of course, people have always toiled at home—on farms, where work beckoned on both sides of the back door; on plantations, where white masters and mistresses extracted the labor of African American enslaved people inside the big house and outside in the fields; and in the early days of industrialization, when many workers toiled before most of their labor shifted to factories. Then there are domestic workers as well as housewives who have long done domestic labor, in the former case underpaid and in the latter unpaid.

In the early twenty-first century, new technologies opened up other possibilities. Abroad, people in nations where English was commonly spoken could work for call centers, often from their own residences. Similarly, in the United States, increasingly around the start of the twenty-first century, more and more people worked at home on a part-time basis as employees of decentered call centers. For example, FlexJobs lists "call center jobs" that are "perfect for people who enjoy helping others, can use a computer and telephone well and can 'think on their feet' to find solutions to meet customer needs," to say nothing of their own need to make financial ends meet while remaining at home, even though many of the benefit-less positions pay only ten dollars an hour. People who host Airbnb clients lose some of their privacy (more so if they are renting a room in their home), subject spaces they have curated to the judgments of outsiders, and turn domestic spaces into sites of work they have to clean or arrange to be cleaned.

More momentous were the changes that came when companies allowed increasing numbers of employees with relatively high levels of skills to work more or less full time from their residences—something the internet and other technologies made both possible and increasingly common. One estimate is that, globally, in 1995, by the most capacious and inclusive measurement, the percentage of those working remotely stood at 9 and by 2015 had quadrupled.[51] More recently, Gallup in 2017 reported that 43 percent of people spent at least some time working remotely, were doing so for more extended periods of time, and believed that doing so helped make them more productively engaged in their work and with coworkers and managers.[52] Such people may well include freelancers, part-time and contract workers, and even digital nomads who prefer working from cafés and on trains as they travel the world. Moreover, there is a wide range of models deployed for remote workers, including teams spread across the world whose members never or rarely meet in person, and locational hybrids that involve people who divide their time between home offices and corporate offices in a range of possible mixtures.

For the employee, remote work is attractive for many reasons, especially given the downsides of the *Dilbert* world of privacy-compromised cubicles. Among the advantages are flexibility and convenience, the saving of time and money by not having to commute, the ability to more easily care for family members, and a more favorable work-life balance. Having a remote work force can enable employers to recruit and retain talent in competitive labor markets. Reduced costs and increased profits stem from the ability to lower personnel expenses by hiring less costly workers from abroad, lower overhead expenses that come from dramatically reducing the costly need for office space, and the ability to more easily change the mixture and numbers of employees. Especially if it is possible to shift from time-orientation to a focus on results, enhanced productivity can result from having more satisfied employees.

Of course, for all parties, technologically enabled and geographically distanced work is hardly problem free. For employees, it is difficult to navigate the tensions between office demands and domestic obligations. Working alone away from an office makes collective social or political action difficult. Nor is it easy to ensure privacy from either supervisors or family members. By lowering their real estate costs, bosses have shifted the burden to those they employ, often necessitating more room (or more crowding) and higher expenses at home. The advocates of working remotely claim it is possible to overcome problems associated with physical isolation with technological tools such as FaceTime. Yet there are downsides to new arrangements. The much-maligned water cooler conversations do have their advantages, among them the way personal contacts can facilitate communication, the exchange of useful information, and even serendipitous discoveries. For employers, relying on workers located remotely raises issues of how to effectively supervise and manage individuals and teams, handle conflict resolution, facilitate decision-making, and foster morale that relies on camaraderie.[53]

I researched a hefty portion of this book at home, remotely distanced from the library stacks that I have long enjoyed wandering through as I cast my eyes over rows of books to discover what technology might have caused me to miss. In retirement, I also miss the on-campus conversations—casual as well as intense, with students and colleagues. In contrast, much of what I have written while working remotely finds echoes in the sometimes exaggerated claims in Lisette Sutherland and Kirsten Janene-Nelson's 2020 *Work Together Anywhere: A Handbook on Working Remotely and Successfully from Anywhere for Individuals, Teams, and Managers*. Although much of what they write is data-driven and practical, at moments they speak too enthusiastically. If it would be advantageous to "make location the variable—indeed, immaterial," they insist, then it would be possible to "have the constant be the far more important concern: qualification, including enthusiasm. Employers could hire the best, the brightest, and the most dedicated—wherever those workers happen to be." Because technology could make it "so that everyone could engage in work that jazzes them," the authors wax with undue optimism "about how people from all corners of the globe have figured out how to flourish working remotely—and how in doing so have achieved marvels previous thought impossible."[54]

Even before the COVID-19 pandemic, the impact of these changing patterns reverberated in so many ways. They could involve the rearranging or reallocation of domestic spaces. They affected the relationships of at-home workers to their spouses or domestic partners and their children. They could upend traditional patterns of allocation of time; indeed, there is some evidence that working remotely intensifies work commitments as employees reciprocally benefit their employers by offering more effort in exchange for greater flexibility.[55] These changes could challenge established relationships of employers to employees as well as of employees to each other. On the one hand, they raise questions about authority and surveillance, and on the other, about the danger of eroding or at least complicating the bonds among coworkers. The home as workplace decreased the reliance on means of transportation other than walking from one room to another and in doing so might in some small ways lessen the dangers of climate change. It had an immense and growing impact on commercial office space, as corporations realized that they could save money on rent, taxes, and utilities by relocating staff members to their homes. Although working remotely may exacerbate class and racial divides, it might lessen those driven by gender and bicoastal geography.[56]

With finding a place to live or use on a vacation, managing life in a residence through the life cycle, and treating the home as sanctuary or workplace, new technologies powerfully disrupted patterns of buying, selling, working, gather information, relating to others, and navigating the relationships between public and private worlds. The economic historian Robert J. Gordon has argued that the technological innovations of the years from 1870 to 1940 in areas such as housing, transportation, and manufacturing fundamentally improved the lives of hundreds of millions in the United States. Since then, he insists, what the nation has experienced are more modest increases in productivity and greater increases in inequality, accompanied by innovations "channeled into a narrow sphere of human activity having to do with entertainment, communications, and the collection and processing of information."[57] Innovative enterprises did transform how people gathered information, often substituting searches on the Web for reliance on word-of-mouth and classified advertisements. Ironically, with homeschooling serving as an alternative to public schools and Netflix emptying our movie theaters, the reliance on publicly available technologies fostered the erosion of public spaces and intensified the seeming isolation of private ones. As the CEO and chief economist of Zillow remarked in their jointly written book *Zillow Talk*, homes now "embody the privatization of a whole host of activities that used to be exclusively commercial—from the gym, to the movies, to coffee shops, to the workplace itself. And, yes, Robert Putnam, we even *bowl* at home—on our TVs and in our living rooms, thanks to the magic of Wii and Xbox."[58]

Moreover, creative destruction helped cause many brick-and-mortar stores to close and substantially weakened the market for commercial real estate. Shopping on Amazon may be more convenient in some ways, but getting advice from a knowledgeable person in a store also has its advantages. Platform enterprises weakened the market for midlevel jobs in organizations (and compromised the lives of many middle-class citizens), with greater numbers of people working in the gig economy without benefits and steady incomes. Lyft and Uber were not alone among the sectors of the sharing economy that defined those who worked under its auspices not as employees with benefits but as contract workers without benefits and a range of protections for workers. Making one's way through a phone tree, waiting online at an 800 number, and following on-screen instructions are just a few of the irritating examples that reflect the shift in labor to the struggling self. Living in a house found through Zillow, designed with the help of an influencer, and outfitted through Wayfair has its pleasures but also its costs. As one observer noted in 2020, "Over the past decade, Silicon Valley has been at the center of an energetic campaign to convince people that this insecure status is, in fact, desirable—than an independent contractor is a member of the 'sharing economy' or even, like Zuckerberg or Musk, an entrepreneur."[59] One group of entrepreneurs made fortunes creating new technologies, while others farther down the hierarchy between wealth and poverty developed home-based businesses.

Overall, many of the changes already discussed strengthened class, racial, geographical, and generational divides, in the process challenging the claims of what one observer calls "innovation-centric futurism" and another "techno-optimists."[60] Easy access to and ample use of the internet raised lifestyle aspirations without necessarily providing the means of satisfying them. Where you live and how much wealth and income your family has significantly affects internet access, with rural and poor people on the short end of the router's stick. Less fortunate than those who owned multiple homes or lived in McMansions were people who resided in crowded and dangerous venues such as prisons and homeless shelters; on the street; or in embattled neighborhoods. People living in bicoastal communities, especially those advantaged by high-tech employment, reap the benefits of new media more than do many who live in flyover communities or labor in factories or warehouses. In a related change, those who benefit from employment in sectors that rely on new technologies can flourish in comparison with those whose lives are shaped by jobs in the manufacturing and extractive sectors. Many members of the baby boom generation could afford to buy homes and then watch their value escalate. In contrast, many of those coming of age in the new century had to rent rather than own and then tend to plants, pets, and crafts rather than kids. Millennials and members of Generation Z may be more tech savvy than those who came before them, but they are nonetheless deeply affected by three transformative events of the twenty-first century: the terrorist attacks of 9/11, the Great Recession toward the end of the same decade, and the COVID-19 pandemic.

CODA

FROM THE GREAT RECESSION TO THE COVID-19 PANDEMIC

On January 20, 2020, the State of Washington and the Centers for Disease Control diagnosed the first case of COVID-19 in the United States. Exactly one year later, in a transition of power mandated by the Constitution and confirmed by democracy, Joseph R. Biden Jr. became the forty-sixth president of the United States. On the very next day, I began to draft this coda. I realized that whatever I wrote then had of necessity to be tentative and outdated by the time the manuscript turned into a book. After all, if we have a pretty good idea of the implications of the Great Recession for housing, the consequences of the pandemic are difficult to chart or predict. Yet, drawing on what others have written, an informed but speculative summary was in order—not only for the specific topics covered in individual chapters, but also about the more general conditions such as social class, gender relations, ethnic and racial divisions; public and private lives; the differences between work, play, shopping, and entertainment; and the intensification of inequalities, especially as they related to housing. Though some things remained roughly the same, by and large the twin crises of the early twenty-first century quickened changes already in motion. How the global financial crisis plus the pandemic would affect the fate of political and economic trends was even more subject to speculation. "Sometime in 2021, life will look a lot more normal," quipped a headline writer the day before Christmas in 2020. "But it won't be the same."[1]

For a historian, writing about yesterday, today, and tomorrow is problematic. So I decided I would draft this coda, relying mostly on what information was available by or soon after mid-March 2021, the time when I and so many others in the United States first began dimly to sense how unpredictable and troublesome the pandemic would be. March 11, 2021, was the date Biden signed the $1.7 trillion American Rescue Plan Act passed by

"You really think they'll come back to the hill after they've gotten used to working remotely?"

First published in the *New Yorker* on October 5, 2020, and used by permission of the artist, Kendra Allenby. © Kendra Allenby

Congress, which included a broad range of provisions to counter the pandemic's impact. To help keep people adequately housed, it provided funds for rental assistance and to lessen the likelihood of foreclosures, evictions, and homelessness. Later on, aware of the lengthy period between finishing a book and seeing it in print, I fixed upon the idea of writing a brief coda to this coda in mid-March 2022, when final copy was due. However, I knew that even this addition would be outdated when the book appeared in print and more so as time marched on.

The 2021 *State of the Nation's Housing* report from Harvard's Joint Center for Housing Studies, based on data available in the first quarter of 2021 and published soon after in June, made clear the profound impact of the pandemic's first year. It emphasized the divisions between households that had thrived (including among them those whose members could afford new homes) and those the pandemic had adversely affected. The number of houses for sale shrank dramatically, and prices escalated. Many households faced dire economic and medical challenges. Renters struggled mightily to pay their landlords, with the federal government stepping in to remedy the situation in ways that helped considerably, even though homelessness increased. The greater number of people working remotely from home sought larger quarters, fueling moves to single-family residences, especially in the suburbs. This also strained the market for labor and lumber as well as the ability of African Americans, Latinx, and people with low to moderate incomes to afford adequate housing.[2]

If we turn our attention to media representations of residential real estate—initially on HGTV, then in workshops, and, finally, in newspapers and magazines—we discover a gossip-filled world. Not surprisingly, with the three HGTV couples, celebrity stories carried the day during the pandemic. We learn that Christina Haack (now divorced from Ant Anstead), and Tarek El Moussa (who in October 2021 married Heather Rae Young) were eager to offer "their coparenting tips," to react "to their ex's new partners," even as they "share the screen post-divorce and continued filming their HGTV show after ending their marriage."[3] And did you hear about Jonathan Scott's romance with Zooey Deschanel, whom he met while filming *Carpool Karaoke*? Or that Chip and Joanna Gaines were "hunkered down with their kids on the family's farm in Waco, Texas, without the distractions classes, work and outside interactions usually provide"?[4] Yet if the three couples were media-savvy celebrities who fed audiences even more hungry for gossip as they, too, hunkered down, they were also perceptive entrepreneurs eager to sustain and expand their empires. Albeit divorced, the El Moussas signed on for a tenth season of *Flip or Flop* even as they worked on their own respective shows, *Flipping 101 with Tarek El Moussa* and *Christina on the Coast*. The Scott brothers enhanced the reach of their imperial projects, an endeavor made easier given how, as one home furnishing publication remarked after a Zoom interview with them, they knew "the pandemic has consumers reimagining their own living spaces now that they are spending so much more time at home."[5] "The Chip and Jo industrial complex, friends, is still growing," remarked pop culture writer Claire McNear on the day of Biden's inauguration. "The real estate impresarios debuted their very own television network, the Magnolia Network," now available on the recently launched streaming service Discovery+, she noted, even as she acknowledged that "calling the couple 'real estate impresarios'" had years ago begun "to feel like calling Jimmy Carter a peanut farmer."[6]

If three of HGTV's star couples could easily leverage pandemic conditions to expand their empires, COVID-19 presented real estate workshops like those of Robert Kiyosaki and Than Merrill with greater challenges, which they met by shifting from in-person workshops to online presentations.[7] With some alacrity but abundant persistence, Merrill's helpers, relying on the email address they captured when I signed up for prepandemic workshops, took advantage of my prior involvement.[8] Beginning at least in May 2020 and then by the summer with considerable persistence, I received a steady stream of emails offering me abundant opportunities to build my fortune. "Hey Daniel! Our Founder just uploaded" an "inspiring new video that you should watch ASAP," I learned. After a picture of the video and a link had come these wise words, from the WealthFit Team, an umbrella organization offering courses by about sixty "World-Class Trainers," including both Kiyosaki and Merrill.[9] A while later, when I clicked on a link to take advantage of my "free trial," apparently to give me access to all the trainers, to proceed I had to sign up with a credit card that would be used after my free weeks. Then I'd pay only $195 for something that would normally cost $588. Here I was again, back where I began during an in-person workshop, faced with a deal I had to take advantage of right away—or else. As with the workshops I attended in person, the purveyors of the online workshops used personal appeals, evocations of expertise, promises, and urgent warnings accompanied by deadlines to capture my interest and my dollars.[10]

As the pandemic took hold, the National Association of Realtors offered practical advice, including tips from Tarek El Moussa and Christina Anstead, who had "tons to teach the rest of us on how to buy, sell, and renovate a house during a pandemic and beyond."[11] More generally, writers for the magazine and website cheered on the industry's agents, who had "displayed resilience, creativity, and drive," even finding that "physical isolation often led to broader and deeper engagement with their clients and contacts than they'd had before the crisis. . . . In a business where social contact is the staff of life," a team of writers insisted in the spring of 2020, "real estate pros have shown just how creative they can be at bridging differences, finding ways to stay connected and positive as they hunkered down," developing "rituals likely to carry on long after the crisis."[12]

Then there were political responses in print media. Those who wrote for the *Nation* worried how the pandemic adversely affected America's most vulnerable, and their counterparts at *Forbes* used adversity to celebrate capitalism's creativity. Writing in late May 2020, the chief content officer and editor of *Forbes* worried that "ideas such as universal basic income, rent amnesties and job guarantees" were increasingly moving "from the fringe to the mainstream." Yet in the end he remained confident that "amid the chaos and disorienting paradigm shifts, though, something profound is also happening: The Invisible Hand is operating on itself with dispatch." To support his confidence, he pointed to three trends. First was that the transformation of "the low-paid heroes previously termed 'unskilled workers'" into workers "now known, with respect, as *essential*" had put the nail in the coffin of Milton Friedman's celebration of "shareholder-first dogma." Secondly, he argued that "the Too Big to Fail playbook from the last meltdown has proven archaic." Finally, he insisted that with the end of "economic incrementalism" there had emerged "Greater Capitalism" built on "systematic solutions greater than what we had before." Ignoring evidence to the contrary, such as the successes of Big Pharma, the failures of millions of small businesses, lobbying efforts by small businesses and large corporations, and massive interventions of the federal government, he instead celebrated "the small businesses and entrepreneurs who ask for a little more than a fair chance and a level playing field."[13]

In sharp contrast to the ways the *Nation* and *Forbes* followed familiar ideological paths, the *Financial Times* stood out for its heralding of a new political economy. In early April 2020, an editorial appeared under the headline "Virus Lays Bare the Frailty of the Social Contract." Below it was a picture of volunteers delivering food donations in London, a gesture that, the caption noted, was symbolic of "the brittleness of many countries' economies." The editorial board identified the "injection of a sense of togetherness into polarised societies" as "a silver living" to the pandemic, which had also helped "shine a glaring light on existing inequalities—and even create new ones." As was true in previous crises such as the Great Depression and World War II, the challenge was "to demand collective sacrifice" and "offer a social contract that benefits everyone." The editors called for "radical reforms" that would reverse "the prevailing policy direction of the last four decades," among them governments taking on more active roles in the economy; seeing "public services as investments rather than liabilities"; devising "ways to make labour markets less insecure"; placing "redistribution," guaranteed basic incomes, and taxes on wealth on the table; and questioning "the privileges of the elderly and wealthy."[14] And then there were the scores of articles by Gillian Tett, the anthropologist turned financial journalist. Many of them echoed themes widely circulating, such as the way the pandemic exacerbated existing inequalities.[15] One of her key articles appeared in early May 2020, a few weeks before the death of George Floyd, an event that intensified the prominence of social divisions in America.

When we shift from the way media from HGTV to the *Financial Times* treated the impact of the pandemic on residential real estate, we encounter a wide range of observations and predictions. We can usefully begin with the vision of the home as an often-problematic safe harbor in the pandemic storm. Tellingly, in March 2020, the *New York Times* launched a weekly online "At Home" section, which in late April first appeared in print. Noting that pandemic conditions resulted in the suspension of the Travel section and significant reduction of Sports, an editor announced that the new "section will be filled with advice and activities to help readers thrive in a setting where work, school, family and recreation come together within a single space."[16] In May 2021, the print edition of "At Home" ended: "With Society Reopening, the At Home Section Is Closing," read the headline announcing the change.[17]

Newspaper coverage, in the *New York Times* and elsewhere, tracked how COVID-19 had shaped the way people sometimes coped and sometimes transformed their domestic lives.[18] Even before the pandemic, the number of people who worked from home, especially among the ranks of white collar and service sector employees, had steadily grown—a phenomenon that now accelerated.[19] The increasing and perhaps somewhat irreversible shift to remote work, one journalist noted, "has the potential to change people's work lives in much more profound ways. It could significantly affect their wages, alter career prospects and restructure organizations. And as with many economic shocks, workers are likely to be affected unevenly."[20] The shift to working from home may well have threatened the welfare benefits of productivity in general and in particular adversely impacted those with some combination of low skills, problematic access to new technologies, children at home, and cramped quarters. On the other hand, it was a boon to the highly skilled, to those who no longer faced long and expensive commutes, who could take advantage of new technologies, who did not have reason to worry about the impact of COVID-19 on them or those they loved, who had no children or could handle childcare without too much difficulty, and who had ample and/or easy-to-refigure domestic spaces. The most fortunate among those now working at home might miss the collegiality of water-cooler conversations, but they soon discovered the benefits of lowered expenses, a room-to-room commute, a more relaxed and flexible schedule, and more time with family members.

For many, the key issue involved the difficulties of caring for and educating children while also working for a living. This was especially so for women in households governed by traditional gender roles who had to navigate taking care of family members at home and others at work away from home in settings like schools, hospitals, and nursing homes. In addition, under pandemic conditions, educating one's own children faced parents with often impossible choices. School districts and those offering advice seemed to forever change plans. As a consequence, parents struggled to balance pandemic risks with educational and social rewards. Sending children to actual classrooms might mean that when they returned home, they'd bring COVID-19 with them. The increased reliance on technology made it difficult for children to find new friends or sustain relationships with old ones. All this was especially trying for families that lacked access to the internet or domestic space ample enough for multiple family members to achieve their goals. Above all, parents and educators had to worry whether 2020 would be, as a September 11, 2020, *New York Times* headline asked, a "Lost Year for America's Children," as "educator experts reckon[ed] with the long-term implications of remote learning, vanishing resources and heightened inequality."[21]

Despite these challenges, or perhaps in response to them, reports circulated about how during the pandemic people turned their homes into self-contained pleasure palaces. "They're Stuck at Home, So They're Making Home a Sanctuary," read the headline of a September 4, 2020, story.[22] Working in PJs or sweats was more comfortable (and less expensive) than dressing up in more formal attire. With plenty of time to plan and supervise projects made possible by the budget relief from not traveling or eating in restaurants, people turned their attention to home improvements—redecorating or adding a room, upgrading systems, or turning a backyard into a vacation retreat. The "At Home" section of the October 25, 2020, *New York Times* captured it all, filled as it was with stories of trying out new cuisines, communicating more effectively with friends and family members, turning your TV set into a movie theater screen, and developing an indoor hydroponic garden. And in the middle of the section stood a two-page ad for an American Airlines Mastercard. It pictured a woman exercising on what appeared to be the wing of an airplane, with both a desert expanse and a living room wall behind her. She promised, shouted the words in large print, "to turn new headphones into sounds of nature."[23]

New or enhanced technologies played essential roles in making living at home during the pandemic more self-contained, though using that hyphenated word glosses over the role of entrepreneurs, venture capitalists, and tech workers around the world who made it all possible. Peloton ($1895 for the basic version or the $1495 Mirror Home Workout System, both with monthly subscription at $39) turned a corner of a room into a gym at a time when commercial gyms were places where you might contract COVID-19. Telemedicine connected patients with health care providers, more successfully with some ailments and, at least initially, more urgently for those confined and/or living remotely from practitioners. Of course, what made remote health care possible were access to technologies and, in the short term, under pandemic conditions and perhaps longer, changes in what insurance providers reimbursed.[24] For students, including adult learners but especially those from kindergarten to college, online learning, sometimes combined with in-person attendance, imperfectly replaced being in the classroom with peers and teachers.

Of all the fields that made living at home at least tolerable under pandemic conditions, none were more transformative than telecommunications through programs like Zoom, Google Meet, and Microsoft Teams, as well as the streaming of entertainment through Netflix and its competitors. Zoom, the nation's most significant teleconferencing platform, was founded in 2009, its software launched two years later, and its initial public offering coming in mid-April 2019. Its market capitalization grew from $25 million in early 2013 to $140 billion in October 2020, and the increase in subscribers and individual users was also dramatic. I am sure my own usage is both typical and idiosyncratic. By late spring of 2020, I had begun to participate in four weekly Zoom meetings and occasional small, one-off gatherings; via the internet started to walk the halls of museums throughout the world to see familiar and for me undiscovered gems; gone to a Thanksgiving dinner and a bar mitzvah, but no weddings or funerals; and attended and even participated in lectures and conferences. Thus, what replaced what friends consider my prepandemic extensive sociability over meals, at meetings, and on long walks was the ability to maintain engagements with friends and family members that Zoom provided. Though, like others, I longed to return to some semblance of normality (whose nature it was difficult for me to imagine), Zoom's technology helped sustain me—and hundreds of millions of others.

If we had not even known of Zoom before the spring of 2020, when my wife and I hunkered down, we had already used streaming services, though such usage paled in comparison with how often we went out into the world to see movies and attend live musical events. Now, the at-home possibilities opened up and expanded for us as they did for others on Netflix, Amazon Prime, Hulu, Apple TV+, Disney+, and HBO Max, among a seemingly unending stream of streaming possibilities. Netflix was founded in 1997, which, by new technology standards, makes it ancient. However, it was only in 2007 that it introduced streaming and about the same time moved beyond rebroadcasting to producing its own series and features. Its revenue grew apace and dramatically, from $682 million in 2005 to $25 billion in 2020. Along the way, as it gathered talent, it exemplified Joseph Schumpeter's process of creative destruction, upending the presentations of Hollywood awards and Hollywood itself, in addition, of course, to providing home entertainment.

"The Week Hollywood Finally, Actually Died," ran an August 16, 2020, headline above an article by *New York Times* media columnist Ben Smith, who had recently jumped to the gray lady of print journalism, tellingly, from his position as editor in chief at BuzzFeed News. Challenges to the traditional studio model had already appeared, he reported, especially surrounding questions about the handling of race and gender, as well as the emphasis on studio blockbusters of interest mainly to moviegoers younger than thirty-five. Added to that were steady or declining revenues from cable and the difficulty old-line studios had in launching their own streaming services. Then came the pandemic, threatening the industry's schmoozing culture and leaving movie theaters empty. Challenging the already weakened and iconic Hollywood empires was a corporation like Netflix, Smith insisted, which upended "everything with a ruthless logic and coldhearted efficiency." What was there for all to see became apparent on August 7, 2020, "when WarnerMedia abruptly eliminated the jobs of hundreds of employees, emptying the executive suite at the once-great studio that built Hollywood, and is now the subsidiary of AT&T. In a series of brisk video calls, executives who imagined they were studio eminences were reminded that they work—or used to work—at the video division of a phone company." Smith went on to note that "much of what's happening now in Hollywood, too, has that feeling of a death so long anticipated that you half assumed you'd just missed the funeral."[25]

If domestic interiors became places where people navigated lockeddown life with various mixtures of difficulty and ease, beyond the walls of a home Schumpeter's creative destruction abounded. While inside homes the pandemic accelerated the powerful reach of all these new technologies, in the wider world COVID-19 posed significant challenges to those involved in the renting, buying, and selling of residential real estate. With vacation travel dramatically curtailed, companies like Airbnb and VRBO struggled to navigate troubled waters of uncertain duration, which they did by shifting from renting vacation homes to offering up longer-term rentals.[26] The pandemic boosted residential real estate prices in many markets, and technology came to the rescue in the buying and selling of homes. With people reluctant to attend open houses, stay-at-home orders in place, social distancing recommended, and long-distance travel inadvisable, virtual tours attracted both lookie-loos and serious house buyers. Zillow was among the pandemic's potential beneficiaries, given how it continued to transform itself into a technologically enabled, full-service home residential real estate site, as was underscored by its February 2021 acquisition of ShowingTime. It remained a powerful force in the business of serving those with time on their hands. As a November 2020 headline announced, "Zillow Surfing Is the Escape We All Need Right Now."[27]

It was possible to see disruption more broadly as the pandemic led to the eviction of people from where they lived; threatened to undermine the ascendency of star, bicoastal cities; prompted people to leave crowded urban areas; weakened the profitability of commercial real estate; continued the transformation of shopping from brick-and-mortar buildings to sites online; and affected people's health and lives unequally. Especially notable and troubling were the racial, class, geographical, and generational dimensions of the impact of disruptive innovations and transformations in residential real estate. "The nation has a plague of housing instability that was festering long before COVID-19, and the pandemic's economic toll has only made it worse. Now," continued an early 2021 story, "the financial scars are deepening and the disruptions to family life growing more severe, leaving a legacy that will remain long after mass vaccinations."[28] Indeed, the disruptions in cities extended well beyond this article's stories of evictions as the pandemic created new problems and intensified preexisting trends. Urban rents plummeted, especially at the high end. At the low end, national eviction moratoria limited the terms under which landlords could evict tenants whose disappearing incomes made it difficult for them to come up with money for the rent. Yet homelessness increased, even as local, state, and federal governments worked to keep people in their homes.

More broadly, the data was mixed on what was happening in once flourishing cities, such as New York, San Francisco, and Washington. There was evidence of how resilient and inventive urbanites were, as they turned empty streets into sites of neighborhood renewal or patronized restaurants that transformed parking lanes into dining spots, outfitted with heaters as cold weather approached.[29] On the other hand, a steady stream of stories appeared that highlighted how multiple forces—the fear of contagion in crowded urban areas, the switch to remote learning, the triumph of Amazon and Grubhub over Neiman Marcus and McDonald's, and the closing of cultural institutions such as museums and concert halls—were turning cities into ghost towns. So much seemed up for grabs. Walking or bicycling replaced getting from here to there on public transportation or in private automobiles, prompting some observers to hail or lament the end of car culture. "I've Seen a Future without Cars, and It's Amazing" shouted a July 2020 headline.[30]

Surely it is more accurate to point out that, even if the long-heralded disappearance of cars from cities actually happened, car culture thrived in suburbs whose population and home prices increased due to the flight of considerable numbers of well-to-do families from cramped apartments in cities to expansive interior and exterior spaces in suburbs. "The real estate market is beginning to show signs of a 'great shuffling,'" Zillow's CEO Rich Burton observed in August 2020 as he cited a number of forces driving changes. People were spending more time at home, with Zoom gatherings transforming "the way families think about space and privacy." The elimination of commuting opened up more choices of where to live. Suburbs appealed, as people searched for better public schools and sought space inside for office work and outside for backyards that replaced gyms and presumably dangerous urban spaces.[31] As a result, if in some quarters the cost for renting or buying an urban residence softened, prices in suburbs, small towns, exurbs, and even vacation locations boomed, driven by low interest rates for mortgages and bidding wars. Beginning in the spring of 2020, stories dramatizing all these changes were common—well, as common as postwar split-level ranch houses and the criticism of the lives lived within them. Yet what remained unclear was, once the dust had settled, what would be the impact of the pandemic on the relationship between urban and suburban residential living, especially the extent, uniqueness, and permanence of what COVID-19 had wrought.[32]

The same uncertainty is true of two other frequently discussed topics: the shift from bicoastal cities where taxes and home prices were high to cities and towns in flyover country, and dramatic shifts in commercial real estate that affected how many people shopped and some lived. Social distancing and the benefits some employers and employees reaped from remote work threatened, as a reporter noted in mid-2020, "the assets that make America's most successful cities so dynamic—not only their bars, museums and theaters, but also their dense networks of innovative businesses and highly skilled workers, jumping among employers, bumping into one another, sharing ideas, powering innovation and lifting productivity."[33] Venture capitalist and private equity dollars, economy-minded executives, and tech workers in search of less stressful and more economical lifestyles threatened to shift resources and people from Silicon Valley, San Francisco, and Manhattan to Austin, Denver, and even less cosmopolitan and less crowded locations.

Again, how significant such changes would be in the long run instead of how they appear in attention-grabbing headlines remained unclear.[34] Much more certain were the implications of the pandemic for commercial real estate, seen with the acceleration of longer-term trends that affected where people lived and how they shopped. To begin with, though it was too early to assess long-term consequences, there were reports that the demand for urban office space decreased, and real estate developers turned abandoned floors and buildings into apartments. More significant to residential life was the way lockdowns accelerated preexisting trends in the interactions between the purveyors and purchasers of retail goods. "The retail industry was in the midst of a transformation before 2020," remarked two reporters for the *New York Times* shortly after Christmas shopping that year confirmed what was happening. "But the pandemic accelerated that change, fundamentally reordering how and where people shop, and rippling across the broader economy."[35] The shift to big-box stores and online shopping had already weakened the hold of small-town stores and suburban shopping centers, non-luxury malls especially; now their operators continued to turn them into locations that contained colleges, offices, health care or logistical facilities, and places that purveyed experiences as well as goods. Disappearing from malls (and elsewhere) were fabled name brand retailers such as J. C. Penney, Neiman Marcus, Ann Taylor, and Brooks Brothers, which filed for bankruptcy while others struggled by closing stores and/or beefing up their online operations. If to some observers the rapid near-collapse of WeWork's office-sharing empire signaled the crisis in office space, then nothing more dramatically captured changes underway in commercial real estate than the 2020 news that the Manhattan flagship store of Lord & Taylor would soon house Amazon employees.

People increasingly bought home furnishings from Wayfair; clothes from L. L. Bean; groceries through Instacart; meals from Grubhub, Hello Fresh, or Blue Apron; and virtually everything from Amazon. If Amazon boxes, with their simple but distinctive logo, became ubiquitous at people's front doors, so did the corporation's fleet of delivery vans on American streets. Accompanying this were struggles by Amazon's workers to protect themselves from COVID-19 and gain their just rights and compensation; the building of fulfillment centers of more than 1 million square feet as critical components of an extraordinary supply chain; and the development of technologies that made shopping as easy of clicking on a mouse (which you could also buy through Amazon); and the increasing power of Amazon Web Services.[36] All of this is not to mention that the net worth of Jeff Bezos was approaching $200 billion. Soon after he announced in early February 2021 that he was stepping down as CEO, a clever commentator speculated on what he might do with his fortune. At $3,000 a month, he could fund Jared and Ivanka's bathrooms for 5 million years. Or, better yet, at $25 billion annually, he could choose to end hunger in America for almost eight years.[37]

In late December 2020, Geoffrey A. Fowler, the *Washington Post*'s technology columnist, looked backward and forward as he surveyed "what worked, what flopped—and what's the new normal." He pointed out the inequalities that the pandemic intensified, such as the exploitation of those workers who made it possible for consumers to have all those packages delivered to their front doors. He also underscored the fact that a significant number of Americans did not have access to the broadband that would enable them to study or work at home, an issue that the Biden administration was committed to remedying. He also perceptively noted the failure of smartphones to counter the power of the virus, and he might have gone on to emphasize the problematic role of technology, at least initially, in connecting suppliers of vaccines with people eager to get vaccinated. When he turned to the future, he concluded that the pandemic had accelerated the shift to remote work, and that its future impact on telemedicine was still uncertain. On the other hand, he thought it unlikely that in a postpandemic world, families shopping for groceries online and, even more surely, children going to school online would persist at anywhere near the levels experienced during lockdowns. He was even more confident that what the Warner Brothers studio had announced in December—that it would simultaneously debut features online and in theaters—would persist. As for the future of streaming more generally, he noted that "Netflix has primed us to get what we want, right away."[38]

So many of the changes under discussion so far—remote work, telemedicine, shopping online instead of at a store, the shuttering of cultural and entertainment venues—underscore how the pandemic undermined the public and strengthened the private or at least blurred the lines between the two. In-person contacts with colleagues in the work world and potentially romantic partners in the dating sphere became less frequent and more dangerous epidemiologically. However technologically powerful, Zoom meetings were poor substitutes for adults having dinner parties or houseguests and children, playmates. Indeed, in February 2021, one shrewd observer lamented that so much of our locked-down lives got "squeezed into the same two-dimensional space: our screens," which blurred the distinction between "work and everything else" and dramatically reduced the "natural pauses like commuting, elevator rides, hallway chats, caffeine runs."[39] Likewise, going to museums, concerts, movies, or athletic events online or on television provided relief to household budgets. Yet experiencing the world through virtual reality deprived us of the pleasures that actual reality provided, among them the sights, smells, sounds, and personal connections that we missed. On Black Friday, the day after Thanksgiving (so named because it supposedly marked the day when black ink replaced red on the books of retailers), one article talked of "The Loneliness of One-Click Shopping." Below was a 1974 picture of Christmas shopping from an earlier period, with the caption evoking a time "when shopping was a communal experience."[40]

If, before the pandemic, I did not often shop in stores except for groceries, having lunch or dinner at a restaurant with friends or family members provided the lifeblood of my social life. Soon, however, with the ravages of COVID-19 seeming to go on forever, I was walking past shuttered restaurants and could not help wondering when or if they would come back. Of course, I was not alone in speculating about what the pandemic would do to our public lives. "We're Losing More Than We Know," read one headline. "If Restaurants Go, What Happens to Cities," read another, and a third noted "Apps Are Helping Gut Restaurants."[41] I am surely not the only person who senses a loss of familiar pleasures when eating takeout food at home or sitting outdoors at a restaurant as a warm summer turned into a chilly fall. And even the incomplete shift of 2020 national political conventions from the physical to the virtual raised the possibility that this historic, once-every-four years circus might change substantially or altogether disappear.[42] As transformed Christmas holidays approached in December 2020, a *New York Times* reporter wrote that the dramatic growth in imports, especially from China, was "another byproduct of the coronavirus, with Americans channeling money they might have spent on vacations, movies and restaurant dining to household items like new lighting for home offices, workout equipment for basement gyms and toys to keep their children entertained."[43]

Measuring the increased usage of Peloton, Grubhub, Zoom, and Amazon is easy enough, but figuring out the impact of the pandemic on our emotional and cognitive lives, short and long term, is much more difficult. Early on my friend Monroe Price suggested we were all victims of Stockholm syndrome—not in the literal sense of identifying with COVID-19 as our captor or abuser, but more figuratively: we had come to accept our captivity as normal and in the process squeezed from our memories what life was like before and from our anticipatory thoughts what it will be like after. What, one had to wonder, given the importance of social connections, were and would be the consequences of social distancing? How would days and weeks that seemed identical and unending affect our sense of time? As a mother of four in her thirties put it on May 30, 2020, "Right now feels like every other minute of the day, of the week, of the month. Right now feels like forever."[44] How would confinement in relatively small spaces affect our sense of more expansive distances? If lockdown disrupted familiar routines, what would it be like to develop new ones? As a writer observed and recommended in late November 2020, "Too many people are still longing for their old routines. Get some new ones instead."[45] When so much was virtual, how could we know anymore what was real? Many of us, someone noted, spent much of 2020 longing for a normal night out and "a normal president. In 2021 we may get both of those wishes. But what," this writer continued, "will 'normal' look like? What should it look like?"[46]

Though in the spring of 2021 much in the future was uncertain, one thing was for sure as the past turned into the present: the pandemic exposed and intensified troublesome inequalities in American society, including in housing. While the most fortunate might thrive as they traveled less, worked remotely, and watched the value of their investments in stocks and real estate rise, millions of others suffered. Less fortunate were people of color, poor whites, folks living in institutions, the undocumented and immigrants more generally, and even many in the middle class. They faced a greater risk of danger from COVID-19 contracted where they worked or lived, more cramped quarters, and at worst foreclosure, eviction, homelessness, or death. I was among the most fortunate: hunkered down in a well-protected condo building; living with the woman I still love after almost sixty years of marriage; using Zoom mainly for pleasure; and, in writing this book, having abundantly meaningful work.

If the holdings of Harvard's Widener Library, located half a mile from where I lived, were unavailable to me, the same was not true of the research into the connections between housing and the pandemic carried out by Harvard's Joint Center for Housing Studies, located at a similar distance but experienced virtually. I could not go there to hear talks and attend in-person seminars, but the results of its work were easily available to me online. Even a small sampling of their studies underscores the multiple forces that revealed how inequalities made housing so precarious for so many Americans as the pandemic's power spread. In its *State of the Nation's Housing*, which usually appears in June but was issued in November 2020 because so much was changing so swiftly, the center assessed the pandemic's impact. "The economic disruption caused by the COVID-19 pandemic," its authors asserted, has "underscored the stark—and growing—differences between financially secure households and those living paycheck to paycheck." The more fortunate could "retreat to their homes and work remotely," contrasted with those in low-income households who faced unemployment, eviction, and/or foreclosure. A disproportionate share of those at risk were people of color, given the intensification of the "wide racial and income disparities between the nation's haves and have-nots" that were "the legacy of decades of discriminatory practices in the housing market and in the broader economy."[47]

The ways the pandemic revealed and accelerated social and economic injustices prompted some to wonder if this would result in the undermining of commitments to ideologies and public policy grounded in the importance of self-reliance and free markets. In response to the Great Recession, despite the realization in some quarters that such approaches were problematic, by and large these commitments persisted.[48] "There was a brief moment," wrote a media scholar in 2010, "when we seemed to be on the verge of a paradigm shift worthy of the name. A tiny window opened, offering a glimpse of a fundamental rethink of one of the dominant ideologies of our age. In a metaphorical nanosecond, one that seemed to slip away almost as it appeared, the enormity of the 'credit crunch' had the potential to bring the whole edifice of neoliberal capitalism crashing down."[49]

Some observers wondered whether this time would be different, with the nation embracing vigorous government action to address long-standing economic and social problems, especially inequalities based on gender, class, race, and ethnicity. Several things fed such hopes. The pandemic had exacerbated these inequalities and dramatically revealed that the poor, including people of color among them, suffered unduly. Less because he saw the light than because he aligned himself with the forces of darkness, Donald Trump, while president, in the words of Samuel Moyn, "accelerated the search for a credible policy framework after neoliberalism."[50] After all, although Trump advanced tax cuts for the rich and powerful, he opposed free trade and globalization, attacked elites, and mouthed angry populism. What would follow was not entirely clear, and not only the future of Trump, the Republican Party, and white nationalism. While the record time in which corporations, scientists, and the federal government developed successful vaccines underscored the importance of collective action, the faltering early shift from vaccines to vaccinations made clear the consequences of a weakened federal government—and the persistence of the evocation of freedom over commitments to social obligations. What happened in 2020 and into 2021 revealed the dire consequences of the hollowing out of the federal government during the Trump presidency that followed decades of government-limiting policies.[51]

Some observers thought or hoped that the failure of the Trump administration to meet the challenges of the pandemic, the way COVID-19's powerful spread intensified social problems, and the election of Biden raised the possibility of a new social and economic order. Remember that, early on, in April 2020, the editorial in the *Financial Times* asserted that the "virus lays bare the frailty of the social contract" and called for "radical reforms" that would reverse "the prevailing policy direction of the last four decades." Then, in October 2020, David Brooks, a longtime advocate of action at the community level and a Burkean conservative, countered what President Bill Clinton had asserted in his 1996 State of the Union Address when he announced that "the era of big government is over." Instead, the *New York Times* columnist insisted, "The era of big government is here." Citing what he saw as the widespread, bipartisan support for a public option in health care, Biden's commitment to promote renewable green energy, and the new administration's proposal of massive spending for COVID-19 relief, Brooks observed that the pandemic had "pushed voters to the left" because it "made Americans feel vulnerable and more likely to support government efforts to reduce that vulnerability." After "a vigorous debate that lasted many decades," he noted, "the liberal welfare state had won—a robust capitalist economy combined with generous social support."[52]

We can also see similar calls and observations in some of the first books that focused on the consequences of the pandemic. As far as I can tell, the earliest in print was the September 2020 *Wake-Up Call: Why the Pandemic Has Exposed the Weakness of the West and How to Fix It* by John Micklethwait and Adrian Wooldridge, respectively the editor in chief of *Bloomberg News* and a columnist for the *Economist*. They wrote that "the Coronavirus has made government important again. Not just powerful again (look at those once-mighty companies begging for help), but also vital again. It matters enormously whether your country has a good health service and competent bureaucrats. The arrival of the virus was like an examination of state capacity."[53] More predictably, from the left came not dissimilar observations, such as from the computer keyboard of Grace Blakeley, a staff writer for Britain's democratic socialist *Tribune*. The advertisement for her *The Corona Crash: How the Pandemic Will Change Capitalism*, which appeared from the radical publisher Verso in October 2020, insisted that, with the death of "free market, competitive capitalism," there was no going "back to business as usual." She wanted to avoid "a new era of monopoly capitalism" seen as "the corporate economy collapses into the arms of the state." Instead, she advocated a "radical response" that involved "the transformation of our political, economic, and social systems based on the principles of the Green New Deal."[54]

Then there is the case of Fareed Zakaria, host of a weekly CNN show, writer of opinion pieces in the *Washington Post*, and author of the October 2020 book *Ten Lessons for a Post-Pandemic World*. Earlier, writing for *Salon* in 2014, Jim Sleeper had noted how Zakaria, who comforted but rarely challenged elites, offered up "his well-practiced, faux-democratic grace notes and smoke-screens, crafted to secure the approval or at least the acquiescence of the mass audiences he brings to the neoliberal consensus."[55]

As his book revealed, though Zakaria clearly preferred the quality of government action over its quantity, the pandemic nonetheless prompted him to rethink his commitments. He acknowledged that "the pandemic laid bare fissures that have been persistently widening" as well as the fact that America's "deep anti-statist" tradition imperiled the nation's ability to handle the COVID-19 crisis. He noted growing support for government action, on both the left and the right, with the global financial crisis having earlier begun "the process of reevaluation" of government's role. In a chapter titled "Markets Are Not Enough," Zakaria laid out the causes for widespread "disillusionment." If "the liberation of markets" had brought "growth and innovation," it had also "produced an impoverished public sector, rising inequality, a trend toward monopolies, and a political system that has been bought by the rich and powerful." And now, he continued, Americans had "seen these shortcomings laid bare in the pandemic," what with "a weak, malfunctioning state, highly unequal access to health care, relief mechanisms that help people with capital and connections much more than those who work for their wages." He found the solution in the vast territory between his commitments as a member of the Party of the Right as an undergraduate at Yale and what he saw as the corrupt state socialism he had known growing up in India. He admired the example of Denmark, because Danes understood "that markets were amazingly powerful, yet not sufficient; that they needed supports and buffers and supplements" the national governments provided.[56]

As I return to finish this coda in early March 2022, I am struck by how much of what I observed eleven months before has changed and how much remains more or less the same.[57] I have hunkered down for almost two years, still cautious and safe—my fate more fortunate than that of so many of the people I write about.

I've found some surprises, clarifications, and uncertainties. For example, in the fall of 2021 Zillow announced it was halting its iBuying efforts, having lost a billion dollars in three and a half years on that venture. Peloton's sales have faltered as people have returned to gyms, competition has emerged from lower-priced brands, and stories have circulated about problems with its products. E-companies such Tulip and Solace have narrowed the gap between the home and the crematorium by enabling you to arrange all aspects of the cremation of a loved one online. New studies have explored what might be the long-term impacts of lockdown on our emotional lives as depression, anxieties, and burnout have intensified, especially among the young and the economically vulnerable. Yet as the sociologist Viviana A. Zelizer has pointed out, though charitable giving decreased during the Great Recession, it increased significantly in response to the pandemic. "When We Were Socially Distant, Money Brought Us Closer" ran the headline of her late-February 2022 op-ed.[58]

Changes in the job and housing markets—as well as a greater awareness of racial inequalities—underscore the persistence of trends already in play. Although the "great resignation" began earlier in the pandemic, Anthony Klotz at Texas A&M coined the term in May 2021 as many people quit their jobs, changed careers, or retired early. Reports have circulated about how difficulties with the supply chain are complicating the building and furnishing of homes. In addition, a symposium planned for late March 2022 at Harvard's Joint Center for Housing Studies promises to explore how digital technologies are "spurring fundamental change in the way housing is produced, marketed, sold, financed, managed, and lived in" and to "assess whether these changes are likely to further (or hamper) efforts to address economic, social, and environmental challenges, such as housing affordability, discrimination, and climate change."[59] More than in the wake of the Great Recession, considerable numbers of citizens are aware of the threats to democracy posed by the far right and the challenges African Americans face. Moreover, just when the pandemic will become endemic remains uncertain. The number of COVID-19 deaths, which stood at just over five hundred thousand in March 2021, is now, a year later, nearing 1 million, and variants have disrupted what seemed to be progress, dashing many plans and hopes.

The pandemic continues to shape our lives in many ways that were already familiar. Institutional investors continue to pose problems for home buyers and renters. Efforts to increase the housing stock are running up against zoning regulations and resistance by homeowners. The shift from major cities on either coast to places in between, and nationwide to suburbs and to small towns, continues, even though cities such as New York and San Francisco are not becoming ghost towns because many homeowners have reversed plans they made earlier.[60] Not without hesitation and vacillation, people have resumed traveling, eating at restaurants, and going to plays, movies, concerts, and museums. Home prices have soared even higher than rents, leaving low- and middle-income families, people in their twenties and thirties, African Americans, the homeless, and others in precarious situations. Corporations like Amazon and Netflix continue their ascendancy in ways that challenge brick-and-mortar stores and Hollywood studios. New enterprises and new technologies continue to fray the social fabric, persist in shifting the balance between public and private, and promise to make homes havens in a heartless world. Schools keep changing their rules about in-person attendance and masks. Masking mandates for students and workers are a political issue. Employers have started, stopped, and then resumed calling their employees back to work, even though the balance between remote and in-person work has likely changed irreversibly.

As was true after the Great Recession, it is unclear how, over time, the pandemic will affect the balance between self-reliance and reliance on robust government action, between self-regulating markets and collective action. Even more than in 2008, the federal government has deployed massive fiscal and monetary resources to combat the adverse effects of a crisis. And this time, President Joe Biden has struggled to achieve even more, especially with his proposal to "build back better."

In a book published in September 2021, the historian Adam Tooze remarked, "It was hard to avoid the sense that a turning point had been reached. Was this, finally, the death of the orthodoxy that had prevailed in economic policy since the 1980s? Was this the death knell of neoliberalism?" Tooze also reminded me of the risk I am taking in offering my own conclusions: "Any effort to cast a narrative frame over the tumult we are still living through," he acknowledged, "is bound to be partial and subject to revision." If he composed his analysis "from the safety of an Upper West Side apartment," I do so harbored in a protected condo in Cambridge, Massachussetts. Writing in the March 10, 2022, issue of the *New York Review of Books*, Paul Krugman both praised Tooze's skills as a writer and asserted that his "book already seems hugely dated, overtaken by events." Fair warning for the risk I am taking here. After all, Tooze ended his book by saying, "If our first reaction to 2020 was disbelief, our watchword in facing the future should be: 'We ain't seen nothing yet.'"[61]

As I began writing this conclusion, I returned to an issue raised at the book's outset: how to place in perspective the events and trends that have so powerfully shaped housing—and our lives more generally—in the twenty-first century. Prominent among these are the rise of social media specifically and of new technologies more generally; the terrorist attacks of 9/11 and the war on terror; the Great Recession; the COVID-19 pandemic; the murder of George Floyd; the acceleration of climate change; the Russian war on Ukraine; and the threats that authoritarian leaders and social movements pose to democracy, the rule of law, and world peace. In this book, I've reflected on how these events, among others, have shaken our ideas about homeland, housing, and homes. Our challenge now is to reimagine how we can achieve long-held dreams of living comfortably and safely at home in the new reality we face.

NOTES

PREFACE

1. Author to Amanda Seligman, March 11, 2020.
2. Laura Spinney, *Pale Rider: The Spanish Flu of 1918 and How It Changed the World* (New York: Public Affairs, 2017), 3–4.
3. Randolph S. Bourne, "The State," in *War and the Intellectuals: Collected Essays, 1915–1919*, ed. Carl Resek (New York: Harper & Row, 1964), 71.

INTRODUCTION

1. J. Hector St. John Crèvecœur, *Letters from an American Farmer*, www.public-library.uk/pdfs/7/567.pdf.
2. Betty Friedan, *The Feminine Mystique* (New York: W. W. Norton, 1963).
3. In *The American Dream: A Short History of an Idea That Shaped a Nation* (New York: Oxford University Press, 2003), 133–57, Jim Cullen discusses "the dream of homeownership" as one of a handful of variants on American aspirations. For a critique of such aspirations for their lack of realism, see Kristen D. Adams, "Homeownership: American Dream or Illusion of Empowerment?," *South Carolina Law Review* 60 (Spring 2009): 573–616. In *Behold, America: The Entangled History of "America First" and "The American Dream"* (New York: Basic Books, 2018), 196 and 199, Sarah Churchwell locates the preliminary but growing connection between the American dream and homeownership in the mid-to-late 1930s, in part because of FDR's clarion call.
4. Jeffrey M. Hornstein's *A Nation of Realtors: A Cultural History of the Twentieth-Century American Middle Class* (Durham, N.C.: Duke University Press, 2005) explores the major role played by the NAR as an organization in shaping ideas about the middle class. On efforts of governments to control housing, see Bernard J. Frieden, *The Environmental Protection Hustle* (Cambridge, Mass.: MIT Press, 1979); and Edward L. Glaeser and Bryce A. Ward, "The Causes and Consequences of Land Use Regulation: Evidence from Greater Boston," *Journal of Urban Economics* 65 (2009): 265–78.
5. Aaron Glantz, *Homewreckers: How a Gang of Wall Street Kingpins, Hedge Fund Magnates, Crooked Banks, and Venture Capitalists Suckered Millions Out of Their Homes and Demolished the American Dream* (New York: HarperCollins, 2019), xxiv–vii. Gwendolyn Wright's *Building the American Dream: A Social History of Housing in America* (New York: Pantheon, 1981) explores a wide range of housing options throughout American history.
6. For histories of residential living, see Erik Avila, *Popular Culture in the Age of White Flight: Fear and Fantasy in Suburban Los Angeles* (Oakland: University of California Press, 2004); Robert A. Beauregard, *When America Became Suburban* (Minneapolis: University of Minnesota Press, 2006); Marijoan Bull and Alina Gross, *Housing in America: An Introduction* (New York: Routledge, 2018); Clifford E. Clark Jr., *The American Family Home, 1800–1960* (Chapel Hill: University of North Carolina Press, 1986); Lizabeth Cohen, *A Consumer's Republic: The Politics*

of Mass Consumption in Postwar America (New York: Knopf, 2003); Maria Krysan and Kyle Crowder, *Cycle of Segregation: Social Processes and Residential Stratification* (New York: Russell Sage Foundation, 2017); Robert J. Gordon, *The Rise and Fall of American Growth: The U.S. Standard of Living since the Civil War* (Princeton, N.J.: Princeton University Press, 2016); Dolores Hayden, *Building Suburbia: Green Fields and Urban Growth, 1820–2000* (New York: Pantheon, 2003); Kenneth T. Jackson, *Crabgrass Frontier: The Suburbanization of the United States* (New York: Oxford University Press, 1985); James A. Jacobs, *Detached America: Building Houses in Postwar Suburbia* (Charlottesville: University of Virginia Press, 2015); Destin Jenkins, *The Bonds of Inequality: Debt and the Making of the American City* (Chicago: University of Chicago Press, 2021); Nicholas Lemann, *Transaction Man: The Rise of the Deal and the Decline of the American Dream* (New York: Farrar, Straus & Giroux, 2019), 178–81; Stacey Moncrieff, ed., *100 Years of Celebration of the American Dream* (Chicago, Ill.: Wiley, 2007); Marina Moskowitz, *Standard of Living: The Measure of the Middle Class in Modern America* (Baltimore, Md.: Johns Hopkins University Press, 2004); Richard Rothstein, *The Color of Law: A Forgotten History of How Our Government Segregated America* (New York: W. W. Norton, 2017); and Justin P. Steil, Nicholas F. Kelly, Lawrence J. Vale, and Maia S. Woluchem, eds., *Furthering Fair Housing: Prospects for Racial Justice in America's Neighborhoods* (Philadelphia, Penn.: Temple University Press, 2021). For a recent critique of the single-family suburban home on ecological and communitarian grounds, see Diana Lind, *Brave New Home: Our Future in Smarter, Simpler, Happier Housing* (New York: Bold Type, 2020).

7. David M. Kennedy, *Freedom from Fear: The American People in Depression and War, 1929–1945* (New York: Oxford University Press, 1999), 368–71. On the history of public housing, see Lawrence J. Vale, *From the Puritans to the Projects: Public Housing and Public Neighbors* (Cambridge, Mass.: Harvard University Press, 2000).

8. Rothstein, *Color of Law*, viii, xxx. Most scholarship on housing discrimination focuses on African Americans, but it is more than likely that these patterns also pertain to others in contemporary America: the poor and other people of color.

9. Jackson, *Crabgrass Frontier*, 219.

10. For important background information on redlining, see LaDale C. Winling and Todd M. Michney, "The Roots of Redlining: Academic, Governmental, and Professional Networks in the Making of the New Deal Redlining Regime," *Journal of American History* 108 (June 2021): 42–69.

11. Ira Katznelson, *When Affirmative Action Was White: An Untold History Of Racial Inequality In Twentieth-Century America* (New York: W. W. Norton, 2005).

12. For a rare dissent from the postwar celebration of homeownership, see John P. Dean, *Home Ownership: Is It Sound?* (New York: Harper, 1945). Steve Swidler, "Home Ownership: Yesterday, Today, and Tomorrow," *Journal of Financial Economic Policy* 3 (January 2011): 5–11, casts doubt on the connection between homeownership, social well-being, and the American dream.

13. For a notable exception, see Wright, *Building the Dream*, which includes discussions of row houses, slave quarters, factory towns, tenements, and planned communities.

14. Congressional Declaration of National Housing Policy, 1949, www.law.cornell.edu/uscode/text/42/1441.

15. Wright, *Building the Dream*, 246, 253.

16. Richard Lacayo, "Suburban Legend: William Levitt," *Time*, July 3, 1950.

17. In "Only Washington Can Solve the Nation's Housing Crisis," *New York Times*, July 10, 2019, and her book *Saving America's Cities: Ed Logue and the Struggle to Renew Urban America in the Suburban Age* (New York: Farrar, Straus & Giroux, 2019), Lizabeth Cohen uses Logue's career in urban renewal to argue for a more positive evaluation of its impact than the widely accepted view of such efforts. For a work that is not as confident as Cohen's about the benign effects of urban renewal, see Alan Altshuler and David Luberoff, *Mega-Projects: The Changing Politics of Urban Public Investment* (Washington, D.C.: Brookings Institution, 2003).

18. Hayden, *Building Suburbia*, 128. On the roles and visions of property developers, see Peter Hendee Brown, *How Real Estate Developers Think: Design, Profits, and Community* (Philadelphia: University of Pennsylvania Press, 2015). For a study of factors shaping postwar cities, see Robert Fishman, "The American Metropolis at Century's End: Past and Future Influences" *Housing Policy Debate* 11 (2000): 199–213.

19. Don Layton, "Learning from the History of the Homeownership Rate," Joint Center for Housing Studies of Harvard University, August 19, 2021, www.jchs.harvard.edu/blog/learning-history-homeownership-rate); PK, "Historical Homeownership Rate in the United States, 1890–2021," DQYDJ, https://dqydj.com/historical-homeownership-rate-in-the-united-states-1890-present.

20. In "'Great Recession': A Brief Etymology," *New York Times*, March 11, 2009, Catherine Rampell noted that the term took hold in December 2008, even though it was also used to describe every significant downturn since the mid-1970s.

21. Tracy Jan, "Redlining Was Banned 50 Years Ago. It's Still Hurting Minorities Today," *Washington Post*, March 28, 2018.

22. Keeanga-Yamahtta Taylor, *Race for Profit: How Banks and the Real Estate Industry Undermined Black Homeownership* (Chapel Hill: University of North Carolina Press, 2019), 5, 7, 255. The literature on these forces is extensive, but among the good starting places, in addition to sources cited elsewhere, are N. D. B. Connolly, *A World More Concrete: Real Estate and the Remaking of Jim Crow South Florida* (Chicago: University of Chicago Press, 2014); Paige Glotzer, *How the Suburbs Were Segregated: Developers and the Business of Exclusionary Housing, 1890–1960* (New York: Columbia University Press, 2000); Dianne Harris, *Little White Houses: How the Postwar Home Constructed Race in America* (Minneapolis: University of Minnesota Press, 2012); Kevin M. Kruse and Thomas J. Sugrue, eds., *The New Suburban History* (Chicago: University of Chicago Press, 2016); Beryl Satter, *Family Properties: How the Struggle over Race and Real Estate Transformed Chicago and Urban America* (New York: Picador, 2009); Thomas J. Sugrue, *The Origins of the Urban Crisis: Race and Inequality in Postwar Detroit* (Princeton, N.J.: Princeton University Press, 1996); Thomas J. Sugrue, *Sweet Land of Liberty: The Forgotten Struggle for Civil Rights in the North* (New York: Random House, 2008); and Chloe N. Thurston, *At the Boundaries of Home Ownership: Credit, Discrimination, and the American State* (New York: Cambridge University Press, 2018).

23. "Expanding Home Ownership," President George W. Bush Record of Achievement, The White House, https://georgewbush-whitehouse.archives.gov/infocus/achievement/chap7.html. An excellent source for tracking housing, past and present, is the work of Harvard's Joint Center for Housing Studies(www.jchs.harvard.edu), especially its annual report, *The State of the Nation's Housing*.

24. For this data, see "Homeownership Rates Show That Black Americans Are Currently the Least Likely Group To Own Homes," USA Facts, July 28, 2020, https://usafacts.org/articles/homeownership-rates-by-race/. Other factors may be in play for these and other disparities, such the relationship between the urban and the rural and racial and ethnic differences.

25. Thomas M. Shapiro, "Race, Homeownership, and Wealth," *Washington University Journal of Law and Policy* 20 (January 2006): 53–74, quote on 65. A useful source of statistics on which I have drawn is Laurie S. Goodman and Christopher Mayer, "Homeownership and the American Dream," *Journal of Economic Perspectives* 32 (Winter 2018): 31–58. Some observers, including Goodman and Mayer but also Thomas Sowell, contest the impact of these factors; see Thomas Sowell, *The Housing Boom and Bust* (New York: Basic Books, 2009). For a more general conservative take on the housing market, see Randall G. Holcombe and Benjamin Powell, eds., *Housing America: Building Out of a Crisis* (New Brunswick, N.J.: Transaction, 2009); and Johan Norberg, *Financial Fiasco: How America's Infatuation with Homeownership and Easy Money Created the Economic Crisis* (Washington, D.C.: Cato Institute, 2009), who note that conservatives and others argue that NIMBY and zoning laws are responsible for a housing shortage.

26. There is an abundant literature of this topic, including Brian J. McCabe, "Why Buy a Home? Race, Ethnicity, and Homeowner Preferences in the United States," *Sociology of Race and Ethnicity* 4 (October 2018): 452–72; Darrick Hamilton and William Darity, "Can 'Baby Bonds' Eliminate the Racial Wealth Gap in Putative Post-racial America?" *Review of Black Political Economy* 37 (January 2010): 207–16; Brad Plumer and Nadja Popovich, "How Decades of Racist Housing Left Neighborhoods Sweltering," *New York Times*, August 24, 2020; Debra Kamin, "Black Homeowners Face Discrimination in Appraisals," *New York Times*, August 25, 2020; Michele Lerner, "One Home, A Lifetime of Impact," *Washington Post*, July 23, 2020; and Dorothy A. Brown, *The Whiteness of Wealth: How the Tax System Impoverishes Black Americans—and How We Can Fix It* (New York: Crown, 2021).

27. On public housing, see, for example, John Baranski, *Housing the City by the Bay: Tenant Activism, Civil Rights, and Class Politics in San Francisco* (Stanford, Calif.: Stanford University Press, 2019). Sheelah Kolhatkar, "What Happens When Investment Firms Acquire Trailer Parks," *New Yorker*, March 15, 2021, explores how the affordability crisis drives people into manufactured homes, located in communities that investment firms purchase and exploit. See also Esther Sullivan, *Manufactured Insecurity: Mobile Home Parks and Americans' Tenuous Right to Place* (Oakland: University of California Press, 2018); and Matthew Desmond, *Evicted: Poverty and Profit in the American City* (New York: Crown, 2016). On the impact of automatic decision-making on housing for the unhoused, see Virginia Eubanks, *Automating Inequality: How High-Tech Tools Profile, Police, and Punish the Poor* (New York: St. Martin's, 2017).

28. Ezra Klein, "'The Queen of Versailles': The Best Film on the Great Recession," *Washington Post*, November 12, 2012.

29. For a trenchant discussion of the film, see Kirk Boyle and Daniel Mrozowski, "Introduction: Creative Documentation of Creative Destruction," in *The Great Recession in Fiction, Film, and Television: Twenty-First-Century Bust Culture*, ed. Kirk Boyle and Daniel Mrozowski (Lanham, Md.: Lexington, 2013), xvii.

30. For thoughtful analyses of the global financial crisis, on which I have drawn in this paragraph, see David Harvey, *The Enigma of Capital and the Crises of Capitalism* (New York: Oxford University Press, 2010); Lisa Adkins, Melinda Cooper, and Martijn Konings, *The Asset Economy: Property Ownership and the New Logic of Inequality* (Medford, Mass.: Polity, 2020); Boyle and Mrozowski, eds., *Great Recession*; and Nick Srnicek, *Platform Capitalism* (Malden, Mass.: Polity, 2017). For a collection of probing essays, see Manuel Castells, João Caraça, and Gustavo Cardoso, eds., *Aftermath: The Cultures of the Economic Crisis* (Oxford, UK: Oxford University Press, 2012). In *Niagara of Capital: How Global Capital Has Transformed Housing and Real Estate Markets* (Washington, D.C.: Urban Land Institute, 2007), Anthony Downs explores the nature and implications of the massive inflow of funds into real estate through new financial instruments since 1997.

31. On the situation millennials face, see Francesca Mari, "Madhouse," *New York Times Magazine*, November 14, 2021. Maureen Ryan, *Lifestyle Media in American Culture: Gender, Class, and the Boundaries of Ordinariness* (New York: Routledge, 2017), 91–127, explores how lifestyle programming operated, as well as the larger ideological and intellectual contexts that shaped experiences with housing.

32. On this concept, see Randy Martin, *Financialization of Daily Life* (Philadelphia, Pa.: Temple University Press, 2002). For later considerations of the connections between the financial crisis, media representations, and ideological formations, see two collections of essays: *Journal of Communication Inquiry* 34 (October 2010); and *Cultural Studies* 24 (May 2010). Of course, though financialization intensified beginning in the 1970s, it was hardly a new force; for a discussion of recent work, see Elizabeth Tandy Shermer, "Whither the History of Capitalism?," *Reviews in American History* 49 (September 2021): 452–59. See also Jonathan Levy, *Freaks of Fortune: The Emerging World of Capitalism and Risk in America* (Cambridge, Mass.: Harvard University Press, 2012).

33. Adam Tooze, *Crashed: How a Decade of Financial Crises Changed the World* (New York: Viking, 2018).

34. "S&P/Case-Shiller U.S. National Home Price Index," Federal Reserve Economic Data, https://fred.stlouisfed.org/series/CSUSHPINSA. This study relies on Case/Shiller National Home Price Index, now one of the the S&P CoreLogic Case-Shiller Indices.

35. See figure 2 in *The State of the Nation's Housing 2021*, Joint Center for Housing Studies of Harvard University, 2021, 2, https://www.jchs.harvard.edu/state-nations-housing-2021.

36. Harvey, *Enigma*, 6.

37. For advocacy of housing as a right, not a commodity, see David Madden and Peter Marcuse, *In Defense of Housing: The Politics of Crisis* (New York: Verso, 2016).

38. Among the most cogent explorations of the promise and problems of the term are Daniel T. Rodgers, "The Uses and Abuses of 'Neoliberalism,'" *Dissent* 65 (Winter 2018): 78–87; Kim Phillips-Fein, "The History of Neoliberalism," in *Shaped by the State: Toward a New Political History of the Twentieth Century*, ed. Brent Cebul, Lily Geismer, and Mason B. Williams (Chicago: University of Chicago Press, 2018), 347–62; and Bruce J. Schulman, "Post-1968 U.S. History: Neo-Consensus History for the Age of Polarization," *Reviews in American*

History 47 (September 2019): 479–99. Moreover, in his magisterial *Age of Fracture* (Cambridge, Mass.: Harvard University Press, 2011), Daniel T. Rodgers explores the larger phenomena of which neoliberalism is an important part. Among the key texts that explore neoliberalism are Wendy Brown, *Undoing the Demos: Neoliberalism's Stealth Revolution* (Brooklyn, N.Y.: Zone, 2015); and David Harvey, *A Brief History of Neoliberalism* (New York: Oxford University Press, 2005).

39. There are elsewhere, however, extensive discussions of the impact of housing policies and choices on the environment such as urban sprawl, open spaces, water quality, and excessive uses of energy.

40. For example, see Justin Lewis, "Normal Viewing Will Be Resumed Shortly: News, Recession and the Politics of Growth," *Popular Communication* 8 (July–September 2010): 161.

41. Jamie Peck, Nik Theodore, and Neil Brenner, "Neoliberalism Resurgent? Market Rule after the Great Recession," *South Atlantic Quarterly* 111 (Spring 2012): 265–66.

42. Michelle Naomi Chihara, "Priceless: Fiction, Finance, and the Fantasy of Home" (PhD diss., University of California, Irvine, 2012), 4.

CHAPTER 1

1. On how networks adjusted their programing when the housing market tanked, see Brian Stelter, "Housing Slump Helps the Draw of Fixer-Upper TV," *New York Times*, June 12, 2008. On a change in programming on reality television, albeit one not related to real estate, see Rebecca M. Curnalia, "Frugal Reality TV during the Great Recession: A Qualitative Content Analysis of TLC *Extreme Couponing*," in *Reality Television: Oddities of Culture*, ed. Alison F. Slade, Amber J. Narro, and Burton P. Buchanan (Lanham, Md.: Lexington, 2014), 101–22.

2. Steven Kurutz, "The Housing Bubble Burst All Over Reality TV," *New York Times*, September 12, 2018; Moe Tkacik, "The Real Housing Crisis of Orange County," in *Bad News: How America's Business Press Missed the Story of the Century*, ed. Anya Schiffrin (New York: New Press, 2011), 122–47, connects various genres of reality television to an epicenter of the financial crisis.

3. According to a 2016 survey of HGTV's reality television real estate shows based on the number of viewers, *Fixer Upper* ranked number one; *Flip or Flop*, number two; *Brother vs. Brother*, number three; and *Property Brothers*, number five: Tony Maglio, "From 'Flip or Flop' to 'Fixer Upper,' 25 HGTV Shows Ranked By Ratings," The Wrap, December 23, 2016. www.thewrap.com/flip-or-flop-fixer-upper-hgtv-ratings/.

4. Jean Bruce and Zoë Druick, "Haunted Houses: Gender and Property Television After the Financial Crisis," *European Journal of Cultural Studies* 20 (October 2017): 483. Their essay introduces the journal's October 2017 issue, which contains a series of articles on "Gender and Property TV after the Financial Crisis." Though the articles do not focus on the three shows discussed in this chapter, they nonetheless are useful in understanding the nexus of political economy, gender, and reality television.

5. Gwynn Guilford, "House Flippers Triggered the US Housing Market Crash, Not Poor Subprime Borrowers," Quartz, August 29, 2017, https://qz.com/1064061

/house-flippers-triggered-the-us-housing-market-crash-not-poor-subprime-borrowers-a-new-study-shows/. Guilford was reporting on a paper three economists published in 2017 for the National Bureau of Economic Research that made clear that prominent among those who took advantage of more plentiful credit beginning in 2001 were investors with relatively strong credit ratings who purchased multiple homes by relying on easy-to-obtain funding: Stefania Albanesi, Giacomo De Georgi, Jaromir Nosal, "Credit Growth and the Financial Crisis: A New Narrative," National Bureau of Economic Research, Working Paper No. 23740, August 2017.

6. Bruce and Druick, "Haunted Houses," 484.

7. In discussing HGTV, I am drawing on Shawn Shimpach, "Realty Reality: HGTV and the Subprime Crisis," *American Quarterly* 63 (September 2012): 515–42. He criticized those who see a direct causal link between reality television's real estate shows and the Great Recession. This issue of *American Quarterly* focused on the connections between the financial crisis, race, and globalism.

8. Ian Parker, "HGTV Is Getting a Renovation: In the Streaming Era, Does HGTV Need to Be More Than Wallpaper?" *New Yorker*, March 29, 2021, discusses HGTV's history, approaches, and offerings, including not only shows under discussion here but also possibly more controversial ones such as "Meth-House Makeover." Maureen Ryan, *Lifestyle Media in American Culture: Gender, Class, and the Politics of Ordinariness* (New York: Routledge, 2017), 91–127, includes HGTV in her analysis, albeit ending before the time under consideration here.

9. Ronda Kaysen, "Who Doesn't Love to Hate-Watch HGTV?," *New York Times*, April 6, 2018. For other discussions of the genre, see Philip Maciak, "Why Do So Many People Watch HGTV?," Pacific Standard, September 29, 2014, https://psmag.com/social-justice/many-people-watch-hgtv-91461; Ronda Kaysen, "For House Flippers, Reality Meets Reality TV," *New York Times*, June 15, 2018; and Jennifer Barger, "As Seen on TV: Home Makeover Shows Have Totally Upended Homeowners' Expectations," *Washington Post*, May 10, 2018.

10. Brian Stelter, "Reality Check for Real Estate Shows," *New York Times*, May 21, 2009; Alessandra Stanley, "On HGTV: Fixing Homes and Hearts," *New York Times*, March 17, 2010.

11. Stelter, "Reality Check"; Ron Becker, "Horribly Guilty Television: HGTV and the Promotion of America's Ownership Society," Flow Journal, April 24, 2008, www.flowjournal.org/2008/04/horribly-guilty-television-hgtv-and-the-promotion-of-americas-ownership-society/.

12. Jim Sollisch, "Blame Television for the Bubble," *Wall Street Journal*, January 3, 2009.

13. Shimpach, "Realty Reality," 515.

14. Stelter, "Reality Check"; Samples and Mike Aubrey (host of *Real Estate Intervention*) quoted in same.

15. The programs on which this chapter concentrates are among the most popular among the huge, ever-shifting, and varied number of television real estate shows. To learn about more of these offerings, see Anthony McKenzie, "7 TV Shows about Flipping Houses," Medium, November 25, 2018, https://medium.com/@tonykenziewrites/7-tv-shows-about-flipping-houses-4824edeac4b6; Taylor Tobin, "12 of The Best Home Makeover Shows Ever Made. Ranked," Insider, April 5, 2018,

www.insider.com/home-makeover-shows-ranked-2018-4; and "Top Real Estate Reality TV Shows," Off the MRKT, January 27, 2019, www.offthemrkt.com/blogs/top-real-estate-reality-tv-shows. TLC, Bravo, and A&E were also major players, with CNBC in early 2019 coming late to the game. Television shows are hardly the only places that focus on real estate investing. For a discussion of real estate podcasts, see "16 Real Estate Podcasts We Love," FlipNerd, September 8, 2016, https://flipnerd.com/blog/16-real-estate-podcasts-love/.

16. For information on their lives, I am relying on Jonathan Scott and Drew Scott, *Dream Home: The Property Brothers' Ultimate Guide to Finding and Fixing Your Perfect Home* (New York: Houghton Mifflin Harcourt, 2016); and Jonathan Scott and Drew Scott, *It Takes Two: Our Story* (New York: Houghton Mifflin Harcourt, 2017).

17. Julie Creswell, "When the Real Estate Game Cost $9.95," *New York Times*, April 18, 2009.

18. Mark Wilson, "You Cannot Escape The Property Brothers," *Fast Company*, June 21, 2017.

19. For the narrative, albeit with a chronology that remains vague, see Scott and Scott, *Takes Two*, 148.

20. Creswell, "Real Estate Game."

21. For studies of the impact of house flipping on the Las Vegas residential real estate market, see Craig A. Depken II, Harris Hollans, and Steve Swidler, "Housing Bubbles and Foreclosures That Follow: The Case of Las Vegas," in *Challenges of the Housing Economy: An International Perspective*, ed. Colin Jones, Michael White, and Neil Dunse (Hoboken, N.J.: Wiley-Blackwell, 2012), 47–57; Craig A. Depken II, Harris Hollins, and Steve Swidler, "Flips, Flops, and Foreclosures: Anatomy of a Real Estate Bubble," *Journal of Financial Economic Policy* 3 (April 2011): 49–65; and Craig A. Depken II, Harris Hollans, and Steve Swidler, "An Empirical Analysis of Residential Property Flipping," *Journal of Real Estate Finance and Economics* 39 (July 2009): 248–63.

22. Gretchen Morgenson and Joshua Rosner, *Reckless Endangerment: How Outsized Ambition, Greed, and Corruption Led to Economic Armageddon* (New York: Times Books, 2013), 224.

23. On their story of wisely protecting themselves from the vagaries of the real estate market while in Las Vegas, see Scott and Scott, *Dream*, 19; and Scott and Scott, *Takes Two*, 145–48, quote on 146.

24. The figures, in inflation-adjusted prices, come from http://www.jparsons.net/housingbubble/las_vegas.html.

25. Wilson, "You Cannot Escape."

26. Wilson, "You Cannot Escape."

27. For biographical information, I am relying on Chip Gaines, *Capital Gaines: Smart Things I Learned Doing Stupid Stuff* (New York: HarperCollins, 2017), which is less helpful than Chip Gaines and Joanna Gaines, with Mark Dagostino, *The Magnolia Story* (New York: HarperCollins Christian, 2016).

28. Chip Gaines, *Story*, 112. The book's format involves alternating sections by Chip and Joanna, marked by different typefaces.

29. Joanna Gaines, *Story*, 85.

30. Joanna Gaines, *Story*, 116, 130.

31. Chip Gaines, *Story*, 133–35.

32. Joanna Gaines, *Story*, 140. See also Mike Copeland, "Waco Couple Rewarded for Risk with Subdivision Development," *Waco Tribune-Herald*, November 4, 2011.

33. Gaines, *Capital*, 76

34. The exact chronology of realizations and shifts is somewhat murky, especially for the period between late 2008 and early 2012: see, for example, Gaines and Gaines, *Story*, 133–60; and Gaines, *Capital*, 76–80.

35. Joanna Gaines, *Story*, x; Katie Neff quoted in same.

36. Joanna Gaines, *Story*, xv.

37. Julia Moskin, "For Joanna Gaines, Home Is the Heart of a Food and Design Empire," *New York Times*, May 4, 2020.

38. On the impact the Gaineses have had on Waco, see Anne Helen Petersen, "'Fixer Upper' Is Over, but Waco's Transformation Is Just Beginning," Buzzfeed, April 20, 2019, www.buzzfeednews.com/article/annehelenpetersen/waco-texas-magnolia-fixer-upper-antioch-chip-joanna-gaines.

39. Among the impacts that the Gaineses had on Waco were rising property taxes and house prices: Clare Trapasso, "Are 'Fixer Upper' Stars Chip and Joanna Gaines Saving Waco or Destroying It?," Realtor, February 10, 2020, www.realtor.com/news/trends/did-fixer-upper-stars-chip-and-joanna-gaines-save-or-destroy-waco/. For additional information about the impact they have had on Waco, an article that hardly merits the headline above it, see Amanda Harding, "'Fixer Upper': Some Fans Believe Chip and Joanna Gaines Are 'Destroying' Waco," CheatSheet, February 22,2020, www.cheatsheet.com/entertainment/fixer-upper-some-fans-believe-chip-and-joanna-gaines-are-destroying-waco.html/.

40. Petersen, "Transformation Is Just Beginning."

41. Drew Scott, quoted in Wilson, "You Cannot Escape."

42. Kurutz, "Housing Bubble."

43. Moskin, "Home Is the Heart."

44. Daniel Langhorne, "Local Couple Star in HGTV Reality TV Show on Flipping Houses," *Orange County Register*, April 4, 2013.

45. Kurutz, "Housing Bubble."

46. However, note that the El Moussas' favorite contractor Israel (Izzy) Battres is Latinx.

47. According to Brenda Bradshaw, a Florida real estate agent, the profits the El Moussas report are questionable: see Maddy Sims, "The Most Realistic HGTV Shows, According To Real Estate Pros," Apartment Therapy, September 6, 2019, www.apartmenttherapy.com/hgtv-shows-ranked-real-estate-professionals-262676.

48. One can never be sure when the list ends, given, for example, the limited series *Property Brothers Take On New Orleans*.

49. On the web, there is a good deal of information on Jonathan's divorce from Kelsy Ully and his later romances: Taysha Murtaugh, "Property Brother Jonathan Scott Opens Up about His Divorce for the First Time Ever," *Country Living*, September 14, 2017, www.countryliving.com/life/entertainment/news/a44801/jonathan-scott-opens-up-about-divorce/.

50. Candace Braun Davison, "What Is the Property Brothers' Net Worth?," *House Beautiful*, February 28, 2019, www.housebeautiful.com/lifestyle/a20075507/property-brothers-drew-jonathan-scott-net-worth, with the estimate coming

from www.CelebrityNetWorth.com. Another source, which also describes scandals and staging, estimates their net worth at a "cool $500 million," a figure that is questionable: Amanda Harding, "These 'Property Brothers' Scandals Almost Destroyed the Show," CheatSheet, December 3, 2019, www.cheatsheet.com/entertainment/these-property-brothers-scandals-almost-destroyed-the-show.html/.

51. Petersen, "Transformation Is Just Beginning"; Amanda Harding, "You Won't Believe the Crazy Number of Businesses and Projects Chip and Joanna Gaines Actually Have," CheatSheet, May 6, 2018, www.cheatsheet.com/culture/you-wont-believe-the-crazy-number-of-businesses-and-projects-chip-and-joanna-gaines-actually-have.html/

52. Tricia Gross, "A Look Inside Chip and Joanna Gaines' Empire," Simplemost, March 18, 2019, www.simplemost.com/inside-chip-and-joanna-gaines-magnolia-empire/

53. Charles Morris, "The Faith of Chip and Joanna Gaines," Haven Today, September 20, 2017, www.haventoday.org/blog/2017/09/20/faith-chip-joanna-gaines/.

54. Petersen, "Transformation Is Just Beginning."

55. Megan Angelo, "As 'Fixer Upper' Ends, HGTV Builds a Roster of Power (Tool) Couples," *New York Times*, April 3, 2018.

56. Brooks Barnes, "Are HGTV's Tarek and Christina the New Brad and Jen?," *New York Times*, June 3, 2017.

57. "Heather Rae Young," IMDb, www.imdb.com/name/nm3927891/bio.

58. Jessica Napoli, "Christina Anstead's Upcoming HGTV Series to Feature New Husband, Blended Family," Fox News, April 16, 2019, www.foxnews.com/entertainment/christina-anstead-hgtv-christina-on-the-coast.

59. Joanna Gaines, *Story*, 164.

60. See, for examples, Nicki Swift, "A Closer Look at Why Property Brothers Is Totally Fake," YouTube, 4:46, May 19, 2019, www.youtube.com/watch?v=n3BAjb8CtB0; and Itay Hod, "The 'Property Brothers' Are Reality Television's Crack Cocaine," Daily Beast, July 11, 2017, www.thedailybeast.com/the-property-brothers-are-reality-televisions-crack-cocaine. On the artifice of reality TV, see Mimi White, "House Hunters, Real Estate Television, and Everyday Cosmopolitanism," in *A Companion to Reality Television*, ed. Laurie Ouellette (Malden, Mass.: Wiley, 2014), 386–401. In a different but relevant context, Pierre Bourdieu, *The Social Structures of the Economy*, trans. Chris Turner (Malden, Mass.: Polity, [2000] 2005), 148, suggestively explores what such visualizations of staged interactions hide, especially "the social space within which they are located."

61. On the staging of real estate shows, see Shimpach, "Realty Reality," 526–32. For a behind-the-scenes analysis of the unreality of house hunting shows, see Mary Ellen Podmolik, "The Realities of Reality Real Estate Television," *Philadelphia Inquirer*, December 20, 2009. For an early exploration of how television shapes experiences, see Mimi White, *Tele-Advising: Therapeutic Discourse in American Television* (Chapel Hill: University of North Carolina Press, 1992).

62. Petersen, "Transformation Is Just Beginning."

63. For a study of representations of African Americans on reality television shows, including on HGTV, see Tia Tyree, "African Americans Stereotypes in Reality Television," *Howard Journal of Communications* 22 (2011): 394–413. On the tension

between racial diversity and gender stereotyping on HGTV shows—offered less frequently in these three than in others—see Mimi White, "Gender Territories: House Hunting on American Real Estate TV," *Television & New Media* 14 (May 2013): 228–43. On the limited attention given to African Americans and Latinx in Great Recession–related television programs, see Maryann Erigha, "And They Lived Happily Ever After . . . or Not At All: (Un) Imagining African Americans in Recession-Era Popular Culture," and Charli Valdez, "Latino Liminality, Exclusion, and Erasure in Great Recession Television: The Case of Treme and Friday Night Lights," in *The Great Recession in Fiction, Film, and Television: Twenty-First-Century Bust Culture*, ed. Kirk Boyle and Daniel Mrozowski (Lanham, Md.: Lexington, 2013), 135–47 and 149–62, respectively. Daniel Mrozowski, "From *Hoarders* to *Pickers*: Salvage Aesthetics and Reality Television in the Great Recession," in Boyle and Mrozowski, eds., *Great Recession*, 189–208, focuses not on fashionable homes but on the results of collapsed excesses. Michelle Chihara, "Extreme Hoards: Race, Reality Television, and Real Estate Value during the 2008 Financial Crisis," *Postmodern Culture* 27 (May 2017), doi:10.1353/pmc.2018.0002, provides a probing discussion of *Extreme Home Makeover* and *Hoarders*. For the larger work on which this draws, see Michelle Naomi Chihara, "Priceless: Fiction, Finance, and the Fantasy of Home," PhD diss., University of California, Irvine, 2012.

64. Shimpach, "Realty Reality," 519.

65. Kelly Corbett, "Erin and Ben Napier Explain Why They Stayed Quiet on Social Media During Protests About Racial Injustice," *House Beautiful*, June 29, 2020, www.housebeautiful.com/lifestyle/a32999191/erin-ben-napier-respond-racial-injustice-protests-performative-social-media/.

66. u/FWEngineer, "Home Town Seems Like White Town," Reddit, www.reddit.com/r/HGTV/comments/il7bet/home_town_seems_like_white_town/.

67. Dustin Seibert, "The Downing Twins Showcase Attainable, Middle-Class Chicago House-Flipping on HGTV with *Double Down*," The Grio, March 14, 2019, https://thegrio.com/2019/03/14/the-downing-twins-showcase-attainable-middle-class-chicago-house-flipping-on-hgtv-with-double-down/. The pilot is available at https://vimeo.com/318241793.

68. Ken Lipartito, written communication to author, July 21, 2021.

69. "About Us," Downing Brothers, https://thedowningbrothers.com/about-us.

70. Joanna Gaines, *Home Body: A Guide to Creating Spaces You Never Want to Leave* (New York: HarperCollins, 2018); Joanna Gaines with Marah Stets, *Magnolia Table: A Collection of Recipes for Gathering* (New York: HarperCollins, 2018); Scott and Scott, *Dream Home*.

71. James D. Stone, "Horror at the Homestead: The (Re)possession of American Property in *Paranormal Activity* and *Paranormal Activity II*," in Boyle and Mrozowski, *Great Recession*, 52, highlights in another context—but one that might apply to these three shows—the power of "consumerist narcissism, the desire to see ourselves wedded with our possessions."

72. Katherine Madden, "Father, Son, and the Holy Dollar: Rebuilding the American Dream in Post Recessionary Reality Television and Mommy Blogging" (PhD diss., University of Southern California, 2016), 6.

73. Jess Bolluyt, "New Details about Chip and Joanna Gaines' Church Will Shock You," CheatSheet, March 10, 2018, www.cheatsheet.com/culture/new-details-about-chip-and-joanna-gaines-church-will-shock-you.html/. Petersen,

"Transformation Is Just Beginning," discusses the controversial aspects of this church's commitments, including those of Chip and Joanna. For a summer 2021 report on these and other issues, see Nate Day, "Joanna Gaines Addresses Allegations of Racism, Homophobia: 'So Far from Who We Really Are,'" Fox News, July 1, 2021, www.foxnews.com/entertainment/joanna-gaines-addresses-allegations-racism-homophobia. For the story of how the couple did not follow through on their promise to preserve a historically important church that was to be moved to the Silo complex, see Kenneth Hafertepe, "Magnolia's Reassembled Historic Church Sure Won't Be Historic Anymore," *Waco Tribune-Herald*, March 14, 2020.

74. You can listen to Joanna Gaines talking of God speaking to her and inspiring her with a calling on a 2015 video she recorded which has attracted at least six million listeners: "The Gathering Testimony: Joanna Gaines," YouTube, 4:17, April 1, 2015, www.youtube.com/watch?v=t7iPEDnqwmo.

75. Gaines, *Home Body*, 8–9, 285–86.

76. Chip Gaines, *Story*, 167.

77. Joanna Gaines, *Story*, 178, 182. Of the history of the Christian home, see Catharine Beecher and Harriet Beecher Stowe, *American Woman's Home* (New York: J. B. Ford, 1869); and Colleen McDannell, *The Christian Home in Victorian America, 1840–1900* (Bloomington: Indiana University Press, 1986). For a history of housing and domesticity, see Witold Rybczynski, *Home: A Short History of an Idea* (New York: Viking, 1986). Laurie Ouellette, "Bare Enterprise: US Television and the Business of Dispossession (Post-crisis, Gender, and Property Television)," *European Journal of Cultural Studies* 20, no. 5 (October 2017): 499, explores the tension between Christina's uncaring competitiveness and her traditional roles as mother.

78. For a discussion of these gender distinctions in different contexts, see, Diane Negra and Yvonne Tasker, "Introduction: Gender and Recessionary Culture," in *Gendering the Recession: Media and Culture in an Age of Austerity*, ed. Diane Negra and Yvonne Tasker (Durham, N.C.: Duke University Press, 2014), 1–26.

79. Gaines, *Capital Gaines*, 17–18. Determined to learn Spanish so he could more effectively communicate with those with whom he worked, early in his career he set out for Mexico to take a three-month language immersion program; however, he had to return prematurely to Waco in order to attend to his multiple businesses (18–29).

80. I am grateful to Ken Hafertepe for pointing this out to me.

81. Ouellette, "Bare Enterprise," 494. For an introduction to the later contexts in which HGTV operates, see Laurie Ouellette, *Lifestyle TV* (New York: Routledge, 2016).

82. James Hay, "Too Good to Fail: Managing Financial Crisis through the Moral Economy of Reality TV," *Journal of Communication Inquiry* 34 (November 2010): 382–402. For a discussion of neoliberalism's impact on a different genre of reality television's real estate shows, see John McMurria, "Desperate Citizens and Good Samaritans," *Television and New Media* 9 (July 2008): 305–32.

83. Negra and Tasker, "Gender and Recessionary Culture," 8.

84. Of the eight shows evaluated by realtors, *Flip or Flop* ranked as the sixth most realistic, *Fixer Upper* as the third, and *Property Brothers* as the second: see Sims, "Most Realistic."

85. Robert Bianco, "Critics Corner," *USA Today*, June 27, 2011.

86. Although not prominent on these three shows, others do feature domestic conflicts: Mimi White, "'A House Divided,'" *European Journal of Cultural Studies* 20 (October 2017): 575–91.

87. Terry Castle, "Home Alone: The Dark Heart of Shelter-Lit Addiction," *Atlantic*, March 2006. For another discussion of property porn, see Bianca London, "Property Porn: The UK's Favourite New Guilty Pleasure," *Daily Mail*, September 10, 2012, www.dailymail.co.uk/femail/article-2200949/Property-porn-The-UKs-favourite-new-guilty-pleasure.html. Marjorie Garber, *Sex and Real Estate: Why We Love Houses* (New York: Pantheon, 2000), explores the erotic dimensions of residential real estate.

CHAPTER 2

1. Peter S. Goodman and Gretchen Morgenson, "Saying Yes, WaMu Built Empire of Shaky Loans," *New York Times*, December 27, 2008.

2. "All-Transactions House Price Index for Phoenix-Mesa-Chandler, AZ (MSA)," Saint Louis Federal Reserve Bank, https://fred.stlouisfed.org/series/ATNHPIUS38060Q.

3. Karl E. Case and Robert J. Shiller, "Full House," *Wall Street Journal*, August 30, 2006.

4. Robert J. Shiller, "How Tales of 'Flippers' Led to a Housing Bubble," *New York Times*, May 18, 2017. For a discussion of how interest in residential real estate intensified in the late twentieth century and early in the next one, see Daniel McGinn, *House Lust: America's Obsession with Our Homes* (New York: Doubleday, 2008).

5. Gary Keller, Dave Jenks, and Jay Papasan, *The Millionaire Real Estate Agent: It's Not about the Money . . . It's about Being the Best You Can Be!* (Austin, Tex.: Rellek, 2003). What comes after the ellipses did not appear in the 2003 edition, but by 2004 it was there.

6. Rick Villani and Clay Davis, *FLIP: How to Find, Fix, and Sell Houses for Profit* (New York: McGraw-Hill, 2007), 3, 8, 15.

7. Laurie Ouellette, "Bare Enterprise: US Television and the Business of Dispossession (Post-Crisis, Gender, and Property Television)," *European Journal of Cultural Studies* 20 (October 2017): 490–508; Daniel Mrozowski, "From *Hoarders* to *Pickers*: Salvage Aesthetics and Reality Television in the Great Recession," in *The Great Recession in Fiction, Film, and Television: Twenty-First-Century Bust Culture*, ed. Kirk Boyle and Daniel Mrozowski (Lanham, Md.: Lexington, 2013), 189–208.

8. On this tension, see Pamela Walker Laird, *Pull: Networking and Success since Benjamin Franklin* (Cambridge, Mass.: Harvard University Press, 2006).

9. Robert T. Kiyosaki, *Rich Dad, Poor Dad: With Updates for Today's World*, 20th anniversary ed. (Scottsdale, Ariz.: Plata, [1997] 2017), 6. Robert T. Kiyosaki, with Sharon L. Lechter, *The Cashflow Quadrant: Rich Dad's Guide to Financial Freedom* (New York: Warner, [1998] 2000), covers much of the same territory as *Rich Dad, Poor Dad*. The focal points of this chapter—the sprawling empires of Robert T. Kiyosaki and Than Merrill—are but the tip of the iceberg in the worlds of books and workshops on real estate investing. For a discussion of the broader genre, see Ashley E. Faulkner, "Financial Literacy Education in the United States:

Exploring Popular Personal Finance Literature," *Journal of Librarianship and Information Science* 49 (September 2017): 287–98. See also Michael Corbett, *Find It, Fix It, Flip It! Make Millions in Real Estate—One House at a Time!* (New York: Penguin, 2006).

10. Sharon Lechter, "Pay Your Family First," https://sharonlechter.com/blog/2014/09/30/for-families/.

11. Home page of the Napoleon Hill Foundation, Naphill.org.

12. Napoleon Hill, *Outwitting the Devil: The Secret to Freedom and Success*, annotated by Sharon Lechter (New York: Sterling, 2011), 5, 37, 141.

13. Sharon Lechter and Greg S. Reid, with the Napoleon Hill Foundation, *Three Feet from Gold: Turn Obstacles into Opportunities!* (New York: Sterling, 2009), 25, 49–51, 87, 217, 221.

14. Robert Kiyosaki, from speech quoted in Ethan Vanderbuilt, "Robert Kiyosaki Is a Scam? Yes, He Is in My Opinion," January 20, 2014, https://ethanvanderbuilt.com/2014/01/20/robert-kiyosaki-scam-artist-yes-opinion.

15. For some of the biographical information on the years from the late 1960s to the late 1970s, I am relying on Robert T. Kiyosaki with Sharon Lechter, *Rich Dad, Poor Dad: What the Rich Teach Their Kids about Money—That the Poor and Middle Class Do Not!* (New York: Warner, [1997] 2000), 134–35; this edition is different from the twentieth anniversary edition published by Plata. Donald J. Trump and Robert T. Kiyosaki, respectively, with Meredith McIver and Sharon Lechter, *Why We Want You to Be Rich: Two Men, One Message* (n.p.: Rich Press, 2006) provides valuable—though perhaps mythologized—information about his life.

16. Kiyosaki, *Why We Want*, 169.

17. Robert Kiyosaki, "The 4 Wealth-Stealing Forces That Make You Poorer . . . and Others Richer," Rich Dad, August 2, 2012, www.richdad.com/4-wealth-stealing-forces-make-you-poorer.

18. Kiyosaki, *Why We Want*, 170; on the consequences of going off the gold standard and changes in retirement planning, see 260.

19. Vanderbuilt claims that Thurber, and not the friend of Kiyosaki's father, was the real Rich Dad, but David D., "Real Life," more convincingly shows that the successful real estate investor Richard Wassman Kimi was the real Rich Dad. Nonetheless, Thurber's approach may well have taught Kiyosaki valuable lessons, and in the metaphorical sense Thurber may have been his father. Having said that, I have to acknowledge that the story of Kiyosaki's Rich Dad, as well as the identity of that person, is open to question. See, for examples, a May 2006 *20/20* investigation, Abdul Ershad, "Who Is Robert Kiyosaki's Real Dad?," Quora, July 15, 2013, https://www.quora.com/Who-is-Robert-Kiyosakis-rich-dad; and Robert Farrington, "The Ultimate Hypocrite: Robert Kiyosaki and His Company's Bankruptcy," The College Investor, November 8, 2018, https://thecollegeinvestor.com/4726/ultimate-hypocrite-robert-kiyosaki-companys-bankruptcy.

20. Kiyosaki with Lechter, *Rich Dad*, 16, 35, 40, 48, 100. For critiques of Kiyosaki, see John Reed, "John T. Reed's Analysis of Robert T. Kiyosaki's book Rich Dad, Poor Dad," September 3, 2015, www.johntreed.com/blogs/john-t-reed-s-real-estate-investment-blog/61651011-john-t-reeds-analysis-of-robert-t-kiyosakis-book-rich-dad-poor-dad-part-1 and https://johntreed.com/blogs

/john-t-reed-s-real-estate-investment-blog/61651331-john-t-reeds-analysis-of-robert-t-kiyosakis-book-rich-dad-poor-dad-part-2. Daniel Fridman, *Freedom from Work: Embracing Financial Self-Help in the United States and Argentina* (Stanford, Calif.: Stanford University Press, 2017), 49, makes clear that Kiyosaki divides opportunities into four choices: employees, the self-employed, business owners, and the fourth that he prefers—people whose money works for them.

21. "Road to Rich Dad," Canadian Broadcasting Corporation, January 29, 2010, www.cbc.ca/marketplace/episodes/2010-episodes/road-to-rich-dad.

22. "Road to Rich Dad." From what I can tell, the franchise operator is currently the Legacy Education Alliance: "Rich Dad Education," pamphlet in author possession; and the website of the Alliance, https://legacyeducationalliance.com/.

23. Allan Roth, "Rich Dad, Poor Dad's Bankrupt Company," CBS News, January 19, 2013, www.cbsnews.com/news/rich-dad-poor-dads-bankrupt-company/. Fridman, *Freedom from Work*, 123, makes clear that those who follow Kiyosaki "reframe . . . either as trivial or even positive" the fact that he made money by selling products to them.

24. Olivier Garret and Stephen McBride, "'Prosperity Gospel': What America's Rich and Successful (Including Donald Trump) Really Believe In," *Forbes*, March 27, 2017, www.forbes.com/sites/oliviergarret/2017/03/27/prosperity-gospel-what-americas-rich-and-successful-including-donald-trump-really-believe-in/#76e86cab1095.

25. Kiyosaki, *Why We Want*, 292. For other Trump-related advice books, see David Lindahl, *Commercial Real Estate 101: How Small Investors Can Get Started and Make It Big* (Hoboken, N.J.: Wiley, 2008), copyrighted by Trump University, with a foreword by Donald J. Trump; Donald J. Trump, with Meredith McIver, *Trump: Think Like a Billionaire: Everything You Need to Know about Success, Real Estate, and Life* (New York: Random House, 2004); Donald J. Trump and Robert T. Kiyosaki, *Midas Touch: Why Some Entrepreneurs Get Rich—and Why Most Don't* (Scottsdale, Ariz.: Plata, 2011).

26. Kiyosaki, *Why We Want*, 298.

27. Kiyosaki, *Why We Want*, 293, 317, 318.

28. "Phoenix, AZ Homes for Sale and Real Estate," Trulia, www.trulia.com/real_estate/Phoenix-Arizona/market-trends/.

29. Trump and Kiyosaki, *Why We Want*, 155.

30. Advertisement in Trump and Kiyosaki, *Why We Want*, 339.

31. Playbook, quoted in Steven Brill, "What the Legal Battle over Trump University Reveals about Its Founder," *Time*, November 5, 2015, https://time.com/4101290/what-the-legal-battle-over-trump-university-reveals-about-its-founder/.

32. Brill, "Legal Battle."

33. Jason Nicholas, quoted in Jeanne Sahadi, "Trump University Controversy . . . In Two Minutes," CNN, June 2, 2016, https://money.cnn.com/2016/03/08/news/trump-university-controversy-donald-trump/. Trump-affiliated workshops were hardly the only ones to face legal scrutiny. The El Moussas ventured into this business, with the Federal Trade Commission calling some of their techniques into question: Bruce Haring, "HGTV's 'Flip or Flop' Stars Tarek El Moussa, Christina Anstead Named in FTC Complaint on 'Bogus' Real Estate Seminars," Deadline,

October 4, 2018, https://deadline.com/2019/10/hgtv-flip-or-flop-stars-tarek-el-moussa-christina-anstead-named-ftc-complaint-1202752855/.

34. David Berson, summarized by Steve Berges, *The Complete Guide to Flipping Properties* (Hoboken, N.J.: Wiley, 2004), 8–10.

35. Berges, *Complete Guide*, 4, 6–7.

36. Jeff Gitlen, "How Much Do House Flippers Make?," LendEDU, March 7, 2017, https://lendedu.com/blog/much-house-flippers-make/. According to Fridman, *Freedom from Work*, 17, there is no data on the efficacy of Kiyosaki's workshops.

37. David D., "The Real Life Rich Dad of Robert Kiyosaki," Entrepreneurship Facts, August 15, 2018, https://entrepreneurshipfacts.com/the-real-life-rich-dad-of-robert-kiyosaki/.

38. Helaine Olen, *Pound Foolish: Exposing the Dark Side of the Personal Finance Industry* (New York: Penguin, 2012), 192.

39. Allan Roth, "Rich Dad Education—The Ultimate Emotional Investment," CBS News, March 4, 2010, www.cbsnews.com/news/rich-dad-education-the-ultimate-emotional-investment/.

40. This becomes clear in "Road to Rich Dad."

41. Josh J., "I paid $524 to Rich Dad Education . . .," comment on "Rich Dad Education," Yelp, August 4, 2016, www.yelp.com/biz/rich-dad-education-cape-coral.

42. In "The Emergence of a Finance Culture in American Households, 1989–2007," *Socio-Economic Review* 13 (July 2015): 575–601, Neil Fligstein and Adam Goldstein explore how broad social forces such as increasing inequality and job insecurity encourage Americans to adopt new financial strategies.

43. "James M. Smith Net Worth," Wallmine, July 22, 2019, https://wallmine.com/people/99318/james-m-smith.

44. The African American Downing Brothers, whose HGTV show I discuss in chapter 1, also offer online courses: https://thedowningbrothers-e-learning.teachable.com/.

45. Than Merrill, *Real Estate Wholesaling Bible: The Fastest, Easiest Way to Get Started in Real Estate Investing* (Hoboken, N.J.: Wiley, 2014), 3–4.

46. Merrill, *Bible*, 1–3, 9, 14, 230. Along with Michael E. Gerber and Paul Esajian, his name appears as one of the authors of *The E-Myth Real Estate Investor: Why Most Real Estate Investment Businesses Don't Work and What to Do about It* (Carlsbad, Calif.: Prodigy Business, 2015). This book is part of a series of more than twenty Gerber has produced under the E-Myth banner, designed to transform operators of small businesses (including accountants, bookkeepers, and dentists) from technicians into entrepreneurs.

47. For statistics on how rates of house flipping change, see ATTOM Staff, "U.S. Home Flipping Returns Drop to Seven-Year Low in 2018," February 26, 2019, www.attomdata.com/news/most-recent/2018-year-end-u-s-home-flipping-report/.

48. For a critique of these enterprises, see "FortuneBuilders.com Reviews—Legit or Scam?," Opportunity Checker, www.opportunitychecker.com/fortunebuilders-com-reviews-is-fortunebuilders-legit/. For a list of Merrill's programs, see the FortuneBuilders website, www.fortunebuilders.com. For examples of FortuneBuilders case studies, see "Student Success," FortuneBuilders, www.fortunebuilders.com/student-success/.

49. Robert Farrington, "The Ultimate Hypocrite: Robert Kiyosaki and His Company's Bankruptcy," The College Investor, October 19, 2019, https://thecollegeinvestor.com/4726/ultimate-hypocrite-robert-kiyosaki-companys-bankruptcy/.

50. Sarah Fenske, "Rich Dad? Poor Dad!: BBB Urges Caution on Kiyosaki-Inspired Seminars," *River Front Times*, May 20, 2011, www.riverfronttimes.com/newsblog/2011/05/20/rich-dad-poor-dad-bbb-urges-caution-on-kiyosaki-inspired-seminars. See also Vanderbuilt, "Kiyosaki."

51. Helaine Olen, "Rich Dad, Poor Dad, Bankrupt Dad?," *Forbes*, October 10, 2012, www.forbes.com/sites/helaineolen/2012/10/10/rich-dad-poor-dad-bankrupt-dad/#32e409b8633a; Olen, *Pound Foolish*, 173.

52. "Undercover: Than Merrill's Fortune Builders," The Frugal Vagabond, October 26, 2015, https://frugalvagabond.com/undercover-than-merrills-fortune-builders/. For complaints sent to the Better Business Bureau, similar to ones found for Rich Dad, Poor Dad, see www.bbb.org/us/ca/san-diego/profile/real-estate-consultant/fortunebuilders-inc-1126-172000368/complaints. YouTube offers critiques of both programs: see, for examples, "Than Merrill Wealth Builders Seminar Total Scam! Team Thayer Real Estate," YouTube video, 8:08, July 17, 2015, www.youtube.com/watch?v=bt_dtDj_dVU&t=329s; and "Robert Kiyosaki's Advice Is for Losers + Rich Dad Education Scam," YouTube video, 8:51, February 22, 2019, www.youtube.com/watch?v=_AoOpulGSUw.

53. Elizabeth Youngling, "'You Are the Architect of Your Own Success': Selling Financial Freedom through Real Estate Investment after the Foreclosure Crisis of 2008," *Economic Anthropology* 7 (January 2020): 108–19, quotes on 108 and 109; see also Elizabeth Youngling, "The Homeownership Complex: The Role of Housing Stakeholders in the Remaking of the U.S. Housing Market" (PhD diss., University of Illinois, 2018).

54. Youngling, "You Are the Architect."

55. "Return of House Flipping Eases Affordable Housing Crunch in Some States," *Chicago Tribune*, October 24, 2016.

56. Steven Swidler, email to author, February 17, 2020. For empirical investigations of flipping, see Craig A. Depken II, Harris Hollins, and Steve Swidler, "An Empirical Analysis of Residential Property Flipping," *Journal of Real Estate Finance and Economics* 39 (May 2009): 248–62; and Craig A. Depken II, Harris Hollins, and Steve Swidler, "Flips, Flops, and Foreclosures: Anatomy of a Real Estate Bubble," *Journal of Financial Economic Policy* 3 (April 2011): 49–65. For a mathematically driven examination of the relationships between flipping and real estate markets, see Charles Ka Yui Leung and Chung Yi-Tse, "Flippers in Housing Market Search" (Working Paper 2015059, Department of Economics and Finance, City University of Hong Kong, January 2011).

57. Patrick Bayer, Christopher Geissler, Kyle Mangum, and James W. Roberts, "Speculators and Middlemen: The Strategy and Performance of Investors in the Housing Market," NBER Working Paper 16784, February 2015, 3, 36, www.nber.org/papers/w16784.pdf. For a revised version, see Patrick Bayer, Christopher Geissler, Kyle Mangum, and James W. Roberts, "Speculators and Middlemen: The Strategy and Performance of Investors in the Housing Market," *Review of Financial Studies* 33 (April 2020): 5212–47. In their *Review of Financial Studies* essay, Bayer, Mangum,

and Roberts rely on data for the Los Angeles market from 1988 to 2012 to explore how information about the activity of neighbors fueled what they call "investor contagion" among amateurs whose performance paled in comparison with that of professionals.

On the ideological and cultural factors that motivate individuals to invest in rental properties, see Philip M. E. Garboden, "Amateur Real Estate Investing," *Journal of Urban Affairs* (2021), doi: 10.1080/07352166.2021.1904781.

58. Bayer et al., "Speculators and Middlemen," 6, 31, 36.

59. Ben Casselman and Conor Dougherty, "Want a House Like This? Prepare for a Bidding War with Investors," *New York Times*, June 20, 2019.

60. Casselman and Dougherty, "Want a House Like This?"

61. In an email of October 11, 2021, Kyle Mangum helped me understand these possibilities.

62. "Than Merrill's Fortune Builders: Scam, or Legitimate?," Scams Galore, June 26, 2020, www.scamsgalore.com/than-merrill.html.

63. Susan S. Collins, "Opening Statement: HUD's Government-Insured Mortgages: The Problem of Property 'Flipping,'" June 29, 2000, www.govinfo.gov/content/pkg/CHRG-106shrg66088/pdf/CHRG-106shrg66088.pdf.

64. Tim Henderson, "Six Years after the Great Recession, House Flipping Is on the Rise," *PBS NewsHour*, October 18, 2016, www.pbs.org/newshour/nation/six-years-great-recession-house-flipping-rise.

65. See, for example, Robert T. Kiyosaki, "It Was 20 Years Ago Today . . . ," in Kiyosaki, *Rich Dad*, 1–7 (Plata edition). For a sober yet enthusiastic real estate death-and-rebirth story, see Marty Boardman, *Fixing and Flipping Real Estate: Strategies for the Post-Boom Era* (Berkeley, Calif.: Apress, 2013). See also J. Scott, *The Book on Flipping Houses: How to Buy, Rehab, and Resell Residential Properties*, rev. ed. (Denver, Colo.: Bigger Pockets, 2019).

66. Ryan Dezember, "KKR Doubles Down on House Flippers with Additional $250 Million Stake in Toorak Capital," MarketWatch, June 12, 2019, www.marketwatch.com/story/kkr-doubles-down-on-house-flippers-with-additional-250-million-stake-in-toorak-capital-2019-06-12; see also Ryan Dezember, "Wall Street Can't Get Enough Fixer-Upper Houses," *Wall Street Journal*, September 7, 2021. For a later story about private equity investments in residential real estate, see Francesca Mari, "The Great Wall Street Housing Grab," *New York Times Magazine*, March 8, 2020, 30–35, 57–59; see also Francesca Mari, "The Housing Vultures," *New York Review of Books*, June 11, 2020. For a fall 2019 report on recent (but prepandemic) trends, see Diana Olick, "Lending to House Flippers Hits a 13-Year High as Prices and Competition Heat Up," CNBC, September 27, 2019, www.cnbc.com/2019/09/27/lending-to-house-flippers-hits-13-year-high.html.

67. Fridman, *Freedom from Work*, 6–10, quotes on 5 and 10. In most ways his fieldwork is deeper and broader than mine, even though he pays little attention to the presentations like the ones I went to. Among the key issues Fridman explores are Cashflow, a board game Kiyosaki and his colleagues developed as another way people learn neoliberal lessons; the role of cooperative group efforts online or in person; the impact and reconfiguration of Kiyosaki's contributions outside the United States; the historical and social theories Kiyosaki offers; and the importance of gender in the world of financial self-help venues.

68. "Earnings and Income Disclaimers," FortuneBuilders, www.fortunebuilders.com/earnings-and-income-disclaimers/.

CHAPTER 3

1. Dean Starkman, "No, Americans Are Not All to Blame for the Financial Crisis," *New Republic*, March 9, 2014. Here I am also relying on Dean Starkman, email to author, October 25, 2021. For a cautionary note on the role of subprime mortgages, see James Conklin, W. Scott Frame, Kristopher Gerardi, and Haoyang Liu, "Villains or Scapegoats? The Role of Subprime Borrowers in Driving the U.S. Boom," Federal Reserve Bank of Atlanta, August 2018, www.atlantafed.org/research/publications/wp/2018/10-villains-or-scapegoats-the-role-of-subprime-borrowers-in-driving-the-us-housing-boom-2018-08-28.

2. John Lancaster, *I.O.U.: Why Everyone Owes Everyone and No One Can Pay* (New York: Simon & Schuster, 2010), 45.

3. Barbara Ballinger, "Great Partnerships: Finding the American Dream," *Realtor Magazine*, June 1, 2006. A more independent publication is *Realty Times*, whose audience includes both real estate agents and homeowners. Unfortunately, when I researched its online archives using relevant search terms, I encountered a crucial gap in its coverage during the relevant years; for an early assessment that was far more pessimistic than anything appearing in *Realtor Magazine*, see "Realty Viewpoint: Fed, Bear Stearns Deal Could Bail Out Taxpayers," *Realty Times*, March 31, 2008, whose unnamed author speculated that the current crisis could end up making "the Great Depression look like a mild recession." *Popular Communication* 8 (July–September 2010) offered a series of articles focused on the relationships between the global economic crisis and new media, including the way television covered the situation. Among the relevant contributions are Cornel Sandvoss, "Conceptualizing the Global Economic Crisis in Popular Communication Research," 154–61; Justin Lewis, "Normal Viewing Will Be Resumed Shortly: News, Recession, and the Politics of Growth," 161–65; Jeffrey P. Jones, "More Than 'Fart Noises and Funny Faces': *The Daily Show*'s Coverage of the US Recession," 165–69; Bill Grantham and Toby Miller, "The End of Neoliberalism," 174–77; Amanda D. Lotz, "US Television and the Recession: Impetus for Change?," 186–89; Matthew P. McAllister, "But Wait, There's More! Advertising, the Recession, and the Future of Commercial Culture," 189–93; and Mark Deuze, Phoebe Elefante, and Brian Steward, "Media World and the Recession," 225–31. A key moment, which I cover in a later chapter, is the March 12, 2009, exchange between Jim Cramer and Jon Stewart, as part of *The Daily Show*'s critique of coverage by CNBC.

4. "About Us," *Realtor Magazine*, https://magazine.realtor/about-us.

5. David Lereah, *Are You Missing the Real Estate Boom? Why Home Values and Other Real Estate Investments Will Climb through the End of the Decade—and How You Can Profit from Them* (New York: Doubleday, 2005), 1, 17–18, 25, 226.

6. David Lereah, quoted in Robert Freedman, "Beneath Market Punditry: On the Road to Recovery," *Realtor Magazine*, January 2007.

7. David Lereah, "The Subprime Reckoning," *Realtor Magazine*, May 1, 2007.

8. "25 People to Blame for the Financial Crisis: David Lereah," *Time*, probably early February 2009, http://content.time.com/time/specials/packages/article/0,28804,1877351_1877350_1877336,00.html.

9. Seth Jayson, "Hiding the Ugly Truth about Housing," *Motley Fool*, September 11, 2007, www.fool.com/investing/general/2007/09/11/hiding-the-ugly-truth-about-housing.aspx and Seth Jayson, "Housing Worse, despite Yelping NAR," *Motley Fool*, November 14, 2007, www.fool.com/investing/general/2007/11/14/housing-worse-despite-yelping-nar.aspx.

10. The quotes are from Robert Freedman, an official at NAR, in his introduction to an interview with Yun, who was somewhat more guarded than Freedman: Robert Freedman, "Beneath Market Punditry: Underlying Strength," *Realtor Magazine*, November 1, 2007. *Realtor Magazine* also blamed "the destabilizing presence of predator lenders" for trouble in the residential real estate market; in response, NAR supported legislation to curb abuses, wanted to protect buyers from problematic practices, and worked to make sure realtors sold homes to immigrants, the elderly, and minorities: quote from Robert Freedman, "Legislative Outlook for 2002," *Realtor Magazine*, March 1, 2007; Marie Spodek and Jerome Mayne, "3 Signs for 2007 of Predatory Lending," *Realtor Magazine*, March 1, 2007.

11. Blanche Evans, "Getting Case-Shillered: Can You Spell Conflict of Interest?," *Realtor Magazine*, June 1, 2008.

12. Suzie Orman, "Financial Power," *Realtor Magazine*, August 1, 2007.

13. Lawrence Yun, "Loan Affordability," *Realtor Magazine*, February 1, 2008.

14. Lawrence Yun, "Economy: A Year of Repair, Then a Year of Growth," *Realtor Magazine*, July 1, 2008.

15. G. M. Filisko, "2008 Cost vs. Value Report: Still Many Happy Returns for Home Rehabs," *Realtor Magazine*, cover of December 2008 issue.

16. Stacey Moncrieff, "Still Believing in Real Estate," *Realtor Magazine*, November 1, 2008.

17. "House Price Index Datasets," Federal Housing Finance Agency, www.fhfa.gov/DataTools/Downloads/Pages/House-Price-Index-Datasets.aspx#mpo.

18. In a telephone conversation on April 21, 2020, John Petrowsky, a realtor with whom I have worked, helped me understand the importance of optimism to real estate agents.

19. For examples of NAR's legislative agenda, see Meg Burns, "Summary of Enhanced Subprime Lending Policy," *Realtor Magazine*, April 16, 2007.

20. The sources I examined are representative but hardly exhaustive. Among the other possible ones are two traditional business media, *Barron's* and *American Banker*, as well as the newer *Entrepreneur* and *Business Insider*, and, on National Public Radio, Kai Ryssdal's *Marketplace* and Adam Davidson's *Planet Money*, including the May 9, 2008, episode "The Giant Pool of Money," https://www.thisamericanlife.org/355/the-giant-pool-of-money. Also of note are the *Huffington Post*, *Mother Jones*, the *Motley Fool*, and *Rolling Stone* (especially the work of Matt Taibbi), as well as *ProPublica*'s "Magnetar Series" (especially Jessie Eisinger and Jake Bernstein). On CNBC, David Faber offered an award-winning report, "House of Cards," on June 4, 2008, https://www.cnbc.com/id/28984151.

Had I focused on new media, a more complicated picture would have emerged, something Max Fraser reminded me of in an email on October 20, 2021. My reliance on print media for a time when new media played such a significant role means that this chapter gives more prominence to writers who failed to understand the gravity and extensiveness of what was happening, instead of those who early on were prescient. Of special relevance are sites or blogs such as Calculated Risk, Marginal Revolution, The Big Picture, Baseline Scenario, Naked Capitalism, and commentators such as Rich Toscano. A preliminary search of *Mother Jones*, using the terms "financialization" and "Lehman Brothers," turned up surprisingly little that is relevant. On a YouTube short documentary on the crisis, see Matt Davies, "The Aesthetics of the Financial Crisis: Work, Culture, and Politics," *Alternatives: Global, Local, Political* 34 (November 2012): 317–37. With *Fortune* there are often several dates for an article, sometimes when initially written (and perhaps available online) and then when published in an issue; when dating entries for *Fortune*, I use the magazine's publication date.

21. Though they share much in common, these four publications vary in their approaches and explanatory powers. More so than the others, perhaps due in part to its being a monthly publication, *Inc.* paid relatively little attention to macroeconomic issues and instead focused largely on individual firms, practical advice, and feel-good narratives.

22. To a lesser but still striking extent, when writers for *Forbes* underscored the dangers in the financing of residential real estate, they could seem as interested in the wisdom of investing in individual stocks or specific sectors as they were in warning about the economy's future: for example, A. Gary Shilling, "Implosion," *Forbes*, June 19, 2006.

23. For these years, issues of *Business Week* were not digitized, which made researching the publication under pandemic conditions difficult. For a sampling of its coverage, see "Subprime Implosion," July 2, 2007, 32; James C. Cooper, "Prognosis: Mild Recession, Slow Recovery," March 24, 2008, 12; Peter Coy and Mara Der Hovanesian (with illustrations by another Daniel Horowitz), "The Housing Abyss, Growing," 32–36, July 7, 2008; Mara Der Hovanesian, "Where to Invest/Stash Your Money" (cover story), October 6, 2008; Peter Coy, "Back on Track—or Off the Rails? The Fannie-and-Freddie Takeover Might Work. Or Darker Days Lie Ahead. Imagining the Best and Worst Scenarios," September 22, 2008, 22–28.

24. *Fortune*, often the most prescient of business publications, nonetheless proved capable of backpedaling when one writer provided fulsome warning and then another proved unduly optimistic. Compare the April 20, 2007, article by Bethany McLean cited below with Rik Kirkland, "The Greatest Economic Boom Ever," *Fortune*, July 23, 2007.

25. Greg Ip and Damian Paletta, "Regulators Scrutinized in Mortgage Meltdown," *Wall Street Journal*, March 22, 2007. For more perceptive reporting, see two articles in the *Wall Street Journal*: Randall Smith and Jed Horowitz, "Merrill Takes $8.4 Billion Credit Hit," October 25, 2007; and Carrick Mollenkamp and Serena Ng, "Wall Street Wizardry Amplified Credit Crisis," December 27, 2007.

26. Steven Rattner, "The Coming Credit Meltdown," *Wall Street Journal*, June 18, 2007. Kate Kelly, "A 'Subprime' Fund Is on the Brink," *Wall Street Journal*, June 16, 2007, was an early and prescient warning of trouble at Bear Stearns. As late as early 2008, writers in the *Wall Street Journal*, more than any other group of American journalists, explained securitization and believed that a recession was avoidable: Michael Connolly, "Investors Hope Write-Downs Signal Crunch's End Is Near," *Wall Street Journal*, April 1, 2008. It took the collapse of Lehman Brothers and AIG for writers to sound a full alarm: see Jon Hilsenrath, Serena Ng, and

Damian Paletta, "Worst Crash Since '30s, With No End in Sight," *Wall Street Journal*, September 18, 2008.

27. Amy Feldman, "Recessionade," *Inc.*, February 2008, 19-20.

28. Ethan Penner, "Can the Financial Markets Make a Comeback?," *Wall Street Journal*, August 27, 2007.

29. Kenneth L. Fisher, "Never Before!," *Forbes*, May 7, 2007.

30. A. Gary Shilling, "Bear Bust," and Ernesto Zedillo, "Summer of Setbacks," *Forbes*, August 13, 2007. In some instances, writers in *Forbes* continued to be optimistic well into 2008, with the collapse of Lehman Brothers and AIG not very far off in the future: Ken Fisher, "Five Blue Chips," *Forbes*, September 1, 2008.

31. Jeremy Grantham, "Danger: Steep Drop Ahead," *Fortune*, September 27, 2007.

32. Carrie Coolidge, "Mortgage Madness," *Forbes*, June 19, 2007.

33. Jason Dean and Peter Stein, "The Man Who Saw It Coming," *Wall Street Journal*, August 29, 2007. Earlier and more fully than most other business publications, writers in *Forbes* focused on the dangers of subprime lending and sometimes more broadly on the possibility of trouble in financial markets: see, for example, A. Gary Shilling, "The Deadbeat Economy," *Forbes*, December 23, 2003.

34. Compare, in the April 14, 2008, issue of *Fortune*, Allan Sloan, "On the Brink of Disaster," with Scott Cendrowski, "Investing Safe Haven: Collectible Watches."

35. Peter Eavis, "Subprime: Let the Finger Pointing Begin," *Fortune*, September 17, 2007. The scholar Olivia Nicol is exploring the use of the blame game in financial reporting in this period.

36. Steve Forbes, "How Capitalism Will Save Us," *Forbes*, October 10, 2008.

37. Forbes, "How Capitalism." This was later expanded into Steve Forbes and Elizabeth Ames, *How Capitalism Will Save Us: Why Free People and Free Markets Are the Best Answer in Today's Economy* (New York: Crown, 2009); by then he seemed to have forgotten his earlier embrace of unprecedented government interventions, as he returned to his position that state action caused but did not solve crises. See also Johan Norberg, *Financial Fiasco: How America's Infatuation with Homeownership and Easy Money Created the Economic Crisis* (Washington, D.C.: Cato Institute, 2009).

38. Bethany McLean, "Is Enron Overpriced?," *Fortune*, March 5, 2001; Bethany McLean and Peter Elkind, *The Smartest Guys in the Room: The Amazing Rise and Scandalous Fall of Enron* (New York: Penguin, 2003).

39. Bethany McLean, "The Dangers in Investing in Subprime Debt," *Fortune*, April 20, 2007; Bethany McLean, "Enron All Over Again," *Fortune*, November 26, 2007; Bethany McLean, "Short's Story," *Fortune*, April 30, 2008. See also Elizabeth Spiers, "Putting Lipstick on a Pig," *Fortune*, September 29, 2008.

40. Nina Easton, "Main Street Turns against Wall Street," *Fortune*, September 28, 2008.

41. In "The Great American Recession: Sociological Insights on Blame and Pain," *Sociological Perspectives* 53 (Winter 2010): 3-17, Judith Treas explores how the emphasis on blaming the victim overlooked the long-standing structural problems that had already made Americans vulnerable.

42. Thomas Sowell, "A 'Sound' Economy?," *National Review*, November 4, 2008. In *The Housing Boom and Bust* (New York: Basic Books, 2009), Thomas Sowell reiterated much of what he wrote in *National Review*: that government programs (including local restrictions on building and national policies aimed

at making housing affordable) were largely responsible for the crisis; that critics exaggerated housing discrimination based on race; and that greed, Wall Street, and securitization were not consequential factors. The aim of the 1977 Community Reinvestment Act was to counter the discriminatory impact of redlining on minority and low-income households.

43. Charles Krauthammer, "Prudence or Punishment?," *National Review*, September 26, 2008.

44. Stan J. Liebowitz, "Anatomy of a Train Wreck: The Causes of the Mortgage Meltdown," *National Review*, October 20, 2008.

45. Thomas Sowell, "Cycle of Dependency," *National Review*, October 30, 2007.

46. Victor David Hanson, "Populism of the Privileged," *National Review*, February 21, 2008. Later, with hindsight, some conservatives writing in the *National Review* reluctantly embraced government intervention to prevent the worst from happening: Stephen Spruiell and Kevin D. Williamson, "The Least-Bad Option: Under Current Conditions, Government Seizure of Shaky Firms May Be a Necessary Evil," *National Review*, April 20, 2009.

47. Stephen Spruiell, "Cavuto's Start-Up," *National Review*, October 19, 2007. For analyses of the ideology that drove how Fox News covered the crisis, see Brandon Reese Peck, "Fox Populism in the Great Recession" (PhD diss., University of California–San Diego, 2012); and Reese Peck, "'You Say Rich, I Say Job Creator': How Fox News Framed the Great Recession," *Media, Culture, and Society* 36 (May 2014): 526–35.

48. Larry Kudlow, "Despite the Gloom, More Bush Boom," *National Review*, October 31, 2007.

49. Donald L. Luskin, quoted in "An NRO Symposium," *National Review*, January 23, 2008.

50. Sowell, "'Sound' Economy."

51. Ellen Schloemer, Wei Li, Keith Ernst, and Kathleen Keest, *Losing Ground: Foreclosures in the Subprime Market and Their Cost to Homeowners* (Durham, N.C.: Center for Responsible Lending, 2006). Founded in 2002, the nonprofit center worked to educate the public about predatory lending.

52. Thomas Sowell, "Magic Numbers," *National Review*, April 17, 2009.

53. Catherine R. Squires, "Coloring in the Bubble: Perspectives from Black-Oriented Media on the (Latest) Economic Disaster," *American Quarterly* 64 (September 2012): 543–70. See also Catherine R. Squires, "Bursting the Bubble: A Case Study of Counter-Framing in the Editorial Pages," *Critical Studies in Media Communication* 28 (March 2011): 30–49.

54. Squires, "Coloring in the Bubble," 543–44.

55. Squires, "Coloring in the Bubble," 546.

56. Squires, "Coloring in the Bubble," 558–59.

57. Squires, "Coloring in the Bubble," 552, 565.

58. Danny Schechter, "Market Media Meltdown," *Nation*, May 26, 2008.

59. "The Blame Game," *Nation*, December 22, 2008; see also Peter Dreier and John Atlas, "The GOP's Blame-ACORN Game," *Nation*, November 10, 2008.

60. B.[obbi] M.[urray], "Wall Street's Soiled Hands," *Nation*, July 15, 2002. This essay and others appear in Katrina Vanden Heuvel, *Meltdown: How Greed and Corruption Shattered Our Financial System and How We Can Recover* (New York: Nation Books, 2009).

61. Garrett Ordower, "The Loan Shark Lobby," *Nation*, April 9, 2007.

62. Max Fraser, "Subprime Cribs," *Nation*, June 30, 2008. In ascribing this and other entries to Fraser, I am relying on what appears in the online version, which may be different in the published version. Indeed, as Max Fraser pointed out to me in an email of October 20, 2021, authorship of some entries was not simple and he authored some that do not appear with his byline.

63. Alexander Cockburn, "The Spitzer Sting," *Nation*, March 31, 2008.

64. The editorial "Subprime Politics," *Nation*, December 31, 2007, called into question how George W. Bush promoted the "Ownership Society." Max Fraser, "Subprime Obama," *Nation*, January 28, 2008, found the future president's plan "tepid."

65. Max Fraser, "Million Mortgage March," *Nation*, January 28, 2008.

66. Kai Wright, "The Subprime Swindle," *Nation*, July 14, 2008.

67. Jesse Jackson, "For the 'FDR,'" *Nation*, April 7, 2008.

68. To this list, I'd add, among others, Geoff Colvin and Shawn Tully of *Fortune*. Dean Starkman, *The Watchdog That Didn't Bark: The Financial Crisis and the Disappearance of Investigative Journalism* (New York: Columbia University Press, 2014), 211–40, covers the work of Michael Hudson, Gillian Tett, and Richard Lord in a chapter titled "Three Journalism Outsiders Unearth the Looming Mortgage Crisis." Starkman, *Watchdog*, 223, notes that "even Tett's work, as singular as it was, reads today as somewhat tentative, given the calamity to come." For a different and more theoretical analysis of how journalists wrote about the global financial crisis that usefully focuses on references to crises, cycles, and trauma, see Amin Samman, *History in Financial Times* (Stanford, Calif.: Stanford University Press, 2019).

69. Paul Krugman's essays in the *New York Times* were admirably smart: for example, "The Big Meltdown," March 2, 2007; and "How Did Economists Get It So Wrong?," September 2, 2009. For an example of the contrast between dire news and a relatively confident conclusion, see Geraldine Fabrikant, "A Home Loan Trap," *New York Times*, September 13, 2007.

70. "The 2002 Pulitzer Prize Winner in Beat Reporting: Gretchen Morgenson of the *New York Times*," The Pulitzer Prizes (website), www.pulitzer.org/winners/gretchen-morgenson.

71. Gretchen Morgenson, "Home Loans: A Nightmare Grows Darker," *New York Times*, April 8, 2007.

72. Gretchen Morgenson, "Mortgages May Be Messier Than You Think," *New York Times*, March 7, 2007.

73. Gretchen Morgenson, "Crisis Looms in Mortgages," *New York Times*, March 11, 2007; Gretchen Morgenson, "Behind Biggest Insurer's Crisis, a Blind Eye to a Web of Risk," *New York Times*, September 27, 2008, focused on the corruption of major Wall Street firms.

74. Jon Birger, "The Woman Who Called Wall Street's Meltdown: Star Bank Analyst Meredith Whitney Says the Economy Is About to Sink into a Deep Recession," *Fortune*, August 18, 2008.

75. At the *Financial Times*, the editor and economics commentator Martin Wolf also wrote astutely. Because articles in the *Economist* are unsigned, it is impossible to tell which of the many perceptively important ones were written by women; however, in the first decade of the twenty-first century, two women played

prominent roles in covering financial markets: Zanny Beddoes (beginning in 1996, its economics editor; then business affairs editor; and, since 2015, its editor in chief) and Pam Woodall, who preceded Beddoes as economics editor and early in the new century was responsible for the magazine's coverage of the housing crisis and other events: Zanny Beddoes, email to author, May 10, 2020. For its early focus on securitization, see "Rough Ride Ahead: America's Banks Are Not as Healthy as They Look," *Economist*, July 8, 1999. Its writers focused, more and earlier than others elsewhere, on the global dimension of any future crisis: "Abandon Ship: Investors Sail into a Credit Storm amid Worries about the Debt Market," *Economist*, August 2, 2007.

76. Gillian Tett, *Anthro-Vision: A New Way to See in Business and Life* (New York: Simon & Schuster, 2021), 24.

77. Laura Barton, "On the Money," *Guardian*, October 30, 2008.

78. Gillian Tett, *Saving the Sun: A Wall Street Gamble to Rescue Japan from Its Trillion-Dollar Meltdown* (New York: HarperCollins, 2003).

79. Barton, "On the Money." For a feminist article she wrote while in Japan, see Gillian Tett, "Time for Office Flowers to Learn Girl Power," *Financial Times*, January 8, 2001.

80. Gillian Tett, "Silence and Silos: The Problems of Fractured Thought in Finance" (address at the 109th Annual Meeting of the American Anthropological Association, November 19, 2010, https://vimeo.com/17854712). See also Gillian Tett, "The (JP) Morgan Mafia," *Inside Job*, March 7, 2011, www.youtube.com/watch?v=moCrR2DQ43k. For other versions of this story, see Gillian Tett, "Silos and Silences: Why So Few People Spotted the Problems in Complex Credit and What It Implies for the Future," *Financial Stability Review* 14 (July 2010): 121-29; and Gillian Tett, "Icebergs and Ideologies: How Information Flows Fueled the Financial Crisis," *Anthropology News* 50 (October 2009): 6-7. In *Anthro-Vision*, 77-97, Tett offers one of her fullest discussions of her career, her coverage of the financial crisis, and the way she used anthropology to analyze what she witnessed.

81. Barton, "On the Money."

82. Gillian Tett, "The Dream Machine: Invention of Credit Derivatives," *Financial Times*, March 24, 2006.

83. Barton, "On the Money."

84. Gillian Tett, "Innovative Ways to Repackage Debt and Spread Risk Have Brought Higher Returns But Have Yet to Be Tested Through a Full Credit Cycle," *Financial Times*, April 19, 2005; Gillian Tett, "Clouds Sighted Off CDO Asset Pool," *Financial Times*, April 18, 2005; these are two slightly different versions that cover the same territory. For other early warnings, see articles she cites in Tett, *Anthro-Vision*, 250nn11-12.

85. Gillian Tett, "The Unease Bubbling in Today's Brave New Financial World," *Financial Times*, January 19, 2007.

86. Gillian Tett, "Does It All Add Up? Worries Grow about the True Values of Repackaged Debt," *Financial Times*, June 28, 2007.

87. Gillian Tett, "The Big Freeze: A Year That Shook Faith in Finance," *Financial Times*, August 4, 2008.

88. Gillian Tett, "Insight: Zombie Curse of Europe's CLOs," *Financial Times*, April 2, 2009. Kirk Boyle and Daniel Mrozowski, "Introduction: Creative Documentation

of Creative Destruction," in *The Great Recession in Fiction, Film, and Television: Twenty-First-Century Bust Culture*, ed. Kirk Boyle and Daniel Mrozowski (Lanham, Md.: Lexington Books, 2013), ix–xxv, note the frequency and prominence of references to zombies in discussions of horror films and threatening weather. From the start of 2007 to the end of 2009, writers for the *Wall Street Journal* used the word "zombie" 121 times, and in about two-thirds of the cases the references were to failed corporations, especially financial ones.

89. Felix Rohatyn, quoted in Ruth Sunderland, "They Had Parties, We Got the Hangover," *Guardian*, June 6, 2009.

90. Joshua Rosner, "A Home without Equity Is Just a Rental with Debt," SSRN, June 29, 2001, https://papers.ssrn.com/sol3/papers.cfm?abstract_id=1162456.

91. Dean Baker, "The Run-Up in Home Prices: Is It Real or Is It Another Bubble?," Center for Economic Policy and Research, August 5, 2002, www.cepr.net/documents/publications/housing_2002_08.htm.

92. Michael Hudson, "Banking on Misery: Citigroup, Wall Street, and the Fleecing of the South," *Southern Exposure* 31 (Summer 2003).

93. Raghuram G. Rajan, "Has Financial Development Made the World Riskier?," NBER Working Paper No. 11728, November 2005, www.nber.org/papers/w11728, 4, 26.

94. Satyajit Das, *Traders, Guns, and Money: Knowns and Unknowns in the Dazzling World of Derivatives* (Harlow, UK: Prentice Hall, 2006), xiv, 320.

95. Bill Ackman, "Who's Holding the Bag?," www.scribd.com/document/52252937/Who-s-holding-the-bag.

96. Mark Pittman, "S&P, Moody's Hide Rising Risk on $200 Billion of Mortgage Bonds," June 29, 2007, Bazaar Model, https://bazaarmodel.net/phorum/read.php?1,4124. For an appropriately positive assessment of Pittman's work, see Dean Starkman, "The Pittman Way: A Financial Reporter Who Combined Data and Attitude," *Columbia Journalism Review*, November 30, 2009, www.cjr.org/the_audit/what_ill_remember_about_mark_p.php.

97. Stephen Mihm, "Dr. Doom," *New York Times Magazine*, August 15, 2008.

98. Alan Sloan, "House of Junk," *Fortune*, October 29, 2007.

99. Robert J. Shiller, *The Subprime Solution: How Today's Global Financial Crisis Happened and What to Do About It* (Princeton, N.J.: Princeton University Press, 2008), 2.

100. Peter S. Goodman, "The Quiet Crisis," in *Bad News: How America's Business Press Missed the Story of the Century*, ed. Anya Schiffrin (New York: New Press, 2011), 97–98.

101. Barton, "On the Money." For an interview in Davos in which she warned about the dangers of opaqueness and the proliferation of new financial instruments, see Gillian Tett, "Davos 2007," July 18, 2007, www.ft.com/video/c059c7eb-2710-32e3-80f7-345ac8446ec6. At a forum at Davos on July 17, 2007, with the exception of Nouriel Roubini participants in a roundtable discussion were generally optimistic about the future of the global economy: "Davos Annual Meeting—2007 Update: The Global Economy," YouTube video, 1:20:36, July 17, 2007, www.youtube.com/watch?v=1868JAyqRK8.

102. Gillian Tett, 2007, quoted in Lourdes Benería, Güseli Berik, and Mario Flors, *Gender, Development, and Globalization: Economics As If All People Mattered* (New York: Routledge, [2003] 2016), 103; Gillian Tett, *Fool's Gold: How the Bold Dream of*

a Small Tribe at J. P. Morgan Was Corrupted by Wall Street Greed and Unleashed a Catastrophe (New York: Free Press, 2009), 167–68, describes this meeting in Barcelona.

103. Howard Kurtz, "Press May Own Share in Financial Mess," *Washington Post*, October 6, 2008.

104. This summary draws on Alyt Damstra, Mark Boukes, and Rens Vliegenthart, "The Economy: How Does the Media Cover It and What Are the Effects: A Literature Review," *Sociology Compass* 12 (May 2018): 1–14; Matthew Fraser, "Five Reasons for Crash Blindness," *British Journalism Review* 20 (December 2009): 78–83; Francesco Guerrera, "Why Generalists Were Not Equipped to Cover the Complexities of the Crisis," *Ethical Space: The International Journal of Communication Ethics* 6 (2009): 44–49; John Huxford, "Reporting on Recession: Journalism, Prediction, and the Economy," *International Business and Economics Research Journal* 11 (March 2012): 343–56; Lewis, "Normal Viewing," 161–65; Sandvoss, "Conceptualizing," 154–61; Danny Schechter, "Credit Crisis: How Did We Miss It?," *British Journalism Review* 20 (February 2009): 19–26; Anya Schiffrin, "The Press and the Financial Crisis: A Review of the Literature," *Sociology Compass* 9 (August 2015): 639–53; Anya Schiffrin and Ryan Fagan, "Are We All Keynesians Now? The US Press and the American Recovery Act of 2009," *Journalism* 14 (February 2013): 151–72; Dean Starkman, "Power Problem: The Business Press Did Everything but Take On the Institutions That Brought Down the Financial System," *Columbia Journalism Review* 48 (May–June 2009): 22–30; Louis Uchitelle, "The Uses and Misuses of Economics in Daily Journalism," *History of Political Economy* 43 (Summer 2011): 363–68; Tett, "Icebergs and Ideologies," 6–7; and Tett, "Silos and Silences," 121–29.

105. Thomas l. Palley, "Financialization: What It Is and Why It Matters," Levy Economics Institute, Working Paper No. 525, December 2007, www.levyinstitute.org/pubs/wp_525.pdf, 7.

106. Simon Johnson, "The Quiet Coup," *Atlantic*, May 2009.

107. Schiffrin, ed., *Bad News*, contains essays that were important precursors of what Starkman would reveal in his book three years later; see especially Anya Schriffrin, "The U.S. Press and the Financial Crisis," 1–21; Joseph E. Stiglitz, "The Media and the Crisis: An Information Theoretic Approach," 22–36; Dean Starkman, "Power Problem: The Business Press Did Everything but Take On the Institutions That Brought Down the Financial System," 37–53; Ryan Chittum, "Missing the Moment," 71–93; and Goodman, "Quiet Crisis," 94–121.

108. Starkman, *Watchdog*, 4; for his chart that highlights the differences, see 143.

109. My research suggests a more mixed assessment than Starkman's statement that "the business press responded with vigor from mid-2007 onward": Starkman, *Watchdog*, 285.

110. Starkman, *Watchdog*, 171, 199–200.

111. Starkman, *Watchdog*, 199, 242–43.

112. Fraser, "Five Reasons," 79.

113. Jon Talton, "Journalism's Culpability in the Economic Crisis," *Encyclopedia Britannica Blog*, March 4, 2009, http://blogs.britannica.com/2009/03/journalisms-culpability-in-the-economic-crisis/.

114. Tett, "Iceberg," 6.

115. Schiffrin and Fagan, "All Keynesians," 152.

116. Tett, "Icebergs," 6–7.

117. The statistics come from Starkman (this and following citations are from his article), "Power Problem," 25.

118. Fraser, "Five Reasons," 80–81.

119. Schriffrin and Fagan, "All Keynesians," 164.

120. Tett, "Icebergs," 7.

121. Schiffrin and Fagan, "All Keynesians," 151.

122. Starkman, "Power Problem," 24.

123. Damstra, Boules, and Vliegenthart, "Economy," 5.

124. Tett, "Silos," 121, 124.

125. Schiffrin, "Financial Crisis," 643; Starkman, "Power Problem," 29.

126. Starkman, "Power Problem," 29.

127. Dean Starkman, "How Could 9,000 Business Reporters Blow It?," *Mother Jones*, January–February 2009, www.motherjones.com/politics/2009/01/how-could-9000-business-reporters-blow-it/.

128. For these changes, see Bob Franklin, "The Future of Journalism," *Journalism Studies* 13 (2012): 663–81.

129. Schiffrin, "Review," 650.

130. Lewis, "Normal Viewing," 161–63; in this article Lewis offers a probing and fundamental critique of how journalists, limited by institutional and intellectual blinders, failed.

CHAPTER 4

1. For information on the Cramer/Stewart exchanges, see "Jon Stewart–Jim Cramer Conflict," Wikipedia, accessed Feburary 28, 2022, https://en.wikipedia.org/wiki/Jon_Stewart%E2%80%93Jim_Cramer_conflict; and "The Listening Post—Jon Stewart vs. CNBC—20 March 2009," YouTube, 11:19, March 21, 2009, https://www.youtube.com/watch?v=N3LCZ3wTD0Q. For the larger contexts, see two articles in *Popular Communication* 8 (July–September 2010): Cornel Sandvoss, "Conceptualizing the Global Economic Crisis in Popular Communication Research," 154–61; and Jeffrey P. Jones, "More Than 'Fart Noises and Funny Faces': *The Daily Show*'s Coverage of the US Recession,"165–169; as well as Jeffrey P. Jones, *Entertaining Politics: Satiric Television and Political Engagement*, 2nd ed. (Lanham, Md.: Rowman & Littlefield, 2010), 136–41. For a contrasting approach, see Reece Peck, "'You Say Rich, I Say Job Creator': How Fox News Framed the Great Recession through the Moral Discourse of Producerism," *Media, Culture, and Society* 36 (May 2014): 526–35. The focus of my research is on print media, with only occasional examinations of television coverage. Moe Tkacik, "The Real Housing Crisis of Orange County," in *Bad News: How America's Business Press Missed the Story of the Century*, ed. Anya Schiffrin (New York: New Press, 2011), 122–47, quote on 137, explores how the role that Cramer—who was "paid to peddle harmless urgency and benign hysteria"—played in CNBC's failure to cover the financial crisis.

2. Steven Perlberg, "Rick Santelli Started the Tea Party with a Rant Exactly 5 Years Ago Today—Here's How He Feels Now," BusinessInsider, February 19, 2014, https://www.businessinsider.com/rick-santelli-tea-party-rant-2014-2.

3. The relevant portion of *The Daily Show with Jon Stewart* of March 12, 2009, is at www.cc.com/video-clips/iinzrx/the-daily-show-with-jon-stewart-jim-cramer-pt-2.

4. *The Daily Show*, March 12, 2009.

5. The quote appears in Sam Stein, "Economists, Progressives Petition CNBC For Coverage Overhaul," *Huffington Post*, April 16, 2009, www.huffpost.com/entry/economists-progresses-pet_n_175249.

6. Jon Stewart, "Wall Street Bonuses," *The Daily Show with Jon Stewart*, January 12, 2010.

7. Michael Lewis, *The Big Short: Inside the Doomsday Machine* (New York: W. W. Norton, 2011). For a critique of the work of Lewis, see Michelle Chihara, "The Rise of Behavioral Economic Masculinity," *American Literary History* 32 (Spring 2020): 77–110.

8. Lewis, *Big Short*, 2.

9. Chihara, "Behavioral Economic Masculinity," 88.

10. Lewis, *Big Short*, 96.

11. Lance Rubin, "'We Are the Walking Dead': Zombie Literature in Recession-Era America," in *The Great Recession in Fiction, Film, and Television: Twenty-First-Century Bust Culture*, ed. Kirk Boyle and Daniel Mrozowski (Lanham, Md.: Lexington Books, 2013), 69–94, explores the Zombie theme. See also Andrew Lawson, "Foreclosure Stories: Neoliberal Suffering in the Great Recession," *Journal of American Studies* 47 (February 2013): 49–68, which discusses Paul Reyes's *Exiles in Eden: Life among the Ruins of Florida's Great Recession* (2010) and Paul Auster's novel *Sunset Park* (2010).

12. Gillian Tett, "The Dream Machine," *Financial Times*, March 25, 2006.

13. Diane Negra and Yvonne Tasker, "Introduction: Gender and Recessionary Culture," in *Gendering the Recession: Media and Culture in an Age of Austerity*, ed. Diane Negra and Yvonne Tasker (Durham, N.C.: Duke University Press, 2014), 16. For explorations of the gendering of finance in performances, see Melissa S. Fisher, "Wall Street Women on Film," Public Books, September 1, 2006, www.publicbooks.org/wall-street-women-on-film/; and Melissa S. Fisher, "Performing Beyond the Gendered Zombie Economy," openDemocracy, July 26, 2016, www.opendemocracy.net/en/opendemocracyuk/performing-beyond-gendered-zombie-economy/.

14. Jon Birger, "The Woman Who Called Wall Street's Meltdown: Star Bank Analyst Meredith Whitney Says the Economy Is about to Sink into a Deep Recession," *Fortune*, August 6, 2008.

15. Lewis, *Big Short*, xiii–xiv.

16. The one notable exception was Baum's wife.

17. Of course, the films under discussion here are not the only important ones that explored these issues; for more information, see Kirk Boyle and Daniel Mrozowski, eds., *The Great Recession in Fiction, Film, and Television: Twenty-First-Century Bust Culture* (Lanham, Md.: Lexington Books, 2013); Jeff Kinkle and Alberto Toscano, "Filming the Crisis: A Survey," *Film Quarterly* 65 (Fall 2011): 39–51. Nor, of course, are the books under discussion the only ones a historian, with world enough and time, might discuss. Among the scores of others published by 2010, arranged by the year of publication, are: Philip Augar, *The Greed Merchants: How the Investment Banks Played the Free Market Game* (2005); John C. Bogle, *The Battle for the Soul of Capitalism* (2005); Mohamed El-Erian, *When Markets Collide: Investment Strategies for the Age of Global Economic Change* (2008); Charles Morris,

The Trillion-Dollar Meltdown: Easy Money, High Rollers, and the Great Credit Crash (2008); Mark Zandi, *Financial Shock: A 360° Look at the Subprime Mortgage Implosion, and How to Avoid the Next Financial Crisis* (2008); Barry Ritholtz with Aaron Task, *Bailout Nation: How Greed and Easy Money Corrupted Wall Street and Shook the World Economy* (2009); Peter S. Goodman, *Past Due: The End of Easy Money and the Renewal of the American Economy* (2009); David Faber, *And Then the Roof Caved In: How Wall Street's Greed and Stupidity Brought Capitalism to Its Knees* (2009); Carmen M. Reinhart and Kenneth S. Rogoff, *This Time Is Different: Eight Centuries of Financial Folly* (2009); Andrew Ross Sorkin, *Too Big to Fail: The Inside Story of How Wall Street and Washington Fought to Save the Financial System from Crisis and Themselves* (2009); Johan Norberg, *Financial Fiasco: How America's Infatuation With Homeownership and Easy Money Created the Economic Crisis* (2009); William Greider and Katrina Vanden Heuvel, *Meltdown: How Greed and Corruption Shattered Our Financial System and How We Can Recover* (2009); Shari B. Olefson, *Foreclosure Nation: Mortgaging the American Dream* (2009); Michael Hudson, *The Monster: How a Gang of Predatory Lenders and Wall Street Bankers Fleeced America—and Spawned a Global Crisis* (2010); Joseph E. Stiglitz and Dick Hill, *Freefall: America, Free Markets and the Sinking of the World Economy* (2010); and Roger Lowenstein, *The End of Wall Street* (2010). For assessments coming from Harvard University's Joint Center for Housing Studies of some key elements of the crisis and its aftermath, see Erik S. Belsky and Nela Richardson, "Understanding the Boom and Bust in Nonprime Mortgage Lending," Joint Center for Housing Studies of Harvard University, September 1, 2010, https://www.jchs.harvard.edu/research-areas/reports/understanding-boom-and-bust-nonprime-mortgage-lending; and Eric Belsky, Christopher E. Herbert, and Jennifer H. Molinsky, *Homeownership Built to Last: Balancing Access, Affordability, and Risk after the Housing Crisis* (Washington, D.C.: Brookings Institution, 2017). Among the most recent entries on a long list is Aaron Glantz, *Homewreckers: How a Gang of Wall Street Kingpins, Hedge Fund Magnates, Crooked Banks, and Vulture Capitalists Suckered Millions Out of Their Homes and Demolished the American Dream* (New York: HarperCollins, 2019), which, unlike the work of the journalists I discuss, focuses on both elites—including members of the Trump family and administration implicated in the real estate crisis—and the ordinary people adversely impacted by their actions. For another approach, see Edmund L. Andrews, *Busted: Life Inside the Great Mortgage Meltdown* (New York: W. W. Norton, 2009), which weaves together the story of the global economic crisis and another story closer to home due to his own venture into homeownership that relied on a combination of his own faulty financial decisions and the reckless behavior of financial institutions. Also of note is Ryan Dezember, *Underwater: How Our American Dream of Homeownership Became a Nightmare* (New York: St. Martin's, 2020).

18. Gretchen Morgenson and Joshua Rosner, *Reckless Endangerment: How Outsized Ambition, Greed, and Corruption Led to Economic Armageddon* (New York: Times Books, 2011). The second "s" in the book's title appeared as a dollar sign falling over.

19. Morgenson and Rosner, *Reckless Endangerment*, xiv, 85–88, 240–41. Maxine Waters is a member of the House of Representatives from California, whom the

authors very briefly viewed skeptically for what they considered riskily advocating expanded opportunities for homeownership (192-92, 247-47).

20. Morgenson and Rosner, *Reckless Endangerment*, xiv. For a useful corrective to the book's analysis of the role of GSEs that also emphasizes the role of private mortgage insurers, see Wayne Passmore and Shane M. Shurland, "FHA, Fannie Mae, Freddie Mac, and the Great Recession," *Real Estate Economics* 49 (Autumn 2021): 733-77.

21. Morgenson and Rosner, *Reckless Endangerment*, 10. For his advocacy of affordability, see James A. Johnson, *Showing America a New Way Home: Expanding Opportunities for Home Ownership* (San Francisco: Jossey-Bass, 1996).

22. Morgenson and Rosner, *Reckless Endangerment*, 143, 263.

23. Morgenson and Rosner, *Reckless Endangerment*, 126.

24. An exception was their focus on the Jordan family in Atlanta, African American victims of predatory lending. However, since the source of their story is not clear, it is likely that the authors did no reporting outside the New York–Washington corridor: Morgenson and Rosner, *Reckless Endangerment*, 208-10.

25. Morgenson and Rosner, *Reckless Endangerment*, xiv.

26. Morgenson and Rosner, *Reckless Endangerment*, xiv-xv, 7.

27. Bethany McLean and Peter Elkind, *The Smartest Guys in the Room: The Amazing Rise and Scandalous Fall of Enron* (New York: Penguin, 2003). For a study of the broader context, see Christine L. Williams, *Gaslighted: How the Oil and Gas Industry Shortchanges Women Scientists* (Oakland: University of California Press, 2021).

28. McLean and Elkind, *Smartest Guys*, vii, 406.

29. McLean and Elkind, *Smartest Guys*, xiii-xvii, 407.

30. McLean and Elkind, *Smartest Guys*, 52, 70-72.

31. McLean and Elkind, *Smartest Guys*, 73-84, 247, 250, 253, 263.

32. McLean and Elkind, *Smartest Guys*, 358.

33. Bloomberg News, "Severance Package at Enron Is Set," *New York Times*, August 29, 2002; "Enron Paid Managers $744M," CNN Money, June 17, 2002, https://money.cnn.com/2002/06/17/news/companies/enron_pay/index.htm.

34. Peter Bradshaw, review of the movie *Enron: The Smartest Guys in the Room*, *Guardian*, April 27, 2006.

35. Bethany McLean and Joe Nocera, *All the Devils Are Here: The Hidden History of the Financial Crisis* (New York: Penguin, 2010).

36. Blythe Masters is the one woman they mention whom they saw as problematically involved in securitization.

37. "In the end, this drama is a human one, a tale about the fallibility of people who thought they themselves were too big to fail," writes the journalist Andrew Ross Sorkin in his *Too Big to Fail: Inside the Battle to Save Wall Street* (New York: Penguin, 2009, 7), a statement typical of journalists who use capsule biographies and dramatic stories to drive a narrative. In contrast, David Harvey, *The Enigma of Capital and the Crisis of Capitalism* (New York: Oxford University Press, 2010), focuses not on individual failures but on systematic ones.

38. Harvey, *Enigma of Capital*; and Nick Srnicek, *Platform Capitalism* (Malden, Mass.: Polity, 2017).

39. McLean and Nocera, *All the Devils*, 218.

40. For a list of acronyms, see McLean and Nocera, *All the Devils*, xvii–xviii.

41. McLean and Nocera, *All the Devils*, 359–61, 363–64. In *Shaky Ground: The Strange Saga of the U.S. Mortgage Giants* (New York: Columbia Global Reports, 2015), Bethany McLean covered much of the ground as she had in the earlier book she wrote with Nocera, but now focused on the lingering and momentous problems of the status of Fannie Mae and Freddie Mac.

42. According to her IMDb entry, McLean appeared as a talking head in eighteen television shows and documentaries but served as a writer only in the film on Enron. Her most recent appearance was in *Fishing with Dynamite* (2019), which focused on the difference between stakeholder and shareholder capitalism. "Bethany McLean," IMDb, www.imdb.com/name/nm1628322.

43. Nina Easton, "Main Street Turns against Wall Street," *Fortune*, September 28, 2008.

44. "Panic: The Untold Story of the 2008 Financial Crisis," Vice News Reports, 2018, YouTube video, www.youtube.com/watch?v=wyz79sd_SDA (no longer available); "Panic: The Untold Story of the 2008 Financial Crisis (2018)—Transcript," Scraps from the Loft, November 13, 2020, https://scrapsfromtheloft.com/movies/panic-the-untold-story-of-the-2008-financial-crisis-transcript/.

45. Gillian Tett, "'Guardians of the Faith'? Gender and Religion in an (Ex) Soviet Tajik Village," in *Muslim Women's Choices: Religious Belief and Social Reality*, ed. Camillia Fawzi El-Solh and Judy Mabro (Oxford: Berg, 1994), 129, 143, 146, 148. Tett offered her most extensive discussions of her early work in Gillian Tett, *Anthro-Vision: A New Way to See in Business and Life* (New York: Simon & Schuster, 2021), 3–7, 13–27.

46. Gillian Tett, *The Silo Effect: The Peril of Expertise and the Promise of Breaking Down Barriers* (New York: Simon and Schuster, 2015), 49.

47. Gillian Tett, *Saving the Sun: A Wall Street Gamble to Rescue Japan from Its Trillion-Dollar Meltdown* (New York: HarperCollins, 2003), xi.

48. Tett, *Saving the Sun*, x, 321–22.

49. Tett, *Saving the Sun*, 200, 280, 289.

50. Gillian Tett, *Fool's Gold: How the Bold Dream of a Small Tribe at J. P. Morgan Was Corrupted by Wall Street Greed and Unleashed a Catastrophe* (New York: Free Press, 2009), x.

51. Ruth Sunderland, review of Tett's *Fool's Gold*, *Guardian*, June 6, 2009.

52. Tett, *Fool's Gold*, 43, 249. Note, however, that Tett ended a key section on Masters with a quote from journalist Paula Froelich about a nongendered group who thought, incorrectly, that "they were the smartest guys on the planet" (56; see also 141–42).

53. For some discussion of Tett as an anthropologist, see these articles in the *Financial Times* by Gillian Tett: "The Grandees Shift Into 'Blame the Media' Mode," October 5, 2007; "Anthropology That Explains Varying Banking Behaviours," January 18, 2008; "Tribal Analysis: An Anthropologist Observes the Behavior of Wall Street Bankers," October 3, 2009.

54. Tett, *Fool's Gold*, 99, 129.

55. Tett, *Fool's Gold*, 252–54.

56. Tett, *Fool's Gold*, 252–54.

57. Tett made more than two dozen appearances as a talking head in movies and on television. See her IMDb entry: www.imdb.com/name/nm3842799/.

58. In "Silos and Silences," Tett mentioned the Madam and Lagarde but not Born.

59. The film also featured Martin Wolf of the *Financial Times*.

60. Press kit for *Inside Job*, www.sonyclassics.com/insidejob/_pdf/insidejob_presskit.pdf, 8 and 15. Four weeks before the collapse of Lehman Brothers and AIG, Sloan authored what, looking back, seems like a relatively reassuring assessment of the ability of federal officials to solve the financial crisis: Allan Sloan, "Washington's Ultimate Solution," *Fortune*, August 18, 2008, https://money.cnn.com/2008/08/15/news/economy/Sloan_washingtons_solution.fortune/index.htm. The film's director, Charles Ferguson, followed up in *Predator Nation: Corporate Criminals, Political Corruption, and the Hijacking of America* (New York: Crown, 2012). In many ways the book resembled the film. Both were hard hitting in their accusations of criminality and global in their reach; both paid more attention to Sloan than Tett and worked around the refusal of powerful people to grant interviews. Yet the movie was more successful in dramatizing the impact of the global financial crisis on the lives of ordinary people as well as the system's corruption (including the availability of prostitutes to Wall Street financiers by the "Wall Street Madam").

61. David Mattingly, "Crash Fiction: American Literary Novels of the Global Financial Crisis," in Boyle and Mrozowski, eds., *Great Recession*, 109. Miroslaw Aleksander Miernik, *Rethinking Fiction after the 2007/8 Financial Crisis: Consumption, Economics, and the American Dream* (New York: Routledge, 2021), focused on four novels: those by Elizabeth Strout, Philipp Meyer, Sophie McManus, and William Gibson.

62. April Miller, "Reel-to-Reel Recessionary Horrors in *Drag Me to Hell* and *Contagion*," in Boyle and Mrozowski, eds., *Great Recession*, 36. Karen Ho critiques Hollywood films and documentaries on the Great Recession, including *The Big Short*, in "Finance, Crisis, and Hollywood: Critique and Recuperation of Wall Street in Films about the Great Recession," in *Global Finance on Screen: From Wall Street to Side Street*, ed. Constantin Parvulescu (New York: Routledge, 2018), 89–104, but she makes no mention of McLean, Tett, or Whitney; by and large she confines her gendered analysis to different styles of masculinity.

63. Tett, *Silo Effect*, 43–46.

64. Gillian Tett, "Icebergs and Ideologies: How Information Flows Fueled the Financial Crisis," *Anthropology News*, 50 (October 2009): 6–7.

65. Gillian Tett, "Silos and Silences: Why So Few People Spotted the Problems in Complex Credit and What It Implies for the Future," *Financial Stability Review* 14 (July 2010): 121–22; she was drawing on Pierre Bourdieu, *Outline of a Theory of Practice* (1977). For another statement of Bourdieu's influence in alerting her to the importance of silences, see Gillian Tett, "What Pierre Bourdieu Taught Me," *Financial Times*, July 26, 2013. In *The Social Structures of the Economy*, trans. Chris Turner (Malden, Mass.: Polity, [2000] 2005), Pierre Bourdieu analyzed the housing market.

66. Tett, *Silo Effect*, 49–50.

67. Tett, *Silo Effect*, 108, 193.

68. Tett, *Silo Effect*, 109–10. Philip Mirowski, *Never Let a Serious Crisis Go to Waste: How Neoliberalism Survived the Financial Meltdown* (New York: Verso, 2013) critiques members of the economics profession and those involved in the Mont Pèlerin Society.

69. Tett, *Silo Effect*, 251. Elsewhere she wrote that anthropologists "tend to take a 'bottom up' view of the world, looking at life from grassroots, often by getting their feet dirty with participant observation," and that "taking a bottom-up, immersive approach to analyzing financial markets, that tries to join up the disparate pieces, explore what participants are not saying, and look at how this props up the people who are in power, has enabled me to see striking patterns that some of my colleagues have missed." Gillian Tett, "Anthropology and Power to the People?," *Journal of Business Anthropology* 3 (Spring 2014): 133–34.

70. Tett, *Anthro-Vision*, 77–97.

71. Tett, *Anthro-Vision*, xix–xv.

72. Sorkin, *Too Big To Fail*, xi, 539.

73. For another compelling documentary that relied on the contribution of Mark Pittman, see *American Casino* (2009). J. C. Chandor's *Margin Call* (2011) provides a dramatic fictionalized story of what happened in one day at an investment bank.

74. For a discussion of how, in response to the recession, popular culture texts strove "to preserve verisimilitude in their representations of economic inequalities while doggedly refraining from systemic critique," see Negra and Tasker, "Introduction," 25.

75. Christopher L. Foote, Kristopher S. Gerardi, and Paul S. Willen, "Why Did So Many People Make So Many Ex Post Bad Decisions? The Causes of the Foreclosure Crisis," in *Rethinking the Financial Crisis*, ed. Alan S. Blinder, Andrew W. Loh, and Robert M. Solow (New York: Russell Sage Foundation, 2012), 137. See also Christopher L. Foote, Lara Loewenstein, and Paul S. Willen, "Cross-Sectional Patterns of Mortgage Debt during the Housing Boom: Evidence and Implications," NBER Working Paper 22985, December 2016, www.nber.org/papers/w22985, 25; Manuel Adelino, Antoinette Schoar, and Felipe Severino, "The Role of Housing and Mortgage Markets in the Financial Crisis," *Annual Review of Financial Economics* 10 (2018): 25–41; Manuel Adelino, Antoinette Schoar, and Felipe Severino, "Loan Organizations and Defaults in the Mortgage Crisis: The Role of the Middle Class," *Review of Financial Studies* 29 (2016): 1635–70; Greg Kaplan, Kurt Mitman, and Giovanni L. Violante, "The Housing Market Boom and Bust: Model Meets Evidence," *Journal of Political Economy* 128 (2020): 3285–45; Robert J. Shiller, *Narrative Economics: How Stories Go Viral and Drive Major Economic Events* (Princeton, N.J.: Princeton University Press, [2019] 2020) and *The Subprime Solution: How Today's Global Financial Crisis Happened, and What To Do about It* (Princeton, N.J.: Princeton University Press, 2008); and Nicola Gennaioli and Andrei Shleifer, *A Crisis of Beliefs: Investor Psychology and Financial Fragility* (Princeton, N.J.: Princeton University Press, 2018). I am grateful to Chandler Lutz for alerting me to this body of work and to Paul S. Willen and Christopher L. Foote for email exchanges on these issues during early November 2021.

76. Foote, Gerardi, and Willen, "Why Did So Many People," 136.

77. Susan Faludi, "The Reckoning: Safeway LBO Yields Vast Profits but Exacts a Heavy Human Toll," *Wall Street Journal*, May 16, 1990; Dean Starkman, *The Watchdog That Didn't Bark: The Financial Crisis and the Disappearance of Investigative Journalism* (New York: Columbia University Press, 2014), 130.

78. Melissa S. Fisher, *Wall Street Women* (Durham, N.C.: Duke University Press, 2012), 158.

79. For a list of differences, see Starkman, *Watchdog*, 143.

CHAPTER 5

1. Gillian Tett, *The Silo Effect: The Peril of Expertise and the Promise of Breaking Down Barriers* (New York: Simon & Schuster, 2015), 48.

2. Knut M. Rio and Bjørn Enge Bertelsen, "Anthropology and 1968: Openings and Closures," *Anthropology Today* 34 (April 2018): 9.

3. For a general discussion of foreign correspondents and anthropologists, see Ulf Hannerz, *Foreign News: Exploring the World of Foreign Correspondents* (Chicago: University of Chicago Press, 2004).

4. Gillian Tett, "Silence and Silos: The Problems of Fractured Thought in Finance" (address at the 109th Annual Meeting of the American Anthropological Association, November 19, 2010), https://vimeo.com/17854712. Among the other examples are Gillian Tett, "Silos and Silences: Why So Few People Spotted the Problems in Complex Credit and What It Implies for the Future," *Financial Stability Review* 14 (July 2010): 121–29; Gillian Tett, "Icebergs and Ideologies: How Information Flows Fueled the Financial Crisis," *Anthropology News* 50 (October 2009): 6–7; and Gillian Tett, "Anthropology and Power to the People?," *Journal of Business Anthropology* 3 (Spring 2014): 132–35. One of the earliest examples of the emergence of how anthropologists were turning their attention to finance came in 2003 when Melissa Fisher and Karen Ho organized a session at the 2003 annual meeting of the AAA on "Corporate Ethnography in the New Economy": *Anthropology News*, April 2004, 15. Another piece of evidence of what was happening while Tett was developing her own pathbreaking work was, similarly, *Frontiers of Capital: Ethnographic Reflections on the New Economy*, edited by Greg Downey and Melissa S. Fisher (Durham, N.C.: Duke University Press, 2006) which grew out of a 2001 workshop they organized.

5. Brian McKenna, "Bestselling Anthropologist 'Predicted' Financial Meltdown of 2008," *News: A Publication of the Society of Applied Anthropology* 22 (February 2011): 21–25. In her 2009 talk at a meeting of anthropologists, Tett remarked that it was not entirely accurate to say that she "predicted" the financial crisis. Soon after, McKenna offered a more extensive evaluation of Tett's work in which he wondered out loud about the compromises she made because of her close relationships to the sources among the powerful: Brian McKenna, "How Will Gillian Tett Connect With the Natives of the US Left?," *Counterpunch*, March 4, 2011, www.counterpunch.org/2011/03/04/how-will-gillian-tett-connect-with-the-natives-of-the-us-left/. Another evaluation of Tett's work as a journalist trained as an anthropologist is Michael G. Powell, "Anthropologist as Prognosticator: Gilliam Tett and the Credit Derivatives Market," *American Anthropologist* 112 (March 2010): 142–43.

6. McKenna, "Anthropologist."

7. Gillian Tett, review of *Liquidated: An Ethnography of Wall Street*, by Karen Ho, *Financial Times*, October 2, 2009.

8. Tett, review of *Liquidated*.

9. For information on her work, see Michael F. Bernstein, "Margaret Mead Meets Morgan Stanley," *Princeton Alumni Weekly*, September 23, 2009. In "Situating Global Capitalisms: A View from Wall Street Investment Banks," *Cultural Anthropology* 20 (February 2005): 68–96, Karen Ho juxtaposes the problematic ways both Wall Street denizens and many social scientists construct the global as a powerful force. See Karen Ho, "Disciplining Investment Bankers, Disciplining the Economy: Wall Street's Institutional Culture of Crisis and the Downsizing of

American 'Corporate America,'" *American Anthropologist* 111 (June 2009): 177–89, for her discussion of the role of investment banks in the 2001 market crash. Among other relevant publications is Laura Bear, Karen Ho, Anna Lowenhaupt, and Sylvia Yanagisako, "Gens: A Feminist Manifesto for the Study of Capitalism," Society for Cultural Anthropology, March 30, 2015, https://culanth.org/fieldsights/gens-a-feminist-manifesto-for-the-study-of-capitalism.

10. Karen Zouwen Ho, "Liquefying Corporations and Communities: Wall Street Worldviews and Socio-Economic Transformations in the Postindustrial Economy," PhD diss., Princeton University, 2003, i, xiii, xiv, 62.

11. Ho, "Liquefying Corporations," 255, 291.

12. Ho, "Liquefying Corporations," 255, 291.

13. Karen Ho, *Liquidated: An Ethnography of Wall Street* (Durham, N.C.: Duke University Press, 2009), 12, 285, 296.

14. Ho, *Liquidated*, 10, 318–24.

15. Ho, *Liquidated*, 13, 321; Gillian Tett, "Innovative Ways to Repackage Debt and Spread Risk Have Brought Higher Returns but Have Yet to be Tested through a Full Credit Cycle," *Financial Times*, April 19, 2005.

16. Karen Z. Ho, "Outsmarting Risk: From Bonuses to Bailouts," *Anthropology Now* 2 (April 2010): 4, 6, 7, 8.

17. Karen Ho, "'Studying Up' Wall Street: Reflections on Theory and Methodology," in *Researching amongst Elites: Challenges and Opportunities in Studying Up*, ed. Luis Aguilar and Christopher Schneider (London: Ashgate, 2012), 42–69. For a broader review of the field, one that briefly mentions the work of Ho and Tett, see Keith Hart and Horacio Ortiz, "The Anthropology of Money and Finance: Between Ethnography and World History," *Annual Review of Anthropology* 43 (2014): 465–82.

18. McKenna, "Anthropologist," 23–24, pointed to Michael Perelman, *The Confiscation of American Prosperity: From Right-Wing Extremism to the Next Great Depression* (New York: Palgrave Macmillan, 2007); Edward LiPuma and Benjamin Lee, *Financial Derivatives and the Globalization of Risk* (Durham, N.C.: Duke University Press, 2004); Alexandra Ouroussoff, *Wall Street at War: The Secret Struggle for the Global Economy* (Malden, Mass.: Polity, 2010); Caitlin Zaloom, *Out of the Pits: Traders and Technology from Chicago to London* (Chicago: University of Chicago Press, 2006); and Annelise Riles, *Collateral Knowledge: Legal Reasoning in the Global Financial Markets* (Chicago: University of Chicago Press, 2011). Among the many other relevant studies, not cited by McKenna, are Bill Maurer, "Repressed Futures: Financial Derivatives' Theological Unconscious," *Economy and Society* 31 (February 2002): 15–36; and Annelise Riles and Hirokazu Miyazaki, "Failure as an Endpoint," in *Global Assemblages: Technology, Politics, and Ethics as Anthropological Problems*, ed. Aihwa Ong and Stephen J. Collier (Chichester, UK: Wiley, 2004), 320–31 (based on research carried out in Tokyo at a time when Tett was reporting from there). For other studies, see Daniel Beunza, *Taking the Floor: Models, Morals, and Management in a Wall Street Trading Room* (Princeton, N.J.: Princeton University Press, 2019); Vincent Antonin Lépinay, *Codes of Finance: Engineering Derivatives in a Global Bank* (Princeton, N.J.: Princeton University Press, 2011); and the works Tett cites in *Anthro-Vision: A New Way to See in Business and Life* (New York: Simon & Schuster, 2021), 96.

19. McKenna, "Anthropologist," 24. Among what McKenna mentioned were Richard Robbins, *Global Problems and the Culture of Capitalism* (1999), Henry Giroux, *The Terror of Neoliberalism: Authoritarianism and the Eclipse of Democracy* (2004), and David Harvey's animated cartoon on his website, davidharvey.org.

20. McKenna, "Anthropologist," 23.

21. Melissa S. Fisher, *Wall Street Women* (Durham, N.C.: Duke University Press, 2012), 2–3. For later reflections on the study of gender, finance, and anthropology, see Melissa S. Fisher, "Notes on the Anthropology of Gender in Finance," *Journal of Business Anthropology* 2 (Spring 2013): 68–73.

22. Fisher, *Wall Street Women*, 15, 104, 107, 156–58, 171, with the quote from Lewis, *Big Short*, on 155.

23. Noelle Stout, *Dispossessed: How Predatory Bureaucracy Foreclosed on the American Middle Class* (Oakland: University of California Press, 2019). In "The Great American Recession: Sociological Insights on Blame and Pain," *Sociological Perspectives* 53 (Winter 2010): 3–17, Judith Treas emphasizes that systematic vulnerabilities, rather than problematic behavior by borrowers, were responsible were responsible for the crisis.

24. Stout, *Dispossessed*, 13, 16, 30. She also writes of "predatory debt extraction—a process through which the most vulnerable Americans are no longer exploited for their surplus labor but now become key to capitalist accumulation through their debts, which are securitized and then sold and resold on global markets" (72).

25. Stout, *Dispossessed*, 7.

26. Ho, *Liquidated*, 329n15; Laura Nader, "Up the Anthropologist—Perspectives Gained from Studying Up," in *Reinventing Anthropology*, ed. Dell Hymes (New York: Pantheon, 1972), 284–311.

27. Keith Hart, quoted in McKenna, "How Will Gillian Tett."

28. Silvia Irina Berástegui, "More Anthropologists on Wall Street Please, Revisited," *Culture and Capitalism* (blog), February 28, 2019, https://cultureandcapitalismblog.wordpress.com/2019/02/28/more-anthropologist-on-wall-street-please-revisited/.

29. Michael Lewis, *The Big Short: Inside the Doomsday Machine* (New York: W. W. Norton, 2011), 70.

30. Gillian Tett, "In with the 'On' Crowd," *Financial Times*, May 24, 2013. In Gillian Tett, "America's Debt-Laden Students Need Better Policy Solutions," *Financial Times*, September 5, 2019, she called Caitlin Zaloom's *Indebted: How Families Make College Work at Any Cost* (2019) "compelling." Yet, as far as I can see, she did not review her *Out of the Pits*. Nor did she take note of other books by anthropologists directly related to her work that were available when she was working on *Fool's Gold*, such LiPuma and Lee's *Financial Derivatives*. Tett did not review Annelise Riles's *Collateral Knowledge*, but she did mention an article Riles wrote: Gillian Tett, "Regulators Should Say Who Calls the Shots," *Financial Times*, February 27, 2014. Although she did not review Ouroussoff, *Wall Street at War* or Noelle Stout's *Dispossessed* in the *Financial Times*, she enthusiastically reviewed Ho's *Liquidated*.

31. See, as examples, Zaloom, *Out of the Pits*, 7, 11, 189, 204; Ouroussoff, *Wall Street*, 1, 9–10, 12, 51–53; and LiPuma and Lee, *Financial Derivatives*. Even in

Perelman's discussion of financialization (107–10) focusing on Enron, he could have mentioned the work of McLean and Elkind in a bibliography two dozen pages in length. Similarly, he mentioned a minor article by Morgenson but not her major, revelatory ones. Ho might have taken note of Tett's work on the Morgan Mafia, which deployed anthropology in order to offer an analysis of the ideology of finance and of an origin myth different from hers.

32. This discussion relies on coverage of her work in *Annual Review of Anthropology*, *Current Anthropology*, *American Anthropologist*, and *American Ethnologist*. Aside from Powell's discussion, the only significant attention was a favorable discussion of her career and books with Y. A. Orr, "Anthropology and Journalism," *Current Anthropology* 51 (October 2010): 573. It is too early to tell if this neglect is also true of Tett, *Anthro-Vision*.

33. Powell, "Anthropologist as Prognosticator," 142–43.

34. For a discussion of cinematic treatments that link horror and economic crises, see Diane Negra and Yvonne Tasker, "Introduction: Gender and Recessionary Culture," in *Gendering the Recession: Media and Culture in an Age of Austerity*, ed. Diane Negra and Yvonne Tasker (Durham, N.C.: Duke University Press, 2014), 19, and, more extensively in the same volume, Tim Snelson, "The (Re)possession of the American Home: Negative Equity, Gender Inequality, and the Housing Crisis Horror Story," 161–80. See also April Miller, "Reel-to-Reel Recessionary Horrors in *Drag Me to Hell* and *Contagion*," 29–49; and James D. Stone, "Horror at the Homestead: The (Re)possession of American Property in *Paranormal Activity* and *Paranormal Activity II*," 51–64, in *The Great Recession in Fiction, Film, and Television: Twenty-First-Century Bust Culture*, ed. Kirk Boyle and Daniel Mrozowski (Lanham, Md.: Lexington Books, 2013). Amin Samman, *History in Financial Times* (Stanford, Calif.: Stanford University Press, 2019), 112–34, discusses other films that responded to financial crises. On films and novels, see also Alberto Toscano and Jeff Kinkle, *Cartographies of the Absolute* (Winchester, UK: Zero Books, 2015); and Miroslaw Aleksander Miernik, *Rethinking Fiction after the 2007/8 Financial Crisis: Consumption, Economics, and the American Dream* (New York: Routledge, 2021).

35. Snelson, "(Re)possession," 161–62.

36. Emma Donoghue, *Room: A Novel* (New York: Little, Brown, 2010), 72, 127–28.

37. S. Nathan Park, "'Parasite' Has a Hidden Backstory of Middle-Class Failure and Chicken Joints," *Foreign Policy*, February 21, 2020, https://foreignpolicy.com/2020/02/21/korea-bong-oscars-parasite-hidden-backstory-middle-class-chicken-bong-joon-ho/.

CHAPTER 6

1. Luke Fernandez and Susan J. Matt, *Bored, Lonely, Angry, Stupid: Changing Feelings about Technology, from the Telegraph to Twitter* (Cambridge, Mass.: Harvard University Press, 2019), 134, explore generational differences in understanding the public-private division.

2. For two critical assessments of the corporation, see Eliot Brown and Maureen Farrell, *The Cult of We: WeWork, Adam Neumann, and the Great Startup Delusion* (New York: Crown, 2021); and Reeves Wiedeman, *Billion Dollar Loser: The Epic Rise and Spectacular Fall of Adam Neumann and WeWork* (New York: Little, Brown, 2021).

3. For an overview of these forces, see Keith Hart and Horacio Ortiz, "The Anthropology of Money and Finance: Between Ethnography and World History," *Annual Review of Anthropology* (October 2014): 13–26. Desiree Fields, "Automated Landlord: Digital Technologies and Post-Crisis Financial Accumulation," *Environment and Planning A: Economy and Space*, May 2019, doi:10.1177/0308518X19846514, explores the connections between financialization and new technologies.

4. Juliet B. Schor, *After the Gig: How the Sharing Economy Got Hijacked and How To Win It Back* (Oakland: University of California Press, 2020), identifies the failed promises of the sharing economy and advocates the use of regulation and cooperation to transform it into what it originally promised to be—a force for promoting racial justice, ecological commitments, and improved labor conditions.

5. On the importance of trust for platform enterprises, see Rachel Botsman, *Who Can You Trust? How Technology Brought Us Together and Why It Might Drive Us Apart* (New York: Public Affairs, 2017).

6. Geoffrey G. Parker, Marshall W. Van Alstyne, and Sangeet Paul Choudary, *Platform Revolution: How Networked Markets Are Transforming the Economy—and How to Make Them Work for You* (New York: W. W. Norton, 2016), 5. Arun Sundararajan, *The Sharing Economy: The End of Employment and the Rise of Crowd-Based Capitalism* (Cambridge, Mass.: MIT Press, 2016) is useful for its historical sense, discussion of cause and effects, and balanced treatment of impact of innovations of what he calls "crowd-based capitalism." Nick Srnicek, *Platform Capitalism* (Malden, Mass.: Polity, 2017) offers a probing analysis of the origins and reach of what he calls platform capitalism. For advocacy of turning the platform economy in a radical direction, see Trebor Scholz and Nathan Schneider, eds., *Ours to Hack and to Own: The Rise of Platform Cooperativism, A New Vision for the Future of Work and a Fairer Internet* (New York: OR Books, 2017). For a critical assessment, see Jonathan Knee, *The Platform Delusion: Who Wins and Who Loses in the Age of Tech Titans* (New York: Penguin, 2021). For a book on the topic geared for managers and entrepreneurs, see Michael A. Cusumano, Annabelle Gawer, and David B. Yoffie, *The Business of Platforms: Strategy in the Age of Digital Competition, Innovation, and Power* (New York: HarperCollins, 2019).

7. Srnicek, *Platform Capitalism*, 36. For a critique of the platform capitalism, see Tom Slee, *What's Yours Is Mine: Against the Sharing Economy* (New York: OR Books, 2016).

8. Joseph Schumpeter, *Capitalism, Socialism, and Democracy* (New York: Harper, 1942), 82–83, 156.

9. Martin Kenney and John Zysman, "The Rise of the Platform Economy," *Issues in Science and Technology* 32 (Spring 2016): 61–62.

10. David S. Evans and Richard Schmalensee, *Matchmakers: The New Economics of Multisided Platforms* (Boston: Harvard Business Review Press, 2016), 1. Jean-Charles Rocher and Jean Tirole, "Platform Competition in Two Sided-Markets," *Journal of the European Economic Association* 1 (June 2003): 990–1029, is an early and influential scholarly discussion.

11. For a guide to websites for prospective homeowners, see Miranda Marquit, "11 Essential Websites to Help You Find a Home," Student Loan Hero, January 23, 2017, https://studentloanhero.com/featured/best-real-estate-websites-home-search/.

12. For an example of a critical assessment of Zillow's statistical methods, see Yanni Loukissas, "All the Homes: Zillow and the Operational Context of Data," in *Transforming Digital Worlds*, ed. Gobinda Chowdhury et al. (Sheffield, UK: Springer, 2018), 272–81. Spencer Rascoff and Stan Humphries, *Zillow Talk: Rewriting the Rules of Real Estate* (New York: Grand Central, 2016) explores the lessons learned from the corporation's data.

13. "The Real-Estate Racket," *Economist*, February 15, 2020, 12; for information on a class action lawsuit, the history of MLS, realtors' fees, and the economics of being a realtor, see Lydia DePillis, "The Internet Didn't Shrink 6% Real Estate Commissions. But This Lawsuit Might," CNN, May 15, 2019, www.cnn.com/2019/05/15/economy/real-estate-commissions/index.html. The Bureau of Labor Statistics reports that in 2019, the median pay for real estate brokers was $50,730: "Real Estate Brokers and Sales Agents," Occupational Outlook Handbook, U.S. Bureau of Labor Statistics, www.bls.gov/ooh/sales/real-estate-brokers-and-sales-agents.htm. For court cases contesting the hold of MLS on commissions as anticompetitive, see Ann Carrns, "A Challenge to Real Estate Commissions," *New York Times*, October 10, 2020.

14. Brent Nyitray, "Zillow Plans to Do for Real Estate What Amazon Did to Retailing," *Motley Fool*, November 23, 2019, www.fool.com/investing/2019/11/23/zillow-plans-to-do-to-real-estate-what-amazon-did.aspx.

15. Ben Casselman and Conor Dougherty, "Real Estate's Latest Bid: Zillow Wants to Buy Your House," *New York Times*, May 7, 2019. In the fall of 2021, Zillow ended its iBuying program.

16. "Tearing Down the House," *Economist*, February 15, 2020, 61–63.

17. Taylor Soper, "Amazon's New Real Estate Partnership with Realogy Promises Homebuyers up to $5k in Credits," GeekWire, July 23, 2019, www.geekwire.com/2019/amazon-moves-real-estate-inks-new-deal-brokerage-conglomerate-realogy/. To follow trends in iBuying, see the ongoing work of Mike DelPrete, who remains skeptical about the sector's profitability: www.mikedp.com/articles/category/ibuyer.

18. Casselman and Dougherty, "Latest Bid."

19. "Your Answers to Zillow's 'Instant Offers,'" *Realtor Magazine*, May 26, 2017.

20. "Tearing Down the House."

21. For a discussion of how access to more data has its advantages and limitations, see a paper presented in 2017 at Harvard's Joint Center for Housing Studies: Ralph McLaughlin and Cheryl Young, "Data Democratization and Spatial Heterogeneity in the Housing Market," www.jchs.harvard.edu/sites/default/files/media/imp/a_shared_future_data_democratization_spatial_heterogeneity.pdf.

22. Kayla Matthews, "Tinder Made Us Pickier About Dating . . . Is Trulia Doing the Same for Home Buying?" *Observer*, March 15, 2018, https://observer.com/2018/03/have-real-estate-apps-trulia-and-zillow-changed-how-people-buy-homes/. Instagram offers Zillow Gone Wild, which features unusual residences.

23. Jeffrey M. O'Brien, "What's Your Home Really Worth?," CNN, February 15, 2017, https://money.cnn.com/magazines/fortune/fortune_archive/2007/02/19/8400262/index.htm; see also "Unusual Housing Porn," *Mike the Mad Biologist* (blog), November 12, 2016, https://mikethemadbiologist.com/2016/11/12/unusual-housing-porn/.

24. Rascoff and Humphries, *Zillow Talk*, 11.

25. Lauren Bretz, "Coming and Going: What Home Views Do, and Don't Reveal about Our Potential Moves," Zillow, September 9, 2016, www.zillow.com/research/home-searches-potential-moves-13192/.

26. Megan Garber, "This Is Awkward, but I Know How Much Your House Cost," *Atlantic*, July 28, 2014.

27. Sarah Mikhitarian, "The Housing Gap Widened the Wealth Gap. Here's How," Zillow, October 4, 2018, www.zillow.com/research/housing-bust-wealth-gap-21543/.

28. The essential book on the history of contingent labor is Louis Hyman, *Temp: How American Work, American Business, and the American Dream Became Temporary* (New York: Viking, 2018). On the role of iBuying, venture capitalism, and PropTech, see Mike DelPrete, *The 2021 Emerging Models in Real Estate Report*, July 6, 2021, https://www.mikedp.com/articles/2021/7/5/the-2021-emerging-models-in-real-estate-report; and Andrew Baum, *PropTech 2020: The Future of Real Estate*, University of Oxford Research, Saïd Business School, Oxford Future of Real Estate Initiative, www.sbs.ox.ac.uk/sites/default/files/2020-02/proptech2020.pdf. Though not focusing on the impact of Airbnb, University of California, Berkeley's Desiree Fields explores the connections between financialization and race; her website leads to the relevant articles: see www.desireefields.org/research. For a careful and nuanced study of the impact of companies like Airbnb on real estate values, see Sophie Calder-Wang, "The Distributional Impact of the Sharing Economy on the Housing Market," the Wharton School, University of Pennsylvania, August 2021, https://papers.ssrn.com/sol3/papers.cfm?abstract_id=3908062.

29. Leigh Gallagher, *The Airbnb Story: How Three Ordinary Guys Disrupted an Industry, Made Billions . . . and Plenty of Controversy* (Boston: Houghton Mifflin Harcourt, 2017), xii. Gallagher chronicles how over time the founders, including its tech whiz Nathan Blecharczyk, developed robust strategies and secured equivalent funding from venture capitalists.

30. Stephen McCauley, "Decoding Your Airbnb: Adventures in Voyeurism," *New York Times*, August 8, 2018. Gallagher, *Airbnb Story*, xvii, describes the website and the decisions that make it successful.

31. Erin Griffith, "Airbnb Was Like a Family, until the Layoffs Started," *New York Times*, July 17, 2020.

32. Gallagher, *Airbnb Story*, 50–55, 80–104.

33. "Airbnb by the Numbers: Usage, Demographics, and Revenue Growth," MuchNeeded, February 12, 2020, https://muchneeded.com/airbnb-statistics.

34. Among them are accuracy of reviews by hosts and guests, charges of racial discrimination, and allegations of problematic offerings.

35. Priceconomics Data Studio, "The Rise of the Professional Airbnb Investor," February 2, 2016, https://priceonomics.com/will-real-estate-investors-take-over-airbnb/.

36. Gallagher, *Airbnb Story*, xiii, xix, 191–92, 207. On its new ventures, see Gallagher, *Airbnb Story*, 191–92.

37. Gallagher, *Airbnb Story*, 75.

38. To sample the current scholarship, begin with Daniel Guttentag, "Assessing Airbnb as a Disruptive Innovation Relative to Hotels: Substitution and Comparative Performance Expectations," *International Journal of Hospitality Management* 64 (July 2017): 1–10.

39. Elaine Glusac, "A New Marriott Division Goes Head-to-Head with Airbnb," *New York Times*, April 29, 1919. On the threats that Airbnb poses to hotels and how they responded, see Gallagher, *Airbnb Story*, 115, 139–58.

40. Daniel Guttentag, "Transformative Experiences via Airbnb: Is It the Guests or the Host Communities That Will Be Transformed?," *Journal of Tourism Futures* 5 (July 2019): 181. For a summary of research in the field that touches of all the issues raised in this discussion, see Daniel Guttentag, "Progress on Airbnb: A Literature Review," *Journal of Hospitality and Tourism Technology* 10 (November 2019): 814–44.

41. William Alden, "The Business Tycoons of Airbnb," *New York Times Magazine*, November 25, 2014. Estimates vary, but the involvement of significantly scaled commercial operators through Airbnb may be as high at 40 percent: Gallagher, *Airbnb Story*, 115. On how those who benefited from gentrification drove out the artists, workers, and immigrants who had made urban living "authentic," see Sharon Zukin, *Naked City: The Death and Life of Authentic Urban Places* (New York: Oxford University Press, 2010).

42. Gallagher, *Airbnb Story*, 105–37, chronicles the controversies Airbnb generated in New York and elsewhere.

43. Patrick Sisson, "How Vacation Homes Went from Private Escape to Investment Opportunities," Curbed, October 2, 2018, www.curbed.com/2018/10/2/17925738/property-airbnb-vacation-home-short-term-rental.

44. Sisson, "How Vacation Homes."

45. For a how-to book on working from anywhere, see Lisette Sutherland and Kirsten Janene-Nelson, *Work Together Anywhere: A Handbook on Working Remotely—Successfully—for Individuals, Teams, and Managers* (Hoboken, N.J.: Wiley, 2020).

46. Geoff Boeing, Max Besbris, Ariela Schachter, and John Kuk, "Housing Search in the Age of Big Data: Smarter Cities or Same Old Blind Spots?," *Housing Policy Debate* 31 (2021): 112–26, doi: 10.1080/10511482.2019.1684336.

47. Alexander Taub, "Everything But the House Takes Its Estate Sale Marketplace Nationwide with New Redesign," *Forbes*, March 15, 2016, www.forbes.com/sites/alextaub/2016/03/15/everything-but-the-house-takes-its-estate-sale-marketplace-nationwide-with-new-redesign/#3dc79dc156e6.

48. Sarah Buckley, "House Design App: 10 Best Home Design Apps," Architecture and Design, April 14, 2020, www.architectureanddesign.com.au/features/list/house-design-app-10-best-home-design-apps#.

49. "8 of the Best Free Home and Interior Design Tools, Apps and Software," *House Beautiful*, May 26, 2020, www.housebeautiful.com/uk/renovate/design/a28461218/best-free-home-interior-design-tools-apps-software/.

50. Libby Plummer, "This Is How Netflix's Top-Secret Recommendation System Works," *Wired*, August 22, 2017, www.wired.co.uk/article/how-do-netflixs-algorithms-work-machine-learning-helps-to-predict-what-viewers-will-like.

51. Janene-Nelson and Sutherland, *Work Together*, 26. The following discussion relies on this book, whose authors tend to emphasize the advantages of remote working, while minimizing the disadvantages.

52. Niraj Chokshi, "Our of the Office: More People Are Working Remotely, Survey Finds," *New York Times*, February 15, 2017.

53. Two books by Melissa Gregg, *Work's Intimacy* (Malden, Mass.: Polity Press, 2011) and *Counterproductive: Time Management in the Knowledge Economy* (Durham, N.C.: Duke University Press, 2018), offer nuanced, ethnographic examinations of what work, domesticity, public and private mean for midlevel employees who work at home and for their employers, and thus provide a good entry point into the abundant amount of scholarship on these topics. On the pleasures of chatting around the water cooler or during a coffee break, see Derek Thompson, "Hard Work Isn't the Point of the Office," *Atlantic*, September 21, 2021.

54. Janene-Nelson and Sutherland, *Work Together*, 1–3. Patricia L. Mokhtarian, who has written extensively on teleworking, emphasizes its long-term slow growth: "Patricia L. Mokhtarian," Faculty Profile, Georgia Tech, https://ce.gatech.edu/people/faculty/6251/overview.

55. Clare Kelliher and Deidre Anderson, "Doing More with Less? Flexible Working Practices and the Intensification of Work," *Human Relations* 63 (January 2010): 83–106.

56. On gender, see Claire Cain Miller, "How to Close a Gender Gap: Let Employees Control Their Schedules," *New York Times*, February 7, 2017. One useful source on how new technologies intensify class and racial inequalities is Virginia Eubanks, *Automating Inequality: How High-Tech Tools Profile, Police, and Punish the Poor* (New York: St. Martin's, 2017).

57. Robert J. Gordon, *The Rise and Fall of American Growth: The U.S. Standard of Living Since the Civil War* (Princeton, N.J.: Princeton University Press, 2016), 2.

58. Rascoff and Humphries, *Zillow Talk*, 11.

59. Vauhini Vara, "The WeWork Guy's Guide to Striking It Rich," *Atlantic*, November 2020, 99.

60. David Edgerton, *The Shock of the Old: Technology and Global History Since 1900* (New York: Oxford University Press, 2007), xvi; Gordon, *Rise and Fall*, xi. We do not yet have enough comprehensive and convincing studies of the relationships between disruptive new technologies and socioeconomic divisions, and what we do have points in multiple directions. For relevant studies, see Jennifer Miller, "Is an Algorithm Less Racist Than a Loan Officer?," *New York Times*, September 18, 2020; Robin Wolfe Scheffler, "Bankrolling Creative Destruction," *Reviews in American History* 48 (September 2020): 470–75; Samuel P. Fraiberger and Arun Sundararajan, "Peer-to-Peer Rental Markets in the Sharing Economy," NYU Stern School of Business Research Paper, September 2017, https://ssrn.com/abstract=2574337; Benjamin G. Edelman and Michael Luca, "Digital Discrimination: The Case of Airbnb.com," Harvard Business School NOM Unit Working Paper No. 14-054, January 10, 2014, https://ssrn.com/abstract=2377353.

CODA

1. "Let's Start Over," *New York Times*, December 24, 2020.

2. *The State of the Nation's Housing, 2021*, Joint Center for Housing Studies of Harvard University, www.jchs.harvard.edu/sites/default/files/reports/files/Harvard_JCHS_State_Nations_Housing_2021.pdf.

3. Riley Cardoza, "Tarek El Moussa, Christina Haack's Quotes about Their Split and Coparenting: We're 'in a Really Good Place,'" *Us Weekly*, January 7, 2021, www.usmagazine.com/celebrity-moms/pictures/tarek-el-moussa-christina-ansteads-quotes-on-split-coparenting/. For a discussion of recent changes at HGTV,

especially those related to the business model, see Ian Parker, "HGTV Is Getting a Renovation: In the Streaming Era, Does the Network Need to Be More Than Wallpaper?," *New Yorker*, March 22, 2021.

4. Ree Hines, "Joanna Gaines Gives an Update on Life at Home with Chip and the Kids," Today, April 8, 2020, www.today.com/home/joanna-gaines-gives-update-life-home-chip-kids-t177940.

5. David Perry, "Scott Brothers Say New Home Focus a Plus for Industry," Furniture Today, September 7, 2020, www.furnituretoday.com/mattress-bedding-news/scott-brothers-say-new-home-focus-a-plus-for-industry/.

6. Claire McNear, "Into the Gaines-verse," The Ringer, January 20, 2021, www.theringer.com/platform/amp/tv/2021/1/20/22240623/chip-joanna-gaines-magnolia-network-streaming-discovery-plus.

7. Not surprisingly, Kiyosaki doubled down on his combination of doom and opportunity: "2021 Predictions: Robert and His Trusted Experts Predict the Future of Investing," Rich Dad World, January 25, 2021, https://experts.richdadworld.com/catalog/live/2021_rich_dad_predictions_with_bonus/rd.

8. If the focus of some of Rich Dad's advice was on investments in cryptocurrencies and precious metals, FortuneBuilders concentrated on opportunities in real estate: Than Merrill, "Best Real Estate Investment Strategies Right Now," FortuneBuilders, www.fortunebuilders.com/best-real-estate-investment-strategies-right-now/.

9. "About Us," WealthFit, https://wealthfit.com/about-us.

10. "WealthFit Premium," WealthFit, https://wealthfit.com/for/real-estate-investors/activate.

11. Jillian Pretzel, "Tarek El Moussa and Christina Anstead's Top Tips on Flipping amid a Pandemic—and Beyond," Realtor, January 6, 2021, www.realtor.com/advice/home-improvement/tarek-el-moussa-and-christina-ansteads-top-tips-flipping-in-a-pandemic/.

12. Erica Christoffer, Christina Hoffmann, Alexandra Stegman, Melissa Tracey, and Graham Wood, "COVID-19 and Real Estate," *Realtor Magazine*, May–June 2020.

13. Randall Lane, "Greater Capitalism," *Forbes*, May 26, 2020. For an example of how, in response to the pandemic, the *National Review* celebrated free market capitalism and denigrated the role of the government, see Nicholas Kerr, "The Private Sector's COVID-Era Triumph," *National Review*, January 11, 2021.

14. "Virus Lays Bare the Frailty of the Social Contract," *Financial Times*, April 3, 2020. See also David Brooks, "Joe Biden Is a Transformational President," *New York Times*, March 11, 2021.

15. In "At a Distance: Gillian Tett on the Risk of Pandemic as an Incredible Blind Spot," May 8, 2020, https://podcasts.apple.com/us/podcast/gillian-tett-on-risk-pandemics-as-incredible-blind/id1504301339, Tett speaks more as a financial journalist than as an anthropologist, though there are hints of what putting on that hat might involve.

16. Adriana Balsamo, "A New Print Section for a New Way of Life," *New York Times*, April 26, 2020.

17. Emmett Linder, "With Society Reopening, the At Home Section Is Closing," *New York Times*, May 30, 2021.

18. This discussion relies on stories in newspapers, mainly the *New York Times*, for the year beginning in late January 2020.

19. One estimate is that about half of Americans worked from home during the pandemic, and that once it was over the percentage would be between 20 and 30, up from 10 percent before 2020: Erik Brynjolfsson, John J. Horton, Adam Ozimek, Daniel Rock, Garima Sharma, and Hong-Yi TuYe, "COVID-19 and Remote Work: An Early Look at US Data," National Bureau of Economic Research Working Paper 27344, www.nber.org/papers/w27344.

20. Noam Scheiber, "Upsides for Some Remote Workers; Lost Pay and Security for Others," *New York Times*, July 26, 2020.

21. Discussion moderated by Emily Bazelon, "Will This Be a Lost Year for America's Children?," *New York Times*, September 11, 2020.

22. Maria Cramer and Aimee Ortiz, "They're Stuck at Home, So They're Making Home a Sanctuary," *New York Times*, September 4, 2020.

23. "At Home" section, *New York Times*, October 25, 2020.

24. On what will happen when the pandemic has passed, see Reed Abelson, "Is Telemedicine Here to Stay?" *New York Times*, August 3, 2020.

25. Ben Smith, "The Week Hollywood Finally, Actually Died," *New York Times*, August 16, 2020. For another funeral notice, see Brooks Barnes, "Hollywood's Obituary, The Sequel. Now Streaming," *New York Times*, November 28, 2020.

26. Danielle Abril, "Airbnb's CEO On How COVID Has Changed Travel Forever," *Fortune*, January 14, 2021.

27. Taylor Lorenz, "Zillow Surfing Is the Escape We All Need Right Now," *New York Times*, November 19, 2020. One estimate is that 63 percent of homebuyers made an offer on a residence they had seen only online: Debra Kamin, "Online Home-Buying Picks Up Speed," *New York Times*, February 21, 2021. The pandemic accelerated the reliance on paperless, digital mortgages, such as those offered by Rocket Mortgage, Quicken Loans, or Loan Depot and increased traffic on Zillow by 41 percent.

28. Conor Dougherty, "Pandemic's Toll on Housing: Falling Behind, Doubling Up," *New York Times*, February 6, 2021.

29. Corina Knoll, "How New Yorkers Found Resolve after 6 Months of Pandemic Hardship," *New York Times*, September 23, 2020.

30. Farhad Manjoo, "I've Seen a Future without Cars, and It's Amazing," *New York Times*, July 9, 2020.

31. Jessica Bursztynsky, "Zillow CEO: Real Estate Market Is Beginning 'Great Reshuffling' as People Seek More Space at Home," CNBC, August 7, 2020, www.cnbc.com/2020/08/07/zillow-were-at-the-beginning-of-a-great-reshuffling-to-space.html.

32. When the dust had settled, it was clear that some fears were overstated: David Faris, "The Death of Cities Was Greatly Exaggerated," *The Week*, April 26, 2021, https://theweek.com/articles/978456/death-cities-greatly-exaggerated; Jed Kolko, Emily Badger, and Quoctrung Bui, "How the Pandemic Did, and Didn't, Change Where Americans Move," *New York Times*, April 19, 2021.

33. Eduardo Porter, "Coronavirus Threatens the Luster of Superstar Cities," *New York Times*, July 21, 2020.

34. David Streitfeld, "The Long, Unhappy History of Working From Home," *New York Times*, June 29, 2020, casts doubt on predictions of skyrocketing shifts of

work from office to home. For a history of the reconfigurations of offices, see John Seabrook, "Office Space: The Post-Pandemic Future of Open-Plan Work," *New Yorker*, February 1, 2021.

35. Sapna Maheshwari and Michael Corkery, "The Retail Industry's Tumultuous Year Began before the Pandemic," *New York Times*, December 29, 2020.

36. Erika Hayasaki, "America's Great Labor Awakening," *New York Times Magazine*, February 21, 2012, explores the impact of the pandemic on real estate and workers in Southern California's Inland Empire.

37. Elizabeth Lopatto, "Some Things Jeff Bezos Can Do With His $193 Billion," The Verge, February 9, 2021, www.theverge.com/22264856/jeff-bezos-worth-amazon-founder-ceo-193-billion-dollars.

38. Geoffrey A. Fowler, "In 2020, We Reached Peak Internet. Here's What Worked—And What Flopped," *Washington Post*, December 28, 2020. For another set of predictions, see Thomas Friedman, "After the Pandemic, A Revolution in Education and Work Awaits," *New York Times*, October 20, 2020. Heather Long, "Millions of Jobs Unlikely to Come Back, Even after Pandemic, Economists Warn," *Washington Post*, February 17, 2021, focused on how less business travel, more people working remotely, and increasing reliance on automation would negatively affect employment.

39. Jenna Wortham, "The Rise of the Wellness App," *New York Times Magazine*, February 17, 2021.

40. Alec MacGillis, "The Loneliness of One-Click Shopping," *New York Times*, November 27, 2020.

41. Frank Bruni, "We're Losing More Than We Know," *New York Times*, December 20, 2020; Eduardo Porter, "If Restaurants Go, What Happens to Cities," *New York Times*, November 3, 2020; Greg Bensinger, "Apps Are Helping Gut the Restaurant Industry," *New York Times*, December 9, 2020.

42. Adam Nagourney and Michael M. Grynbaum, "Flat Polls. Weak Ratings. Do Political Conventions Have a Future?," *New York Times*, September 5, 2020.

43. Ana Swanson, "With Americans Stuck at Home, Trade With China Roars Back," *New York Times*, December 14, 2020.

44. Benedict Carey, "Dear Diary: This Pandemic Has Been A Bear," *New York Times*, February 16, 2021. This quote comes from the Pandemic Journaling Project, suggested by the historian Richard D. Brown and carried out by two anthropologists, Katherine A. Mason of Brown University and Sarah Willen of the University of Connecticut.

45. Kate Murphy, "Pandemic-Proof Your Habits," *New York Times*, November 28, 2020.

46. "Let's Start Over," *New York Times*, December 24, 2020.

47. *The State of the Nation's Housing, 2020*, Joint Center for Housing Studies of Harvard University, www.jchs.harvard.edu/sites/default/files/reports/files/Harvard_JCHS_The_State_of_the_Nations_Housing_2020_Report_Revised_120720.pdf, 40. Lawrence Wright, *The Plague Year: America in the Time of Covid* (New York: Knopf, 2021), 143–45, discusses how the work of Raj Chetty and his colleagues on socioeconomic class differentially impacted work and education.

48. Mark Hayward, "The Economic Crisis and After," *Cultural Studies* 24 (May 2010): 283–94.

49. Justin Lewis, "Normal Viewing Will Be Resumed Shortly: News, Recession, and the Politics of Growth," *Popular Communication* 8 (August 2010): 161.

50. Samuel Moyn, "How Trump Won," *New York Review of Books*, November 9, 2020.

51. After the beginning of Trump's presidency but before the pandemic's arrival, in *The Fifth Risk* (New York: W. W. Norton: 2018), Michael Lewis chronicled what it meant to undermine government agencies in ways that threatened the ability of the federal government to function.

52. David Brooks, "How Democrats Won the War of Ideas," *New York Times*, October 22, 2020. For a later, more mixed, but important discussion, see Michael J. de la Merced, "The Debate: How Is Capitalism Coping in an Era of Populism?," *New York Times*, December 16, 2020.

53. John Micklethwait and Adrian Wooldridge, *Wake-Up Call: Why the Pandemic Has Exposed the Weakness of the West and How to Fix It* (New York: HarperCollins, 2020) 2, published September 15. Other books that appeared early on—albeit ones in which political economy were not central—are Nicholas Christakis, *Apollo's Arrow: The Profound and Enduring Impact of Coronavirus on the Way We Live* (New York: Hachette, 2020), October 27; Scott Galloway, *Post Corona: From Crisis to Opportunity* (New York: Penguin, 2020), November 24; Bob Gordon, *Life after COVID-19: Lessons from Past Pandemics* (New York: Verso, 2020), December 2; and James Rickards, *The Next Great Depression: Winners and Losers in a Post-Pandemic World* (New York: Penguin, 2021), January 12.

54. October 2020 online copy for Grace Blakeley, *The Corona Crash: How the Pandemic Will Change Capitalism* (New York: Verso, 2020), www.versobooks.com/books/3723-the-corona-crash.

55. Jim Sleeper, "Fareed Zakaria's Real Sins: Not Plagiarism But Neoliberalism Know-It-All-Ism," *Salon*, August 28, 2014, www.salon.com/2014/08/28/fareed_zakarias_real_sins_on_plagiarism_and_the_dishonesty_of_our_self_important_pundit_class/.

56. Fareed Zakaria, *Ten Lessons for a Post-Pandemic World* (New York: W. W. Norton, 2020), published October 6, 34, 58, 64, 74.

57. The following relies mainly on material from the *New York Times* and Harvard's Joint Center for Housing Studies.

58. Viviana A. Zelizer, "When We Were Socially Distant, Money Brought Us Closer," *New York Times*, February 21, 2022.

59. "Bringing Digitalization Home: How Can Technology Address Housing Challenges?," Calendar, Joint Center for Housing Studies, Harvard University, https://www.jchs.harvard.edu/calendar/bringing-digitalization-home-how-can-technology-address-housing-challenges.

60. Julie Lasky, "Green Pastures, Rural Problems," *New York Times*, February 27, 2022.

61. Adam Tooze, *Shutdown: How COVID Shook the World's Economy* (New York: Penguin, 2021), 13, 23, 24, and 305; Paul Krugman, "Covid's Economic Mutations," *New York Review of Books*, March 10, 2022.

INDEX

A&E network, 22, 24, 71, 238n15
ACORN, 101, 103, 105
affordable housing: Airbnb's effect on, 197, 199; *Colorlines* on, 104; and COVID-19 pandemic, 212; and Fannie Mae, 135; and global financial crisis, 142; and manufactured homes, 12, 234n27; and subprime mortgages, 105; and technology, 228
African Americans: and COVID-19 pandemic, 212, 228; effect of short-term rentals on employment, 194; enslaved African Americans, 2–4, 205; and foreclosures, 107, 173; and Great Recession, 104; and HGTV, 19, 47–48, 246n44; homeownership rates of, 9–11, 14, 106–7, 228; and housing, 87; and predatory lenders, 102, 107, 261n24; and real estate workshops, 19, 72, 76; and redlining, 6, 102; on residential real estate discrimination, 103; and wealth accumulation, 6, 10–11; whites favored for homeownership over, 3–7
Airbnb: business model of, 196–98; and commercial operators, 199, 272n41; and COVID-19 pandemic, 218; and hospitality industry, 193–94, 196, 197–99, 200; origin of, 195, 271n29; problems associated with, 196–97, 206, 271n34; regulation of, 199–200, 201; and short-term rentals, 184, 186, 193–94, 197–200
Amazon: and COVID-19 pandemic, 219, 221, 223; effect on shopping centers and bookstores, 187; music streaming services of, 204; and online shopping, 184, 201, 208, 221, 229
American Anthropological Association (AAA), 164–65, 166, 265n4
American dream: and homeownership, 3, 9, 21, 52, 54, 80, 104–5, 108, 136,
160, 230, 231n3, 232n12; lure of, 88; and residential real estate, 56; and suburban areas, 6
American International Group (AIG): collapse of, 88, 89, 98, 102, 109, 113, 115, 127, 156, 169, 193, 251n26, 252n30, 263n60; government bailout of, 100
American Rescue Plan Act, 210–11
American Securitization Forum, 130
anthropologists: and ethnographic investigations, 18, 19, 123, 165, 166, 171–74, 273n53; and financial system, 146, 154, 165, 166, 170–71, 175, 265n4; Gillian Tett on, 163–66, 175–76; and global financial crisis, 128, 163, 166; and Great Recession, 2, 163, 171, 175
Asian Americans, 10, 76

baby boomers, 14, 209
Ballinger, Barbara, 89–90
Bank of America, 89, 109
Bear Stearns: collapse of, 93, 97, 102, 108, 126, 134, 144; role of, 89
Bernanke, Ben, 97, 122, 131, 143–46, 158
Biden, Joseph R., Jr., 210, 212, 222, 225–26, 229
Big Short, The (docudrama): and accountability, 162; on employment, 130, 132–33, 183; on financialization, 130, 131–32, 134; gender in, 130, 133, 134, 154, 263n62; on residential real estate, 29, 130–31; shorting in, 128, 130–33, 134, 183
Bloomberg News, 107, 114, 120, 226
Bourdieu, Pierre: anthropologists on, 176; on habitus, 167; on "insider-outsider" pattern, 154–55, 156, 163; social science theory of, 169; on social silences, 111, 120, 155, 263n65
Bourne, Randolph, xiii–xiv
Bradshaw, Peter, 140–41
Buffett, Warren, 62, 68, 143, 145

::: 279

Burges, Steve, 64-65
Bush, George H. W., 140
Bush, George W.: economic policies of, 102, 122; and Enron, 140; and forces for uniformity, xiv; and global financial crisis, 17; and National Economic Council, 152; and 9/11 terrorist attacks, 195; and Ownership Society, 10, 108; in *Panic*, 143, 144, 146
Business Week, 87, 95-96

capitalism: and Airbnb, 198; boom-and-bust nature of, 133, 149, 168, 169; and COVID-19 pandemic, 213-14, 226; and creative destruction, 187, 208, 217, 218; finance capitalism, 88, 166-68; gendered conception of, 172; Great Recession exposing contradictions of, 122, 123; innovative capitalism, 115; ownership as central to, 106; and religion, 76; risks of, 89; *Capitalism* (documentary), 158-60, 162, 183
Case-Shiller Home Price Indices, 92, 94
Center for Responsible Lending, 102, 121, 253n51
Chesky, Brian, 195, 197
Citi Group, 109, 133, 134
Cleveland Clinic, 154, 156
climate change, 20, 208, 228, 230, 236n39
Clinton, Bill, 10, 136, 152, 226
Clinton, Hillary, 101, 106
CNBC, 122, 126-27, 131, 238n15, 258n1
cognitive capture, 120, 126
collateral debt obligations (CDOs), 51, 89, 110-13, 115, 116, 120-21, 130, 132
Colorlines, 103-5Community Reinvestment Act of 1977, 10, 101, 104, 105, 253n42
consumer culture, 2, 20, 26, 52, 116, 201-5, 209
contract workers, 206, 209
Countrywide Financial, 89, 108, 136, 153
COVID-19 pandemic: and commercial real estate, 19, 219, 220-21; context of, xiv-xv, 2, 14, 209, 210, 227-28, 229; disruptions of, xiii, 19, 224; emotional and cognitive effects of, 223, 228; and federal government, 211-12, 219, 225, 226-27; and inequalities of wealth and income, 210, 212, 214, 216, 222, 224-25; precautions, xi-xii, 220, 223, 229; and remote work, 211-12, 215, 216, 222, 229, 275n19, 275-76n34, 276n38; and residential real estate, xi, xii, 19, 218-19, 220, 275n27; and stock market, 97; and technology, 216-17, 222
Cramer, Jim, 105, 121, 126-27, 131, 162, 163, 249n3, 258n1
credit default swaps (CDSs), 89, 112, 129, 132, 149-51, 154, 170, 175
Crèvecœur, J. Hector St. John, 1-3, 21

Daily Show with Jon Stewart, The (TV show), 126-28
Das, Satyajit, 114, 152
Davis, Clay, 55-56
Davison, Candace Braun, 239-40n50
debt: financing of, 14-17, 119, 174; predatory debt extraction, 267n24
democracy, 158-59, 210, 228, 230
deregulation: complexities of, 119; and Enron, 137, 139, 140, 141; of Fannie Mae, 135; of financial institutions, 13, 15-16, 151, 152; and global financial crisis, 114, 116, 123, 128, 159; *Inside Job* on, 152, 153; and neoliberalism, 20
derivatives: in *The Big Short*, 129, 132; in *Capitalism*, 158; Gillian Tett on, 112, 113, 119, 132, 148-50, 155, 168, 171, 176; print media on, 95, 118, 155; risk of, 15-16, 114, 118, 159
domesticity: bankruptcy and foreclosure ending dreams of, 54; Catharine Beecher on, 1-2; and consumer culture, 2, 201-5; and COVID-19 pandemic, 215; and HGTV, 25, 49-50, 52; in horror films, 177, 182-83; and suburban home, 3. *See also* homes
dot-com bubble, 16, 54, 167
Dow Jones Industrial Average, 89, 94, 98
Downing, Anthony, 47-48, 246n44
Downing, Anton, 48, 246n44

Easton, Nina, 100, 107, 145
Eavis, Peter, 97-98

e-commerce enterprises, 201–2
Economist, 87, 88, 189, 190, 226, 254–55n75
economists: on global financial crisis, 55, 81–82, 92, 96, 128, 147, 154, 156, 160–61, 175; on investors taking advantage of credit, 237n5; on manufacturing, 187–88
Eisman, Steve, 130, 132
elites: anthropologists on, 176; in *Capitalism*, 158; Gillian Tett's relationships with, 165, 166, 265n5; and global financial crisis, 12, 19, 145, 155; investigative journalism on, 117, 162; and investment banks, 168; power of, 136, 141, 153, 155, 157, 160, 172; silos of, 175
Elizabeth II (queen), 156
Elkind, Peter, 100, 137–40, 141, 268n31
El Moussa, Tarek: on COVID-19 pandemic, 213; divorce from Christina Haack, 23, 45, 46, 212; as featured host, 18, 23, 27, 42; real estate investments of, 39–40, 83, 84; on real estate market crash, 29, 41; and real estate workshops, 245n33
employment: and automation, 276n38; in *The Big Short*, 130, 132–33, 183; and COVID-19 pandemic, 210, 224, 228; and great resignation, 228; in *Inside Job*, 152–53; market for midlevel jobs, 208; and new media, 184, 186, 187, 205–6; precariousness of, 50, 142, 162, 174, 246n42; shifts in earnings from, 13. *See also* remote work
Enron, 100, 119, 137–41, 176, 268n31
Enron (documentary), 139–41, 154, 262n42entertainment: and COVID-19 pandemic, 210, 217, 222; Netflix, 184, 204, 208, 218, 229; reality television, 43, 51–52; streaming services, 187, 204, 217
entrepreneurship: and Airbnb, 199; and COVID-19 pandemic, 216; government weakened by, 136; and HGTV, 51; and homeownership, 52; housing entrepreneurship, 23, 85; "Mompreneurs," 49; and

neoliberalism, 20; and new media, 184, 209; and real estate workshops, 66, 80, 85, 86
Erhard, Werner, 59
ERISA law, 60
ethnicity, 47, 50–51, 172–73, 210, 225
Etsy, 186, 201
European Central Bank, 16, 149
Evans, Blanche, 92, 94
evictions, 51, 158, 162, 211, 219, 224

Facebook, 154, 156, 186, 193, 194, 202
Fair Housing Act of 1968, 9
Faludi, Susan, 161
Fannie Mae: and blame game, 101, 105; federal government taking over, 25, 109; as government-sponsored enterprise, 5; and housing bubble, 99; on housing industry, 64; hybrid nature of, 141; knowledge of, 89; leadership of, 135–36, 142; status of, 262n41
Federal Aid Highway Act of 1956, 7
federal government: and blame game, 105; corporations rescued by, 143, 145; and COVID-19 pandemic, 211–12, 219, 225, 226–27; and cycle of dependency, 101, 103; deregulation of banking, 13, 15–16, 151, 152; diminished power of, 86; and Donald J. Trump, 225, 277n51; and Enron, 138; and global financial crisis, 16, 18, 20, 25, 98, 227; Great Recession response, 69, 122–23, 229; and housing choices, 3–4; housing policies of, 6, 7, 9–10, 11, 14, 25, 27, 40, 52, 87, 90, 94, 95, 104; monetary policy of, 99; and mortgages, 25, 126; real estate workshops on, 69, 80, 85; regulatory policy of, 99, 122, 149, 150, 155, 186; reliance on, xv, 229
Federal Housing Administration (FHA), 5–6, 93
Federal Reserve, 4, 16, 17, 96, 98, 99, 101
Feldman, Amy, 96
feminism, 146–47, 154, 161, 168–69, 171–72
filmmakers: and documentary films, 2, 12, 18, 115, 139–41, 143–46, 151–54, 159–60, 163, 183, 262n42, 263n62; and global financial crisis, 128, 159, 161, 162;

filmmakers (*continued*)
and Great Recession, 175; relationship between access and accountability, 161–62. *See also specific films*

finance capitalism, 88, 166–68

financial institutions: bailouts of, 100, 122, 170; and Community Reinvestment Act, 10; deregulation of, 13, 15–16, 151, 152; and housing discrimination, 9; influence in private sector, 3; and millennials, 185; mortgages held by, 15, 88, 103, 106, 116; policies of, 27; regulation of, 135–36, 149; rise of, 20; risks taken by, 12–15, 17, 18, 104, 130–31, 136, 153, 160, 260n17; as too big to fail, 170, 214, 261n37. *See also* investment banks

financial instruments: complicated financial instruments, 13, 14, 17, 53, 88–89, 90, 112, 118, 120, 121, 129, 149, 159; development of, 15, 51, 112, 113, 143, 148–49, 161, 170; explanations of, 128; leveraging of, 136; modeled on mutual funds, 84; and residential real estate, 134. *See also* collateral debt obligations (CDOs); credit default swaps (CDSs); derivatives; mortgage-backed securities

financialization: in *The Big Short*, 130, 131–32, 134; complexities of, 119, 120; and Iceland, 152; of news, 118; and racial issues, 271n28; and real estate markets, 51; risks of, 14, 15, 27, 88, 116, 235n32

financial system: and anthropology, 146, 154, 165, 166, 170–71, 175, 265n4; corruption and immorality of, 87, 131, 137, 145–46, 153, 158, 159–60, 174, 263n60; gendered power relationships of, 149, 154, 168, 172; language of, 109, 119, 150, 158

Financial Times: on anthropologists' works, 175; on COVID-19 pandemic, 214, 226; on financial instruments, 120; on Great Recession, 18, 87; Gillian Tett at, 19, 107, 109–11, 113, 132, 146–50, 154, 165, 166, 170, 176; and Martin Wolf, 254n75

Fisher, Melissa S., 161, 163, 171–72, 265n4

Fixer Upper (TV show): and consumerist narcissism, 241n71; episode narratives of, 36–38, 52; and family life, 23–24, 35, 36–39, 45, 49; financial success of, 42–43; gendered division of labor in, 35, 37–38, 50; and Great Recession, 18, 23, 27; impact and meaning of, 80, 83, 239n39; manual laborers of, 34, 38, 41, 50–51, 242n79; popularity of, 23, 44, 51; ranking of, 35, 46, 236n3, 237n15; reality and artifice mixed in, 38, 46, 47, 242n84; and renovation benefits, 23, 45; and stylistic simplicity, 48–49

Flip or Flop (TV show): and consumerist narcissism, 241n71; continuation following divorce, 46, 212; episode narratives of, 40–42, 52; financial success of, 42–43; gendered division of labor in, 40, 41, 50; and Great Recession, 18, 23, 27; impact and meaning of, 80, 83, 189; manual laborers of, 50; origin of, 39–40; popularity of, 23, 51; profits of, 42, 239n47; ranking of, 46, 236n3, 237n15; reality and artifice mixed in, 46, 47, 242n84; and renovation benefits, 23, 46; and stylistic simplicity, 48–49

Flip This House (TV show), 22, 24, 40, 71, 98, 121

Floyd, George, 214, 229–30

Forbes: and blame game, 98, 100, 101; on COVID-19 pandemic, 213–14; on e-commerce enterprises, 202; on financing of residential real estate, 96–97, 251n22; ideologically driven analyses of, 87, 95, 98–100; mixed signals of, 97, 252n30; on subprime mortgages, 252n33

Forbes, Steve, 68, 98–100, 122, 252n37

foreclosures: and African Americans, 107, 173; and American Rescue Plan Act, 211; and COVID-19 pandemic, 224; and federal government, 4–5; and horror films, 177; and house flipping, 82; and inequalities of wealth and income, 193; and real estate workshops, 53, 80; and residential real estate, 17, 58; and systematic vulnerabilities, 267n23; and victims of dangerous financing, 162

Fortune: on Airbnb, 198; and Allan Sloan, 153-54; and Bethany McLean, 137, 139; and blame game, 97-98; coverage of, 88, 98, 100; and Meredith Whitney, 109, 134; mixed signals of, 96, 251n24; observations of, 87, 95; on populism, 145; and Rebecca Mark, 138-39; on residential real estate, 192; on subprime loans, 114

Freddie Mac, 25, 89, 99, 101, 105, 109, 262n41

freelance workers, 186, 206

free markets: and COVID-19 pandemic, 226, 274n13; and global financial crisis, 144; and home ownership, 3; ideology of, 170, 225; and neoliberalism, 20; reliance on, xv, 122

Fridman, Daniel, 84-85, 245n23, 248n67

Friedan, Betty, 2

Friedman, Milton, 214

Gaines, Chip: business success of, 23, 34, 39, 44-45, 83, 84, 212; crew of, 34, 50-51, 242n79; family life of, 23-24, 33, 36-37, 49-50, 56, 212; as featured host, 18, 23, 27, 38, 46; and house flipping, 33, 34-35; on real estate market crash, 29, 34; and renovation shift, 34-35, 239n34

Gaines, Joanna: business success of, 23, 34, 39, 44-45, 83, 84, 212; family life of, 23-24, 33, 36-37, 45, 49-50, 212; as featured host, 18, 23, 27, 38, 46; on real estate market crash, 29, 34; religious language used by, 34, 49-50, 242n74; and renovation shift, 34-35, 239n34

Gebbia, Joe, 195, 197

Geithner, Timothy, 143-46, 148, 152, 158, 173

gender: in *The Big Short*, 130, 133, 134, 154, 263n62; and COVID-19 pandemic, 210, 215, 225; and "Davos Man," 115; and *Enron*, 139; and financial system, 149, 154, 168, 172;

and global financial crisis, 107, 119, 128, 133, 134, 172, 254-55n75; and HGTV, 19, 35, 37-38, 40, 41, 50; and Hollywood, 218; and horror films, 177, 182; and housewives' unpaid labor, 205; and influence of being an outsider, 107, 119, 134, 161; *Inside Job* on, 153-54; and real estate workshops, 19, 67, 72; and reality television, 236n4; and remote work, 208; and rhetoric of power, success, and family, 51; and technology's effect on home, 201. *See also* women

General Motors, 58, 158

generational differences, 10-11, 14, 69-70, 185, 209, 219, 268n1

Get Out (film), 163, 177, 181, 182-83

GI Bill, 5

gig economy, 185, 187, 209

Glass-Steagall Act of 1933, 16, 53

global financial crisis of 2007-8: collapse of global markets, 88; economists on, 55, 81-82, 92, 96, 128, 147, 154, 156, 160-61, 175; and elites, 12, 19, 145, 155; evaluations of, 116, 123, 128-29, 134-37, 141-44; factors influencing, 13, 18, 89, 91, 122, 167, 210; and federal government, 16, 18, 20, 25, 98, 227; and gender, 107, 119, 128, 133, 134, 172, 254-55n75; Gillian Tett on, 19, 109-13, 115, 132, 134, 146, 148, 154-55, 157, 161, 164, 166, 176, 254n68, 265n5; and Global Economic Forum, 115, 256n101; and homeownership rates, 10; and housing bubble, xiv, 14, 23, 67, 82, 83, 105, 114-15, 123, 159, 174; *Inside Job* on, 152-53; legacy of, 20, 23, 128; and new media, 118, 122, 126-27, 249n3, 250-51n20; ordinary people affected by, 19-20, 95, 110, 117, 128, 132, 143, 151-53, 157, 162, 163, 169, 172, 183, 263n60; and populism, 17, 143, 145; print media on, xi, 95, 113-18, 122; and real estate markets, 13, 16-17, 39, 235n30; and real estate workshops, 53; and reality television, 23, 236n2; and securitization, 15, 16, 127, 128; and suburban population shifts, 8;

global financial crisis of 2007-8 (*continued*)
  women's perceptions of, 19, 107, 133, 134
globalization: and Donald J. Trump, 225; and Great Recession, 123; and insecure employment, 174; of mortgage markets, 53; and neoliberalism, 20; world shaped by, 86, 142, 160–61, 187
Goldman Sachs, 15, 100, 134, 136, 152, 165
Google, 184, 186, 187, 204, 217
Great Depression, 56, 58, 122, 158, 169, 170, 214
Great Recession of 2008-2009: and African Americans, 104; and Airbnb, 194, 195, 197, 200; causes of, 14, 16, 18, 26, 53, 54–55, 84, 89, 98–99, 142, 151, 163, 170, 183; charitable giving during, 228; context of, xiv–xv, 2, 12, 18–19, 56, 209, 225, 229; federal government's response to, 69, 122–23, 229; and Great Depression, 158; and HGTV, 2, 18, 22–25, 26, 27, 52; and homeownership rates, 9; and horror films, 2, 18, 163, 173, 177, 179; and housing markets, 24, 163, 210; and inequalities of wealth and income, 193, 201; and neoliberalism, 20; print media's coverage of, xi, 2, 18, 87–88, 89, 121–23, 163, 258n130; and real estate workshops, 2, 18, 53, 54, 56, 80, 85; and reality television, 35, 237n7; recovery from, 42, 44, 46; and residential real estate, xi, xiv, 33, 55, 188, 193, 195; and technology's effect on home, 201; as term, 233n20
Greenspan, Alan, 16, 54, 91, 131
Grubhub, 184, 203, 219, 221, 223
GSEs (government-sponsored enterprises), 5, 99, 135
Guess Who's Coming to Dinner? (film), 181

Haack, Christina El Moussa: on COVID-19 pandemic, 213; design skills of, 50; divorce from Tarek El Moussa, 23, 45, 46, 212; as featured host, 18, 23, 27, 41–42, 46, 242n77; real estate investments of, 39–40, 84; on real estate market crash, 29; and real estate workshops, 245n33
Hansen, Mark Victor, 58
Harvard's Joint Center for Housing Studies, 211, 224, 228, 233n23
Harvey, David, 166, 170–71, 261n37
health care, 15, 174, 204–5, 216, 219, 226, 227
hedge funds, 84, 92, 94, 98, 108, 128
HGTV: and African Americans, 19, 47–48, 246n44; and audience expectations, 161; and celebrity gossip, 43–44, 212; depictions of housing choices, 18, 22, 174, 189, 192; and domesticity, 25, 49–50, 52; expertise promised by, 83; and gender roles, 19, 35, 37–38, 40, 41, 50; and Great Recession, 2, 18, 22–25, 26, 27, 52; and house flipping, 25, 26, 40, 55; programming shifts of, 23, 25–27, 237n8; and real estate workshops, 73–75, 76
higher education, 13, 14, 20
high source dependency, 120, 126
Hill, Napoleon, 18, 56–58, 59, 62
Ho, Karen: on corporate ethnography, 166–69, 170, 175, 265n4; on financial system, 167–68, 265n9; and Gillian Tett, 166–67, 176, 268n31; on Great Recession, 170, 263n62; on habitus, 167, 168, 169; *Liquidated*, 166–70, 172, 175, 267n30; and socioeconomic spectrum, 163; top-down approach of, 174–75
Hollywood, 187, 204, 217–18, 229
Home (film), 163
Home Affordable Modification Program (HAMP), 173
home equity, 6, 10, 14, 15, 54, 64, 113
homeless people: and COVID-19 pandemic, 219, 224; effect of global financial crisis on, 162; and homeownership, 20, 228; and *Parasite*, 179; population of, 12, 209, 211, 219
homeownership: Airbnb's effect on, 197; and American dream, 3, 9, 21, 52, 54, 80, 104–5, 108, 136, 160, 230,

231n3, 232n12; citizenship linked with, 1, 52, 104; factors shaping, xv, 3, 18; increasing rates of, 101, 135–36, 143, 160, 261n19; media representations of, 23; racialized patterns of, 3–7, 8, 9–10, 234n24; rates of, 4, 9, 10, 11, 13, 14–15, 234n24; as replacement for social benefits, 174; and tax advantages, 7, 11, 13; and technology-based enterprises, 191–92

homes: and class conflicts, 179; and COVID-19 pandemic, 214–15, 216; home-based businesses, 209; meaning of, xiv, 1–2, 19, 21, 212, 230; nature of, 3; as remote workplace, 19, 184, 205, 206–8, 215, 216, 273n53, 273n54, 275n19; as sanctuaries, 19, 201–8, 216, 229; as socially and psychologically toxic sites, 177, 178, 181, 182; as tradeable commodity, 17. *See also* domesticity

Homestead Act of 1862, 4

horror films, 2, 18, 163, 173, 177–83. *See also specific films*

hospitality industry, 193–94, 196, 197–99, 200

house flipping: and Chip Gaines, 33, 34–35; economics of, 81–82, 83, 84; guides to, 55–56; and HGTV, 25, 26, 40, 55; in Las Vegas, 29; real estate workshops on, 2, 54, 65, 69, 83; residential real estate market affected by, 24, 40, 55, 81–82, 84, 237n5; Robert T. Kiyosaki on, 62, 63; Steve Burges on, 64–65; and Tarek El Moussa, 40, 41; Than Merrill on, 71; and Zillow, 189–90

Housing Act of 1949, 6–7

Housing and Urban Development Act of 1968, 9

Housing and Urban Redevelopment Act of 1949, 7

housing bubble: and Carleton Sheets, 28; economists on, 160–61; and global financial crisis, xiv, 14, 23, 67, 82, 83, 105, 114–15, 123, 159, 174; and HGTV, 26, 27; print media on, 103; *Realtor Magazine* on, 90–91; Robert J. Shiller on, 54–55, 114–15

housing choices: HGTV's depictions of, 18, 22, 174, 189, 192; impact on climate change, 20, 236n39; and rural areas, 3, 4, 12

housing discrimination, 9, 19, 103, 225

housing markets: African Americans' disadvantaged position in, 104; bets on, 130; collapse of, 23, 24, 26, 27, 29, 39–41, 53, 173, 174, 177; and COVID-19 pandemic, 211, 228; and federal government, 101; and global financial crisis, 16, 17, 95; and Great Recession, 24, 163, 210; and HGTV, 25, 26; and housing prices, 10, 14, 17, 18, 27, 54, 55, 105, 161, 211, 228; and inequalities of wealth and income, 193, 224; and New Deal programs, 5; and new media, 19; racialized discrimination in, 19, 225; and real estate workshops, 53, 54; *Realtor Magazine* on, 91; and securitization, 184; and technology, 228

housing segregation, 5–7, 9, 11, 102, 232n8

Hudson, Michael, 107, 113–14, 119, 183, 254n68

Hulu, 204, 217

iBuying enterprises, 190–91, 227, 270n15

immigrants, xii, 3, 6, 12, 69, 224

Inc., 87, 95, 96, 98, 251n21

In Debt We Trust (documentary), 115

IndyMac, 89, 93, 97, 102, 133

inequalities of wealth and income: and adoption of new financial strategies, 246n42; in *Capitalism*, 158; and COVID-19 pandemic, 210, 212, 214, 216, 222, 224–25; and Great Recession, 193, 201; and American dream, 104–5; and housing markets, 193, 224; increases in, 161, 208; *Inside Job* on, 152, 153; and limits to upward mobility, 146; and New Deal order, 20; racialized lines of, 10–11; and second-home speculation, 201; and short-term rentals, 194, 197;

inequalities of wealth and income (*continued*)
and speculation in real estate markets, 13–14
Inside Job (documentary), 139, 151–54, 160, 162, 165, 183, 263n60
institutional investors, 197, 228
intellectual capture, 118, 119
International Monetary Fund, 17
internet-enabled enterprises, 185, 202–5, 208, 216
investment banks: collapse of, 93; debt-to-capital ratios of, 16; and deregulation, 152; and Enron, 138; and levels of capital reserves, 142; mortgage-backed securities developed by, 15, 169; print media on, 98; and public and private spheres, 141; and real estate industry, 94; shareholder value ideology, 167–70, 214. *See also* Bear Stearns; Lehman Brothers; *and other specific banks*
irrational exuberance, 54, 55, 91, 118, 160
It's a Wonderful Life (film), 11

Jackson, Jesse, 103, 106–7, 168
Japan, 109–10, 113, 147
Jayson, Seth, 91–92
Johnson, James A., 135–36
journalists: deadlines of, 18, 134, 175, 176; and global financial crisis, 128, 134–36, 159–60, 161, 162, 163, 175; and Great Recession, 175; relationship between access and accountability, 116, 117, 118, 119, 120–22, 128, 134, 152, 157, 161–62, 175, 265n5; silos of, 175, 176. *See also* print media; *and specific authors*
J. P. Morgan, 111–13, 148–50, 154, 166, 268n31

Kay, Martin, 82–83
Keller Williams, 191, 198
Kickstarter, 185
Kiyosaki, Robert: Cash Flow board game, 61, 248n67; *The Cashflow Quadrant*, 243n9; corporations launched by, 59–63, 83; on financial freedom, 84–85; franchises of, 61–62, 245n23; and identity of Rich Dad, 244n19; *If You Want to Be Rich and Happy, Don't Go to School*, 60; life story of, 59–60, 65–66, 70, 78; online presentations of, 212, 274n7; on residential real estate, 57, 59, 243n9; *Rich Dad, Poor Dad*, 56–57, 59–62, 65–66, 68, 71, 78; Rich Dad enterprises of, 57, 61, 62–63, 64, 65–68, 84; Rich Dad/Poor Dad workshops, 18, 56–57, 65–70, 72, 73, 77, 78–79, 80, 85, 86, 174, 212, 213, 274n8; *Why We Want You to Be Rich*, 62, 63
Kramer vs. Kramer (film), 163
Kurtz, Howard, 115–16
Kurutz, Steven, 22–23, 36, 40

labor conditions, 20, 221, 222, 269n4, 276n36
labor unions, 13, 20, 199
Las Vegas, Nev., 8, 29, 32–33, 44, 98, 130
Latinx people, 10, 47, 76, 104, 173, 194, 212
Lechter, Sharon L., 57–59, 61, 65, 243n9
Lee, Benjamin, 171, 174, 267n30
Lehman Brothers: aggregation of loans, 106; collapse of, 22, 25, 88, 89, 93, 98, 99, 102, 109, 113, 115, 156, 169, 193, 251n26, 252n30, 263n60
Lereah, David, 90–92
Lewis, Justin, 122–23
Lewis, Michael: *The Big Short*, 29, 128, 130, 131–34, 137, 141, 154, 162, 172, 175; *The Fifth Risk*, 277n51; *Liar's Poker*, 111, 133
LiPuma, Edward, 171, 174, 267n30
loan originators, 95, 128
local zoning boards, 3, 5, 228, 234n25
Lord, Richard, 107, 113, 254n68
Los Angeles, Calif., 81, 83, 248n57
Los Angeles Times, 118
loss aversion, 54
Love It or List It (TV show), 25, 43, 47
Luskin, Donald L., 102
Lyft, 185, 187, 209

Margin Call (film), 264n73
Mark, Rebecca, 138–39

Marx, Karl, 100, 159, 166, 186
mass media, 6, 9, 12, 20, 51, 235n31
Masters, Blythe, 149–50, 261n36, 262n52
Maxed Out (documentary), 114
McCain, John, 102, 106
McKenna, Brian, 165–66, 170–71, 265n5
McLean, Bethany: and access journalism, 162; *All the Devils Are Here*, 141–43, 145, 148, 149, 156, 170, 172, 175, 261n36; in *Enron*, 139, 140–41, 154, 262n42; on financial system, 154; in *Fishing with Dynamite*, 262n42; on global financial crisis, 100, 134, 157, 161; in *Panic*, 143–44; on securitization, 100, 119, 134, 139, 141, 142; *Shaky Ground*, 262n41; *The Smartest Guys in the Room*, 100, 137–40, 141, 268n31; top-down approach of, 174; undergraduate education of, 107, 161
means of production, 155, 186
Merrill, Than: and CT Homes, 71, 83, 84; *The E-Myth Real Estate Investor*, 246n46; and *Flip This House*, 24, 64; FortuneBuilders workshops of, 18, 24, 56, 68, 70, 71–78, 79, 80, 85, 86, 174, 212–13, 274n8; online presentations of, 212; *Real Estate Wholesaling Bible*, 71, 76
middle class: challenges to, 62, 71, 158, 160; and COVID-19 pandemic, 224; and HGTV, 26; and home equity, 10; and homeownership, 1, 5, 8, 20, 228; and inequalities, 14; National Association of Realtors on, 231n4; and overleveraged credit frenzy, 176; and *Room*, 178–81; taxation of, 61; and working class, 173
Milgram, Stanley, 140
millennials, 14, 185, 198, 209, 228
Mishkin, Frederic, 152
Moncrieff, Stacey, 93–94
Moody's Investor Service, 89, 127, 148
Moore, Michael, 158–60, 162
Morgenson, Gretchen: and access journalism, 162; on global financial crisis, 107–8, 116, 134–37, 157, 161; *Reckless Endangerment*, 134–37, 141–42, 148, 149, 156, 170, 172, 175, 260–61n19,

261n24; on securitization, 134, 135, 136; sources of, 118–19, 121; top-down approach of, 174; Wall Street coverage of, 108, 135, 254n73
Morris, Charles, 45, 114
mortgage-backed securities: development of, 15–16, 51, 89, 131, 143, 169; and Fannie Mae, 99; risk level of, 106, 108, 127, 129, 132; subprime mortgages packaged as, 114
mortgage markets, 53, 104, 105, 114, 128–30
mortgages: adjustable-rate, 90, 91, 128, 129, 131; availability of, 10, 14–15, 103; and down payments, 12–13; duration of, 4, 5; and federal government, 25, 126; held by financial institutions, 15, 88, 103, 106, 116; local mortgage originators, 131, 141, 173; and natural disasters, 3; securitization and leveraging of, 15, 16, 87, 88, 127, 128, 129; and suburban areas, 6. *See also* subprime mortgages
Motley Fool, The, 91–92, 189, 190
movie theaters, 184, 204, 208, 218, 222, 228
Mozilo, Angelo, 136, 153
Multiple Listing Service (MLS), 188, 189, 191
Murray, Bobbi, 106–7, 119
mutual funds, 62, 84, 106, 170

Nader, Laura, 174–75
Nation, 87, 98, 105–7, 213, 214
National Association of Realtors (NAR): and COVID-19 pandemic, 213; on global financial crisis, 91–92, 94; individual homeownership advocated by, 4, 94; influence in private sector, 3; on middle class, 231n4; mission of, 90; and Multiple Listing Service, 188; on predatory lenders, 94, 250n10; Zillow's competition with, 189–90, 191. *See also* *Realtor Magazine*
National Bureau of Economic Research (NBER), 56, 237n5
National Review, 87, 98, 100–103, 105, 252–53n42, 253n46, 274n13

Native Americans, 4, 10, 12
neoliberalism: and blame game, 100; and depictions of housing crisis, 103; *Inside Job* on, 165; political economy of, 20, 26, 123, 236n38; and print media, 122; reconsiderations of, 225–27, 229
Netflix, 23, 184, 187, 204, 208, 217–18, 222, 229
network effects, 186
New Century Financial, 56, 88, 89, 91, 108
New Deal, 4, 5, 20, 99
new media: access to benefits of, 209; and global financial crisis, 118, 122, 126–27, 249n3, 250–51n20; and Great Recession, 2; homes affected by, 201; and public-private balance, 184–85, 229; and residential real estate, 18–19, 184, 192; and telemedicine, 185, 204–5; terms for, 185–86
New York City, 95, 136, 199, 219, 220, 221, 228
New York Federal Reserve Bank, 148, 165
New York Times: on Airbnb, 199; business journalists of, 120; on COVID-19 pandemic, 214–15, 216, 218, 221, 223; economy covered by, 87, 107–8; on federal government, 226; on global financial crisis, 115; on housing bubble, 22; on residential real estate, 191
9/11 terrorist attacks, xiv, 16, 195, 209, 229–30
NINJA loans (no income, no jobs, no assets), 131
Nixon, Richard, 60, 67
Nocera, Joe: *All the Devils Are Here*, 141–43, 145, 148, 149, 156, 170, 172, 175, 261n36; *Shaky Ground*, 262n41; top-down approach of, 174

Obama, Barack, 17, 101, 106, 145, 152, 158, 181
Occupy Wall Street, 145
Olen, Helaine, 66, 78
online learning, 215–16, 217, 222
online shopping, 19, 184, 201, 208, 219–23, 229
Oppenheimer, 107, 108–9, 133
Orange County, Calif., 8, 27, 39–41, 46
ordinary people: *Capitalism* on, 158, 162; effect of global financial crisis on, 19–20, 95, 110, 117, 128, 132, 143, 151–53, 157, 162, 163, 169, 172, 183, 263n60; and Enron, 140; and financial knowledge, 121, 132, 151; and Great Recession, 173, 183; *Inside Job* on, 151–53, 263n60; and power of elites, 136, 141, 153
other people's money (OPM), 55, 62–66, 72
Ouroussoff, Alexandra, 171, 174, 175, 267n30
Ownership Society, 10, 136

Panic (documentary), 143–46, 152, 162
Parasite (film), 163, 177, 179–83
Paulson, Henry, 131, 143–44, 146, 152–53, 158
Peale, Norman Vincent, 18, 56, 62, 72
peer-to-peer economy, 185–86, 269n4
Peloton, 216, 223, 227
pension funds, 94, 108, 128
people of color: and COVID-19 pandemic, 224–25; and homeownership, 3, 7, 10, 103, 232n8; and print media, 103–4
Perelman, Michael, 171, 174, 268n31
Petersen, Anne Helen, 214–42n73
Phoenix, Ariz., 9, 54–55, 111, 190
platform economy, 185–88, 196–97, 200–201, 204, 208–9
Plunder (documentary), 115
poor, the: and COVID-19 pandemic, 224, 225; government programs for, 61, 62; and homeownership, 3, 232n8; and internet access, 209; and *Parasite*, 179–80; and predatory lenders, 106; and urban renewal, 7; working poor, 14
Popular Communication, 249n3
populism, 17, 100, 101, 143, 145, 159, 225
post–World War II period, 6–9
predatory lenders: and African Americans, 102, 107, 261n24; and

Center for Responsible Lending, 102, 253n51; greed of, 160; *Inside Job* on, 152;

print media: and access journalism, 117, 118, 121, 161–62; and accountability reporting, 117, 118; attitudes of African American newspapers and magazines, 103–5; attitudes of business publications, 95, 97–101, 117, 118, 123, 134, 251n21; on Bear Stearns, 251n26; and blame game, 87, 88, 97–98, 100–101, 104, 252n35, 252n41; competition from internet-based sites, 118, 122; on COVID-19 pandemic, 213–15; on derivatives, 95, 118, 155; and Facebook, 194; on global financial crisis, xi, 95, 113–18, 122; and gossip, 212; on Great Recession, xi, 2, 18, 87–88, 89, 121–23, 163, 258n130; on Hollywood, 218; on housing markets, 184; and investigative journalism, 117–19, 121, 123, 138; and journalistic conventions, 119–20; on rating agencies, 95, 98; relationship between journalists and sources, 116–22, 128, 134, 152, 157, 161–62, 175, 265n5; on securitization, 95, 96, 184. *See also* journalists; *and specific journals*

prisons, 12, 19, 20, 158, 209

private equity companies, 82–83, 194

private equity funding, 185, 220

Property Brothers (TV show): Canadian premiere of, 28, 30; and consumerist narcissism, 241n71; episode narratives of, 30–32, 52; financial success of, 33, 42–43; and Great Recession, 18, 23, 27; house budgets of, 30–32, 35, 36; impact and meaning of, 80, 83; manual laborers of, 38, 50; popularity of, 23, 51; ranking of, 46, 236n3, 237n15; reality and artifice mixed in, 38, 46, 47, 242n84; and renovation benefits, 23, 45; scandals of, 240n50; and stylistic simplicity, 48–49

public-private balance: and COVID-19 pandemic, 222–23; generational differences in, 185, 268n1; and new media, 184–85, 229

Queen of Versailles (documentary), 12

racial issues: of Airbnb, 196, 271n34; and COVID-19 pandemic, 2, 210, 219, 225, 228; divisions in, 209; and financialization, 271n28; and *Get Out*, 181, 182–83; and Hollywood, 218; and homeownership policies, 4, 5, 7, 9–10; of housing financing, 104; *National Review* on, 102–3; and portrayals of work, 50; racial justice, 47, 269n4; and remote work, 208

Rainbow PUSH Wall Street Project, 168

Rajan, Ragharum G., 114, 152

rating agencies: corruption at, 128; and high-risk mortgages, 127; incentives at, 159; and *Inside Job*, 152; print media on, 95, 98

real estate, commercial, 19, 184, 185, 208, 219, 220–21

real estate, residential: and Airbnb, 193–94, 197, 199–200; and American dream, 56; in *The Big Short*, 29, 130–31; collapse of, 100; and COVID-19 pandemic, xi, xii, 19, 218–19, 220, 275n27; disruptions in, 19, 28, 33, 40, 188–92, 199, 200–201, 218–19, 275n27; in early twenty-first century, xiii, xiv, 4, 14, 27, 64, 66, 80, 229–30; and financial instruments, 134; financing of, 90, 95, 251n22; fluidity of, 195; and Great Recession, xi, xiv, 33, 55, 188, 193, 195; and HGTV, 25, 212; house flipping's effect on, 24, 40, 55, 81–82, 84, 237n5; impact of discriminatory policies and practices, 103, 225; markets for, 82–83, 94, 190, 192–93; and new media, 18–19, 184, 192; and platform enterprises, 196–97; and private equity companies, 82–83, 194; real estate workshops on, 53; and rising home prices, 89, 90, 92, 98, 160, 199, 211, 218; and spectatorship, 192, 193; statistics on, 54; value of, 3, 16–17, 93, 94, 189; and Zillow, 184, 188, 203, 208, 209. *See also* housing bubble

real estate agents: commissions of, 189, 190, 191, 270n13;

real estate agents (*continued*)
on COVID-19 pandemic, 213; home-ownership boosted by, 6, 89–90; influence in private sector, 3; internet-based firms disrupting business of, 188, 192; optimistic mindset of, 94, 250n18; professional value of, 191, 192; and racialized patterns of housing segregation, 5, 7, 9

real estate markets: collapse of, 27, 29–30, 39; economic reality of, 43; evangelism of real estate wealth, 48; and financialization, 51; and global financial crisis, 13, 16–17, 39, 235n30; and Great Recession, 200; residential real estate values, 3, 16–17, 93, 94, 189; speculation in, 13–14, 53, 54–55, 89

real estate workshops: and African Americans, 19, 72, 76; call and response used in, 73, 79; and Carleton Sheets, 28–29; and COVID-19 pandemic, 2, 19, 212–13; critiques of, 66, 78–79, 83; and entrepreneurship, 66, 80, 85, 86; FortuneBuilders workshops, 18, 24, 56, 68, 70, 71–78, 79, 80, 85, 86, 174, 212–13, 274n8; and franchise opportunities, 76–77, 78; and gender, 19, 67, 72; and Great Recession, 2, 18, 53, 54, 56, 80, 85; and HGTV, 73–75, 76; on house flipping, 2, 54, 65, 69, 83; impact and meaning of, 80–81, 83–85, 86, 212; and mentors, 68, 69, 70, 71, 75, 76, 78, 86; and religion, 68, 69, 72, 76, 80, 85; Rich Dad/Poor Dad workshops, 18, 56–57, 65–70, 72, 73, 74, 77, 78–79, 80, 85, 86, 212, 213, 274n8; self-governance emphasized in, 18, 56, 85, 86; on stock market, 68–69, 74, 80; and Tarek El Moussa, 245n33; WealthFit Team, 213

reality television: entertainment value of, 43, 51–52; ethnicity in, 47, 50–51; and gender, 236n4; and global financial crisis, 23, 236n2; and Great Recession, 35, 237n7; impact and meaning of, 80–81, 83–84, 189; and real estate workshops, 53; and same-sex couples, 47, 49; staged aspects of, 46–47, 240n60. See also *Fixer Upper* (TV show); *Flip or Flop* (TV show); HGTV; *Property Brothers* (TV show)

Real Simple, 48, 203

Realtor Magazine: blind optimism of, 87, 89–90, 91, 92–93, 94, 249n3; on COVID-19 pandemic, 213; Great Recession covered by, 18, 90, 93, 95; on predatory lenders, 94, 250n10; on Zillow, 191

Realty Times, 249n3

Redfin, 184, 188, 190

redlining, 5–6, 9, 102, 253n42

Reid, Greg S., 58–59

remote work: and COVID-19 pandemic, 211–12, 215, 216, 222, 229, 275n19, 275–76n34, 276n38; and homes as workplace, 19, 184, 205, 206–8, 215, 216, 273n53, 273n54, 275n19

renters, 3, 130, 133, 192–94, 197, 199–200, 211, 228

REX, 190–91

Robbins, Richard, 170–71

Roberts, James W., 247–48n57

Rohatyn, Felix, 113

Room (film), 177–82

Roosevelt, Franklin D., 4–5, 158, 231n3

Root, 103, 104, 105

Rosner, Joshua: on home equity, 113; as outsider skeptic, 118, 121; *Reckless Endangerment*, 134–37, 141–42, 148, 149, 156, 170, 172, 175, 260–61n19, 261n24

Roubini, Nouriel, 114, 152, 256n101

rural areas, 3, 4, 12, 200–201, 209, 234n24

Salomon Brothers, 15, 111, 133

San Francisco, Calif., 193, 195, 219, 220, 228

Santelli, Rick, 126, 145

savings and loan associations, 6, 15

Schechter, Danny, 105, 115

Schiffrin, Anya, 119, 121–22, 236n2, 257n107, 258n1

Schumpeter, Joseph, 187, 217, 218

Scott, Drew: business success of, 43–44, 48, 83, 84, 239–40n50; and Carleton Sheets, 28–29; family background of, 27–28; as featured host, 18, 23, 30–31,

35, 39; and gendered roles, 50; in Las Vegas, 29, 32–33, 44; in Toronto, 36
Scott, Jonathan: business success of, 43–44, 48, 83, 84, 239–40n50; and Carleton Sheets, 28–29; family background of, 27–28; as featured host, 18, 23, 30–31, 35, 39; in Las Vegas, 29, 32–33, 44; romantic life of, 44, 212, 239n49
securitization: and global financial crisis, 15, 16, 127, 128; and Great Recession, 151; in *Inside Job*, 152; risks of, 1, 16, 88, 105, 112
self-governance, 18, 52, 56, 85, 86, 184
self-regulating markets, 20
self-reliance, 56, 61, 225, 229
sharing economy, 185–88, 197–98, 199, 209, 269n4
Sheets, Carleton, 28–29
Shiller, Robert J., 54–55, 92, 114–15, 160
shorting, 128, 130–33, 134, 183
short-term rentals, 19, 184, 186, 193–94, 197–200
Shreveport, La., 195, 199
Silicon Valley corporations, 196, 209, 220
Sisson, Patrick, 200, 201
Skilling, Jeffrey, 139
Sloan, Allan, 114, 153–54, 263n60
Smith, Ben, 218
Smith, James M., 67–70, 73, 80
Snelson, Tim, 177
social class: conflicts in, 179–80, 209; and COVID-19 pandemic, 210, 219, 225; and *Get Out*, 182–83; higher classes favored over lower classes, 3, 19–20, 163; and *Parasite*, 179–83; and portrayals of work, 50; and public-private balance, 185; and remote work, 208, 215; and *Room*, 178–79, 181, 182–83; and upward mobility, 52. *See also* elites; middle class; poor, the; wealthy, the; working class
social contract, rupture of, 174, 226
social media sources, 122, 161, 209, 229–30
social mobility, 20, 153
social welfare programs, 13, 20
Society for Applied Anthropology, 165

Solace, 227–28
Sorkin, Andrew Ross, 157–58, 162, 261n37
Soros, George, 152, 165
Sowell, Thomas, 101, 102–3, 104, 234n25, 252–53n42
Spanish flu pandemic of 1918–19, xiii, xiv
Squires, Catherine R., 103–5
Srnicek, Nick, 187, 269n6
Starkman, Dean, 87, 107, 116–18, 121, 161, 254n68, 257n107, 257n109
State of the Nation's Housing (2021), 211, 224
Stewart, Jon, 126–28, 162, 163, 183, 249n3
Stockholm Syndrome, 120, 223
stock market: and COVID-19 pandemic, 97; and cycles of boom and bust, 133, 149, 167, 168, 169–70; high prices in, 54, 55, 56; real estate workshops on, 68–69, 74, 80; residential real estate value compared to, 189; speculation in, 13, 53, 120
Stout, Noelle: *Dispossessed*, 172–74, 177, 183, 267n24, 267n30; on global financial crisis, 19–20, 163, 183
streaming services, 187, 204, 217
Streitfeld, David, 275–76n34
subprime mortgages: and New Century Financial, 56, 91; and predatory lenders, 106, 113; print media on, 95, 117; proliferation of, 88, 128; racially based targeting of, 19, 103; *Realtor Magazine* on, 90, 91, 92; and rise in home prices, 160; risks of, 15, 24, 105, 129–30, 142, 154
suburban areas: African Americans excluded from, 10; and COVID-19 pandemic, 19, 212, 219–20; homeownership boosted by, 6, 11; homes of, 3, 5, 178, 179, 182; and Housing Act of 1949, 6–7; population of, 8–9; residential real estate values in, 17; shopping centers of, 3, 221
supply chain, 204, 228
Swartz, Mimi, 139–40
systemic injustice, 20

Tajikistan, 109–11, 146–47, 150, 156
Tarbell, Ida, 117, 161

Taylor, Keeanga-Yamahtta, 9–10
Tea Party, 126, 145, 159
technology: and COVID-19 pandemic, 216–17, 222; disruptive technologies, 184, 185, 187, 188–91, 194, 197–98, 199, 200–204, 273n60; and home as sanctuary, 19, 201–8; and housing markets, 228; and remote work, 19, 184, 205, 206–8, 215, 273n53, 273n54; shifts in, 160, 161, 185, 229–30. *See also* new media
telemedicine, 19, 185, 204–5, 216, 222
Tett, Gillian: anthropological education of, 107, 109, 147, 150, 161, 164, 165; anthropological methods used in financial reporting, 109–11, 121, 146, 148, 150–51, 154, 155–57, 163–65, 175–76, 255n80, 264n69, 265n4, 268n31; *Anthro-Vision*, 157; bottom-up perspective of, 147, 156, 157, 164, 175, 264n69; career combined with motherhood, 149, 165; Charles Ferguson on, 263n60; on COVID-19 pandemic, 214, 274n15; on derivatives, 112, 113, 119, 132, 148–50, 155, 168, 171, 176; on detachment of academic anthropology, 163–66, 175–76; on financial language, 109, 119, 150; on financial system, 149–50, 154, 156, 164–65, 167, 175, 262n52; *Fool's Gold*, 139, 148–51, 154, 156, 162, 166, 169, 170, 171, 172, 175, 176, 262n52, 267n30; on global financial crisis, 19, 109–13, 115, 132, 134, 146, 148, 154–55, 157, 161, 164, 166, 176, 254n68, 265n5; "Iceberg Memos" of, 110, 118; in *Inside Job*, 151, 153–54, 165; as insider/outsider, 165; on Japan's Lost Decade, 109–10, 113, 147; on journalistic conventions, 119–20, 164; and Karen Ho, 166–67, 176, 268n31; on participant observation, 157, 264n69; on power structures, 164, 165; *Saving the Sun*, 109, 147; on securitization, 110, 112, 115, 134, 148, 154; *The Silo Effect*, 154–57, 163; on silos, 111, 118, 120, 150, 154, 155–56, 164–65, 166; on social silences, 111, 120, 150, 155, 156, 157, 164,

263n65; on Tajiks, 109, 110, 111, 146–47, 150, 156; television and film appearances of, 262n57; top-down approach of, 174
Thaler, Richard, 129, 132
Thurber, Marshall, 60, 244n19
Tooze, Adam, 16, 229
travel industry: and Airbnb, 194–96, 198, 199; business travel, 194, 276n38; and COVID-19 pandemic, 19, 215, 216, 218, 224, 228
Treas, Judith, 252n41, 267n23
Troubled Asset Relief Program (TARP), 145
Trulia, 184, 188
Trump, Donald J.: administration of, 260n17; and Larry Kudlow, 102; and polarized politics, xiv; and populism, 145, 225; residences of, 12; rise to power, 157; and Robert T. Kiyosaki, 62–63, 64; and Trump University, 63–64, 77

Uber, 185–86, 188, 199–200, 209
United States Housing Authority, 5
Urban Renewal Act of 1954, 7, 233n17
US Congress, 4–5, 17, 140, 210–11
US Department of Homeland Security, xiv
US Department of Justice, 189
US Department of Labor, 4
US Department of Treasury, 89, 109, 145
US Senate, 83–84
USSR, 109

venture capital, 185, 189, 194, 216, 220, 271n29
Villani, Rick, 55–56
VRBO (Vacation Rentals by Owner), 194, 218

Waco, Tex., 23, 27, 33–39, 44–45, 47, 49–50, 212, 239n39, 242n79
Wall Street: in *Capitalism*, 158; and corruption, 128, 129; and Enron, 138; and global financial crisis, 16, 105, 127, 128, 141, 143, 145; power relationships of,

151, 154, 164; prominence of financial sector on, 116; and residential real estate prices, 92; and securitization, 136
Wall Street Journal, 87, 95-98, 117, 120, 251n26, 256n88
Warren, Elizabeth, 114
Washington, D.C., 95, 135, 136, 142, 219
Washington Post, 103, 118, 222
Waters, Maxine, 260-61n19
Wayfair, 43, 184, 201, 209, 221
WeWork, 185, 186, 221
Whitney, Meredith: on banks and rating agencies, 118; on global financial crisis, 109, 133, 134, 137, 154, 157, 161, 172; at Oppenheimer, 107, 108-9, 133; top-down approach of, 174
Wilson, Woodrow, xiv, 4
Wolden, Woody, 73-77, 80
Wolf, Martin, 254n75, 263n59
women: domestic roles of, 1-2; at *Economist*, 254-55n75; in financial industry, 154, 161, 171-72; and Gillian Tett's analysis of financial system, 149-50, 156, 262n52; in *Inside Job*, 152; perceptions of global financial crisis, 19, 107, 133, 134; and real estate workshops, 19, 67; as whistleblowers, 138
working class, 5, 106, 173, 177, 179, 182
World Economic Forum, 115, 256n101
World War II, 214
Worth, 108

Young, Heather Rae, 45, 212
Yun, Lawrence, 92-93, 250n10

Zakaria, Fareed, 226-27
Zaloom, Caitlin, 171, 174, 176, 267n30
Zillow: business model of, 188-91, 192, 193, 195, 197, 198, 227, 270n15; and COVID-19 pandemic, 218-19, 220; and residential real estate, 184, 188, 203, 208, 209
Zoom, 184, 217, 220, 222, 223, 224

www.ingramcontent.com/pod-product-compliance
Lightning Source LLC
Chambersburg PA
CBHW021650230426
43668CB00008B/578